AF378557

2016
CyberArts

ARS ELECTRONICA

HATJE CANTZ

Hannes Leopoldseder · Christine Schöpf · Gerfried Stocker

CyberArts 2016

International Compendium

Prix Ars Electronica

Computer Animation / Film / VFX – Interactive Art+ – Digital Communities
Visionary Pioneers of Media Art – u19 - CREATE YOUR WORLD

STARTS Prize '16

Grand Prize of the European Commission honoring Innovation in
Technology, Industry and Society stimulated by the Arts

Contents

Prix Ars Electronica 2016

Contents

STARTS Prize'16
Innovation at the nexus of **S**cience, **T**echnology and the **ARTS**

PRIX ARS ELECTRONICA 2016

PRIXARS

A Plea in Opposition to the Discontented Spirit of the Times

Hannes Leopoldseder

> "We live in an extraordinary place
> at an extraordinary time."
>
> William MacAskill, Oxford

If we consider the mood prevailing in our country and throughout Europe at the moment, then we realize how ambivalent these times truly are. People have very different perceptions of the changes society is undergoing. The political parties that form the respective governing coalitions are being punished at the polls; populism flourishes everywhere. We Austrians experienced this in the spring 2016 presidential election in which what had been major parties for 70 years were relegated to the role of marginal factions. Instead of painting optimistic pictures of the future, the business community is busy drawing up nightmare scenarios. Everything has to change. The Digital Revolution that was recognizable on the horizon decades ago—and which Ars Electronica has been elaborating on in ongoing discourses and manifesting in artistic projects since 1979—now constitutes the mainstream in media, business, and politics. In symposia, discussions, and elaborate glossy publications, the private sector is promoting "Industry 4.0."—Europe's response to Silicon Valley, which has built, among other things, a substantial lead in many sectors of the digital economy.

In Austria, this mood has reared its ugly head in the real world as well. Captains of commerce and industry complain of overzealous regulation, tax hikes, bureaucratic red tape, and the hindrance of innovation. Dissatisfaction and mistrust are widespread. Politicians postulate innovation; manufacturers level critique. Prominent corporate executives agree: "I get the impression that government officials are suspicious of efficiency and commitment"; "I've never experienced such pervasive frustration among entrepreneurs"; "You get the feeling you're just beating your head against the wall. This is why you get disenchanted with politics." That's a representative sample.[1]

The more than 3,000 artworks submitted for prize consideration to this year's Prix Ars Electronica competition reflect this day and age across the global spectrum, and here too we encounter feelings of ambivalence, insecurity, anxiety, bafflement, rage, and resentment.

In addition to this worldwide pessimism, there's also confidence, optimism, and a positive outlook on the future. And one particular aspect of this future is "RADICAL ATOMS–the alchemists of our time," the theme of the 2016 Ars Electronica Festival being produced in cooperation with Boston-based MIT Media Lab. This year's theme focuses on a future in which a process of transformation amalgamates the disembodied world of digital data with the physical world of our bodies. This process is destined to change our life and our economy, and also open up fascinating possibilities for artists. One of the pioneers of this development is Hiroshi Ishii, who's been doing intensive research at the MIT Media Lab for more than 20 years–initially with his Tangible Media Group and most recently with his *Radical Atoms* project, which he'll present at Ars Electronica 2016. With their unorthodox approaches and highly inspiring methods, the artists and scientists involved in this project are not only paving the way for new developments, but also opening up totally new ways of regarding the role of science in our society and the interplay of technology and nature.

On the social level, this is a matter of new, positive future scenarios, of new social models. Where are the approaches to a process of rethinking that seeks ways for us to live well without growth? Wherever we look, everything we see is affected by the digital upheaval that's now in full swing. Multiple factors merge here: the growing divergence of rich and poor, the transformation of work, the absence of growth, the strong emergence of political populists, and, of course, the migration of millions of people seeking a new homeland.

When you consider the question of how moods, outlooks, and attitudes towards life change, you come across surprising developments and facts, both negative and positive. Sociologist Heinz Bude, a professor at the University of Kassel, regards research on attitudes as a way "to clearly reveal what's gotten out of hand, what's on the horizon, and what's totally unclear."[2] Moods are a society's feelings. They're ways of being in the world. At present, a general "mood of irritability" characterizes the various social movements of mistrust.

France has long been the avant-garde in matters of intellectual upheaval, but also when it comes to protests by young people such as the student revolts of May 1968 that were triggered by the closure of a college at the Sorbonne in Paris. This revolt subsequently led to mass demonstrations in France that nearly paralyzed the whole country and then spread to other European cities. Back then in Vienna, I was amidst the students on Ringstraße, a cub reporter covering the demonstrations for the ORF–Austrian Broadcasting Company.

Now, once again, it's France where young people are refusing to tacitly accept the social status quo; instead, they're just saying: STOP. The movement has dubbed itself *Nuit Debout* (Up All Night)—one must remain alert due to concerns about ones job and ones income, the diminishing standard of living, and improving the educational system. As "nocturnal activists," these young French people are fighting for a better life. This past spring, thousands gathered in mass demonstrations on Place de la République in Paris. Each demonstration continued through the night and on into the following days. And there were repeated discussions with passers-by about their lives, their concerns, and what should be done. On the night of April 28, 2016, there were huge demonstrations in Paris, Marseille, and Nantes. According to *Le Monde,* there were as many as 500,000 protestors in Paris alone. Rioting, injuries, and arrests were the consequences as the police broke up the demonstration. *Le Monde* and *Le Figaro* published spreads of shocking photos on their front pages. The protest opposed social injustice, unemployment, and the lack of opportunities for young people. One of the main slogans: "We want a society built on something else than just profit and money-making."[3] Worldwide demonstrations have been the upshot.

In any case, what these French people were doing after dark triggered a nationwide wave of protest marches and strikes that, coinciding as they did with the EURO 2016 football championship, threatened to plunge Paris and the rest of the country into chaos. Perhaps the Up All Night crowd is a flash in the pan,

but maybe it's also a symptom for a new awakening by young people fighting for a new future.

In his 500-page book *PostCapitalism: A Guide to Our Future,* British journalist Paul Mason wrote that it just might be the young, smart, urbane Twitter-Facebook-cell phone-internet generation that topples global capitalism's current form of turbo-capitalism.[4] It's gratifying that scholars and media outlet representatives haven't only been propagating negative future scenarios in recent years; a few of them have also been coming up with new takes on the present and the future that point in a different direction and display optimism, confidence, and a spirit that things are going to get better. One of the leading lights of this positive future outlook is Harvard Professor Steven Pinker, a linguist, journalist, experimental psychologist, and cognitive scientist. His theoretical point of departure came as a surprise to many: "Violence has continually declined over the long term, and today we may be living in the most peaceful time in our species' existence."[5] Thus, violence isn't increasing worldwide; it's declining. He draws a picture that's in sharp contrast to currently prevailing opinion. His credo: Data from all over the world show that everything gets better in the long run. In his 1,212-page book, Pinker has assembled statistics and other material supporting his position: on death rates in combat, on genocide, murder and manslaughter, on civil rights and income distribution, as well as data documenting the increase in empathy and altruism aimed at making the world a better place.

Anyone looking to supplement this picture can refer to the detailed and comprehensive data on optimism and pessimism that Mohamed Nagdy and Max Roser have amassed and made available online.[6] Max Roser is an economist, media critic, and research fellow at the University of Oxford, whose research focuses on poverty, income distribution, and global development. The material he provides free-of-charge on the internet impressively demonstrates radical changes for the better. Roser speaks in terms of an amazing success story.

In these times, seeking out what's good has become a subject in its own right. Guido Mingels, the Swiss journalist honored with the 2003 Egon Erwin Kisch

Prize, has been a reporter for German news magazine *DER SPIEGEL* since 2011. Last January, he launched a text-and-graphics feature entitled "Back then, everything was worse."[7] Data going back many years or decades and displayed in graphic form prove that everything's improving—in contradistinction to the currently widespread opinion that it's getting worse and worse. One of the subjects this feature has dealt with is combat casualties. The prevailing view assumes that wars are raging everywhere and it's never been this bad, but the fact is that the last 20 years have been, comparatively, the most peaceful such period in centuries. Executions in the USA have decreased dramatically, literacy rates are steadily rising worldwide, child mortality is declining significantly, air travel has never been so safe, and mishaps due to playground violence in Germany have dropped from 136,000 in 2000 to 80,000 today.

A highly commendable scientific study entitled *Quantifying Global International Migration Flows* performed by Guy J. Abel and Nikola Sander at the Wittgenstein Centre for Demography and Global Human Capital in Vienna and first published in the magazine *Science* has also been made available to wider audiences by Guido Mingels in *DER SPIEGEL.*[8] The results of that study turn the view of migration as propagated in the media completely upside down. The reality is global and, statistically speaking, a far cry from our perception of it. According to Abel and Sander, only 0.6% of the world population has migrated in the last 11 years, which means that 99.4% of humankind remain in their respective homeland. Abel, a social statistician, has also analyzed global migration flows over the past 50 years on the basis of data from 196 countries and concluded that the trend is stable: "Contrary to common belief, our data do not indicate a continuous increase in migration flows over the last two decades, neither in absolute or relative terms."[9] In an interview with Guido Mingels, Abel went into further detail: on the whole, global migration has actually declined in the last five years. In response to the journalist's exclamation "Declined?," Abel reiterated: "Significantly declined." Overall, however, Abel is critical of the UN's statistics, since they mix various areas. Furthermore, the current situation in Central Europe differs from Abel's study, since Abel concentrated on international migration flows.

Accentuating positive current developments is one thing; contributing to it and doing good is the other. One movement dedicated to making the world a better place comes from the USA, and one of its foremost advocates is Peter Singer, the controversial professor of bioethics at Princeton University. In his book,[10] he defines the concept of effective altruism as "a philosophy and a social movement which applies evidence and reason to determining the most effective ways to improve the world."[11] The term "altruism" goes back to Auguste Comte (1798-1857), who juxtaposed it to egotism. Comte is considered the founder of positivism and sociology.

And 29-year-old Oxford philosopher William MacAskill wants to apply effective altruism to change the world. His motto: *Doing good better.* MacAskill's point of departure is global income distribution, and he calculates as follows (I've converted the dollars to euros): Earning a net income of €2,380/month (whereby Austrians get paid 14 times/year) puts you among the richest 1% of the world's population. That means that 99% of human beings are poorer than you.

Every morning, we should remind ourselves of something very important, MacAskill writes in his book *Doing Good Better: How Effective Altruism Can Help You Make a Difference:* "We live in an extraordinary place at an extraordinary time."[12]

When the conversation turns to income distribution, then we also have to come to terms with the idea of an unconditional basic income. The roots of this concept reach back to Antiquity, to Sparta during the reign of King Charilaus around 700 B.C. Peggy Burian[13] of the University of Leipzig has examined the historical record. The king's guardian and uncle, Lycurgus, considered wealth and poverty as diseases. After consulting the Oracle of Delphi, he decided to redistribute Sparta's land and to do so by lot, so that "everyone has enough ... to maintain their wellbeing and their health."[14] The needs were simple, and everyone enjoyed a carefree life. And once again, Lycurgus decided to journey to Delphi, but before he departed, he made every citizen swear an oath that they would abide by the provisions of the constitution until he returned from Delphi. But he never came back; instead, he chose suicide by starvation and thus forced the Spartans to comply with their oath. And that's how the first constitution that guaranteed an unconditional basic income survived for 500 years, no less! This idea has been handed down through the millennia and now, in the early 21st century, it's experiencing a revival. Experiments, projects, and specific legislation already exist in Europe and many other parts of the world. Austria has been a trailblazer when it comes to social commitments displayed by groups and initiatives such as the *Armutskonferenzen* (Anti-Poverty Network) and the Basic Income Weeks, though there have been few expressions of support on the part of politicians—and this despite the fact that it was an Austrian economist, Nobel laureate Friedrich August Hayek, who pioneered the concept of minimum subsistence level.

An especially prominent role is currently being played by Swiss impresario Daniel Häni and Philip Kovce, a German-born author and scholar. In Switzerland, they've launched a cultural campaign that has attracted support from several groups. Their common goal is for every citizen to receive an unconditional basic income, no matter how high their salary or earnings, without doing anything in return, or submitting to any sort of audit. The amount of this basic income is to be determined by a referendum.[15]

The arguments Häni and Kovce advance in favor of a basic income have to do primarily with digitization and the deployment of robots in the workplace. Over the coming decades, robots, machines and computer programs will gradually take over the jobs that human beings currently perform. Some predictions maintain that they'll do up to 70% of the work.

Switzerland put the basic income to a vote in a historic plebiscite held on June 5, 2016. The surprising result: 23.1% of the voters—569,000 people—came out in favor of an unconditional basic income. In the Province of Bern, 40% were for this measure. The initiators spoke in terms of a successful first step. Their aim is a basic income as the "humanistic response" to technological progress.

Will an unconditional basic income be a prerequisite for this future? What's left for people to do? Make full use of our human capabilities; give expression to our humanity, that which sets us apart from machines; give free rein to our human creativity; dedicate ourselves to artistic and cultural pursuits! When our workload diminishes, there's more time for us to enjoy life. A plea in opposition to the discontented spirit of the times can only be an impulse. We have to believe in the future. And we have to regard the times in which we live as extraordinary, as is the place in which we live. Time and location are unique.

1 *trend. Das Wirtschaftsmagazin*, 05/2016, p. 28ff
2 Heinz Bude, *Das Gefühl der Welt. Über die Macht der Stimmungen*, Hamburg 2016, p. 21
3 *Le Monde*, 30. 04. 2016; *Le Figaro*, 30. 04. 2016
4 Paul Mason, *Postkapitalismus. Grundrisse einer kommenden Ökonomie*, Berlin 2016
5 Steven Pinker, *Gewalt: Eine neue Geschichte der Menschheit*, Frankfurt / Main 2013, p. 11
6 *https://ourworldindata.org*
7 Guido Mingels, Früher war alles schlechter. In: *DER SPIEGEL*, ab 1/2016
8 Guido Mingels, Die Welt bleibt zuhause. In: *DER SPIEGEL* 18/2016, p. 52
9 Guy J. Abel, Nikola Sander, Quantifying Global International Migration Flows. In: *http://www.science.org/*
10 Peter Singer, *Effektiver Altruismus. Eine Anleitung zum ethischen Leben*, Berlin 2016
11 Ebenda, p. 9
12 William MacAskill, *Gutes besser tun: Wie wir mit effektivem Altruismus die Welt verändern können*, Berlin 2016, p. 33
13 Peggy Burian, *Das garantierte Grundeinkommen. Grundlagen und Entstehung einer Idee von der Antike bis zum Beginn des 20. Jahrhunderts*, Universität Leipzig 2006
14 Ebenda, p. 21
15 Daniel Häni, Philip Kovce, *Was fehlt, wenn alles da ist? Warum das bedingungslose Grundeinkommen die richtigen Fragen stellt*, Zürich 2015

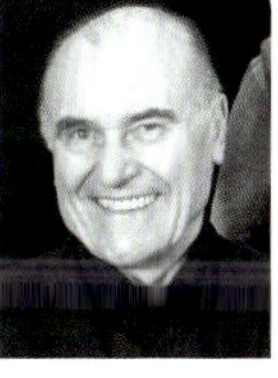

Hannes Leopoldseder (AT), PhD, he has worked as a television journalist for ORF Vienna, as the managing director of ORF Upper Austria (1974–1998), and the information director of ORF Vienna (1998–2002). In 2009 he was appointed honorary professor at the University of Art and Design Linz. He co-founded Ars Electronica and the Linzer Klangwolke in 1979 and initiated the Prix Ars Electronica (1987) and the Ars Electronica Center (1996). He is also the co-editor of Ars Electronica's catalogues.

Prix Ars Electronica 2016

Christine Schöpf, Gerfried Stocker

3,159 entries from 84 countries were submitted for prize consideration to the 2016 Prix Ars Electronica that's celebrating its 30th anniversary this year. The huge number of projects the Prix attracts from across the spectrum of art, science and R&D, as well as the high level of social commitment many of them display, underscore once again the Prix Ars Electronica's excellent international reputation as the oldest continually staged competition in digital media art and, above all, its status as a platform for creative individuals working in a wide range of disciplines and as a meeting place for very diverse cultural positions. Since Hannes Leopoldseder established the Prix Ars Electronica in 1987, this yearly competition in the cyberarts has reflected the current state of the art in digital creativity, and the works it singles out for recognition reflect the trends now pointing the way towards the future.

From its very inception, the intention has been to bring together all the various realms of artistic media design in a single competitive framework, and in 1987 this was a new curatorial approach. Indeed, there were competitions and festivals in the fields of computer music and computer graphics, but the two remained strictly segregated in all of them. The Prix Ars Electronica, on the other hand, has always endeavored to create a *shared* platform and thereby foster dialog between what had previously been discrete disciplines.

When the Prix Ars Electronica was launched 30 years ago, the three competitive categories were Computer Animation, Computer Graphics, and Computer Music. In the wake of increasingly intense discussions about interactivity in art in the late 1980s, a new Interactive Art category was introduced in 1990. In 1995, only a few years after Tim Berners-Lee presented his concept of a World Wide Web developed at CERN, Computer Graphics was replaced by a new competition for Internet-supported projects. This category, in turn, was serially tweaked over the ensuing years until, in 2004, in light of the massive emergence of social networks, it morphed into Digital Communities. Computer Music, for its part, was re-orchestrated as Digital Musics & Sound Art. 1998 saw the addition of u19 – CREATE YOUR WORLD, the category for young people in Austria. The Hybrid Art category, added in 2007, honors excellence on the part of promising collaborations at the nexus of art and science. So, the Prix Ars Electronica has been in a continuous state of experimentation for 30 years now, and is thus still accurately mirroring the dynamic development of the media arts. A wrinkle added this year was the substantive expansion of the Interactive Art category, a plus signaled by the addition of a simple "+" to its title.

The Visionary Pioneers of Media Art award initiated in 2014 is the Prix Ars Electronica's way of honoring those trailblazers whose artistic creativity and experimentation paved the way to media art as it is right now, and what it is today—a central part of our social reality and our specific forms of communication and cultural techniques. These people have been the architects of the still-young history of media art, and this award is meant to give them the recognition and respect they're due.

Of inestimable importance is the fact that, ever since 1987, the Prix Ars Electronica has succeeded in attracting top experts from throughout the world to serve as jurors, men and women whose competence vouches for the quality of each year's verdicts, and whose commitment to these proceedings says a lot about what the Prix is all about.

It was decided in 2014 to conduct the competition in four of the Prix Ars Electronica's seven categories on a biennial basis in order to better manage the process of assessing each and every one of the entries, as well as to continue to showcase the prizewinners in a way that does justice to them at the Ars Electronica

Festival in September. Accordingly, the categories staged in 2016 were Computer Animation/Film/VFX, Interactive Art+, Digital Communities, u19 – CREATE YOUR WORLD and Visionary Pioneers of Media Art. The works singled out for recognition are presented in the CyberArts exhibition produced jointly with the OK Center for Contemporary Art, the Ars Electronica Animation Festival, as well as performances and lectures that, together, constitute a core element of the Ars Electronica Festival. *CyberArts,* a book published annually in conjunction with the Prix, and Ars Electronica's huge online Archive are reference sources in great demand by those performing research on the history of media art.

In 2016, a Golden Nica grand prize (including a cash award of €10,000), two Awards of Distinction, and 12 Honorary Mentions are bestowed in each category. In u19 – CREATE YOUR WORLD, the Golden Nica is endowed with €3,000; additionally, there are the netidee SPECIAL PRIZE 2016 with a value of €1,000, two prizes valued at €800 each, and merchandise prizes for youngsters in the "up to 10" and "11–14" age groups

The Prix Ars Electronica has been sustained by government funding and private-sector sponsors. Gratitude is due, above all, to the City of Linz, which has provided financial support to the Ars Electronica Festival, the Prix Ars Electronica, and the Ars Electronica Center since 1979. We would also like to express our thanks to the Province of Upper Austria and federal ministries of the Republic of Austria for their ongoing support. Our thanks also go to OK Offenes Kulturhaus im OÖ Kulturquartier, KulturKontakt Austria, FH Oberösterreich Campus Hagenberg, Maxon, Central Linz, Casinos Austria, netidee, Rotary Club Linz-Altstadt, Conrad, and Linz AG for their support and cooperation over the years.

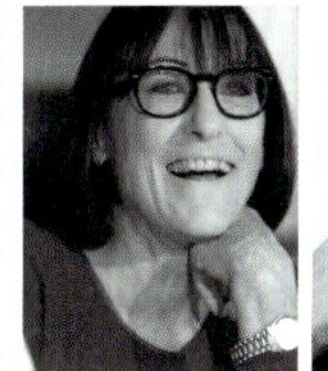
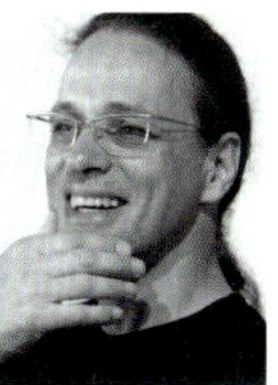

Christine Schöpf (AT), PhD, studied German and Romance Languages. She has worked as a radio and television journalist and was the head of the art and science department at ORF Upper Austria (1981–2008). In 2009 she was appointed Honorary Professor at the University of Art and Design Linz. Since 1979, she has held a number of positions in which she has been able to contribute considerably to the development of Ars Electronica. She was responsible for conceiving and organizing the Prix Ars Electronica from 1987–2003. Together with Gerfried Stocker, she has been the artistic co-director of Ars Electronica since 1996.
Gerfried Stocker (AT) is a media artist and electronic engineer. Since 1995 he has been a managing and artistic director of Ars Electronica. 1995/1996 he developed the groundbreaking exhibition strategies of the Ars Electronica Center with a small team of artists and technicians and was responsible for the set-up and establishment of Ars Electronica's own R&D facility, the Ars Electronica Futurelab. Since 2004 he has been in charge of developing Ars Electronica's program of international exhibition tours. Since 2005 he has planned the expansion of the Ars Electronica Center and implemented the total substantive makeover of its exhibits.

Computer Animation

/ Film / VFX

A mind-blowing Metaphor of Evolution

Mihai Grecu, Bernd Kracke, Erick Oh, Mari-Liis Rebane, Johannes Schiehsl

This year's Prix Ars Electronica saw a record-breaking number of more than 1,300 entries that were submitted to the Computer Animation/Film/VFX category. These entries included individual nominations by the jury members. All entered works were considered in a meticulous pre-selection process before being reviewed together by the jury members Mihai Grecu, Bernd Kracke, Erick Oh, Mari-Liis Rebane, and Johannes Schiehsl at the Ars Electronica Center in Linz.

The jury took on the challenge to narrow the pre-selection of some 300 entries down to the strongest thirty pieces that were representing the rich variety of new and innovative installations, narrative shorts, visual effects, and experimental works. Considering the rapidly expanding ways of digital artistic expression, the jury had to discuss and redefine the role of the Computer Animation category to carefully weigh all projects and find the most outstanding animations, films, and VFX pieces of 2016.

A clear intention of the jury was to search for unseen, original, and innovative work with strong content, a good story, and political impact. In that respect we reviewed and discussed all entries and agreed on the most convincing and accomplished pieces. As there was such a variety of work we established subcategories to create a reasonable comparability. Based on this we generated our list of 30 finalists that was reviewed and discussed again in a lengthy and thorough process, resulting in the 15 finalists. In the end we voted on the candidates for the Golden Nica and the two Awards of Distinction and arrived at a unanimous decision for the winners and the Honorary Mentions.

Golden Nica

RHIZOME · Boris Labbé

The 2016 Golden Nica award for animation, film and visual effects goes to *RHIZOME* by Boris Labbé, a film director and visual artist based in Madrid. *Rhizome* is a very complex and complete piece of artwork, blending complementary techniques in a post-digital painting-like visual poem. Going from fractal-like animation to figures reminiscent of Escher's drawings or even Bosch's universe, it coagulates and redistributes permanently itself in a mind-blowing metaphor of evolution, urbanization, migration, and transcendence of societies. Highly elaborated esthetical research mixes with complex hand-drawn animation and computer crowd-simulation to build a multilayered but very coherent universe.

Awards of Distinction

Nosaj Thing—Cold Stares ft. Chance The Rapper + The O'My's · Daito Manabe, MIKIKO, TAKCOM, ELEVENPLAY, Rhizomatiks Research

An outstanding music video that introduces innovative technologies from 3D scanning, motion capture, and drone controlling, adding a layer of sensitive notion with live recorded choreography and augmented reality. Japanese artist Daito Manabe and his creative collective has come up with a complex artistic concept that introduces the switch between the real and the virtual, blurring the line between human and machine interaction and data analysis. Daito Manabe's work explores the advantages that different fields of art and technology can combine.

Peripheria · David Coquard-Dassault

Peripheria is a beautifully crafted animated film directed by David Coquard-Dassault, a director based in Paris, France. This film is set in the abandoned urban environment where a lonely suspicious group of dogs set the boundaries of their own world. This work has been awarded for its own subtle but strong way of storytelling, cinematography, artistic direction, and technical achievement, which are extremely successful at every level and angle. Especially the artistic skill in both traditionally hand-drawn and computer generated animation pulls the audience right into the core of the film without giving them a chance to question the technique behind the film. This is a great example of a good use of the right medium for the certain narrative, and this is why the work deserves The Award of Distinction for this year's Prix Ars Electronica in the Animation/Film/VFX category.

Honorary Mentions

7001 · Nataša Teofilović

This experimental piece transforms particle crowd simulations into moving abstract paintings. The artist manages to blend fractal dimension-shifting forms into little individual elements, all of which have an individual movement pattern. The result is a mesmerizing composition, where absence and extreme complexity mutually complement and replace each other, and where chaos mutates into a stylized coordinated geometric choreography.

Accidents, Blunders and Calamities

James Cunningham, Media Design School

Accidents, Blunders and Calamities introduces a series of cases and accidents of different animals getting killed by humans. They are described in such a very direct way that we start to care a lot about them by the end of the film. It changes your perspective on nature and how we treat it. It is funny and sad at the same time—which is very difficult to achieve effectively. Also this film is a great example of a good use of VFX technology to tell the story. Despite such amazing achievements in computer animation and VFX technique, they are naturally blended as a part of the story or visual and support the idea of the work.

Bio-Inspire FullDome Performance

Yusuf Emre Kucur, Bahadır Dağdelen / Void

Bio-Inspire FullDome Performance is a monumental work, where physical space is fully used to warp the viewer's perception and transcend contemplation into an immersive abstract universe. From purely geometric forms to organic movements, the exquisite digital animation uses latest technological advancements to distort dimensions of sensorial perception.

Coordinated Movement · Mike Pelletier

Body is personal, body is physical. Body defines us as humans and links to our self and senses. A strong motif, which has prehistoric origins in art, has transformed here into an ethereal form, where movements are morphed as if they would exist in another reality with different physical laws. Mike Pelletier shows us a variety of uncanny motions in a choreographic performance of virtual bodies. By performing these familiar, yet incongruous movements that imitate motions usually not applicable to humans, it creates a certain experience of reality shift.

Die Gegenwart sucht ihren Mund in der Spiegelung der Suppe · Yves Netzhammer

Yves Netzhammer is known for his installations, video projections, and interventions. In his work *Die Gegenwart sucht ihren Mund in der Spiegelung der Suppe* (The present searches for its mouth in the reflection of the soup) the geometric wooden and virtual objects appear almost as if they had secretly sneaked themselves into the Museum, to mingle alongside all the venerable exhibits and have good fun. By setting his simple geometric and plain objects in contrast to the elaborate details of the artifacts of foreign cultures, the artist induces a dynamic that opens up a refreshing approach to the long established understanding of the exhibition to many visitors, and does so by using a good portion of humor and irony.

geist.xyz · ZEITGUISED

ZEITGUISED is a creative collective whose very name reveals its interest in current trends. The zeitgeist reference implies concern with the dominant set of ideals in our contemporary culture, while the wordplay suggests that the artists are making an obvious comment on the fragile line between illusional perception and the virtual and deceptive appearance of our reality. Combining abstract movements with amoeba-like shapes in playful patterns, *geist.xyz* opens up a path to an unknown synthetic territory that fascinates us with its flawless futuristic fiction of the mind. "Fake hacks realism, Small wonders: Sympathy demons / Uncertainty artifacts."

Ghost Cell · Antoine Delacharlery

Ghost Cell takes us to a new reality: Paris as we have never seen it before. Like in some of his previous works, director Antoine Delacharlery mixes reality and CG and uses 3D scans and photogrammetry to capture the real world and re-enact it in virtual space. Houses, cars, people—everything the computer has caught suddenly finds itself in a new abstract connection. Like a bizarre organism these fragments of reality unfold themselves in a breathing polygon matrix and leave us behind with the question: What will remain of us and our relations in an age of total digital acquisition?

Moom · Tonko House
Robert Kondo & Daisuke "Dice" Tsutsumi

We usually call an artwork "innovative" when it explores a new medium. However, fully understanding the grammar of a traditional medium can also bring innovation and a new perspective. *Moom* is a CG animated short film, whose format may seem familiar and conventional to the audience. However, the perfect marriage between a heartwarming, profound story about memories and life and beautifully crafted art absolutely captivates the viewers so that they fully appreciate the beauty of CG animation and film language. It is also very meaningful since the entire production is carried out in Japan. This film could open the door for them, bringing up their CG technique and skill to the level of their amazing 2D animation.

Never Say Never · Saman Kesh, Skunk

Never Say Never is a very well made music video which introduces the fictional dancing robot. It starts like a simple narrative live action short film. In the lab, scientists are in the middle of a serious discussion on developing these robotic devices. Then it suddenly takes a right turn by revealing what they have been making—which turns out to be a dancing robot. Then the music starts and the narrative progresses. It is hilarious and brilliant in terms of the choice of music and way of storytelling. And most importantly, the mixture between computer animation / VFX and the actual physical robots and models they built in real life is absolutely creative and jaw-dropping.

Simulacra · Theo Tagholm

Simulacra takes us to American landscapes to explore the concepts of simulation by flying over hyperrealistic, manipulated landscapes. It shows the fragmented reality, where moments keep expanding beyond the surface and where seconds keep constantly moving on towards infinity. *Simulacra* is a visual metaphor to describe the feeling of the desert of the real, inspired by Baudrillard.

Tehran-Geles · Arash Nassiri

The 18-minute long video stands as a metaphor, a political and poetical statement. Aerial footage of Los Angeles is slowly and progressively colonized by neon signs from Tehran's past. The digital manipulation of the images creates an eerie bridge between past and present, between two antagonistic cultures, mixing them in both senses. Imaginary present and distorted past are different possible readings of this mind challenging art-piece.

Uncanny Valley · AlteredQualia + Fractal Fantasy

Since mankind's discovery of the ability to create images, the central theme was always the same: man himself. In the age of virtual and artificial representation of the human form, engineers and artists encounter an obstructive and yet fascinating phenomenon known as the "Uncanny Valley": when representations look nearly but not exactly like real humans, they appear dead and repellent. The interactive music video of the same name takes us to this infamous valley and lets us interact with perfectly rendered face scans in conjunction with mesmerizing sounds. It enables us to see ourselves in the digital mirror and realize that we are closer to crossing into the valley than we might wish to be.

RHIZOME

Boris Labbé

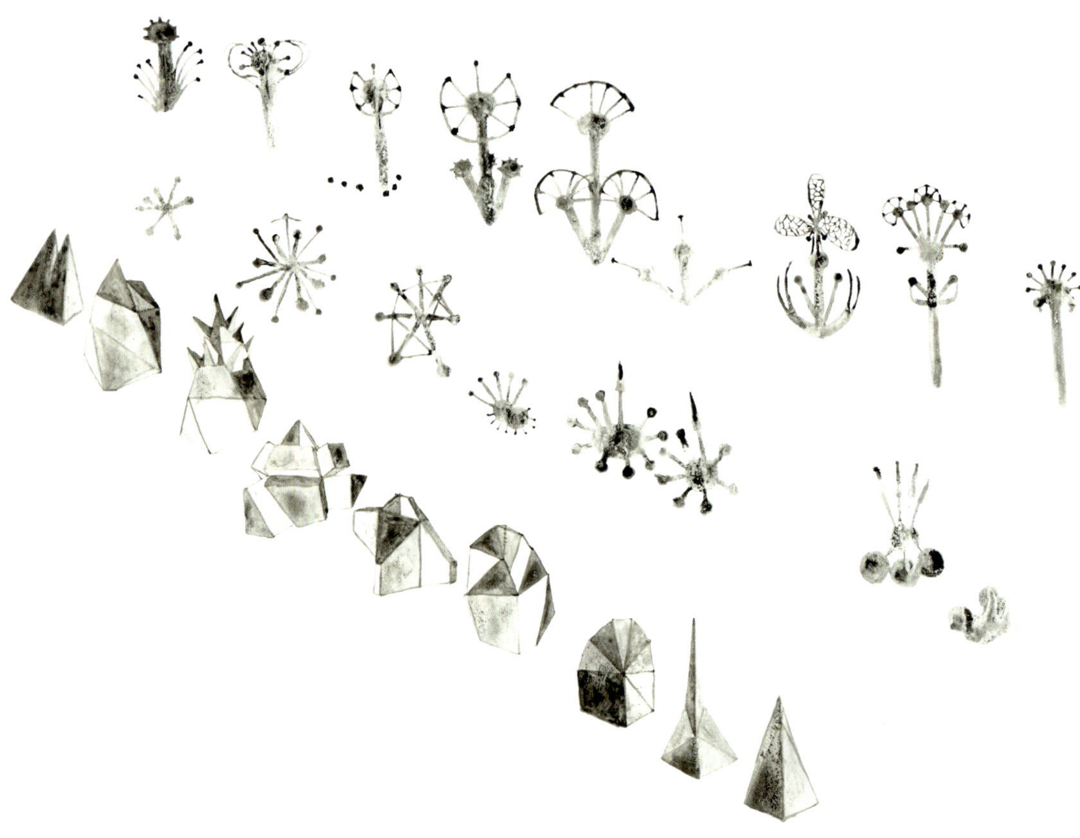

"Unlike trees or their roots, the rhizome connects any point to any other point, and its traits are not necessarily linked to traits of the same nature; it brings into play very different regimes of signs, and even nonsign states. [...] It is composed not of units but of dimensions, or rather directions in motion. It has neither beginning nor end, but always a middle (milieu) from which it grows and which it overspills. [...] What is at question in the rhizome is a relation to sexuality, but also to the animal, the vegetal, the world, politics, the book, things natural and artificial, that is totally different from the arborescent relation: all manner of 'becomings'".
Extract from *A Thousand Plateaus* by Gilles Deleuze and Félix Guattari (translation by Brian Massumi).

RHIZOME is an experimental animated short film that has its foundation in the homonymous philosophical concept, coined and developed by Gilles Deleuze and Félix Guattari, involving research that is close to Steve Reich's repetitive music, Escher's mathematical art work, Bruegel and Bosch's paintings and different scientific theories about the development of life, genetics, the infinitely small and the infinitely large. The film propels us from the beginning to a big zoom over a dimension that is not accessible for us until now, infinitely small, or infinitely far away. There, we attend the birth of an unknown form of life. By repetition, connection, or metamorphosis the organism experiences very fast evolution, giving shape to three big ways of evolution: organic, vegetable, and mineral.

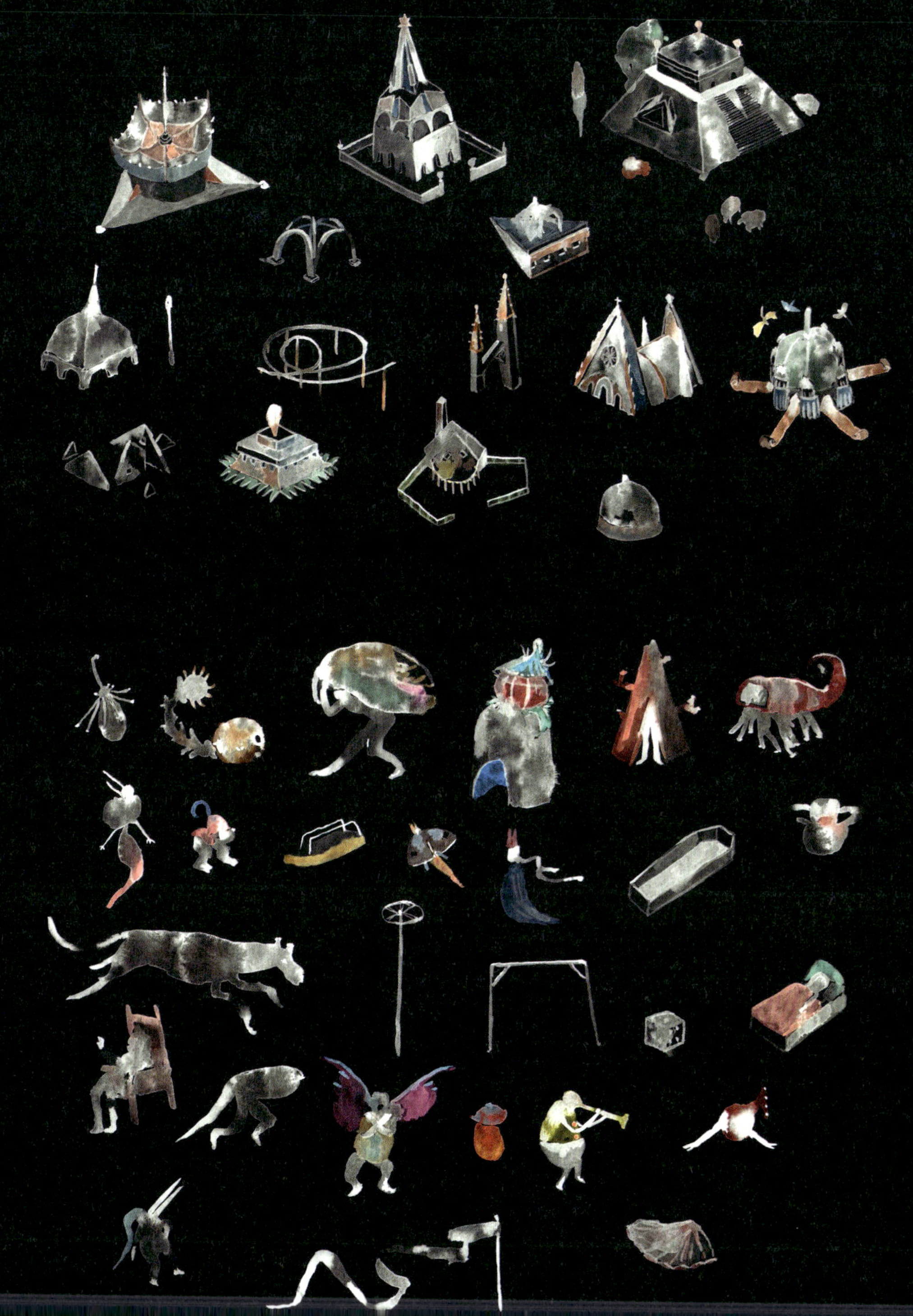

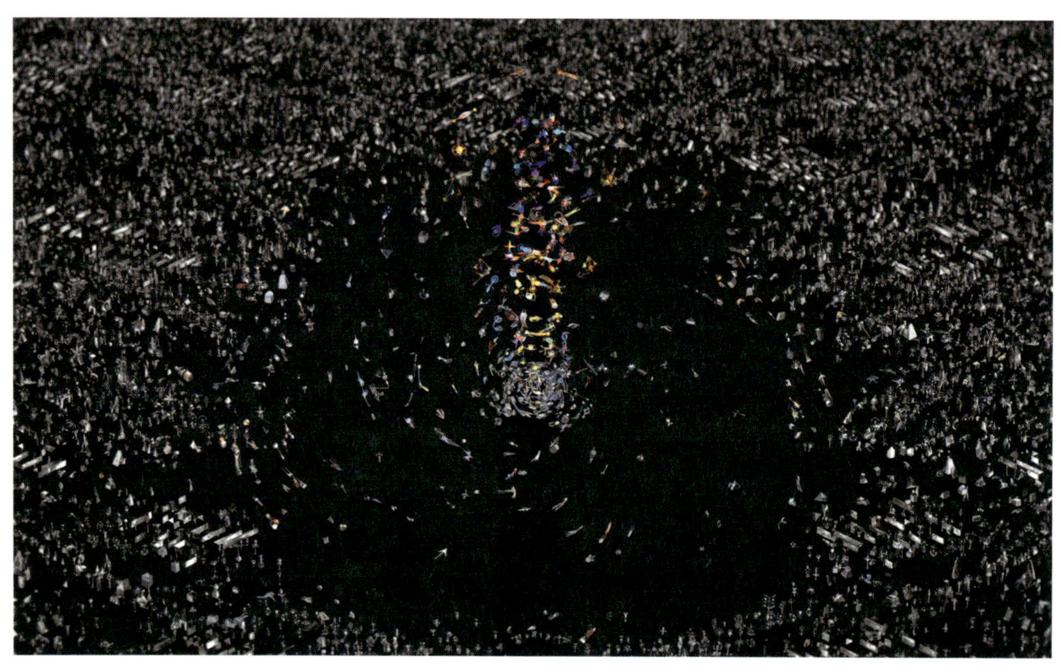

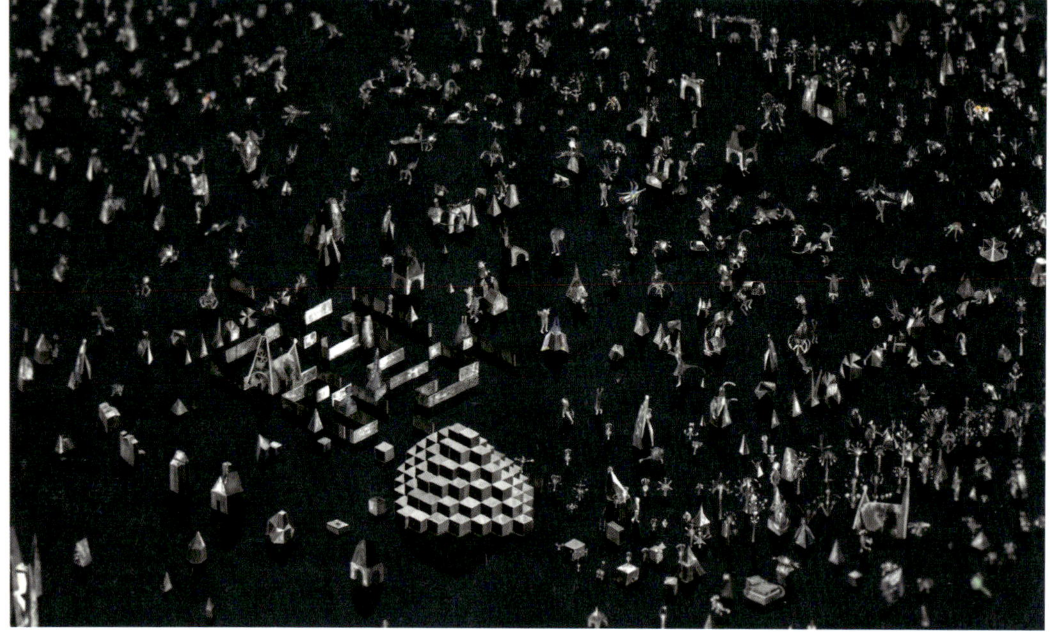

http://www.borislabbe.com/Rhizome
http://vimeo.com/127579635

Really fast, by connection, contact, or mixing, these organisms hybridize and metamorphose until they create a whole society made out of unknown plants, peculiar animals, and archetypal architectures. This scene develops until it creates a constellation, a great ensemble in movement, a wave that spreads towards emptiness. Then the system itself starts a huge revolution: the elements converge in a central point and destroy themselves in order to renew themselves, through pure color and on spiral upward movements to a series of air circles. Finally, we leave this world in a large zoom out, which first seems infinite, huge, but as the distance increases, it becomes microscopic, disappearing from itself again.

RHIZOME was made by a small team of artists and technicians and directed by Boris Labbé. The animation of animated sequences consists of Indian ink and watercolor drawings on paper (21 x 30 cm and 60 x 84 cm). Approximately 2,300 original drawings were needed to create the whole film, with between 1 to 80 elements in each drawing.

The principle of animation runs on a system of loops, which are organized like a canon: modules with multiple inputs and outputs which have the ability to connect with other modules. The drawings were progressively photographed or scanned. Then, a digital treatment of the animation was done (cleaning the images, setting negative, etc.) and the film got its shape due to the work of compositing on the After Effects software (camera animation, compositing image, etc.).

The musical composition was created by Brazilian composer Aurélio Edler-Copes from a series of musical motives analogously recorded from the electric guitar and followed by digital compositing work on the computer (editing, treatment and transformation of the sound). The haunting rhythmic base, acute and repetitive, forms the word R-H-I-Z-O-M-E in Morse code. This pattern is submitted to progressive acceleration and deceleration towards the bass and treble, increasing then the sound spectrum. The ensemble creates an expanding sound constellation that finds its climax with the arrival of the final spiral and the gradual emergence of color.

Produced in France by Sacrebleu Productions, the film received support from the Agence Culturelle d'Alsace during a two-month pre-production residency and from the CICLIC Région Centre during 8 months on a production residency in 2014. The film also received financial support from SACEM, CNC, France Television, and PROCIREP—ANGOA.

11 min 25, Short film 2K, 25 fps, 5.1 surround sound
Technic: Drawing on paper, Indian ink and watercolor, 2D Computer. Approx. 2,300 original drawings, 21 x 30 and 60 x 84 cm.

Director: Boris Labbé
Animation: Boris Labbé, Loïc Sitti, Wen Fan
Compositing: Boris Labbé, Sami Guellaï
Music: Aurélio Edler-Copes
Sound mix: Victor Praud
Producer: Ron Dyens
Sacrebleu Productions 2015

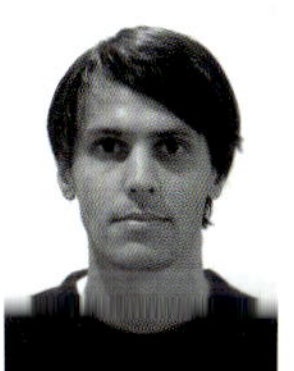

Boris Labbé (FR). After obtaining a DNAP (National Diploma in Visual Arts) at l'École supérieure d'art et de céramique de Tarbes, Boris Labbé continued his studies at the EMCA of Angoulême (École des métiers du cinéma d'animation). At the EMCA, he produced *Kyrielle*, his final film project, which was awarded the Special Jury's prize for Graduation Films at the Annecy International Animated Film Festival in 2012. Simultaneously, he developed an artistic work that is both visual and plastic. He spent a year at the Casa de Velázquez in Madrid. *RHIZOME* is his first professional film.

Nosaj Thing
Cold Stares ft. Chance The Rapper + The O'My's
Daito Manabe, MIKIKO, TAKCOM, ELEVENPLAY, Rhizomatiks Research

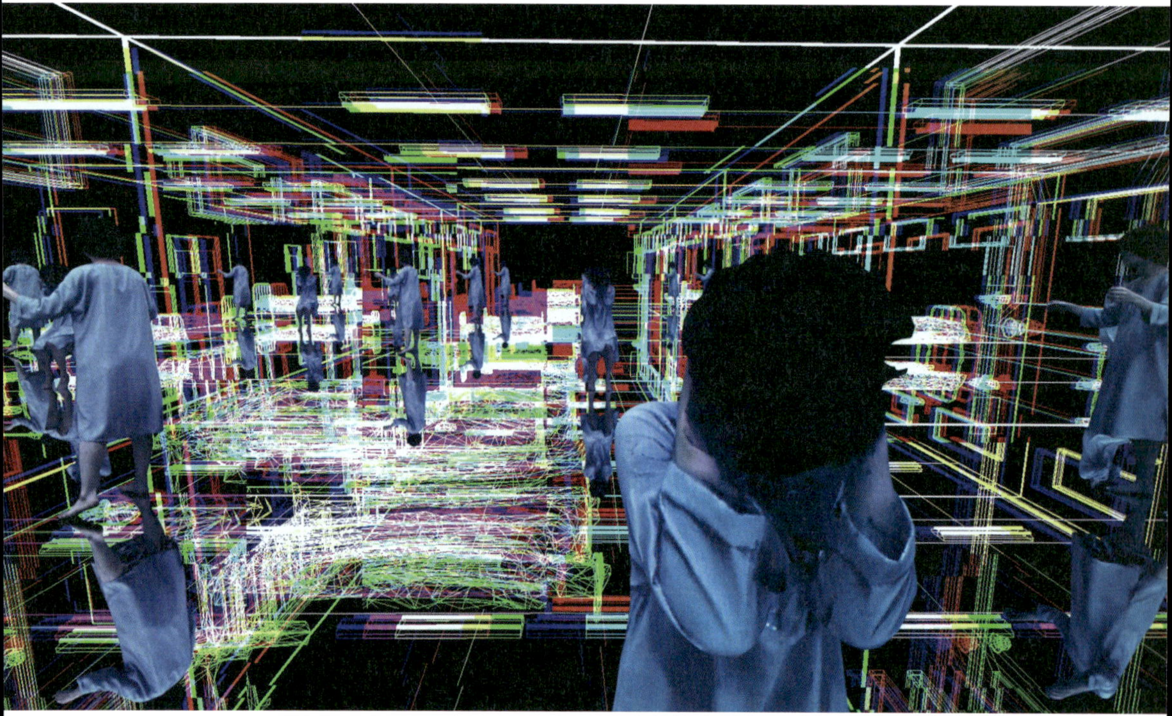

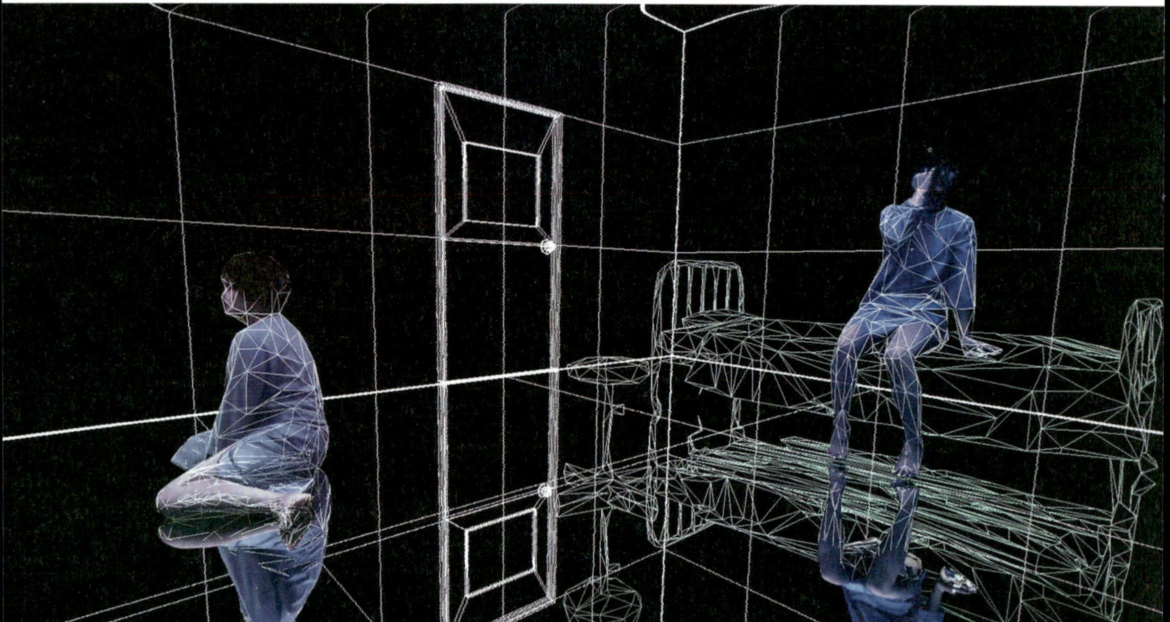

This is a music video of "Cold Stares," a collaboration between Los Angeles-based artist and beatmaker Nosaj Thing, who is actively working around the world, and rapper Chance The Rapper. A dance piece by two dancers was produced to express the message in the lyrics—their mental situation and conflict, searching for reason of being and memories, wandering along the border between reality and illusion. This dance has been shown in two ways: the real world performed by people and the delusional world of CG. A plug-in has been developed to link a drone equipped with a camera for synthesizing video images, drone control, image synthesizing software, and existing CG software (e.g. Maya). While controlling with a program the position and angle of the drone and the camera using the motion capture technology, the camera data for synthesizing CG are recorded at the same time. The significant reduction of the process has been realized by using the acquired data at the time of shooting on the existing CG software.

Dancers in the real world are shot by cameras set on six drones. Dancers in the world of illusion are shot by 48 cameras. Using technology for restoring 3D models from plural 2D data, 3D models with a high quality of texture can be achieved.

Camera motions used for the two worlds of reality and fantasy are identical. It is usually difficult to move a camera motion for the real world as freely as a camera motion for CG due to many restrictions. In this project, however, a system to move drones according to a camera motion created by CG software has been developed. Using this system, we can move drones accurately and freely like a CG camera. What's more, we could achieve a smooth transition between live action and CG.

Rhizomatiks Research: Daito Manabe, Motoi Ishibashi, Yuya Hanai, Katsuhiko Harada, Momoko Nishimoto, Youichi Sakamoto, Tomoaki Yanagisawa
ELEVENPLAY: MIKIKO, Kaori Yasukawa, Erisa Wakisaka
TAKCOM
P.I.C.S.: Takahiko Kajima, Syuhei Harada
McRAY: Akira Miwa, Kohki Okuyama, Akira Iio
Crescent, inc.
Yae-pon

Daito Manabe (JP) is a media artist, DJ and programmer. Daito founded Rhizomatiks in 2006, and since 2015 he has worked with Motoi Ishibashi on Rhizomatiks Research, which conducts projects for the purpose of R&D. **Rhizomatiks Research**, researching into the relationship between human beings and technology, is an organization which introduces art and entertainment projects to the world, through collaborating with creators including artists, researchers, graphic designers, athletes, dancers, choreographers, directors, musicians, and engineers. **MIKIKO** (JP) is a stage director/choreographer, the artistic director and choreographer of world-famous Japanese artists, and choreographer/director of the dance company ELEVENPLAY. **ELEVENPLAY** (JP) was founded by MIKIKO in 2009 in hopes of creating dancers who possess highly artistic sense and creativity on top of exquisite techniques, body and spirit. **TAKCOM** (JP) is a director of the moving image and an artist, based in Tokyo. He has garnered acclaim worldwide with gallery exhibitions and art festivals. From art gallery to advertising, he takes pleasure in pursuing artistic expression in all mediums and forms.

Peripheria
David Coquard-Dassault

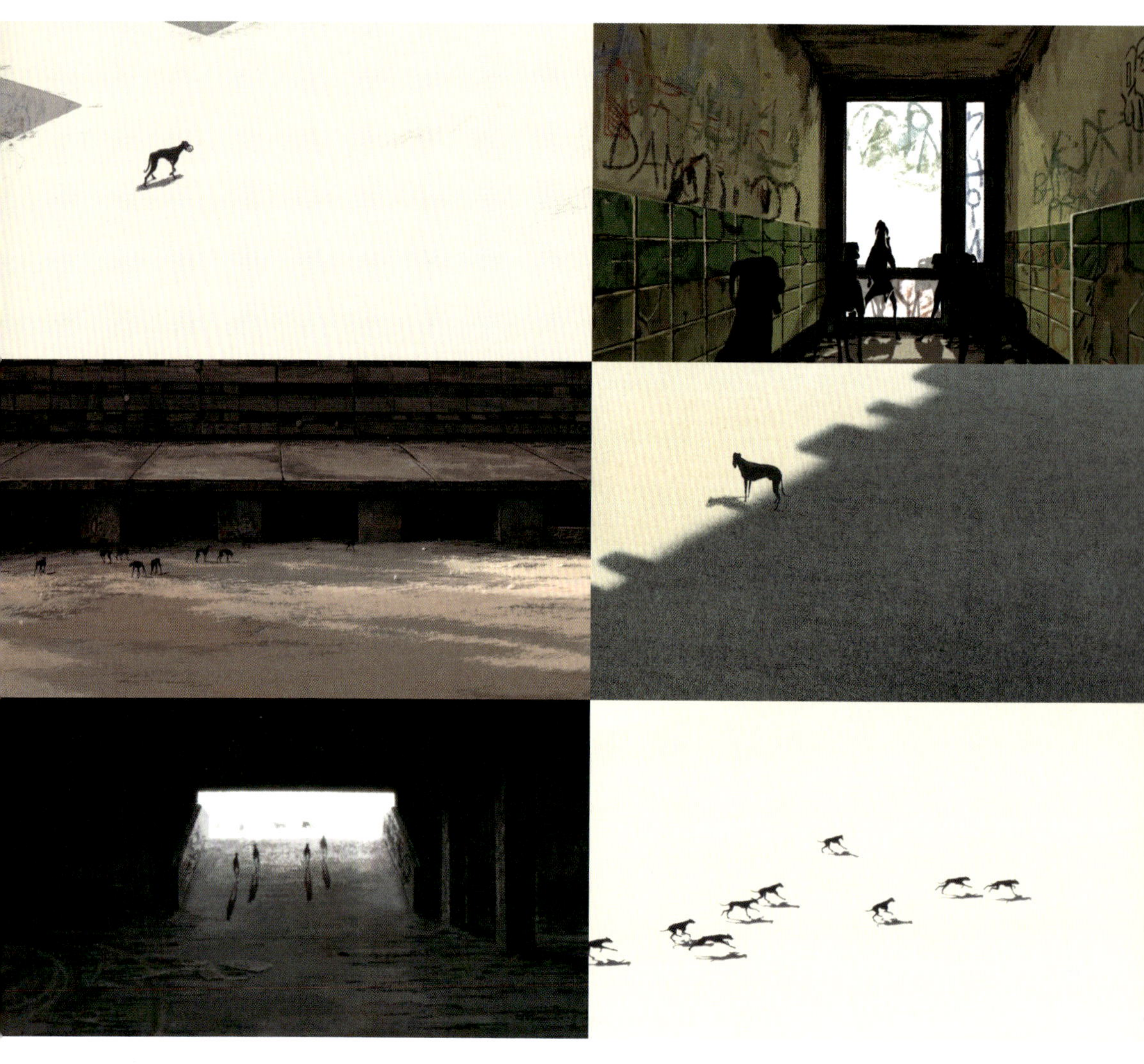

A journey into the heart of a large and abandoned council estate. *Peripheria* portrays an urban environment becoming wild: a modern Pompeii where the wind blows and dogs roam, tailing the remains of human life.

Technics: 2D/3D Animation
Software: Blender, TV Paint, Photoshop, After Effects

Director: David Coquard-Dassault
Screenwriter: David Coquard-Dassault & Patricia Valeix
Executive producer: Nicolas Schmerkin, Autour de Minuit Productions
Executive producer: Thibaut Ruby, Schmuby Productions

Crew
Production manager: Émilie Schmerkin
Animation: Emmanuel Linderer, Florian Durand, Hervé Barberau, Jeanne-Sylvette Giraud, Nicolas Guilloteau, Manuel Raïs, Christophe Seux, Cyril Costa, Paul Szajner
Backgrounds: David Coquard-Dassault
Editing: David Coquard-Dassault
Music: Christophe Heral
Sound design: Nadège Feyrit
Mix: Vincent Cosson, Studio KGB
Color grading: Alexandre Lelaure, Le Pingouin magnifique

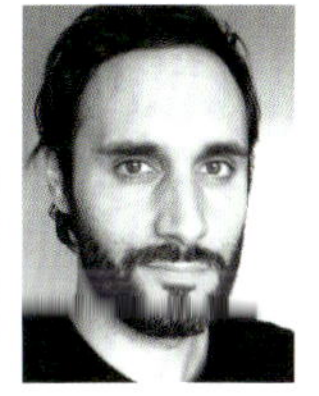

David Coquard-Dassault (FR), born in 1977, graduated from Lyon's Applied Arts program and illustrated novels and children's books and is working now as an artistic director, author, and director of animated films. In 2008 he directed his first short film, *L'Ondée*, which was selected for a number of festivals including La Semaine de la Critique, Ottawa International Film Festival, and Sundance. In 2013 David Coquard-Dassault was awarded the Arte France Prize for his short film *Peripheria* at Annecy International Animated Film Festival.

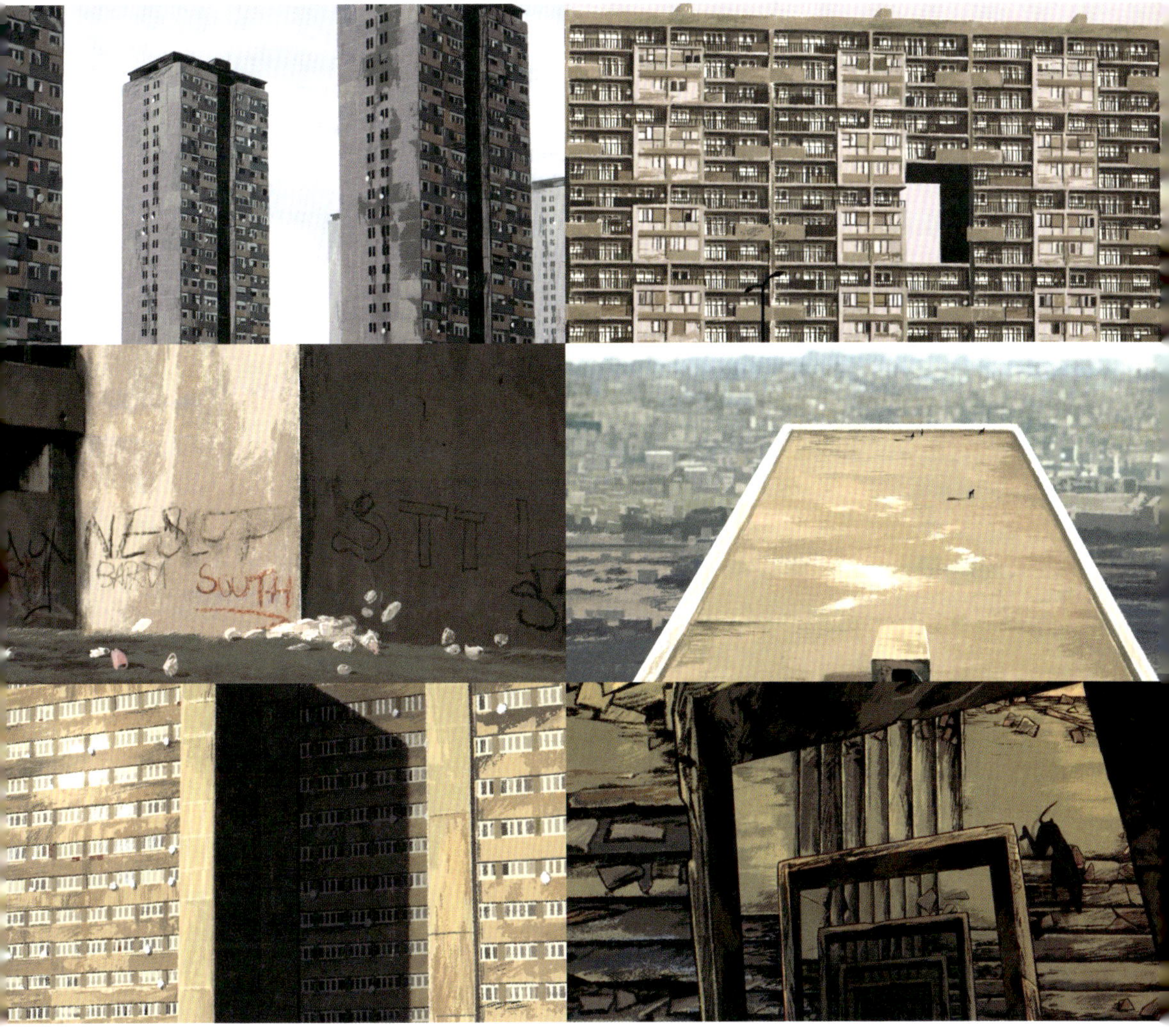

7001

Nataša Teofilović

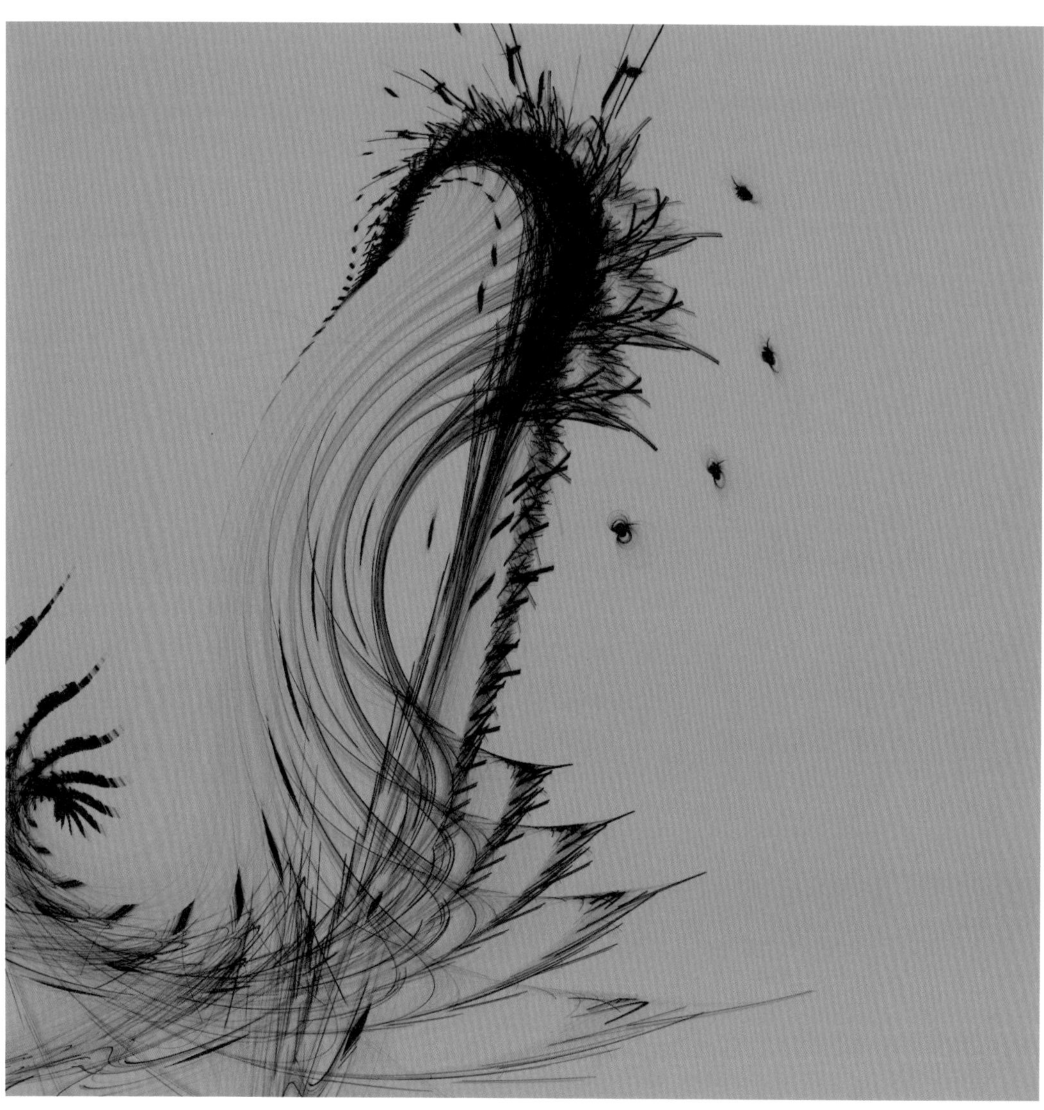

Animation *7001* was produced exclusively by using a fractal generating computer program, i.e. it is based on mathematical formulas. But the final visual result uncovers another, more personal side, reminding us of a free-form, gestural hand drawing and particles in motion. Working with fractals has a poetry of its own. Every part, even the tiniest part, contains information, an image, of the whole. The smallest contains the biggest and vice versa. A similar approach is also evident in science. Scientists who are dealing with the infinitely big, the Universe, are basing their axioms on the results of the physicist who deals with the infinitely small, particle research. Micro and macro universes are mutually reflected and contained. Just like in poetry, the global and the individual, the common and the personal, are intertwined.

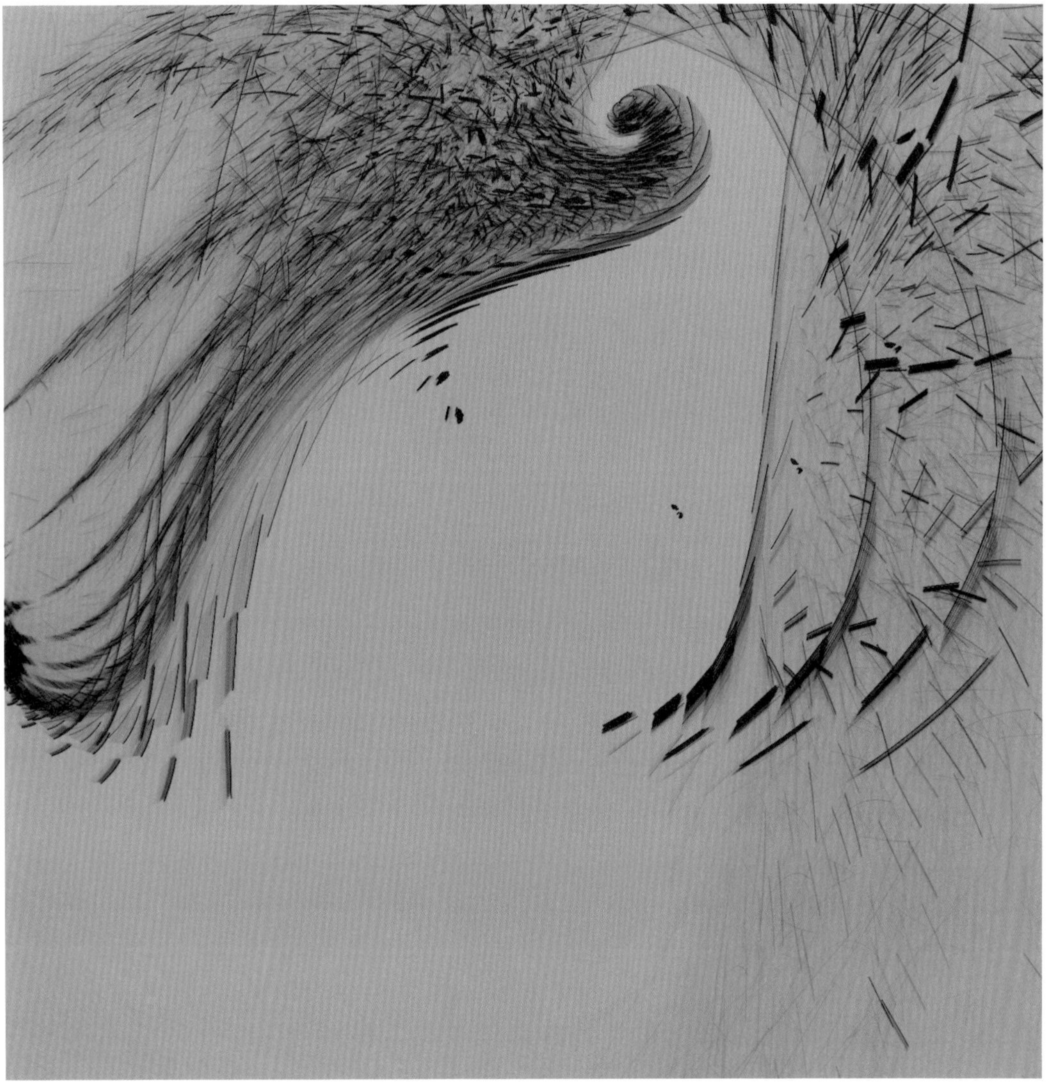

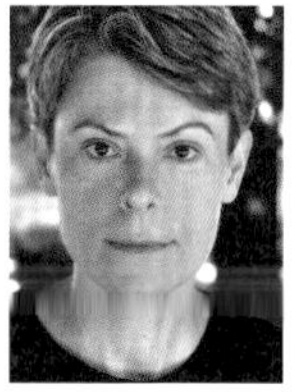

Nataša Teofilović (RS) is a visual media artist. Her artistic approach evolved from neo-conceptual art in the early 90s to digital art in the new century that merges art, science and technology. She works in diverse media including experimental video, 3D animation performance, digital ambiances, and generative art. Conceptually, these works are connected with topics such as the representation of the senses in media art, identity in the void of virtual space, the perception of virtual beings, and the boundaries between virtual and real spaces.

Accidents, Blunders and Calamities

James Cunningham, Media Design School

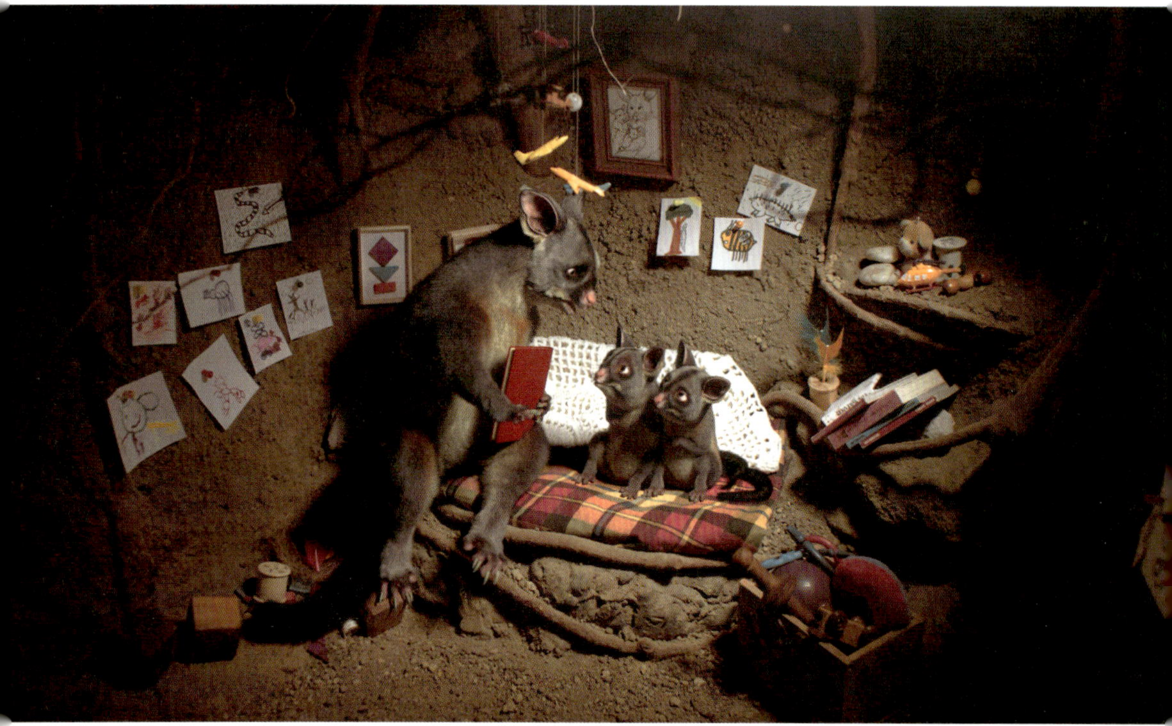

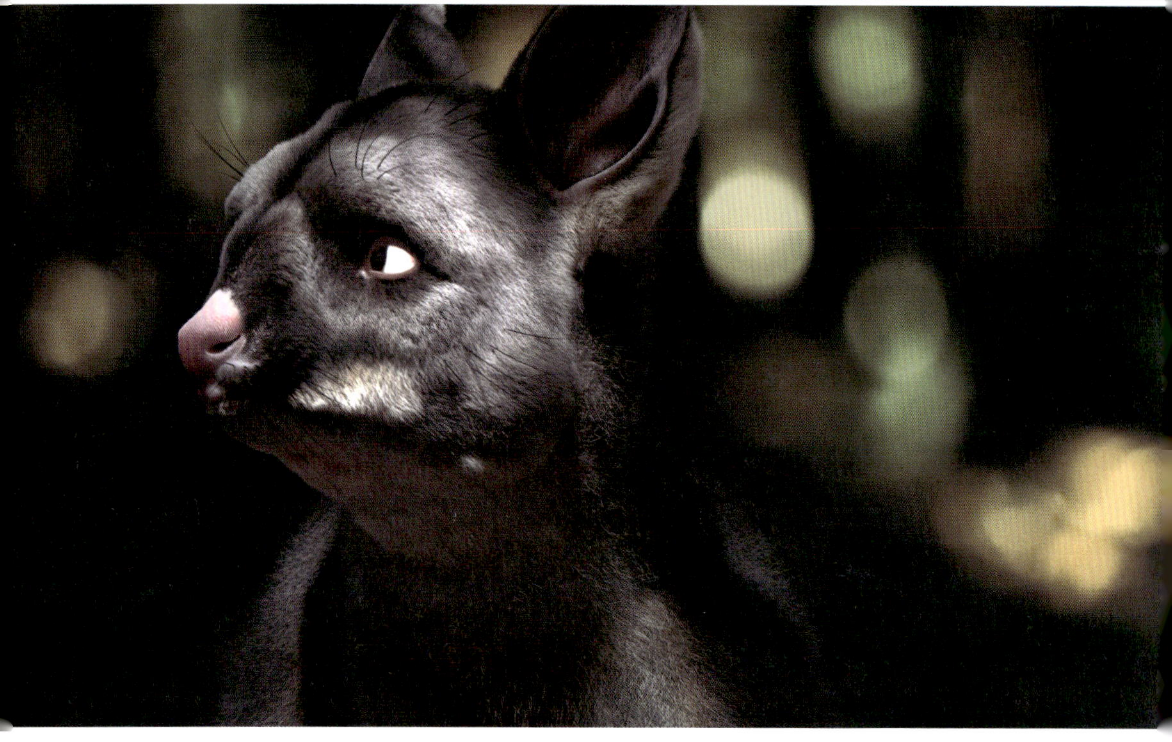

https://vimeo.com/149596663

Synopsis: A father possum reads his kids a story that's an alphabet of the most dangerous animal of all—HUMANS!
This black comedy for kids and parents alike is a hilarious and brutal alphabet of death and mayhem exacted upon animals by ignorant humans. 30 CGI animals were meticulously crafted and killed by a team of 44 students at Media Design School.

Inspiration for Murder: This project was born out of the necessity to make a film with a huge production class of 44 VFX and animation students. Could we make something that was simple to shoot, so production could start immediately? Could we make something that had enough diversity and complexity to give all the students something different to work on? The solution came from an old book from the 1960s called *The Gashlycrumb Tinies* by Edward Gorey. We would show what life is like for animals, continually threatened by brutal and clumsy humans. I set about writing the script. This turned out to be immensely difficult. For each letter I had to decide upon an animal, how it would die and I needed to make that rhyme with the next letter. The final letters were not decided upon until well into production, and yes, X was the hardest.

Production: The shoot was executed with a Sony FS7 camera coupled with an Odyssey external recorder. This allowed 4K ProRes acquisition and gave immense color fidelity. The bulk of the shoot took place over a three-week period and was filmed in, around, and above Auckland city. The crew on most days was just two people, myself and DOP Oliver Hilbert. The performers in most cases were friends, family, and students, but we got in front of the camera too—hitting a golf ball, squashing a newt, and falling in the bath.

Post-Production: The film was edited in Premiere Pro and then brought into HIERO, where we created our post-production EXR plates and exported all this into our pipeline system run through Shotgun.
The class of 44 had three specializations: animation, technical, and compositing. The animators were given plates and started drawing in post-viz of the action.

The key thing here was refining the gag and seeing how much more humor could be milked out of the performance. The animators also filled up the time before they had completed digital rigs doing research into how the animals would move and understanding the body mechanics of all these diverse creatures.
The technical artists were assigned animals to build. This all started with research of real animals, getting the right one approved and then into modeling and texturing. A couple of key students pulled together the rigs for all the creatures. Two of the key creatures that took a lot of time were the Octopus and the Possum. The Octopus was extremely complicated to build then rig and then tear apart. The shading and texturing is very complex with a tricky balance of reflection, diffuse and sub surface illumination. The Possum was even more complex—not just due to the fur but also the range of performance that the rig required—the combined efforts on the Possum would take well over 12 weeks spread across three key artists. The fur was set up using Yeti, donated by Peregrine Labs. Yeti was quick to learn and allowed for easily controlled grooming and a caching system that was reliable and trustworthy. And yes, the face is slightly based upon Liam Neeson.
The compositors had plenty of shots to 3D track in SynthEyes and set up the digital layout scenes. There was also plenty to do in Nuke, like painting out mistakes, combining takes, and adding effects to help sell the humor. But most important was integrating the CGI creatures. The most complex comp shot was X. This was built up from a couple of takes and had to create the explosion and the animation of the X-ray unit. Our key software tools are Maya, V-Ray, Nuke, SynthEyes, Yeti, ZBrush.

Written and directed by James Cunningham
Producers: James Cunningham, Oliver Hilbert
Father Possum: Phillip Greeves
Baby Possum Boy: Drew Cunningham
Baby Possum Girl: Eleanor Cunningham
Visual Effects and animation: Media Design School, Bachelor of Art and Design Class, February 2015
http://www.mediadesignschool.com
Composer: Emile De La Rey

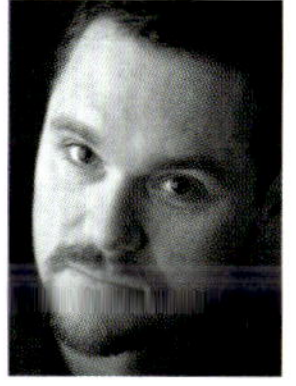

James Cunningham (NZ) born in 1973, is a film director and animator. He has directed eleven award winning short films and is based in Auckland, New Zealand. James is a Senior Lecturer at Media Design School, the premier Animation and Visual Effects new media school in New Zealand, where he produces and directs short films with his students. Prior to that he was Head of 3D at Digital Post working on Visual Effects for local and international TV Commercials, and he was a technical director on *The Lord of the Rings* at Weta Digital. He has a Bachelor of Fine Arts in photography and a Master of Fine Arts in digital animation from Elam School of Fine Arts (Auckland, NZ)

Bio-Inspire FullDome Performance

Yusuf Emre Kucur, Bahadır Dağdelen / Void

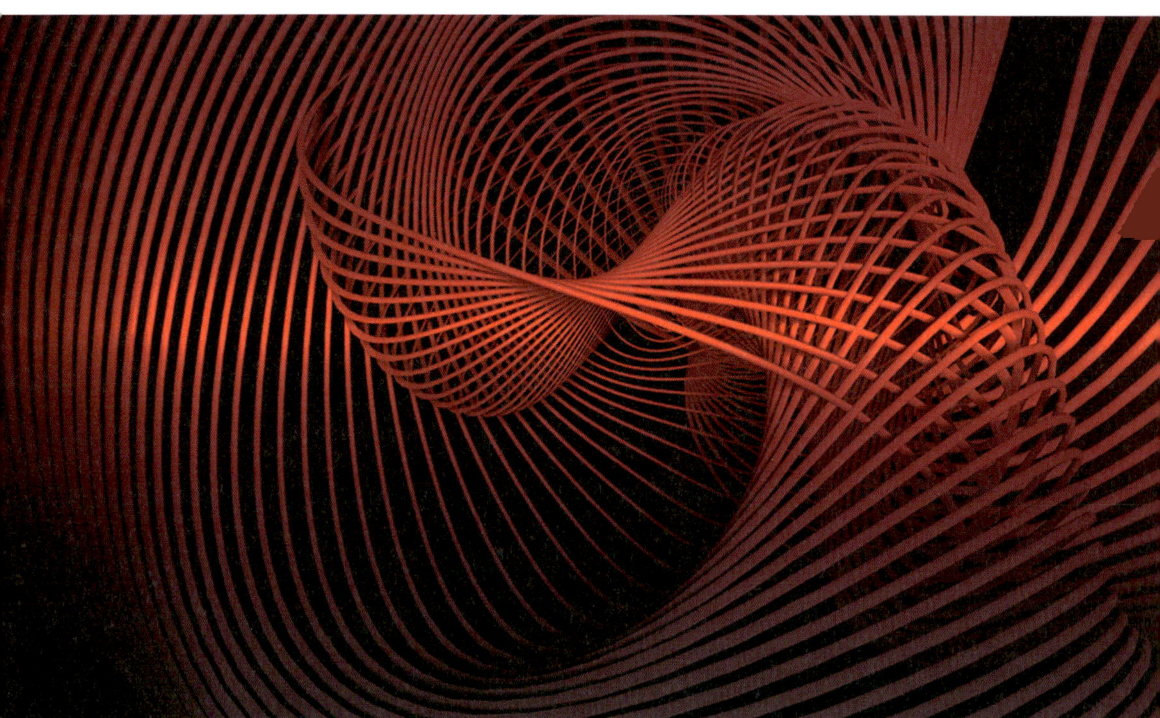

Bio-Inspire is an inspired A/V 3D dome performance which has screened in the Institute of American Indian Arts (New Mexico) and Fiske Planetarium—University of Colorado Boulder (Colorado).
Two A/V artists and two sound designers worked on the project. It is a five minute long mapping video that took three months to be completed. Red, white, and black fractal patterns flutter across the screen. A show of abstract webs and networks of connected organisms visualize artificial neuron connections and the growth & gradual sophistication of neural networks. This is *Bio-Inspire*.
It is mainly inspired by Artificial Neural Networks, which is a widely used method in machine learn-ing and cognitive science. They are human-made versions of biological neural networks, namely the neural system of the animals. The ANNs are com-posed of several nodes, layers, and connections which simulate to some extent the message exchange and processing through a biological neural network. Each function is specific to the learned data according to which the form of the ANN is shaped.
As the quantity of layers, nodes, and connections in an artificial neural network increase, the structure gets more complex. Getting the inspiration from the structure of an ANN, our aim was to redefine the complexity of a neural network using abstract objects and sound referring to its natural form.

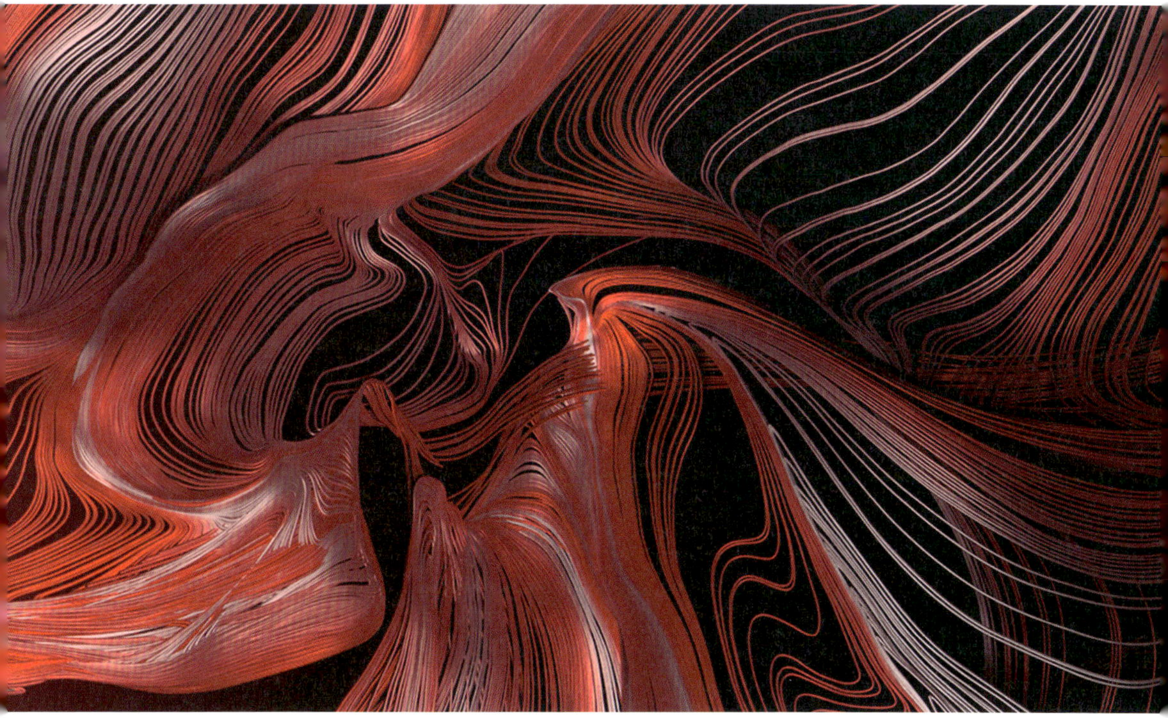

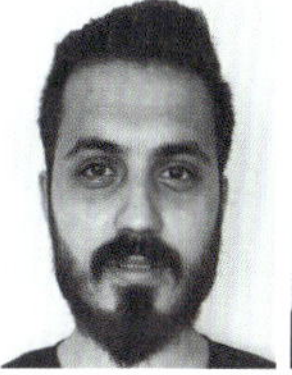

All visuals are made by using C4D, Softimage and ICE.

Direction and animation: Void, *bevoid.co*
Concept development: Şerife Seda Kucur, Selay Karasu, Tuğçe Akkoç
Project manager: Evren Erbaşol

A/V artists and directors: Yusuf Emre Kucur, Bahadır Dağdelen
Documentation: Cüneyt Korkut Keleşoglu
Sound design: Selçuk Can Güven , Erhan Kabakci
Special thanks: Rob Chapman, Barış Serdar, Ali Ata Kavame, Can Bilgin

Bahadır Dağdelen (TR) is a multidisciplinary new media artist based in Istanbul. Influenced by street art and graffiti from an early age, his graffiti paintings have appeared in national and international festivals. His interest in digital art and media led him to study Visual Communication Design (VCD) at Istanbul Bilgi University (IBU). He focused on computer graphics and 3D and took part in national and international projects. Since 2015 he has worked as a designer and is co-founder of Void. **Yusuf Emre Kucur** (TR) is a multidisciplinary designer in Istanbul. He studied Visual Communication Design (VCD) at Istanbul Bilgi University (IBU) and worked on various design projects. From 2011 he worked as a freelancer for different agencies and was involved in art festivals and projects. Since 2015 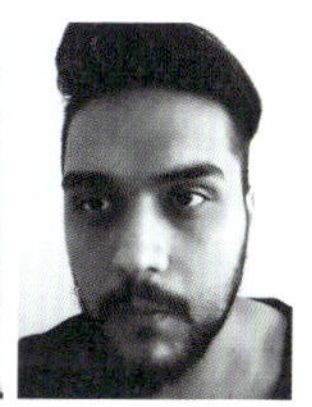 he has worked as a designer and is a co-founder of Void. **Void** (TR) is an Istanbul-based independent creative group that focuses on animation and digital arts and provides support to its customers on different media platforms. Void takes every project as a unique start. It has been involved in national and international digital art activities, and exhibited in various cities in Europe, Russia, America, and Turkey.

Coordinated Movement

Mike Pelletier

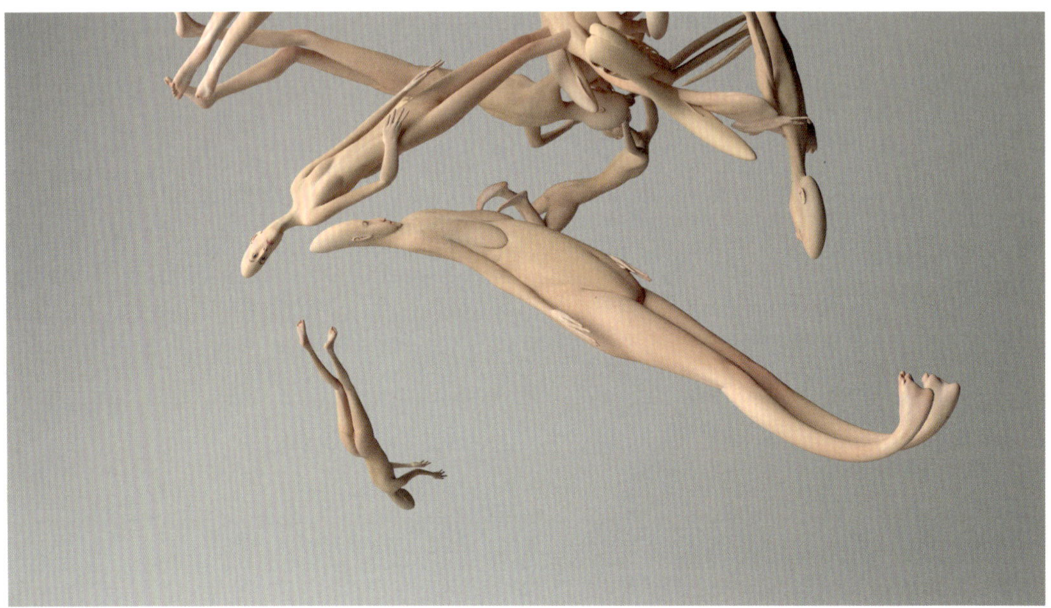

Coordinated Movement is an experimental 3D animation artwork centered around a series of open-source motion capture sequences. In the animation the characters simulate a variety of swimming motions while floating through a digital void. In the absence of liquid to swim through, the bodies of the characters themselves become liquid forms, bending, shifting, and glitching through virtual space.

The impetus for the project came about when encountering a series of swimming motion capture sequences in the Carnegie Mellon University motion capture database. The animation was inspired by the awkward recreation of a person swimming in a motion capture environment. The movements were especially strange as they were performed on dry land without the resistance of water. In the sequences the actors attempt to balance themselves on a beam, and then move their limbs in synch as though they were swimming under water. Equally strange is how in the limited amount of information in the motion capture file where only the joints can be seen as points moving in space, a deep sense of humanity is conveyed in the still flawed data stream.

By translating these physical motions into a 3D animated environment and mapping them onto stock 3D characters with randomly assigned body types and shapes, all nominally different but overall having a similar surface quality suggesting clones or imperfect digital copies, the body is treated as a surface description which information can be mapped onto. They exist in a digital space, where actions are looped and repeated, accurate and repeatable

The bodies are driven along virtual looping paths in a noise field that threatens, distorts, and stretches them until they are almost unrecognizable. They glide almost smoothly through a frictionless space, so much so that figures pass through each other, but at the same time their soft fleshy curves break apart into distorted triangular meshes when rounding extreme corners. In other instances the surface of their bodies are distorted by noise fields, exposing the edges and seams of their virtual construction.

Music: Robot Repair
Composer: Josh Hawkins
Executive producer, robot repair: Doug Darnell
The motion capture data used in this project was obtained from *http://mocap.cs.cmu.edu*.
The database was created with funding from NSF EIA-0196217.

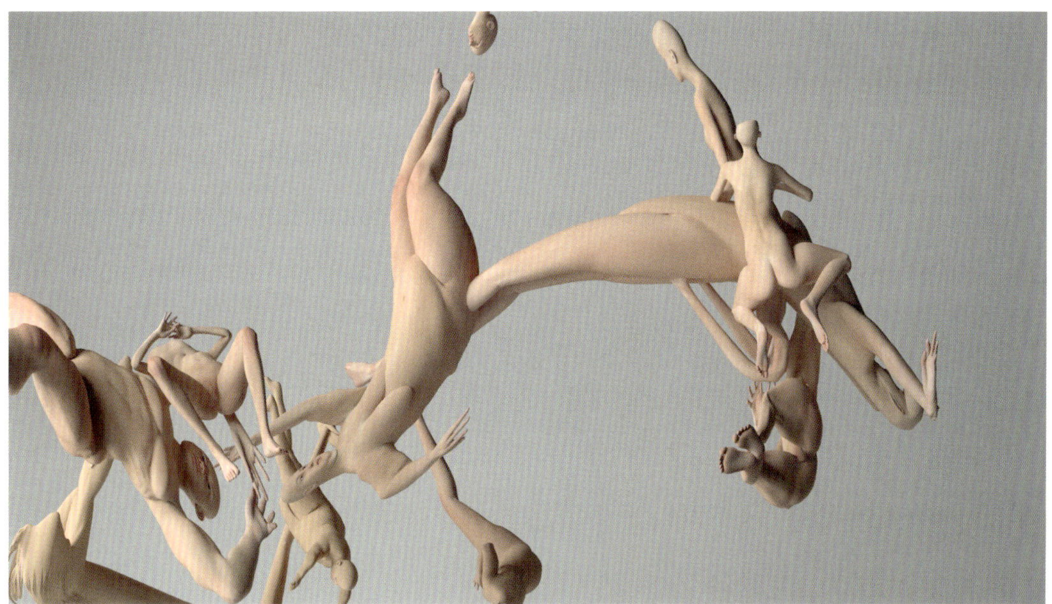

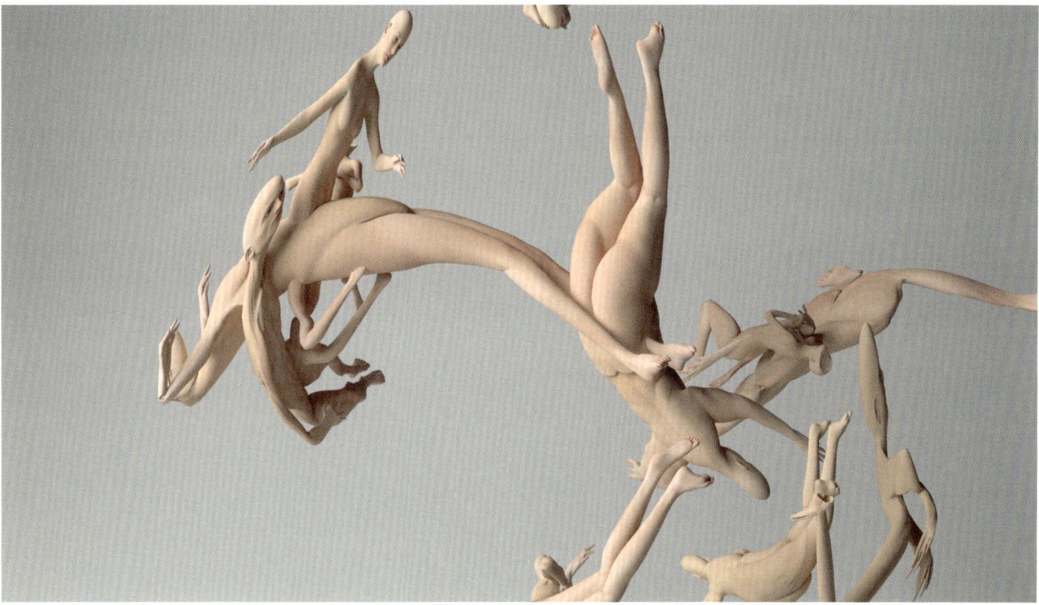

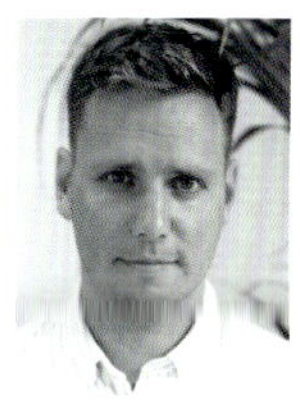

Mike Pelletier (CA), born in 1978, is a Canadian artist based in Amsterdam. Working in mediums such as 3D animation and kinetic installation, his work bridges the divide between digital and physical space. Through different means of technological production, his work explores the various ways in which the human body is represented in art and the social milieu. Using technologies such as motion capture, body scanning, and body tracking, his work examines classical art's obsession with portraiture and adds to it an androgynous, posthuman, and often uncanny protohuman aesthetic.

Die Gegenwart sucht ihren Mund in der Spiegelung der Suppe

Yves Netzhammer

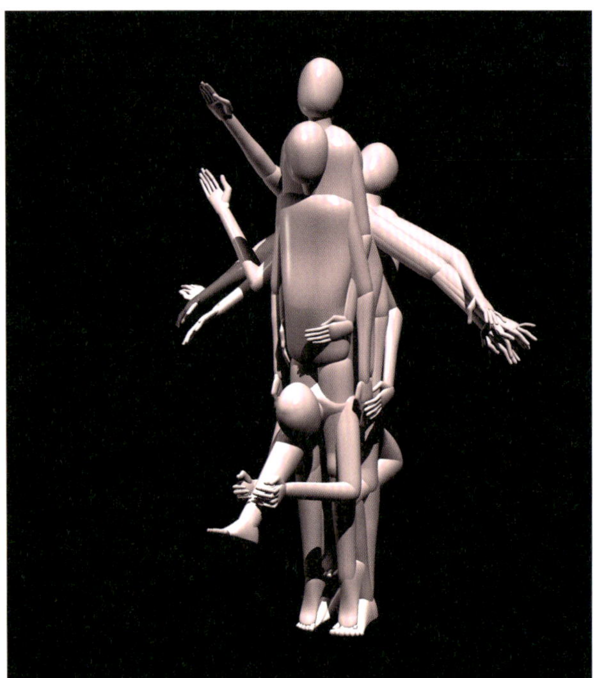

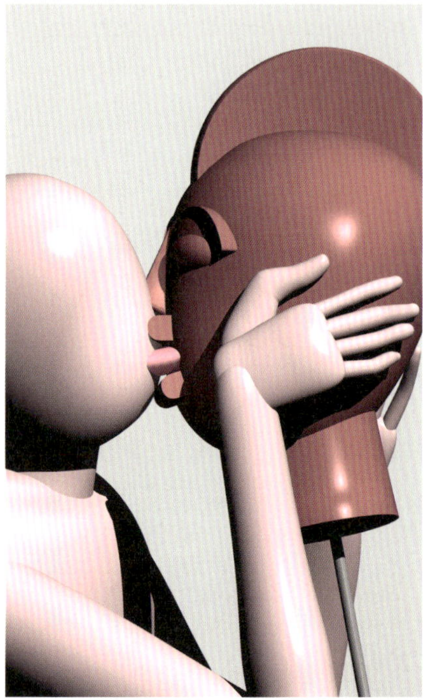

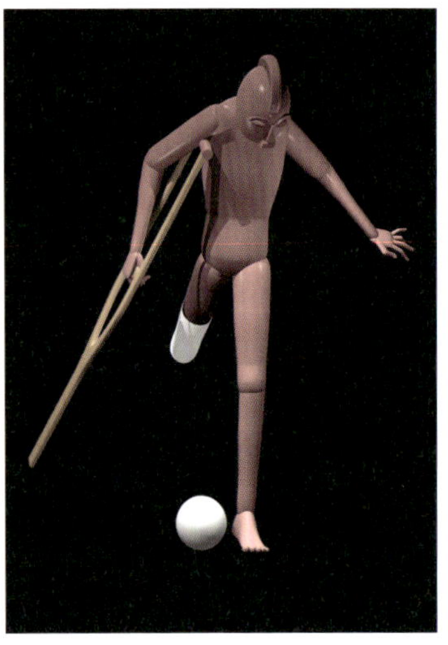

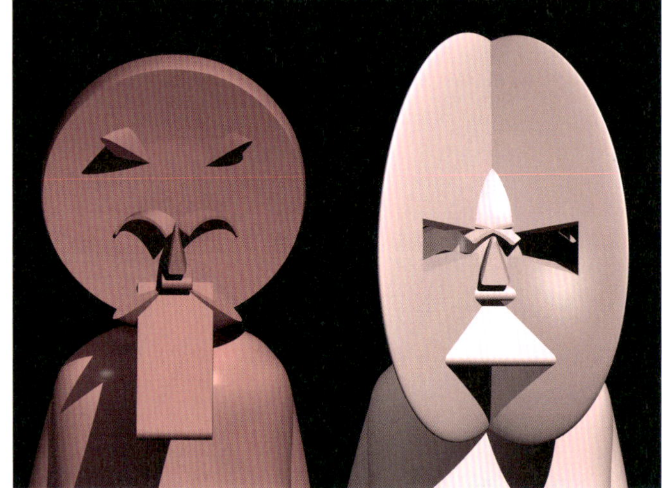

Thomas Krempke, Yves Netzhammer

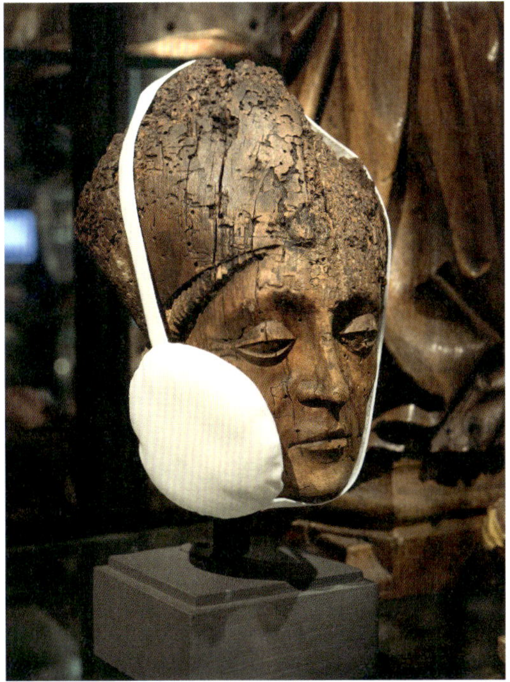

Thomas Krempke, Yves Netzhammer

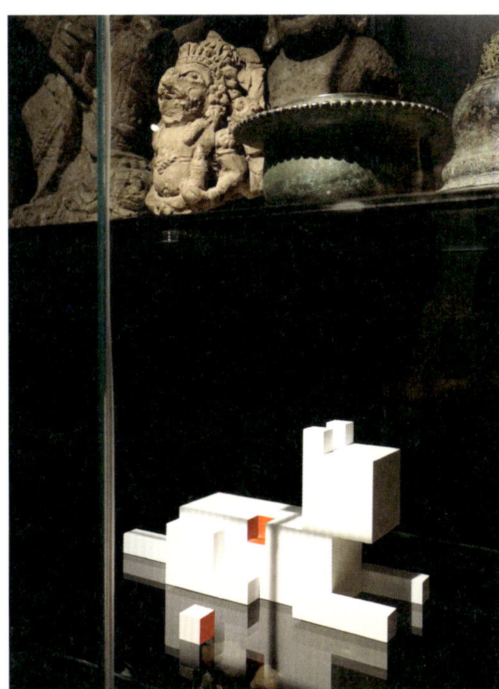

The present searches for its mouth in the reflection of the soup—an artistic intervention in the depot of a Museum of Ethnology, 36 projections and 80 objects in wood or textile.

This playful synaptic prelude intensifies in the dark depot of the Museum Rietberg—an exuberant place of foreign artifacts—into an opulent genuine static, which is manifested in the osculation point of nothing less then birth, life, death, religion, and cult. In this, one finds once more Netzhammer's central theme of assemblage—be it bodily, linguistically, or culturally.

The 36 video works that seem effortlessly and yet very precisely integrated, become just as much an integral part of the visible depot as the innumerable geometrical miniature sculptures which are formally a counterpoint to his opulent formal world. Netzhammer turns us into explorers of our contact with the foreign. And makes us conscious of the fact that the innumerable artifacts that are assembled here have been carefully created by hand in another region and another time. He succeeds in all this with dazzling intensity, gentle irony, and immense empathy.

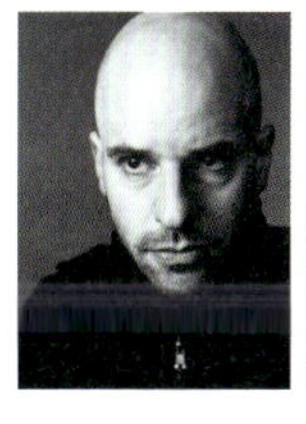

Jörg Leinmetz

Yves Netzhammer (CH), born in 1970, studied Visual Design at Zurich College of Art and Design. Since 1997 he has been working on a widely ramified, poetic cosmos of imagery. His video installations, objects, slide shows, and drawings fascinate through their bodily charisma and their formal clarity. Solo exhibitions include LWL, Munster (2016), Kiev Biennale, Kiev (2015), MONA, Tasmania (2013), Minsheng Art Museum Shanghai (2013), and many others. Yves Netzhammer lives and works in Zurich.

geist.xyz
ZEITGUISED

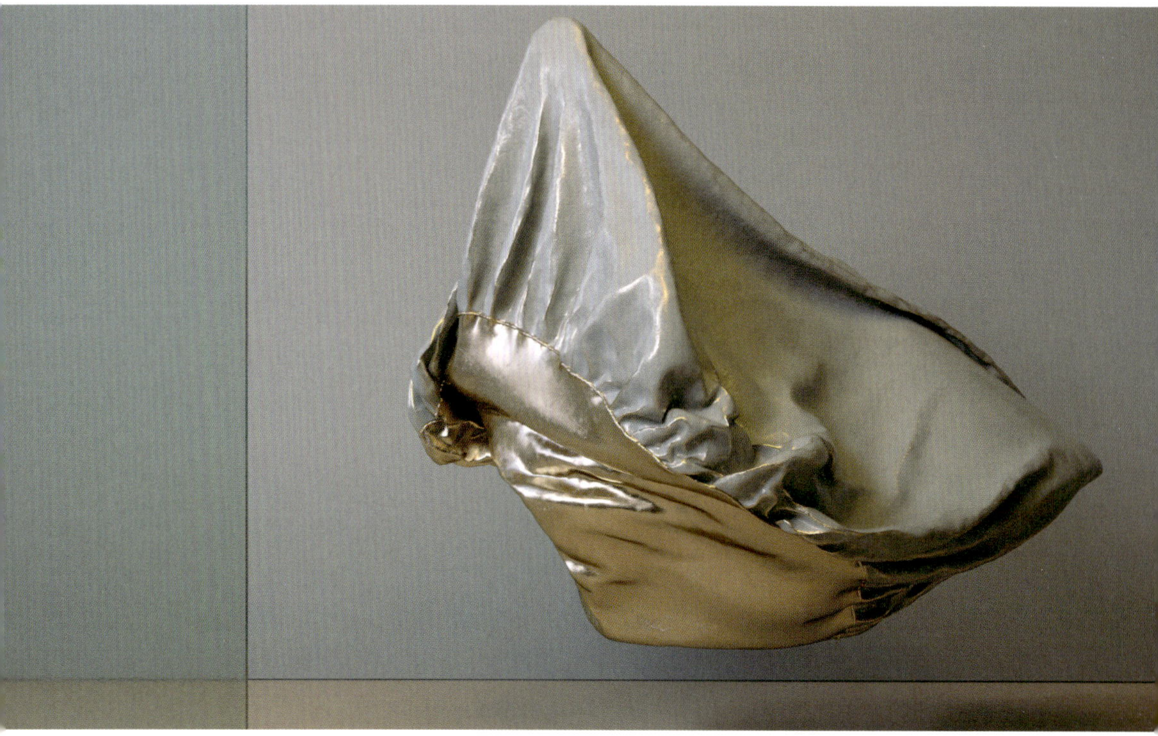

On January 6, 2016, ZEITGUISED released *geist.xyz*, a different kind of fashion project: what looks at first glance like an eccentric tangle of simulated dance and a color-coordinated tumblr exploration turns out to be a study of handcrafted algorithmic textiles and procedural surfaces presented in and for exquisite realities.

A synthetic ghost shifts simulated textiles from passive matter to live organisms. They behave like apparitions in an artificial choreography, with movements that are imaginary, yet familiar. Like a constant metamorphosis, the same sequence gets transformed over and over again. At each step, all aspects of the designs are modified, from algorithmic pattern to color scheme to fabric behavior. The results are meandering layers of style changes. To highlight the open nature of this process we took samples and present them in two forms: One is a grid of moving images on *geist.xyz* that visualizes our conceptual approach. The other is a linear montage showing the intricate details in 4K resolution. Shuffled layers of metronomic sounds emphasize the transformation fluctuating in and out of sync.

We have a background in sculpture and fashion design, and wanted to make this design project for years. We felt that algorithmic design is under-represented in fashion still, due to approaches that are either too nerdy or executions that don't work. We wanted to change that, and bring more design thinking to making patterns with algorithms. We also want to see these patterns being worn, and wear them ourselves—even if self-transforming textiles don't exist yet to the extent that we show. We just simply didn't want to wait for it.

Our focus on algorithmic design stems from an interest in the rules that shape things and how designers can work with a feedback loop of the design intention into emergent results of synthetic processes.

We were infatuated with the idea of algorithm-driven design in general and particularly fabrics and prints for a while. At some point we realized that it will take a while for the current textile technologies to be developed to a state where they are usable in products or even artwork. Visualizing them first in the most enticing way would maybe be a valid precursor of ideas to take shape soon after.

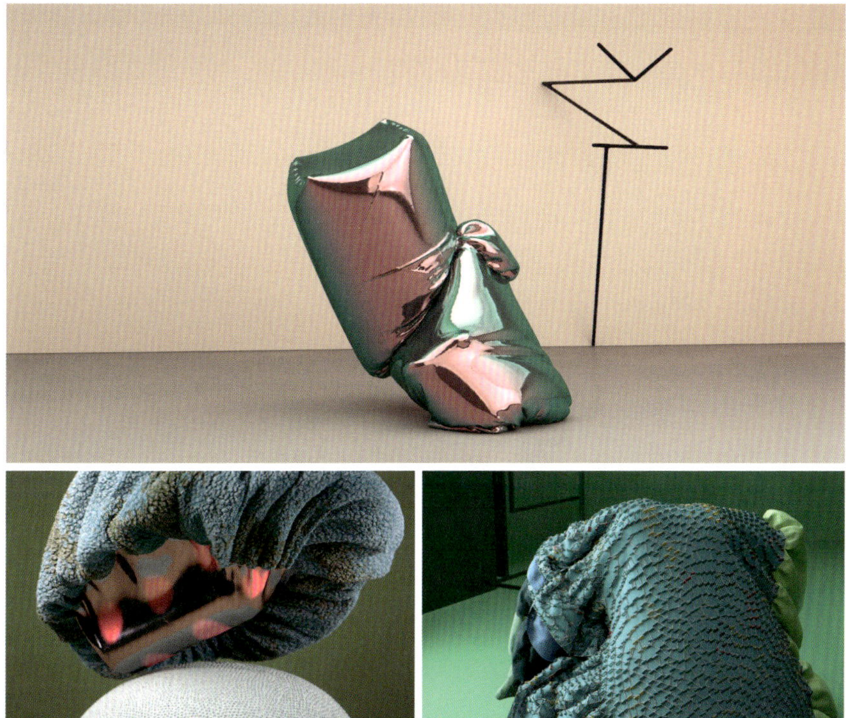

Switching around the initial brief of algorithm-driven design that we used was a choice that presented itself when we thought about textile design. Design-driven algorithms and processes were now the goal. The concept for the final piece was to document and exhibit the process itself—displaying the layered technique of feeding back the results into a design process that is not bound by authenticity and could therefore bear unexpected transformations. We tried to keep it subtle by adhering to a color scheme that we used to guide the manic layered shuffling of design elements. In terms of aesthetics, the resulting sequence bears quite a few moods, from bright to contrasty to dark, from elegant to exuberant, but the flow between those moods was the decisive point we wanted to make, on a micro and a macro level.

On a technical level, we worked with many software packages like Marvellous Designer for the fabric simulations and Houdini for the procedural surfaces and algorithm-driven patterns, and Substance Designer for additional procedural surfaces. It was all put together in Cinema 4D and rendered in Octane in full 4K resolution.

The most challenging part was curbing the sprawling complexity of possibilities. At some point we had oodles of movements, shapes, patterns, and textures that we had to sift through, declutter and recombine in ways that we couldn't have preconceived.

All conceptual, design and production work: ZEITGUISED
Sound track: *geist.xyz* by Superimposed Void
Production outtakes on: instagram/zeitguised

ZEITGUISED (DE) is a studio for consultancy for synthetic art and design with inhouse creative direction and production. The exquisite realities of ZEITGUISED are crafted as a unique blend of tantalizing design, handmade algorithms, and bespoke generative processes. ZEITGUISED was initially founded by Henrik Mauler (DE) and Jamie Raap (US) as a collective of artists, designers, and technologists. Their work has been presented in numerous international new media festivals and selected work has also been shown in galleries and art shows around the world. Their collective is based in Berlin.

Ghost Cell
Antoine Delacharlery

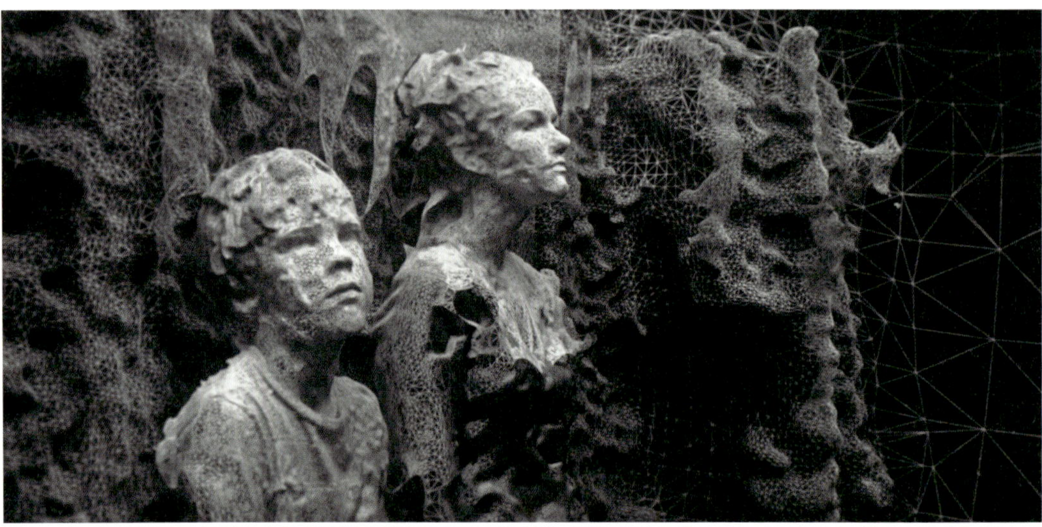

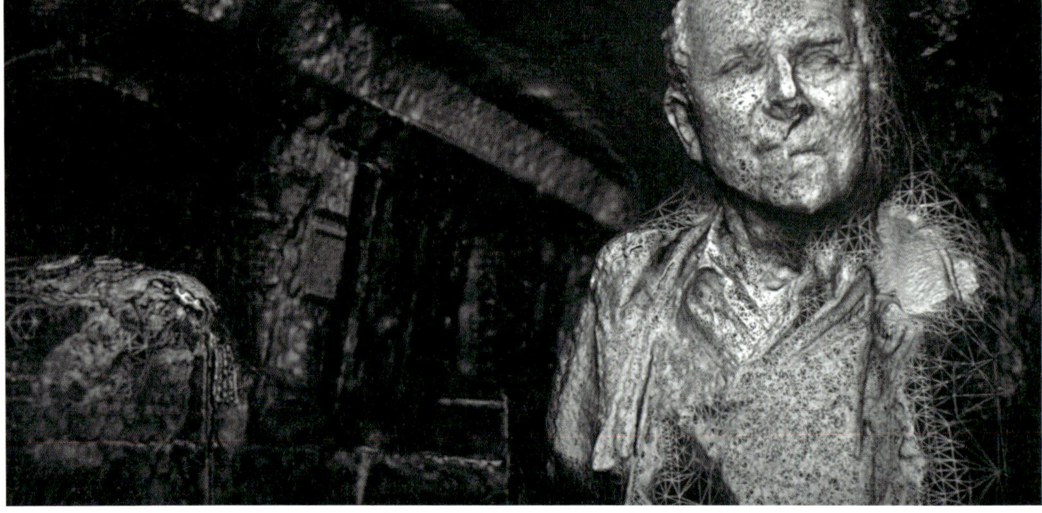

Scientific and dreamlike documentary at once, *Ghost Cell* is a stereoscopic plunge into the guts of an organic Paris seen as a cell through a virtual microscope.

Technics: CGI Animation (Stereoscopic 3D or flat)
Software: 3DS Max / After Effects

Screenwriter and editor: Antoine Delacharlery
Executive producer, line producer: Nicolas Schmerkin, Autour de Minuit Productions
Production manager: Émilie Schmerkin
Crew: Animation: Antoine Delacharlery, Bastien Dubois, Mathieu Bernadat, Jean Delaunay
Editing: Antoine Delacharlery
Music: Bastien Prevosto

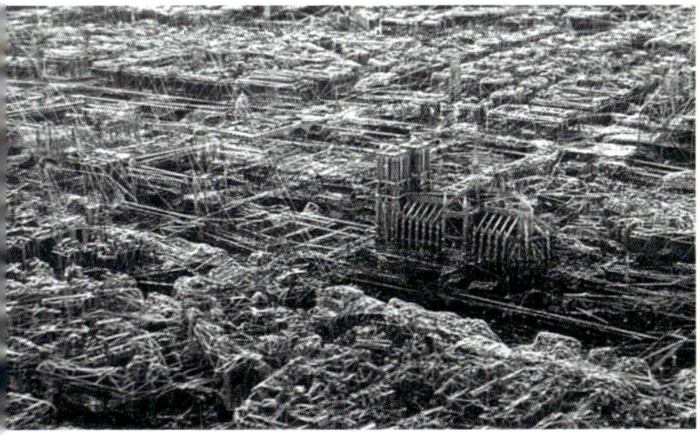

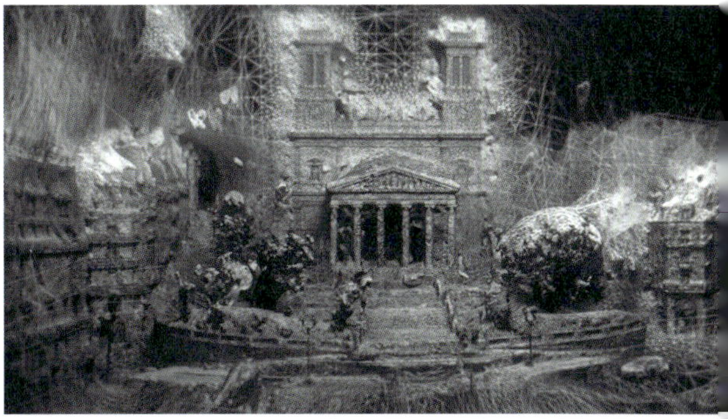

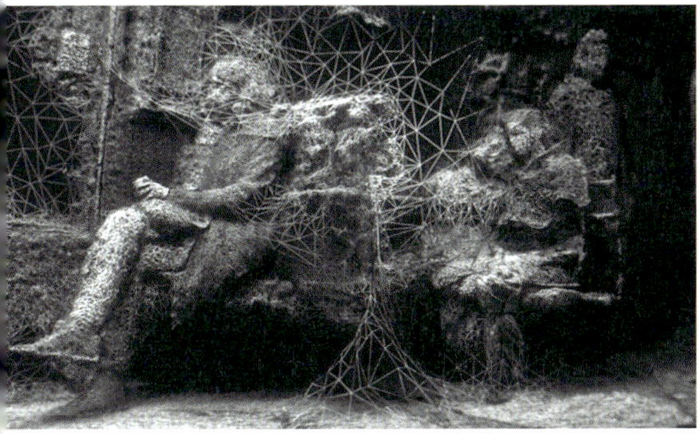

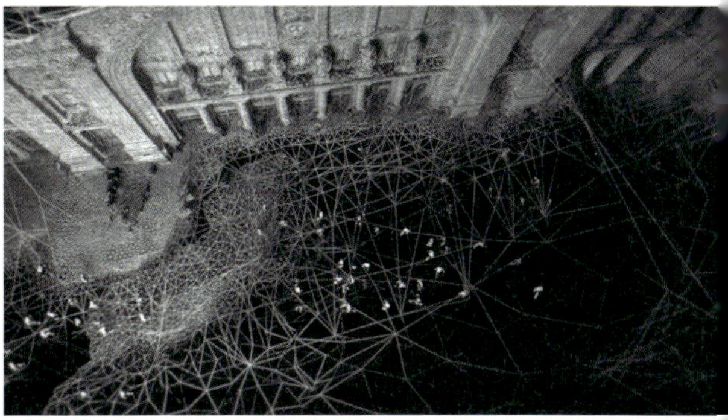

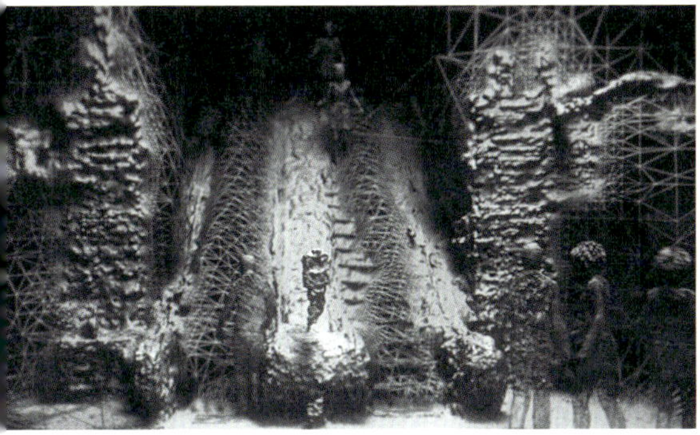

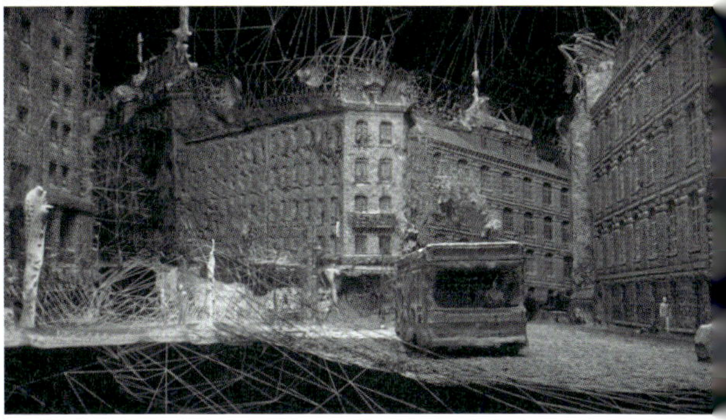

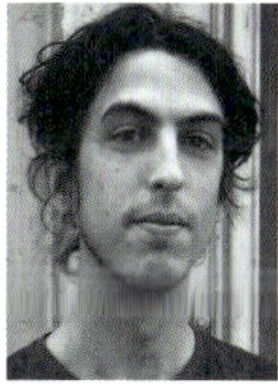

Antoine Delacharlery (FR) studied 3D animation and then turned to the field of animated short filmmaking and digital arts, all the while putting a great deal of manual work into his many projects. Exhibiting consummate versatility, he's equally adept at exploring many different techniques: 3D, camera work, graphic experimentation, and bricolage. His work thus seeks to weave interconnections among the real, the dreamlike, and the organic. In 2010 he received the Prix SCAM for his graduation film from Supinfocom *Telegraphics.*

Moom

Tonko House–Robert Kondo & Daisuke "Dice" Tsutsumi

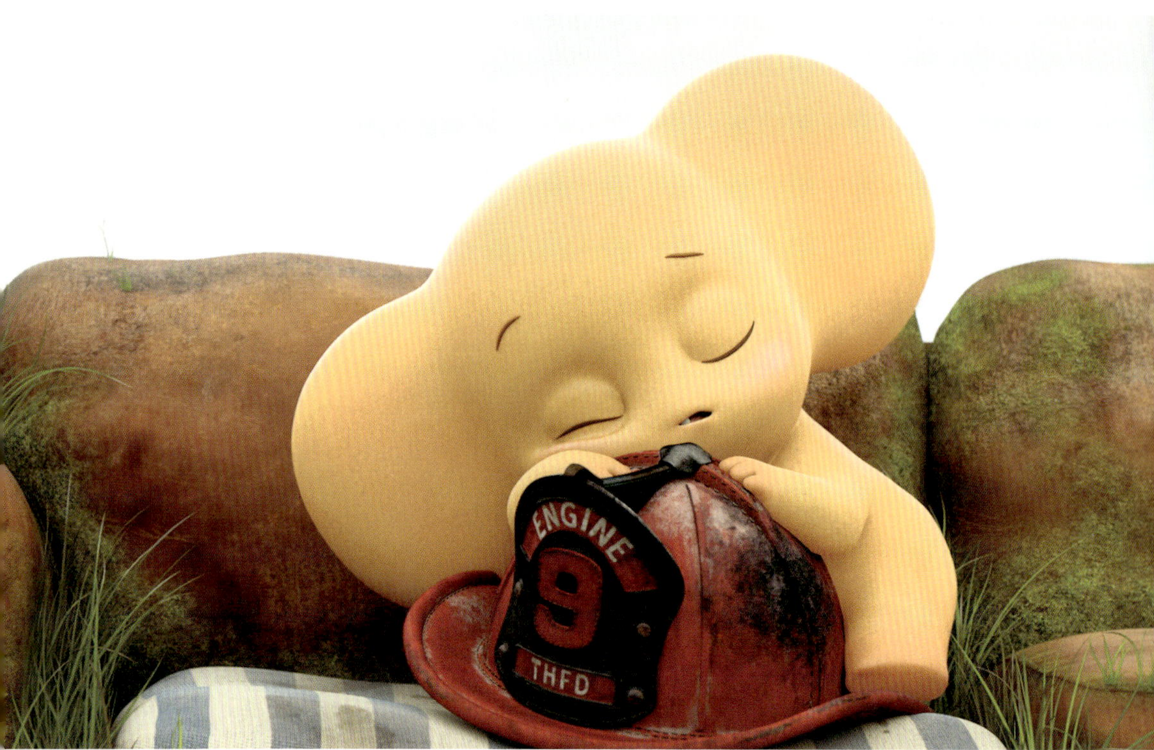

What happens to discarded objects? The old bike or wallet that has served its purpose and is no longer needed, objects we throw out? *Moom* is set in a fantastic land where these discarded objects rise out of a lake with their memories attached. These memories exist as dough-like characters that are the connection between the object and its former owner. When a memory is able to let go of its attachment to the past it rises into the air, dissolving into light and laughter. What happens when a memory can't let go?

We wanted to explore the idea of loss through the story of a stuck memory–Moom. To gain greater insight into the character of Moom, we discussed the earliest experiences of loss in our lives we can remember. Robert remembers losing his great grandmother in a tragic accident when he was four. The feeling of loss was a difficult emotion to process for a four year old. Years later the feeling of sadness and loss would reappear in his life at seemingly random times. It would take time and experience to understand his loss. We all have personal stories of loss and we aren't always able to quickly move on with our lives after experiencing loss. We felt *Moom* was a great opportunity to explore this very human emotion in animation. In the story, Moom cannot let go. Our film is based on a popular contemporary children's book from Japan by Genki Kawamura and Yuuki Mashiko. Genki Kawamura worked as a producer on the film and gave great insight into the story of the children's book. He was very open to the adaptation of the story to best fit the change in medium, from book to film.

Directors: Robert Kondo, Daisuke "Dice" Tsutsumi, Tonko House http://www.youtube.com/watch?v=7Vg4yFnIQSg

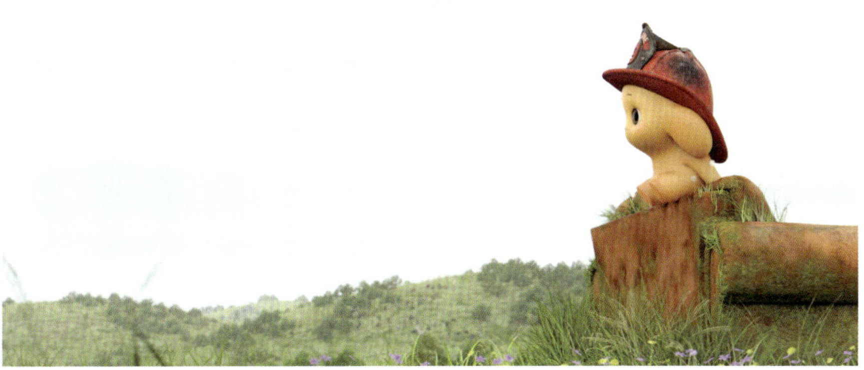

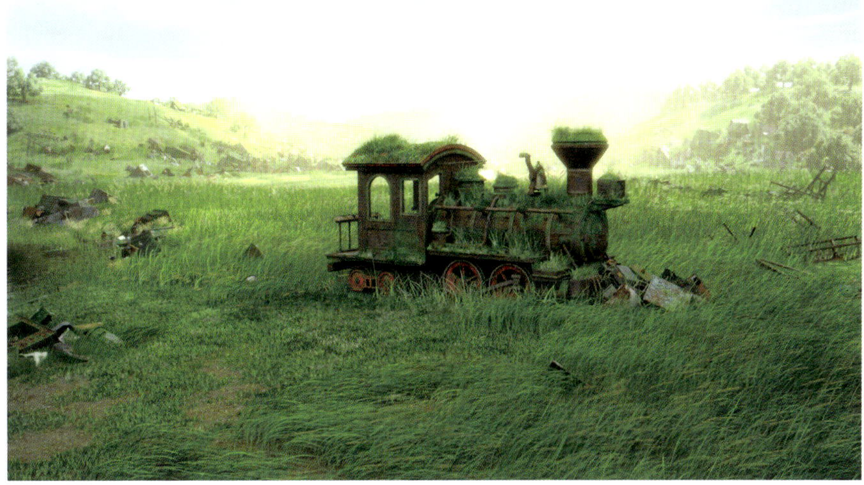

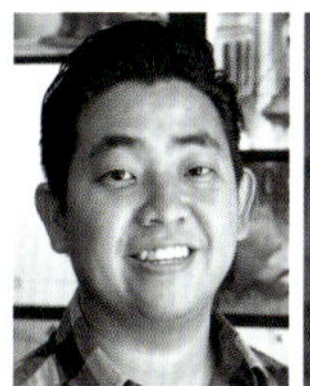

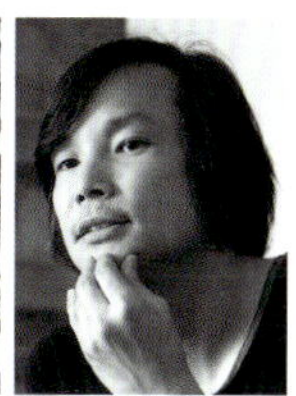

Robert Kondo (US). Originally from Southern California, Robert Kondo graduated with a degree in illustration from the Art Center College of Design in Pasadena. Robert landed his dream job as a sketch artist at Pixar on their 2006 release *Ratatouille*. While at Pixar, his film credits included Sets Art Director for *Ratatouille, Toy Story 3*, and most recently *Monsters University*, and Production Designer on two shorts. In July 2014, Robert left Pixar to start Tonko House, where every day is a challenge and an adventure. **Daisuke "Dice" Tsutsumi** (JP) is a filmmaker, painter, and philanthropist. A graduate from The School of Visual Arts in New York, Dice has worked as a visual development/color key artist at Blue Sky Studios on *Ice Age, Robots* and *Horton Hears a Who!* His credits at Pixar Animation include Lighting Art Director for *Toy Story 3* and *Monsters University*. Dice is passionate about charity work and spearheaded both the *Iotoro Forest Project* and *Sketchtravel*.

Never Say Never
Saman Kesh, Skunk

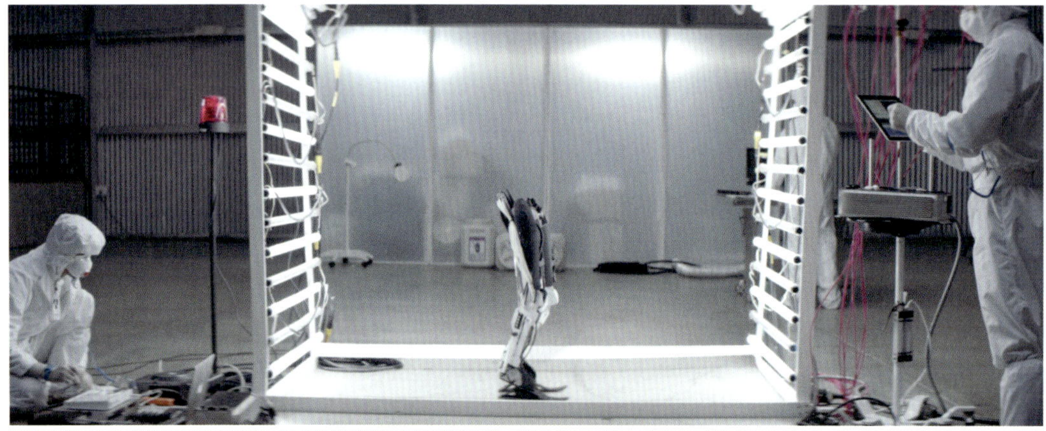

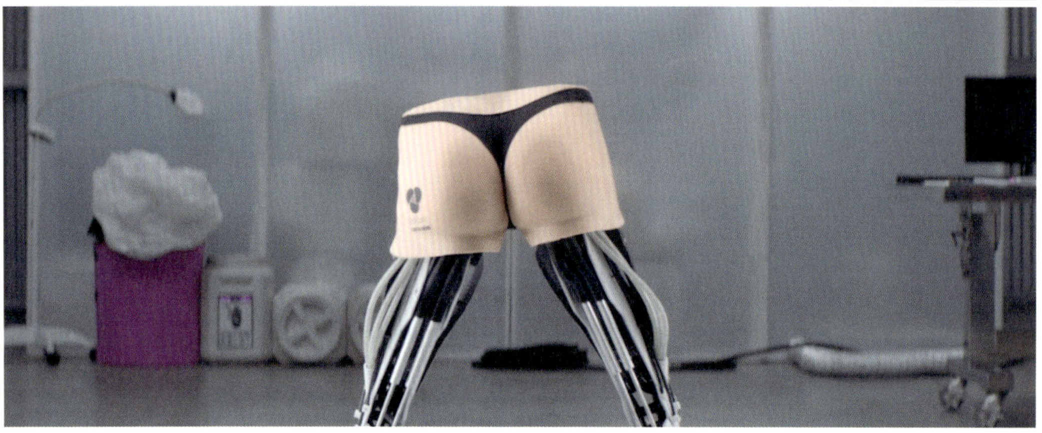

Saman Kesh joined forces with legendary producer duo Felix Buxton and Simon Ratcliffe, known as Basement Jaxx, for a groundbreaking 6-minutes video. *Never Say Never* follows Jaxx Industries in their zealous effort to bring dancing back to mankind via twerking by creating the futuristic TW3RK-BOT1.0.

The Build: My, now, dear friends at Alterian Inc. kicked ass. I brought the idea and a document of a rough mock-up of what I was looking for and what it needed to do as well as the features. They went off and kind of made a little more of a concrete sketch. We then tweaked and adjusted as we went along (since we didn't have a ton of time—eight days to be exact). After visiting the shop almost every day and having our daily pow-wow of evolution, the robot was ready to show its stuff.

The Twerking: I always knew that I didn't want to do CG, but I also didn't want to do full-on robotics. Mostly those two would have been impossible. Instead, I pitched the idea of puppeting the robot and adjusting in post. Alterian bought in and that's what we did. There were three puppeteers. One for the ass pump (the booty shakes). Another for the humping/thrusts (this was a professional Twerker). And finally another animator that worked the legs and knee joints. We later adjusted the "jittery" amount accordingly in post.

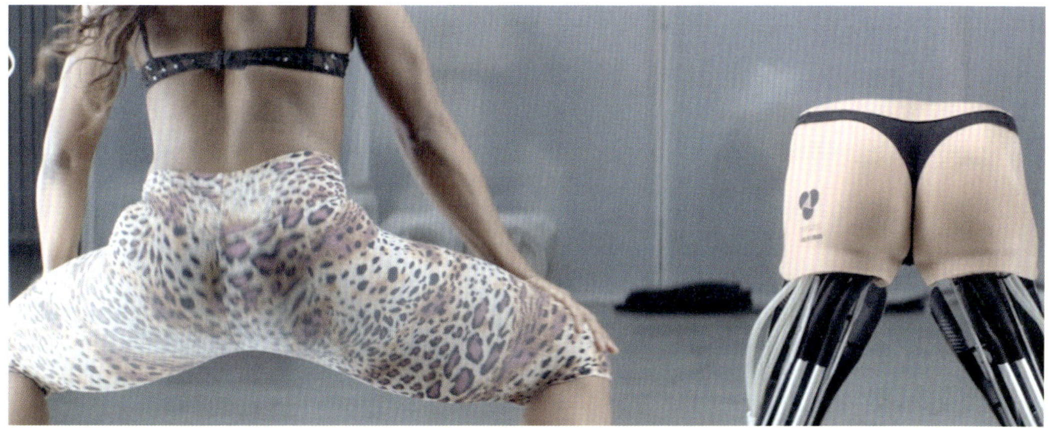

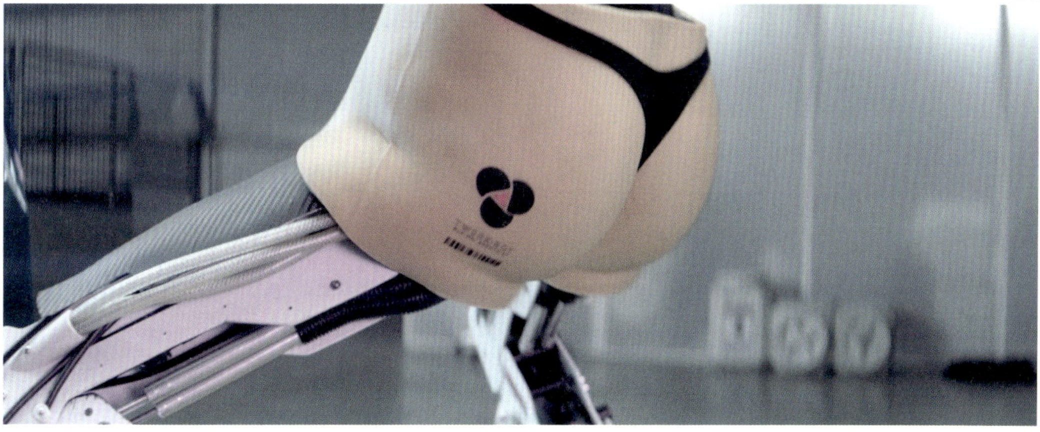

Writer and director: Saman Kesh
Music: Basement Jaxx, *Never Say Never*
Line producer: Courtney Davies
Production company: SKUNK
Executive producer: Shelly Townsend & Matt Factor
Commissioner: John Moule
Twerk-bot design & build: Alterian Inc., Tony Gardner,
Lilo Tauvao, Peter Chevako, *alterianinc.com*

Cinematography: Guillermo Garza
Wardrobe stylist: Michelle Thompson
Editing: Mandy Brown & Saman Kesh
Production design: Greg Lang
Art director: Coran Deloy Oberlin
Colorist: Derek Hansen (MPC)
Sound design: Brent Kiser
Assistant director: Jesse Sternbaum
Director assistant: Brendan Varni

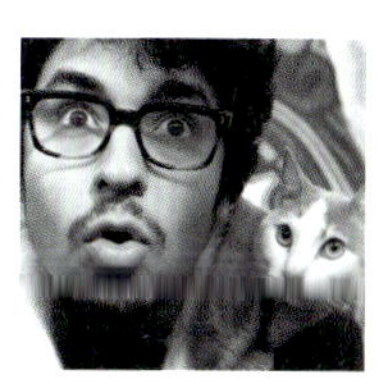

Saman Kesh, Skunk (IR) got his start at the Art Center College of Design, where he won a SXSW 2010 Best Video award for *Cinnamon Chasers*, a road trip shot in POV. While at school, a spec ad for Canon garnered him a Clio and inclusion in the Saatchi New Directors' Showcase. In 2013 he won an additional SXSW Best Video award for Vitalic. Basement Jaxx's *Never Say Never* was nominated for a Grammy (Best Dance Recording) this past year and his newest KYGO music video, *Stole The Show*, was in Creative Review among March's music videos of the month.

Simulacra
Theo Tagholm

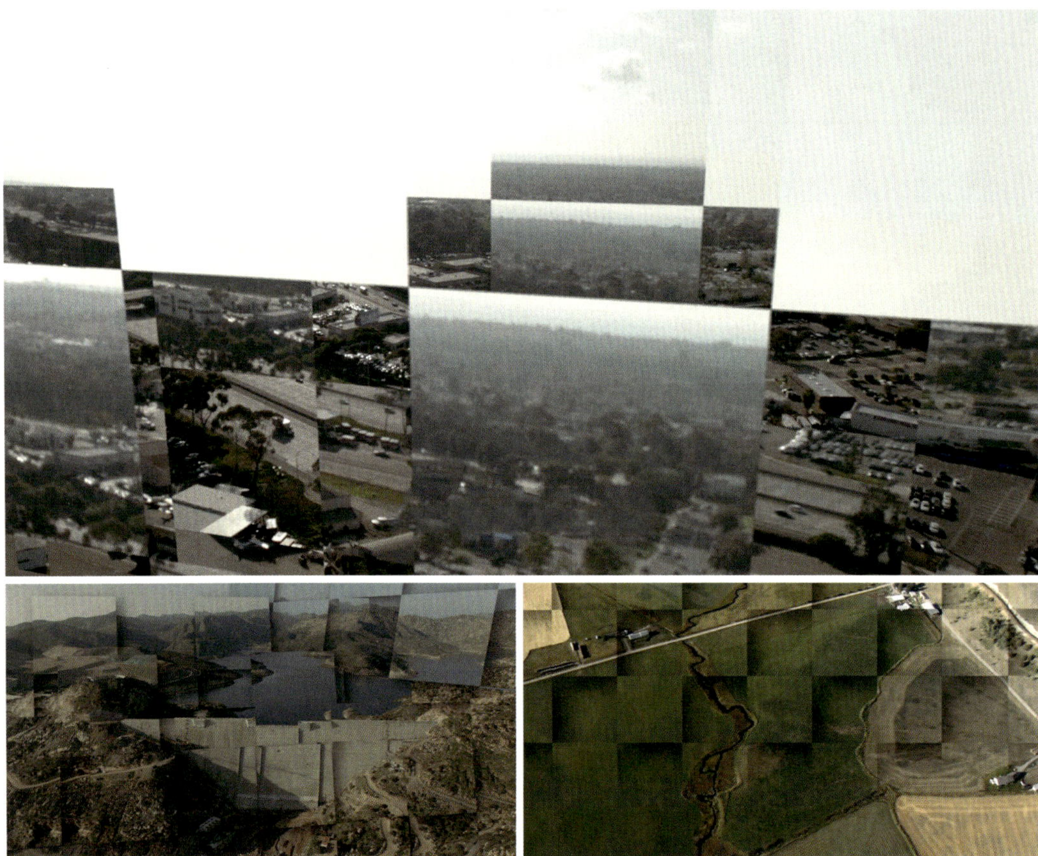

The film *Simulacra* has drawn inspiration from Jean Baudrillard's work *Simulacra and Simulation*.

"Today abstraction is no longer that of the map, the double, the mirror, or the concept. Simulation is no longer that of a territory, a referential being, or a substance. It is the generation by models of a real without origin or reality: a hyperreal. The territory no longer precedes the map, nor does it survive it. It is nevertheless the map that precedes the terri- tory– procession of simulacra–that engenders the territory, and if one must return to the fable, today it is the territory whose shreds slowly rot across the extent of the map. It is the real, and not the map, whose vestiges persist here and there in the deserts that are no longer those of the Empire, but ours. The desert of the real itself."

Simulacra and Simulation by Jean Baudrillard

In *Simulacra* we begin with shots of nature. As we progress through the film we encounter suburbs, the roads that link them, the urban metropolis tipped on its head, and the images become more fractured until a tipping point changes the nature of the city.

Simulacra is about the nature of our bombardment by and relationship to the image. The fracturing surface in the film recalls observations of the field of vision, the act of looking. The surface, the frame, image, origin, original, copy, real and re-real.

The frame of the image is commodifying the ter- rain and framing our relation to it. The signifier and signified become more disparate as the layers seg- ment off, quarantined from the original location they become their own truth. The fragments become a frame in themselves, constituting a new real, a new nature of our cities, that again become processed by

http://vimeo.com/123006429

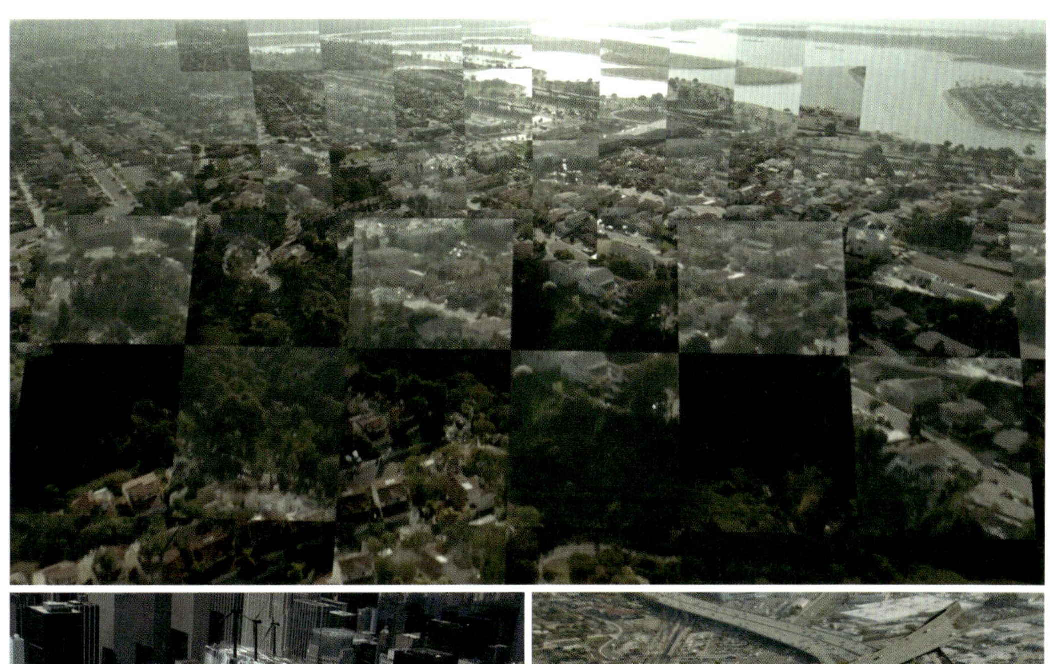

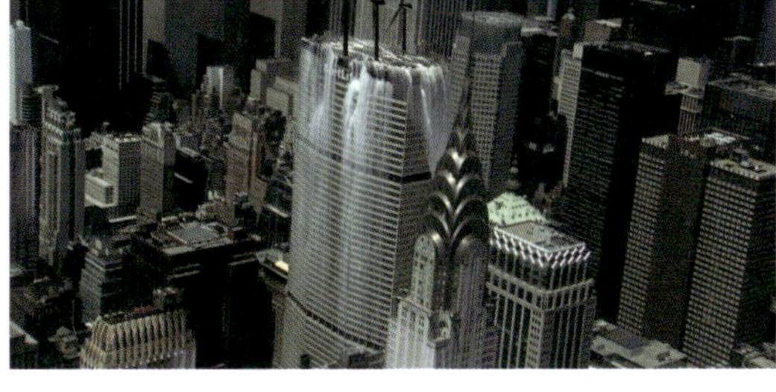

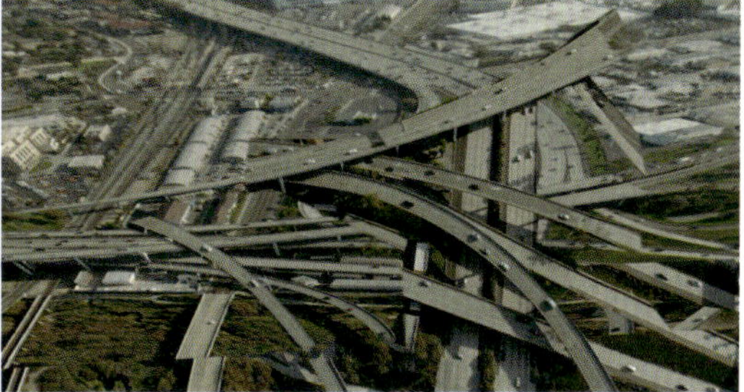

our notions of nature and the state we exist in. A Duchampian notion of the Infra-slim also comes into play here—where the image sits on the real and is separate, but at the same time joined by a shared real. The image becomes a symbol of the construct of our cities, built by ourselves, out of nature becoming a new nature—a habitat of the real, an institution of how we are. So saturated in the image of the city as us and nature as outside the real, we see the wild as all outside the city.

The film was created using Adobe after effects and the music is *A Seated Night* (Ambient), licensed from Moby.

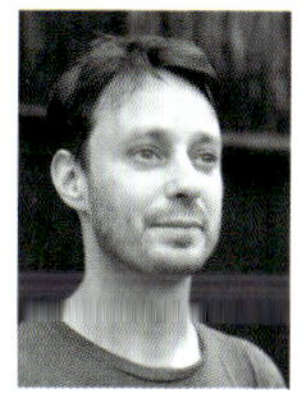

Theo Tagholm (UK) is a London-based artist working in time-based media. He trained at Chelsea School of Art and Middlesex as a painter, which still informs much of his work. Aspects learned in life drawing, the act of looking—which differs from the act of taking a photograph—features heavily in the work. Much of Theo's work begins with a process, often between the subject and the surface, that reveals meaning over time. Previous work and installations include *The Brunswick Project*, the Jerwood Moving Image Award shortlist, South London Gallery—Canada/UK video exchange, and the Rencontres International Festival.

Tehran-Geles
Arash Nassiri

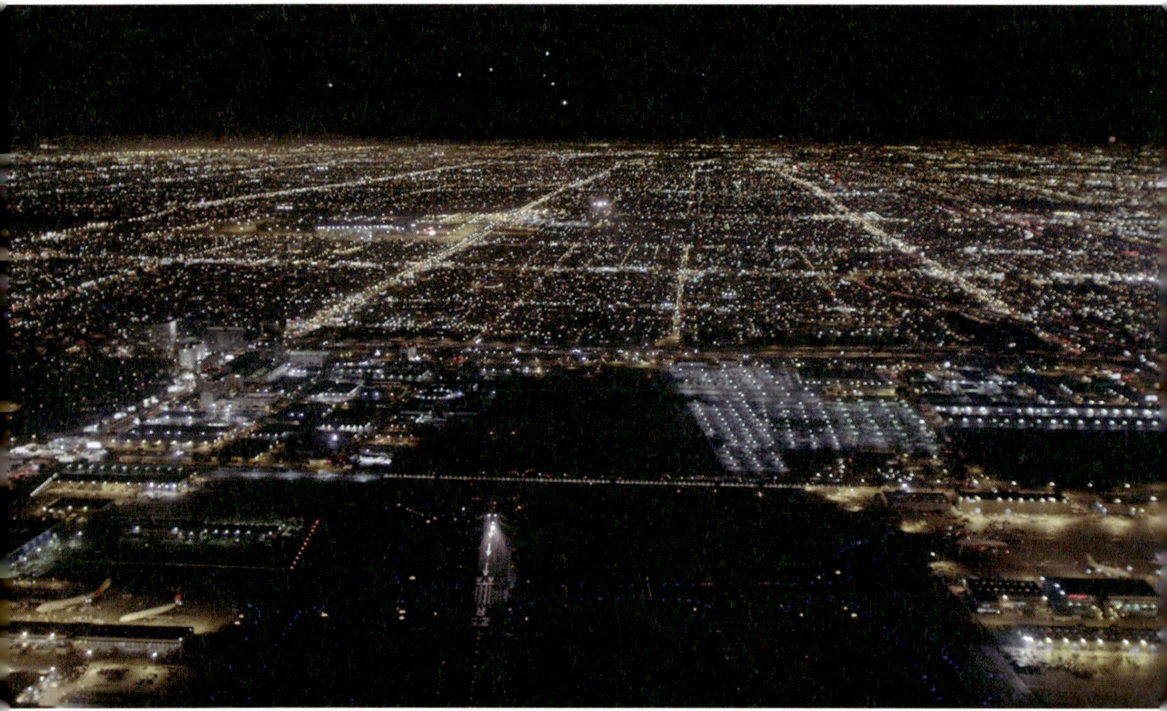

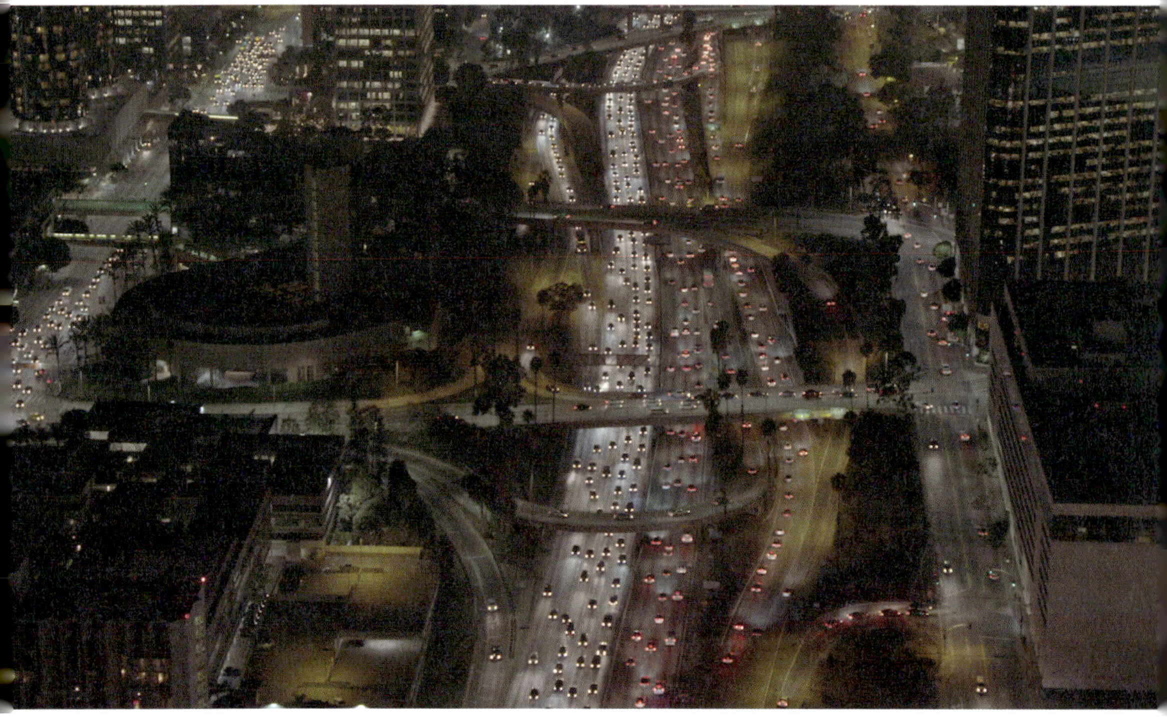

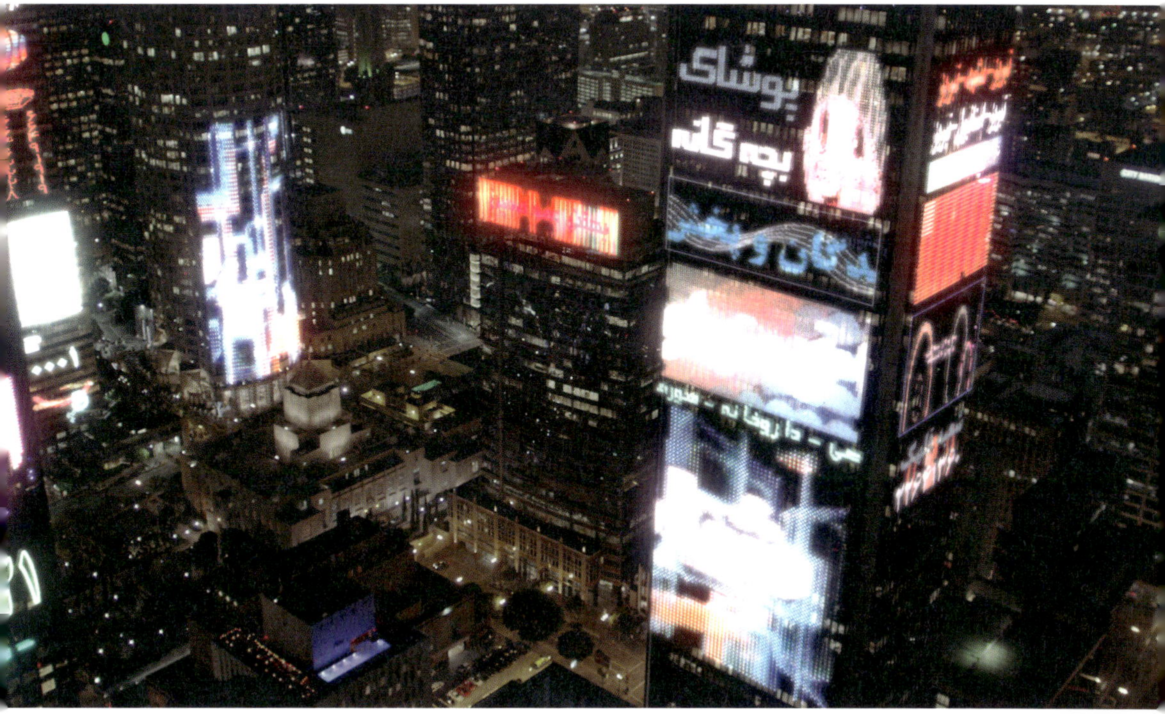

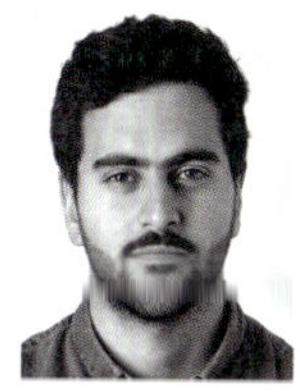

Tehran-Geles is a fictional vision of Tehran, set within the urban landscape of Los Angeles. Through an aerial journey, we discover an architectural transposition of the two cities. While flying over the Los Angeles boulevards, personal migrant testimonies echo the collective story of the Iranian capital. Downtown, the buildings are saturated with neon signs pulsating with voices that take us on a hallucinatory trip.

Parallel to the science fictional genre where the present is projected into the future, this short film projects the past of Tehran into the Western present. The production of this short film generated an audio-visual migration where aerial shots of Los Angeles merge with videos filmed in Tehran and later transported by plane, as well as interviews recorded via Skype in different cities around the world.

Director, scriptwriter: Arash Nassiri
Music: Flavien Berger
Production and distribution: Le Fresnoy,
Studio national des arts contemporains

Arash Nassiri (IR), born in 1986 in Teheran, lives and works between Teheran, Los Angeles, and Paris. Arash studied at the prestigious art schools ENSBA École Nationale des Beaux-Arts de Paris (2008), UdK Berlin (2010), Ensad, Paris (Master's degree, 2012) and Le Fresnoy (Tourcoing, France, 2014). His films include *Voyage / Voyage* (2009), *Tunetracks* (2010), *Lovelock* (2011), *Masters* (2012), *Palais* (2013), and his award-winning film *Tehran-Geles* (2014), which won the Prix RMIT University Award for Best Experimental Short Film at the Melbourne International Film Festival in 2015 and the Grand Prix Art Vidéo at the Festival Côté Court Pantin, Paris, 2014. His current work in progress is the video and installation *Nowruz* (2016)

Uncanny Valley
AlteredQualia + Fractal Fantasy

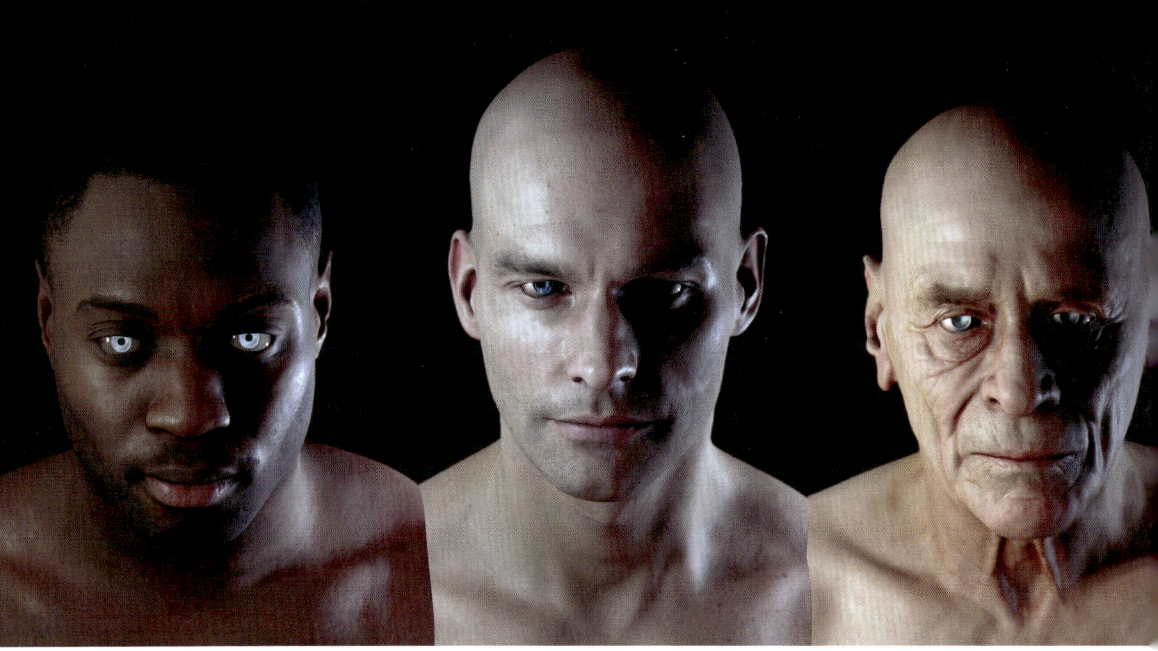

Creating convincing synthetic human beings is a notoriously difficult task. The "uncanny valley" phenomenon is a hypothesis that as you try to increase the realism of your human-like creations, there is a point behind which improvements actually become negative, causing a sense of unease or repulsion.

Something flips in the mind of the observer, and the creature starts to be seen as a "human with which something seems to be wrong" instead of "human-like", a doll becomes a corpse. It takes a lot more effort to climb out of the valley, every little detail that was abstracted away comes back into play.

We created the *Uncanny Valley* project to explore these concepts. It is an interactive webpage experiment with three animated virtual human heads reacting to the user's mouse movements, accompanied by three songs, featuring light sources synchronized to the music. The experiment is trying to find out what can be achieved today on the web, with very limited resources, on a constrained platform.

High-quality 3D scans of human heads (courtesy of Ten24) were adapted for real-time use and rendered in the web browser using JavaScript and WebGL. *Uncanny Valley* features real-time skin and eye shading with a simple subsurface scattering approximation, under dynamic lighting, running on a homebrew WebGL rendering engine called XG.

The three electronic music pieces, which were written specifically for this project, tie music and lighting intrinsically, using a combination of automatic sound frequency analysis and manual beat annotations for modulating light intensities and positions. Synthetic humanoid voices aim to enhance the eeriness of virtual humans visuals.

We used a simple two-lights rig, emulating photography studio lighting and realistic virtual camera with subtle post-processing effects (bokeh depth-of-field, tone mapping, color grading), trying to cheat our way out of uncanny valley by presenting synthetic human beings in a tried-and-tested setting and framing, with a dramatic and flattering presentation.

Special attention was paid to the eyes, both technically and stylistically. A two-layer material is used, with simple approximation of light scattering, refraction, and caustics. Pupils are dynamic, with physiologically-inspired animation depending on the amount of incoming light. Having eyes locked in eye contact with the observer turned out to be a simple yet effective way to induce the illusion of "somebody being there". As an Easter egg we also included several non-human "android" eyes variants.

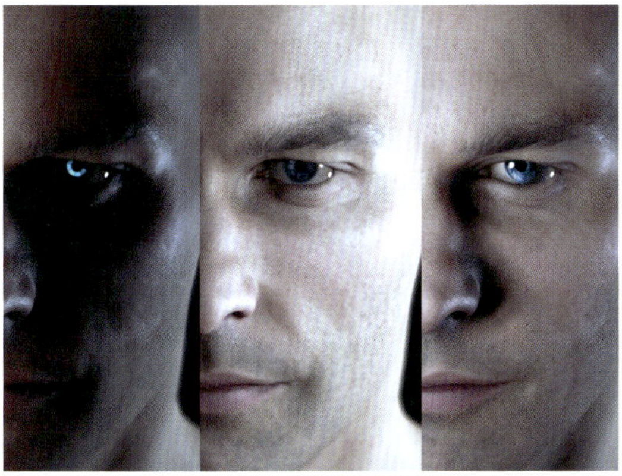

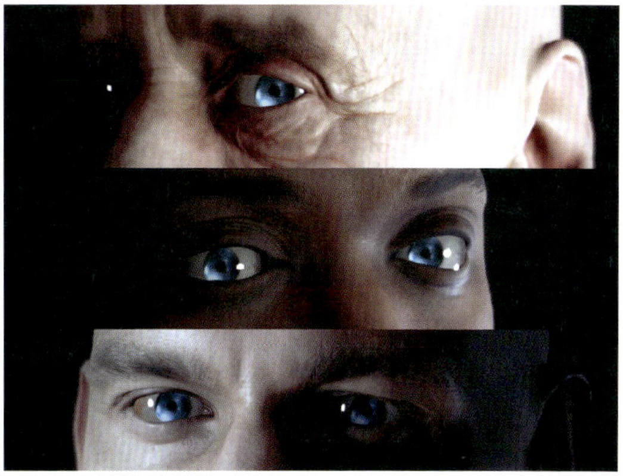

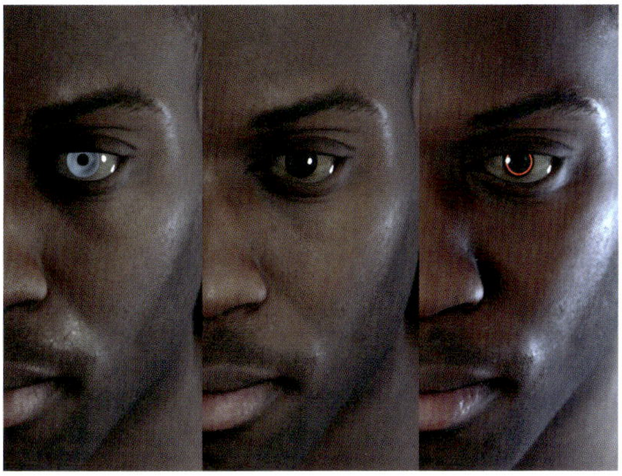

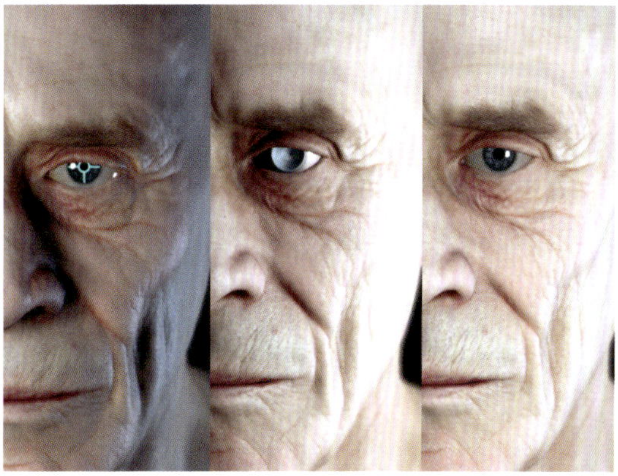

Uncanny Valley is the result of a collaboration between the computer graphics programmer AlteredQualia, and the platform Fractal Fantasy. Head scans courtesy of Ten24.

Visuals, code and rendering: Branislav Ulicny, AlteredQualia, Fractal Fantasy
Songs by: Sinjin Hawke, Martyn Bootyspoon, Zora Jones
http://alteredqualia.com
http://fractalfantasy.net

Branislav Ulicny / AlteredQualia (SK) likes to explore possibilities of real-time computer graphics on the web. Before succumbing to the temptations of dark arts of rendering, he dabbled in academic research of artificial life, crowd simulations, and bioinformatics. He is an alumnus of a popular open source project *three. js* and holds a doctorate in computer science from EPFL. **Fractal Fantasy** (AT/CA) has established itself as an observatory for otherworldly textures, both aural and visual, over the last past years. The brain child of Sinjin Hawke and Zora Jones found life as an outlet for audiovisual pieces in 2013 and has since grown to encompass code experiments and interactive musical works, all the while remaining a fluid and ever-expanding endeavor: "[Fractal Fantasy] is a space to create and evolve freely and not being tied to a mission. It's a platform for us to create whatever we want, whenever we want, with whoever we want, without any restrictions." (Zora Jones, *The FADER*, 13.11.2015)

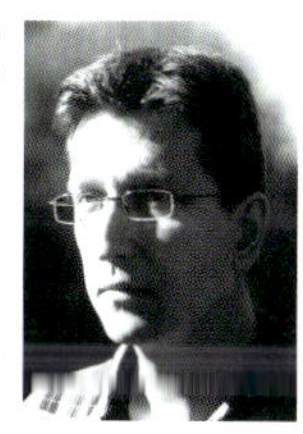

INTERACTIVE ART+

Transcending the Medium

Christophe De Jaeger, Irini Papadimitriou, Michela Ana Magas,
Joachim Sauter, Victoria Vesna

The language of interaction in the realm of art has matured to the extent that it is now able to occupy spaces outside of the artists' laboratory and beyond the confines of the screen. In the era of hyper-connectedness, interaction is the most pervasive medium that allows the art to create a dialogue with every form of human activity. It migrates from the familiar contexts inscribed by artistic jargon to occupy the spaces of social, scientific, and political discourse. The jury selection of Interaction+ reflects this acquired status, demonstrating its effective engagement with this discursive ecosystem and its physical environment.

Significant work from the past two years shows an active engagement with handmade tools and the process of making. It uses the language of making and the associated culture of sharing and openness as an integral part of the intellectual discourse of artistic thought. The ease and portability of the open toolkit allows the artistic dialogue to plant itself at the center of the action, instead of communicating at a distance.

Thus the three top works selected reflect the wide range of interactivity in the arts and each challenges the notion of what we label *art* while engaging in issues that address politics and freedom of speech *(Can you Hear Me?)*, access to advanced medical procedures *(Open Surgery)*, and our relationship with natural systems *(Parasitic Symbiotic)*. That each of these artworks could easily fit into other categories begs the question "What is Interactive Art?" and the answer lies in the + —the interactivity amplifies the message and transcends the medium.

Golden Nica

"Can you hear me?" · Christoph Wachter, Mathias Jud

In a society under constant surveillance, where governments abuse power and act against basic human rights, interactions like *"Can you hear me?"* provide us with powerful tools that challenge these systems and make our voices heard. Following revelations by Edward Snowden about the Brandenburg Gate in Berlin being the focal point of spying on the population, Christoph Wachter and Mathias Jud took a bold step with a minimal DIY installation of can antennas on the roof of the Academy of Arts at Pariser Platz in Berlin, and created an independent WiFi mesh network between the listening posts of the US and the British Embassy, the Swiss Embassy, and the Reichstag, in order to recapture the communication space. The created network was accessible to passers by, giving them equal rights to communicate and send messages to the GCHQ and NSA intelligence.

"Can you hear me?" is a powerful and playful act that engages in questions challenging who gets access to information and data, privacy, and the state of surveillance. It is a testament to the importance of artists who use the medium of interaction in a way that allows them to leave the traditional space for artistic discourse and occupy the space for dialogue currently used by a system of governance known for overriding basic rights of the democratic society—personal privacy and freedom of speech. The jury was particularly impressed with the modest, minimal installation that held a sculptural aesthetic while being a fully active interactive work that challenges the establishment while raising public awareness about our power and powerlessness in the age of digital information.

Awards of Distinction

OpenSurgery—A do-it-yourself surgery robot for domestic laparoscopy · Frank Kolkman

A large number of disturbing YouTube videos of people performing and sharing medical hacks—mainly uninsured Americans—inspired Frank Kolkman to create *OpenSurgery:* a DIY surgical robot that can be used to perform laparoscopic surgery. In the context of the disruptive maker culture, built with ready-made parts and accessible prototyping techniques such as laser cutting and 3D printing, Frank Kolkman's surgical robot presents a potentially accessible and cost-effective alternative to the expensive professional healthcare services, particularly relevant to the public in the US where the gap between those who can afford health insurance and those who cannot is rapidly widening. But more significantly, this critical and conceptual work, which creates new conditions for interaction within the highly regulated and controlled sector of health care, raises important questions about inequality, ethics, and the lack of access to essential health services for a growing number of people around the world.

Parasitic / Symbiotic · Ann-Katrin Krenz

A milling machine installed on a tree moves along the trunk, carving the encoded text of a poem from German Romanticism. With this performative act, Ann-Katrin Krenz explores the impact of the human relationship with nature. The milling machine, as a technological intervention, appears to invade the tree, much like the often aggressive intervention that humans perpetrate on nature. At the same time, this parasitic machine encodes marks derived from a poem about unity and oneness—a non-disturbing act of love—that becomes integrated in nature. As this work of interaction invades the tree, what is accomplished gradually turns into a subtle, even poetic message by a young artist.

Honorary Mentions

Random Darknet Shopper · !Mediengruppe Bitnik

In every realm of human economic activity there exist "dark" markets. This has long been the case in the physical world, and while rarely discussed, they also exist online. The objects for sale are tangible and geographically situated, though the markets that exchange them lie beyond the boundaries of regulation. *Random Darknet Shopper*—automated software designed to randomly purchase items with a set bitcoin budget—goes on weekly shopping sprees from the online dark market. Through its weekly purchases, which have included counterfeit products, a passport, and even drugs, the bot brings to light parts of the hidden world of the deep web that the average person might not ordinarily encounter. The items purchased online are shipped to the exhibition space, unpacked, and their physical manifestation forms the footprint of internet's dark side.
The *Random Darknet Shopper* reveals a hidden sec-

tion of society in an ingenious way, exploring the anonymity of the web, the ways in which products are traded and the extent to which they can be regulated in deepweb markets. It also raises important questions about the ethics in these hidden markets—inaccessible through conventional search engines, but available for purchase and consumption all the same. The bot's seizure by Swiss authorities for purchasing drugs further raises the question of responsibility in the context of these transactions.

Jennifer Lyn Morone™ Inc · Jennifer Lyn Morone

Jennifer Lyn Morone creates a critique of data ownership and personal data worth. She draws attention to the human right to own personal data by turning herself into a corporation—Jennifer Lyn Morone™ Inc. Her identity, physical & mental abilities, her biological functions, and her data are assets only she can exploit and potentially turn into profits. Any data created by Jennifer Lyn Morone™ Inc is trademarked, copyrighted, and therefore protected, a privilege normally unavailable to private individuals. This is a deliberate act that makes us consider the nature of data exploitation by corporations and governments, the issues around data privacy, ownership, and profit. Her interaction invades and exploits the very system that creates the conditions for personal information control by corporations.

Marble Machine · Martin Molin, Wintergatan

Even before digital, it was always possible to make fantastic, programmable musical instruments. In bell towers and church towers that play a melody, they always have a programmable wheel that's like the one that is on the *Marble Machine*. It's also based on the concept of the music box with the pattern playing out on the wheel as it turns. But the *Marble Machine* is definitely a post-digital musical instrument. It uses triggers, sensors, and concepts like grouped sections and digital busses to construct the song as it is played. It's not simply a case of turning the handle like an old-school organ grinder. It brings programming, performance, traditional handcrafting, and digital production together to make a contemporary pop song using ancient techniques, modern tools, and the physics of ballistics. In an age where digital technologies allow almost anyone to participate in the production of music without barriers whether economic, accessibility, or expertise-based, and to do so quickly, simply, and often without significant effort, Molin has labored for over a year to invent an ingenious work that explores the relationship of music to movement, mathematics, physical processes, and systems thinking. In the physical entity of Molin's *Marble Machine* is both the instrument and the song itself–the process of making is embedded within and is inseparable from the process of composition.

Rare Earthenware · Unknown Fields Division

Pottery and clay are very much connected to the soil and the place where they originated; they are also connected to earth, and often remind us of this connection spiritually, physically, but also politically. In the case of the Ming-style vessels that are featured in *Rare Earthenware*–a film showing the extraordinary journey back to their origins–there is something quite unsettling about their presence and connection to their place of origin. The soil and earth they are connected to is in fact a muddy radioactive lake in an industrial city in Inner Mongolia with a high content of heavy metals. The toxic vases have been crafted to represent the amount of waste created in the production of electronics such as a smartphone, a laptop, and an electric car battery, serving as witnesses to our participation in and interaction with this vicious circle of consumerism, and reminding us of the disturbing consequences of our consumerist habits, leading to a toxic future.

Jller · Prokop Bartoníček, Benjamin Maus

Jller is part of an ongoing, multidisciplinary research project in the fields of industrial automation and historical geology. A machine is moving slowly over a group of pebbles, examining them and delicately picking them up one at a time. This is not a random action–the pebbles are sorted meticulously by the machine after being scanned and analyzed for their type and geological age. The machine in *Jller* is performing this act of sorting with a series of beautiful choreographed moves. The work surprises because it confronts nature and technology, beauty and absur-

dity, historical times and immediate actions. The artists don't experiment with technology for the sake of innovation, but adapt an original, infrequently used technology to create a poetic and inspiring piece of interaction.

Exhausting a Crowd · Kyle McDonald

The work refers to a novel in which the writer observed and interpreted one place over a period of time. The artist transfers this situation to the present by using a contemporary interactive medium. *Exhausting a Crowd* presents a 12-hour scene in the busy public Piccadilly area in London, a typical city scene with passers-by, shoppers, tourists, workers, commuters as well as traffic. The events occurring during the 12-hour period are open to anyone to comment upon, annotate, or tag, resulting in a collaborative interpretation of the narrative. Exploring ideas of privacy and the public space, and our society's obsession with commenting on everyday activities, what could initially sound like a captivating tableau vivant of ordinary, everyday scenes, turns out to be an evolving narrative of biased interpretations and altered perceptions–a disturbing futuristic look into a society immersed in mass surveillance.

Inferno · Louis-Phillippe Demers, Bill Vorn

The work *Inferno* by Louis-Philippe Demers and Bill Vorn proposes an interesting interaction between heavy metallic objects and human participants. Humans become an active part of a performance that not only combines different media, but also relates to different disciplines such as literature, music, theatre, and contemporary art. The piece references significant works of media arts from the past and, at the same time, leads the visitors to reflect upon the future impact of technology on our society. *Inferno* addresses the human-machine relationship with a focus on the destructive nature of infinite automation with the human becoming a slave to the machine. The jury recognized the balance that was achieved between the performers, the machine, sound, noise, light, and the interaction with the audience. Demers and Vorn took classical ideas of hell and juxtaposed them with the nature of control within an environment reminiscent of an endless rave party mixed with industrial noise and robotic movements.

Fairy Lights in Femtoseconds · Yoichi Ochiai

The installation *Fairy Lights in Femtoseconds* is the result of a successful collaboration between an artist and three Japanese universities. The ideas of the young computer scientist and media artist Yoichi Ochiai inspire possibilities for the evolution of both computing technologies and our lived experience. The works of Ochiai have a strong sense of beauty, ephemerality, and poetic strength, much in line with the cultural traditions of Japan. At the same time, his experiments with the newest technologies surprise audiences and trigger an interest in scientific evolution. The realization of the 3-dimensional holograph inscribes a dialogue between the physical and immaterial and evokes a magical science fiction narrative, situating the imaginary and the intangible directly within the world of the ordinary.

Architecture of Radio · Richard Vijgen

The *Architecture of Radio* turns the intricate network of radio signals that surround us into a visible and an accurate capture of access points, cell towers, and overhead satellites which provide us with information. The interaction works via a tablet screen and is generated in response to the exact location and direction of the observer. The screen does not augment but simply reveals the hidden activity through a visual language designed to interact with and map out the surrounding radio space. This highly sophisticated data visualization not only shows us the otherwise invisible sources of data around us but also makes us visually aware of how easily and precisely data sources can be traced and tracked.

Pathfinder
Generative approach for conceptual choreography
onformative in collaboration with Christian Loclair

Pathfinder is an abstract geometrical system that stimulates the spontaneous embodiment of visual imagination in the realm of modern choreography. It creates a compelling visual language as an aid to choreographic development. The beautifully animated geometries incite various bodily states driven by an algorithm. Projected onto the floor space surrounding the artist, they result in seamless creative interaction. Much more than just a set of guidelines, the graphic visual language becomes an integral part of the performance dialogue. The jury was particularly impressed by the quality of the visual language, the clarity of communication, and the ease of interaction between the artist and the abstract geometries.

All Things Fall · Mat Collishaw

All Things Fall impressed the jury with the clever use of a zoetrope—usually marveled at for its optical illusions rather than portrayal of political scenes. While mesmerized by the animated characters and the filmic movement of bodies, one becomes aware of the cycle of violence being portrayed, inspired by a work of the Italian painter Ippolito Scarsella. Collishaw uses a Biblical tale of infanticide to bring to the fore the horrific side of humanity that replays these scenes through history and into our contemporary time as we witness tragedies such as the recent events in Syria. The artist thoughtfully combines the language and traditions of art history with technologies in a way that confronts us with our mortality as well as our morality.

Aurelia 1+Hz / proto viva sonification
Robertina Šebjanič, Slavko Glamočanin

Aurelia 1+Hz addresses interspecies communication which could be considered the + sign that was added to the interactive category as this has a growing fascination for artists as well as scientists. Raising awareness about other forms of life and how they react to us is critically important at this time when the environment is in such a dire state. Additionally, we are confronted with the idea of machine and life forms merging, with the potential of a new life form emerging. The artists highlight this issue by creating a way for audiences to have an alternative experience of viewing jellyfish, specifically the common *Aurelia aurita* or moon jellyfish, found in all seas and oceans and used as modular organisms in research laboratories. The performance contains a tracking system that follows the movements and interaction of living jellyfish and the data captured by the camera is transformed in real time into sound via an algorithm that generates sound using the recordings of previous experiments. This is mixed into a soundscape score, which is assembled into immersive sonic and visual experience of machine jellyfish interaction.

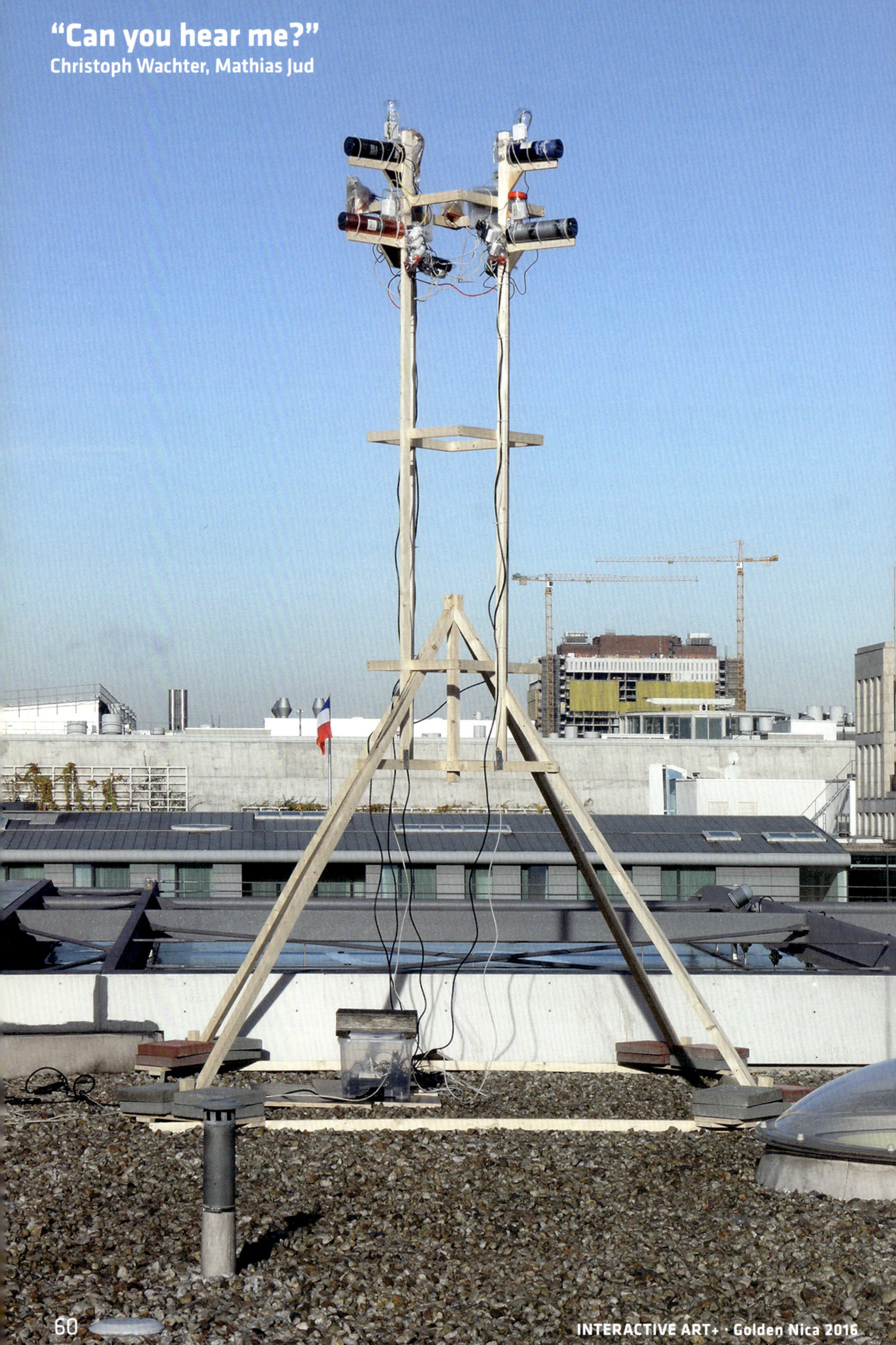

"Can you hear me?"
Christoph Wachter, Mathias Jud
60
INTERACTIVE ART+ · Golden Nica 2016

"Can you hear me?"—an antithesis to surveillance and espionage in Berlin's government district

It all started when the Swiss embassy in Berlin asked Wachter & Jud to present their work. This was not only an honor, it also gave them access to a unique location. The Swiss Embassy in Berlin is located in the government district, next to the German Federal Chancellery. In its neighborhood are Germany's Parliament and other embassies, such as the US and the British Embassy.

According to the revelations of Edward Snowden, this area has become the focal point for surveillance and spying on the population. It was discovered that the US and British secret services were listening in on the entire district, including the Chancellor's mobile phone. Ominous roof structures on the embassy buildings were attracting a global interest. The listening post of the American NSA appeared as a structure with grey, radar-transparent facade elements. Behind it are hidden antennas and listening devices. The British GCHQ also installed eavesdropping antennas behind a white, cylindrical structure, a radome.

Although everyone was talking about the listening devices, this mass surveillance is a situation that leaves us speechless. In this situation, opposition and objection fails, as it is itself always subjected to the criticized surveillance.

But how to address these hidden and disguised forces? Wachter & Jud sought to find out whether other signals could be sent from the roof of an embassy. On the top of the Swiss Embassy, they installed a series of antennas. Their antennas weren't as sophisticated as those used by the Americans and the British, they were makeshift can-antennas, not camouflaged but totally obvious and visible.

The Academy of Arts joined the project, and Wachter & Jud built another large antenna on their rooftop, exactly between the listening posts of the NSA and the GCHQ. Seldom have artists been observed in such detail while building an art installation. A helicopter circled over their heads with a camera registering each and every move they made. And on the roof of the US Embassy, security officers patrolled.

The antennas have become the starting point of an open communication network. Everyone could participate in the network using their Wi-Fi-enabled devices. Chats, text messages, file sharing, and voice chats were possible without Internet connections or wireless service providers. A collective conversation space in which every participant has equal rights has been taking the space of secret wiretapping. Messages could be sent on the frequencies that are intercepted by the NSA and GCHQ.

A different regime of conversation unfolded: If people are spying on us, it stands to reason that they have to listen to what we are saying. At the same time, the participants in the communication network were largely anonymous. It was an inversion.

The independent mesh network in Berlin's Government District recaptured the communication space also on an urban scale. The options for publicly talking and freely assembling are limited in the government district, as it is a non-protest-zone. But there are no special regulations regarding digital communication. This installation was therefore perfectly legal. The Swiss ambassador even informed Chancellor Merkel about it. Within this network, the voices of the people found their way into the closed-off refuges of power as a legal and legitimate response to the constraints, and to a hidden, absolute surveillance by the secret services.

For 33 days this independent and anonymous network was used by thousands of people, and they sent more than 15,000 messages to the NSA and the GCHQ. The personal statements ranged from activist and political contributions to ironic disclosures of embarrassing intimacy to calls for resistance. Some appeals were aimed directly at the surveillants, calling on them to switch sides and become whistleblowers.

The officeholders in the embassies and government centers were invited to join and equally participate in this open network, too. And in fact, they took advantage of this opportunity. Even confidential information from the parliamentary investigation commission about the spying revelations appeared. What started as a playful counter-manifestation with an independent network has become the proof that a free flow of information is vital for a vivid democracy—especially in the digital age.

Supported by: Swiss Embassy, Berlin; Academy of the Arts, Berlin; Swiss Arts Council Pro Helvetia

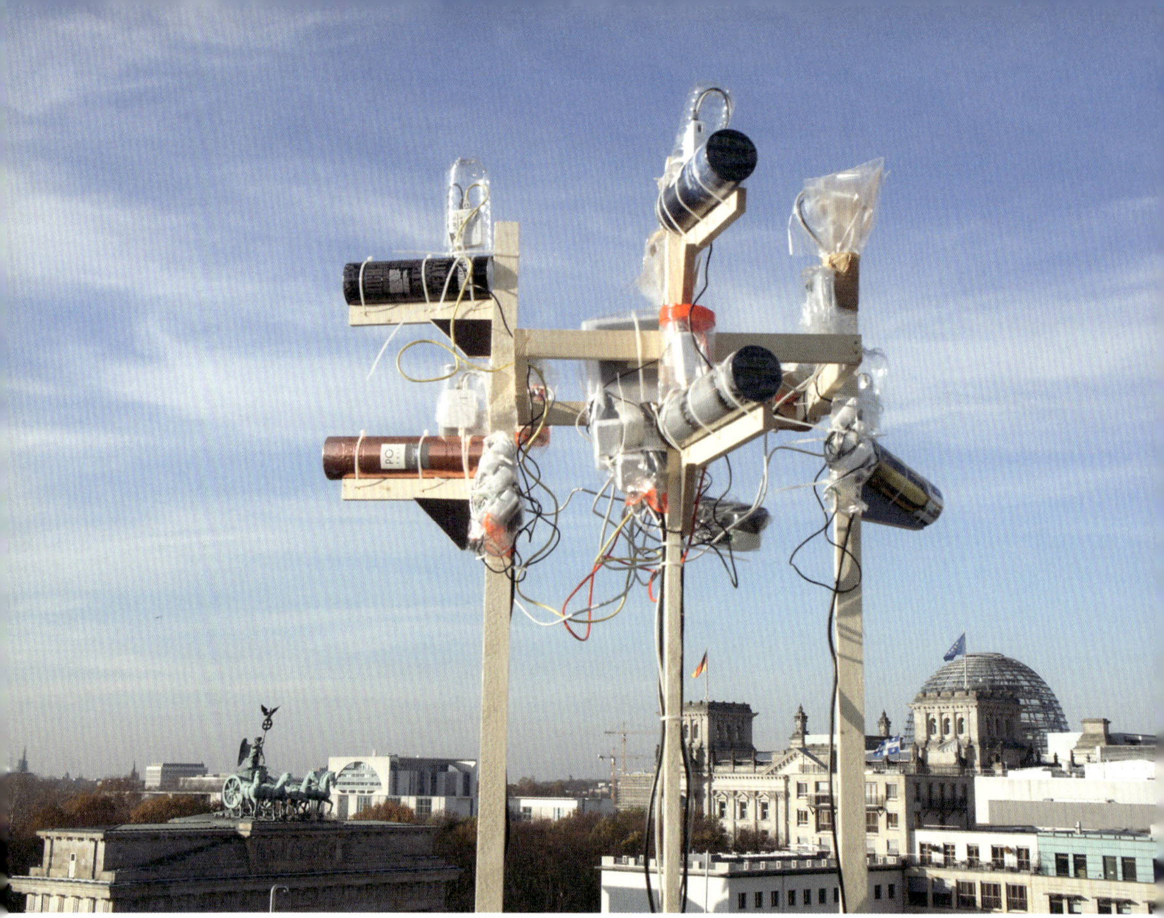

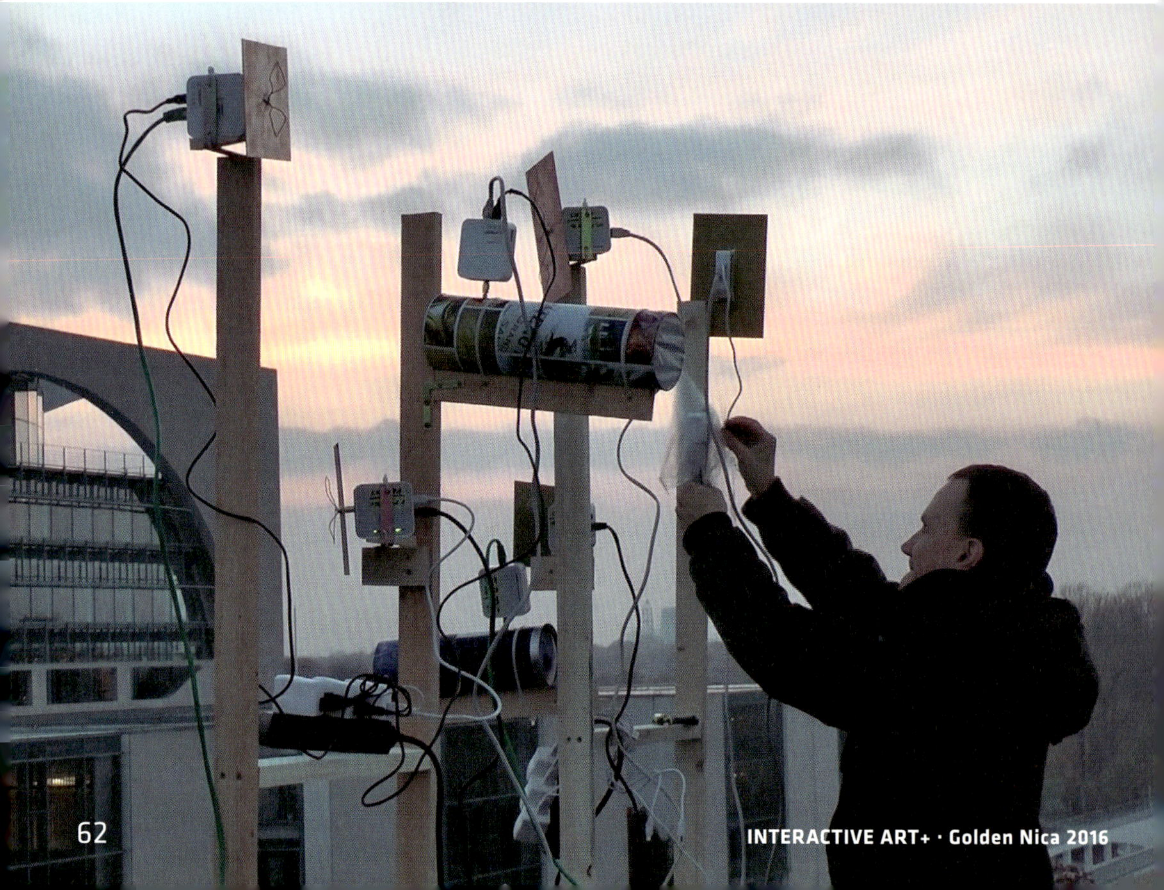

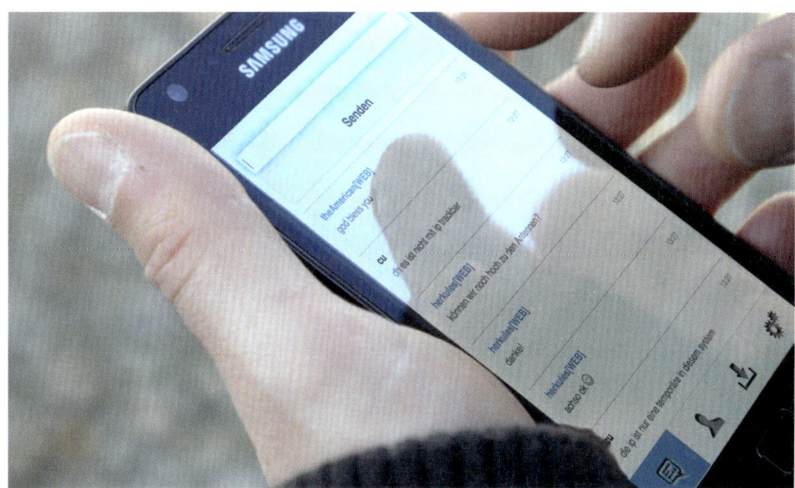

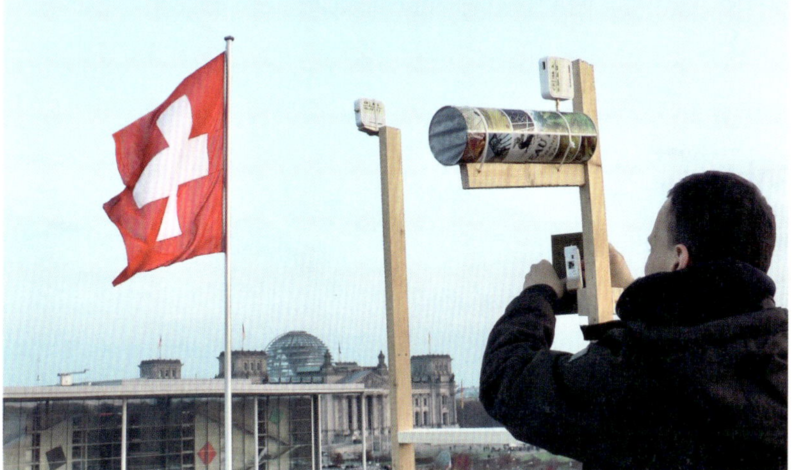

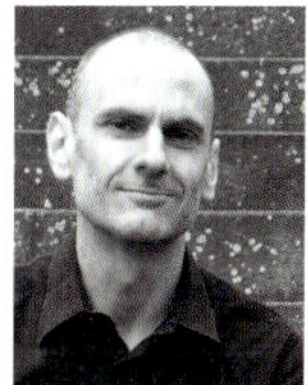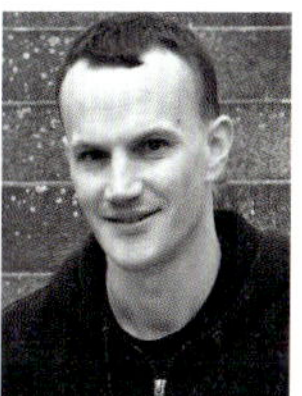

Christoph Wachter (CH) and **Mathias Jud** (CH) were both born in Zurich. They live and work in Berlin. They have participated in numerous international art exhibitions and been awarded many international prizes (Prix Ars Electronica, Swiss Art Award, EMARE, CECEL European Council, Edith Russ Haus, Förderpreis der Kunstministerin des Freistaats Sachsen etc.). In particular, the projects *Picidae* (since 2007), *New Nations* (since 2009) and *qaul.net* (since 2012) have gained worldwide interest. As open-source projects these works uncover forms of censorship of the Internet, undermine the concentration of polit-ical power and even resolve the dependency on infrastructure. The tools, provided by the artists, are used by communities in the USA, Europe, Australia, and in countries like Syria, Tunisia, Egypt, Iran, India, China, and Thailand. Even in North Korea activists participate. But not everyone is fond of these projects. In 2012 the project *HOTEL GELEM* they created with Roma families all over Europe received a Council of Europe award. On this occasion Manuel Valls (now Prime Minister of France) organized a counter-manifes-tation against the art project. The People's Republic of China has denied Wachter and Jud a visa to enter the country since 2013.

OpenSurgery
A do-it-yourself surgery robot for domestic laparoscopy
Frank Kolkman

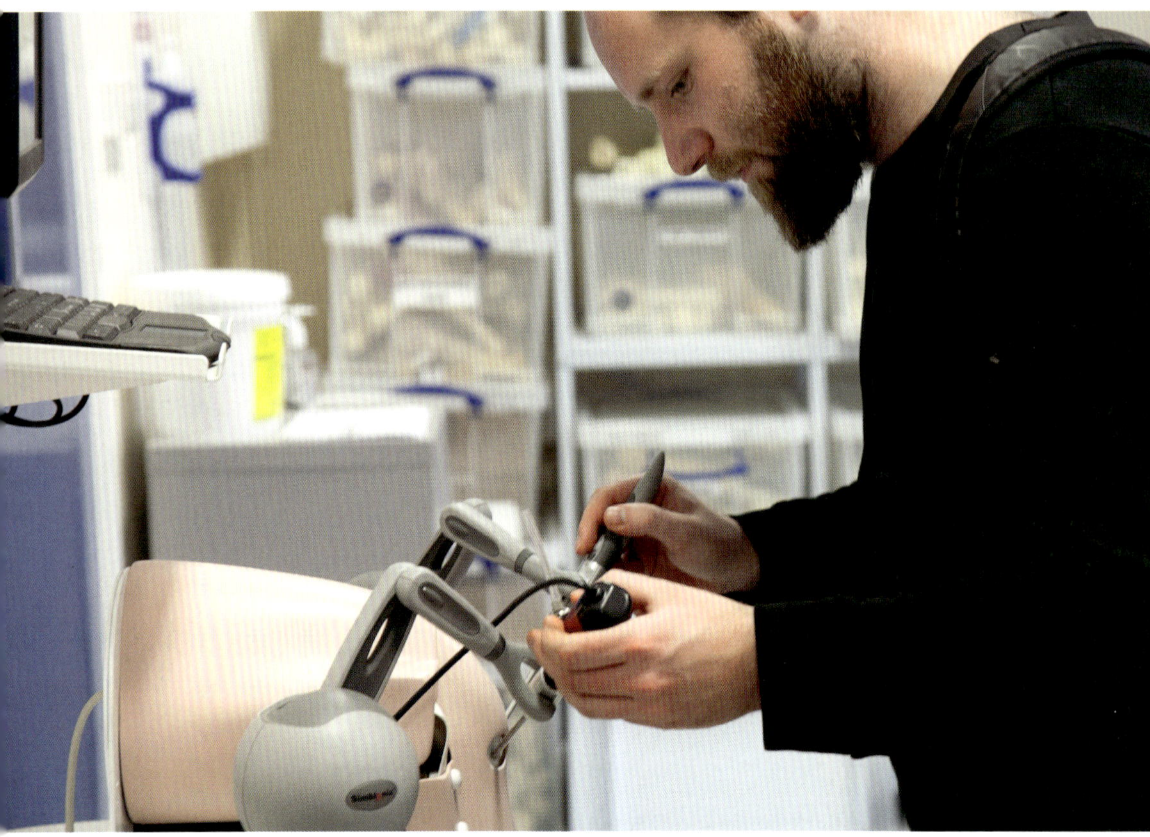

With *OpenSurgery*, Frank Kolkman speculates on the potential for advanced do-it-yourself surgical tools to possibly support more accessible alternatives to the increasingly expensive health services worldwide. Inspiration for the project came from the discovery that uninsured Americans are using YouTube to share videos in which they perform medical and dental hacks on themselves as an alternative to professional care. These videos speak about how the profit-driven medical industries are widening the gap between those who can afford healthcare and those who cannot. Forcing certain groups of people to look for treatment outside of the official systems.

Extrapolating on this phenomenon, *OpenSurgery* proposes a do-it-yourself robot assisted surgery system for use in domestic keyhole surgery. By combining 3D printing and laser cutting with hacked surgical pieces and components bought online, the robot trades medical compliance for accessibility and easy distribution. Although it still requires a surgeon to operate it, with the help of the files, it could theoretically be replicated almost anywhere at a mere fraction of the cost of commercial surgical instruments, challenging many of the assumptions and legally formulated standards that exist within the heavily regulated medical sector.

Even though the current prototype is functional to an extent, it is not nearly stable enough to be used in surgery yet. In its current state however it proves there is potential for alternative communities to assemble around—and explore profoundly different approaches to—medical technologies. Admittedly

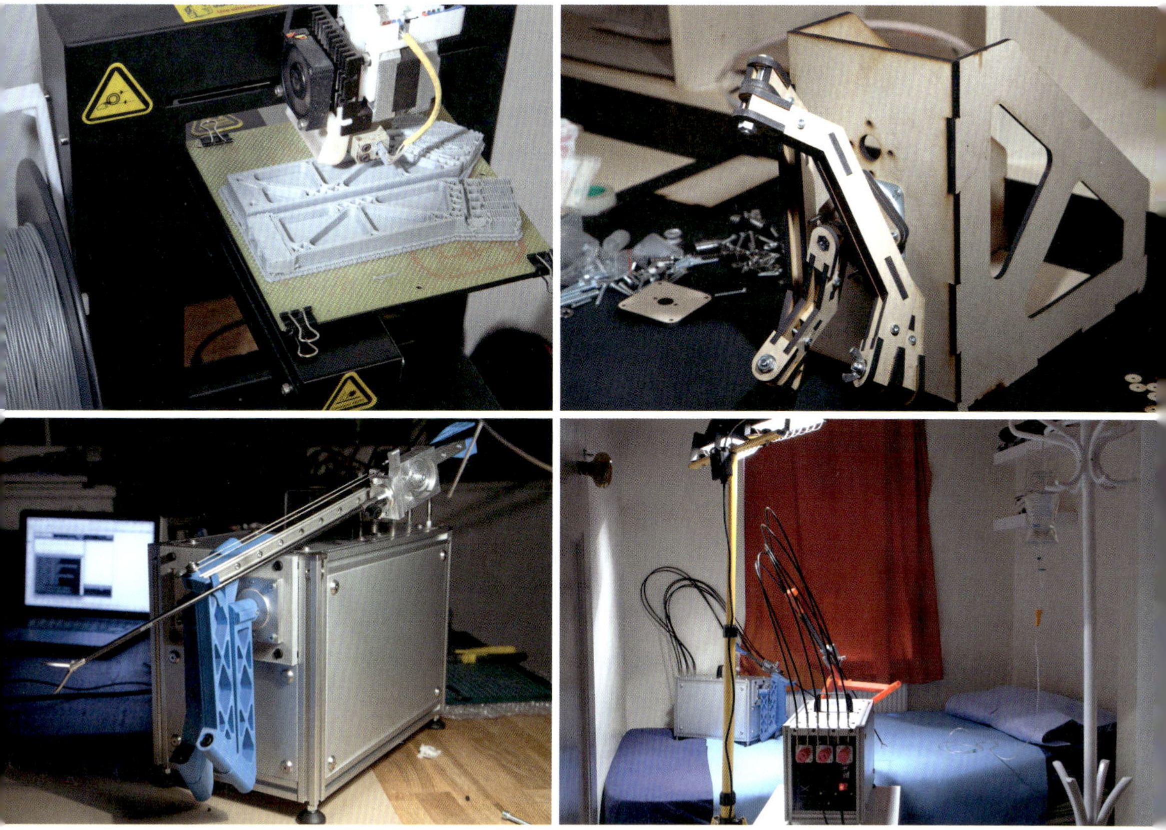

Juuke Schoorl

also raising a number of ethical, psychological, and legal concerns.
Instead of providing an immediate solution, *Open-Surgery* intends to facilitate discussion about alternative models of healthcare. Through provocation it investigates the socioeconomic values associated with medical practice and questions the preferability of the market driven healthcare narratives we have grown so accustomed to.

OpenSurgery was developed as a graduation project at the Design Interactions department of the Royal College of Art (London, UK, 2015), while the initial concept originated from the Healthcare Futures Workshop held at the KYOTO Design Lab (D-Lab) at the Kyoto Institute for Technology (Kyoto, Japan, 2014).

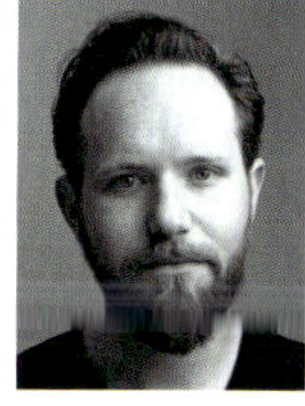

Frank Kolkman (NL) is a Dutch-born artist / designer interested in unpicking the social, economic, and ethical implications of current and near-future technologies. Thematically addressing issues of technological access and ownership, his projects display a broad understanding of design and production. Works include experimental devices, critical prototypes, and fictional scenarios. Frank holds a master's degree in Design Interactions from the Royal College of Art (London, UK) and a bachelor's degree in Product Design from ArtEZ Institute of the Arts (Arnhem, NL). *http://www.frankkolkman.nl*

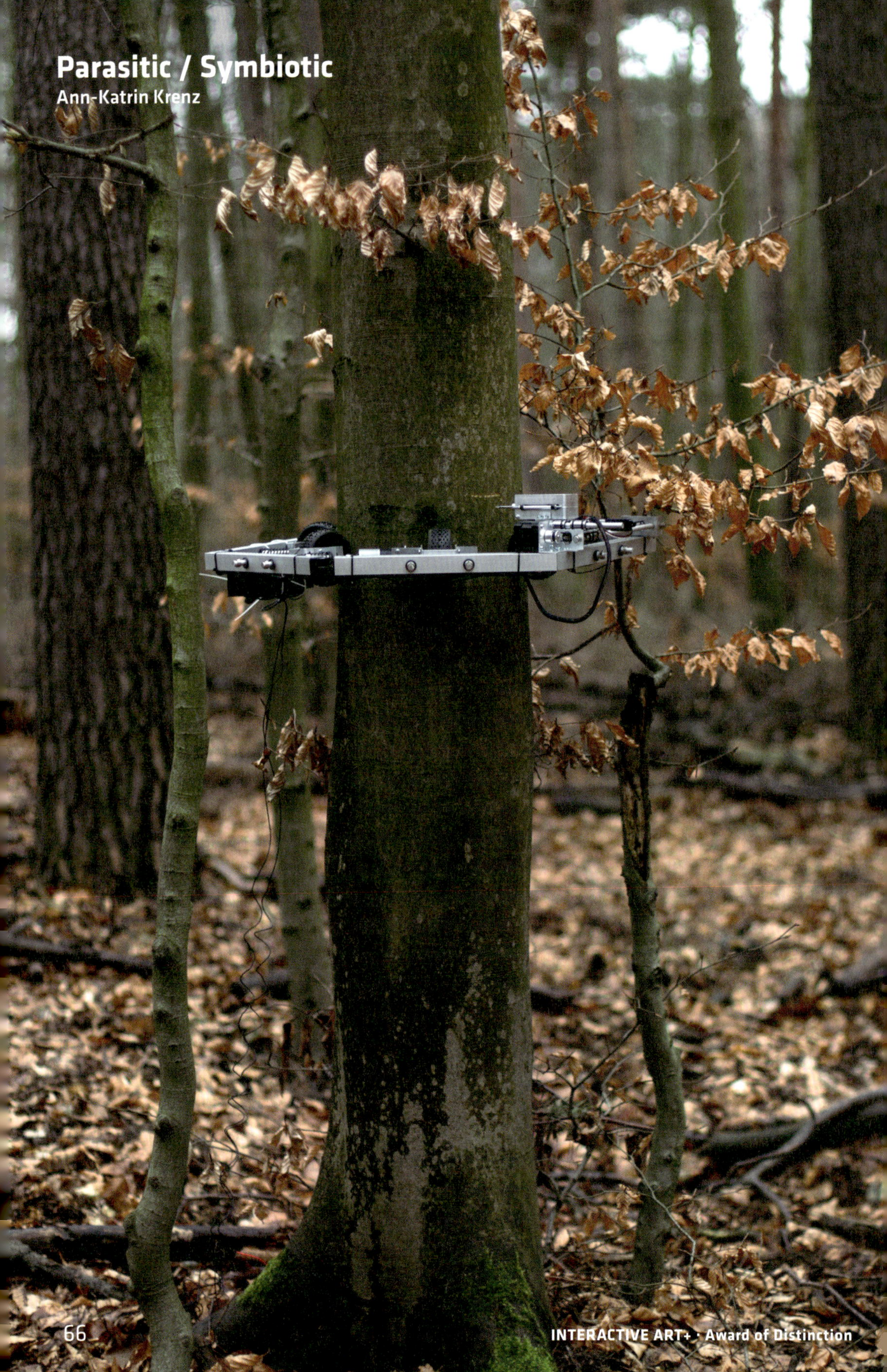

Parasitic / Symbiotic
Ann-Katrin Krenz

The relationship of humans and nature seems to be out of balance. The human, as a being defined by technology, is harming its environment and the very nature on which its existence depends. The focus on advancing technology seems to be contrary to a sustainable, responsible relationship to nature.

But what kind of role does the human being occupy in this area of tension between nature and technology? The human being does not see itself as part of nature, but at the same time has the desire to be close to nature and to become part of the natural persistence. In the project *Parasitic / Symbiotic* this area of tension between nature and technology is addressed.

A scenario is created in which the human being makes use of a technical device, which is sitting like a parasite on a tree. It contains a milling machine, which moves along a tree to carve encoded text into it. For the content of the carving a poem from Romanticism (*Abschied* by Joseph von Eichendorff) is used, which expresses the natural thoughts of unity and oneness and depicts the relation of nature and culture.

The question, whether this act can be considered as natural or artificial and where we as humans are situated, is posed with this action. The project critically discusses this area of tension, as the act of carving into a tree is a paradoxical one on several levels: The forest, in which the act is performed, is actually created artificially for forestry use. But the tree itself still describes nature in its purest form. The human-made technical device interferes with this natural atmosphere. By carving into the tree it even harms nature. This is in contradiction to the content of the poem—the Romantic thought of oneness and the desire of humans for nature. By using this technical device the human can realize parts of this thought. The result is an encoded form of the poem, which clearly refers to digital aesthetics and at the same time becomes part of the living tree.

The project describes a partly parasitic symbiosis between the technical act and the natural tree. This picks up and illustrates the current troubled relationship between humans and nature. The project shows that humans can create something aesthetically valuable and permanent through moderate and thoughtful technical interventions in nature. Even if the procedure is invasive, the damage remains low and it never leads to a fatal disturbance of the natural system; the tree lives on unrestricted and will grow together and merge with the artificial carving and so the artwork becomes one with nature.

Parasitic / Symbiotic was realized with the support of UdK Berlin University of the Arts.

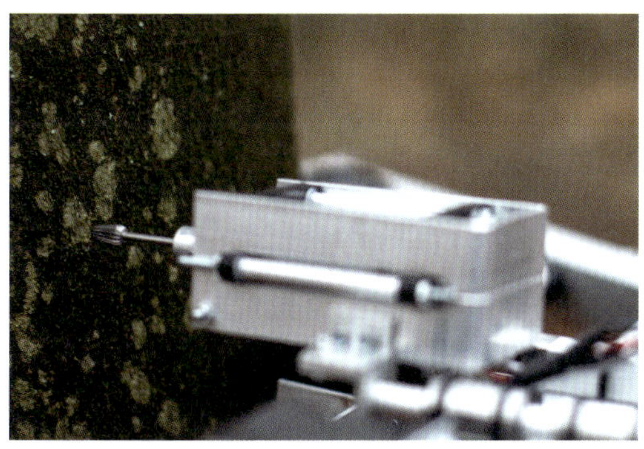

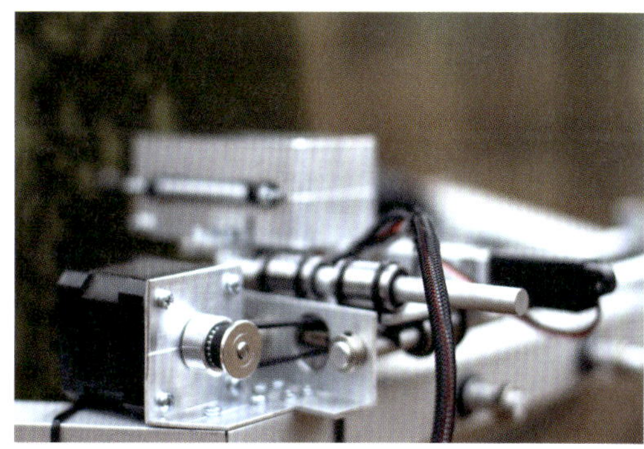

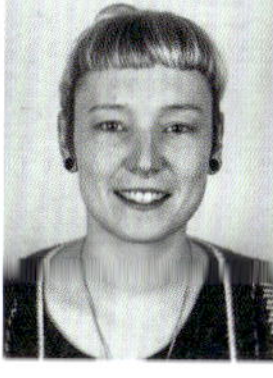

Ann-Katrin Krenz (DE) is an interaction designer and media artist, based in Berlin. Her work ranges from rich interactive installations and environments to generative design and visual explorations with pixels, pen and paper. She finished her master thesis in February 2016 in the "Digitale Klasse" (Visual Communication) under Joachim Sauter and Jussi Ängeslevä at UdK Berlin University of the Arts.

All Things Fall
Mat Collishaw

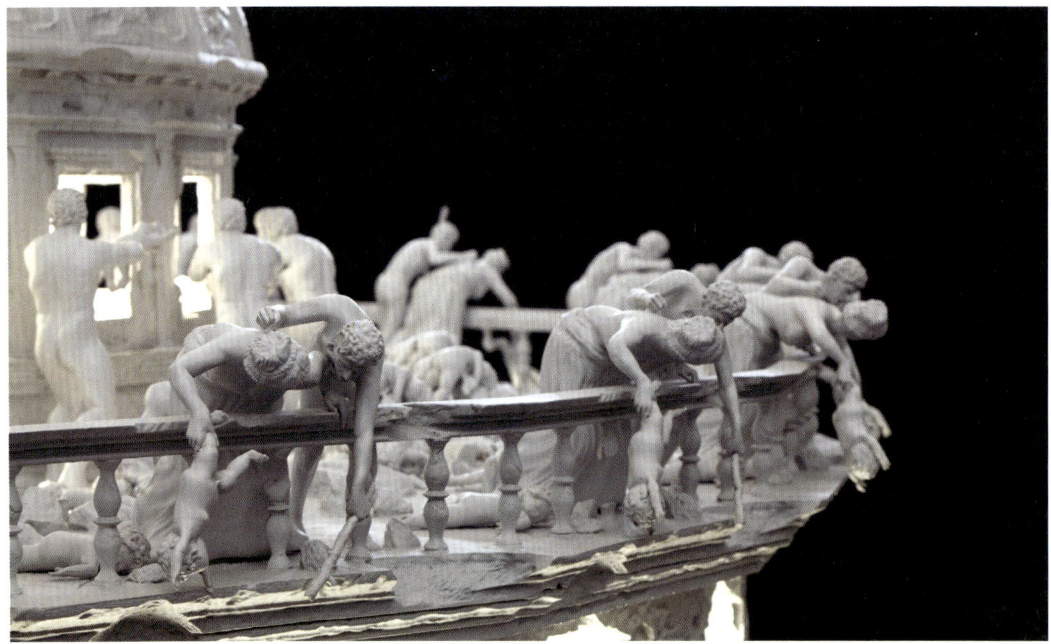

All Things Fall is based on the *Massacre of the Innocents*, a Biblical tale of infanticide, committed by King Herod to avoid losing his crown. The tale has provided dramatic subject matter for artists throughout history, including Rubens, Reni, Giotto, and Tintoretto. Depictions of the subject often show a crowd, in a frenzied and violent orgy of the brutal act of killing children. Rubens' famous depiction (illustrated) was influential for Collishaw's zoetrope, both in its architectural emphasis and complex figural constellations. Apart from being an opportunity to demonstrate the artist's skill in rendering the human body in extreme and dynamic poses, historically the subject of the Massacre of the Innocents has remained a fascination for the public because of its appalling nature. As Collishaw pointed out, in the medieval period the *Massacre of the Innocents* was one of the most popular plays. When looking at these works the eye cannot fixate on one part of the painting, as it's constantly being urged to move on with the ebb and flow of the figures, exploring the multiple bodies in all their contortions. Similarly, in Collishaw's zoetrope, you cannot fixate on one spot, as the carousel of horror whirls around, drawing the viewer into the action. The optical illusion of the zoetrope commands our attention, engaging the audience and in turn, making them complicit in a scene of genocide. The multi-ple characters enhance the feeling of an unremitting onslaught. The work relies on the filmic principle (of a rapidly exposed series of images to suggest animation), which underlines the viewer's involvement, as what you are seeing is not what is actually happening: the eye tricks the mind into seeing an illusion and, in doing so, the viewer becomes the mechanism by which the data is interpreted.

In *All Things Fall* Collishaw combines the old technological form of a zoetrope, an early means of presenting the illusion of a moving image, with new technologies to design and create the work. All of the 300 characters and the architecture have been designed in 3ds Max and ZBrush and then printed as 3D models in resin. The circular sculpture rotates at speeds so high that the static scenes become suddenly animated.

The "carousel" nature of the work adds to the feeling that you are involved in a means of entertainment. In the words of the artist: "It draws you in. As soon as it starts revolving, it's hypnotic, suddenly you are looking at something that is not actually happening, and you engage with it. It becomes this festival of violence, a gory entertaining carousel" (Mat Collishaw in conversation with Andrew Graham-Dixon, *Black Mirror*, Galleria Borghese, 2014).

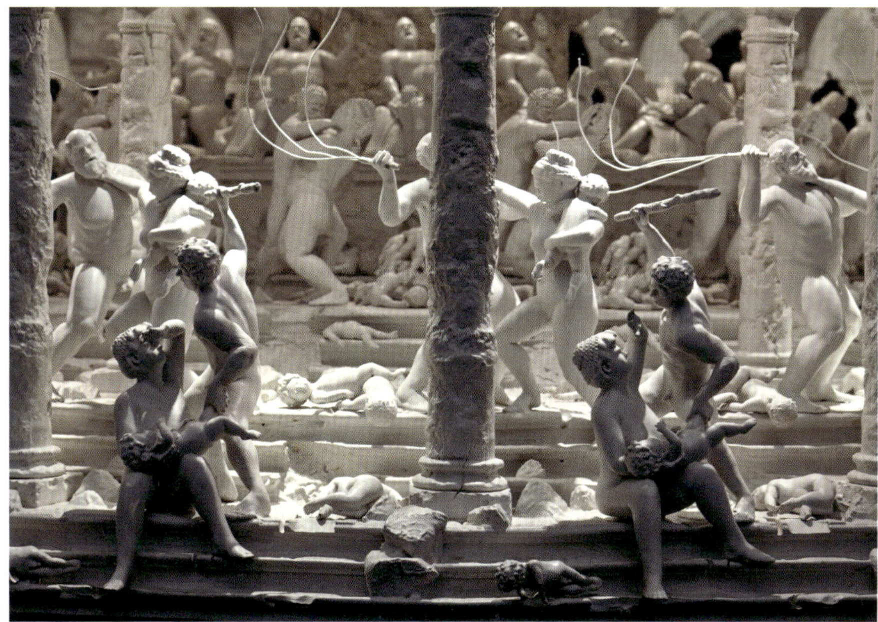

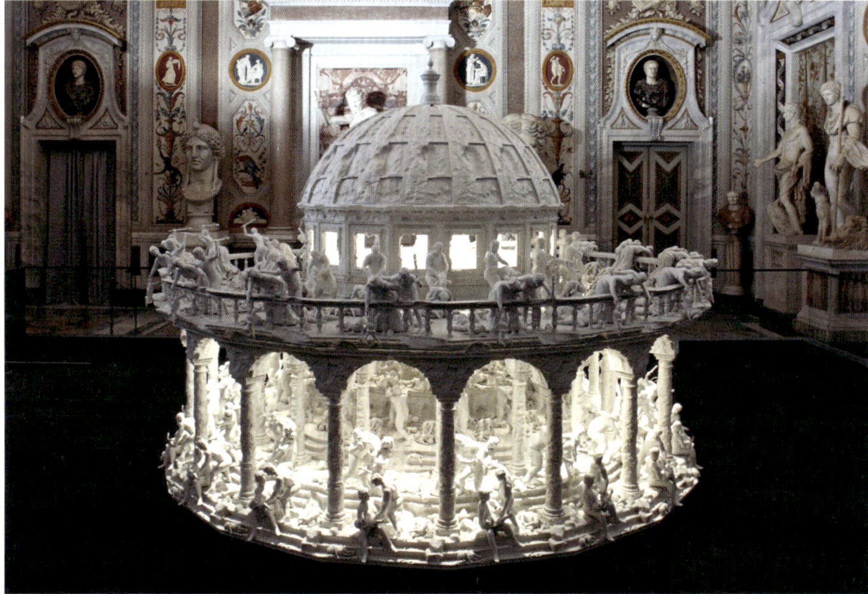

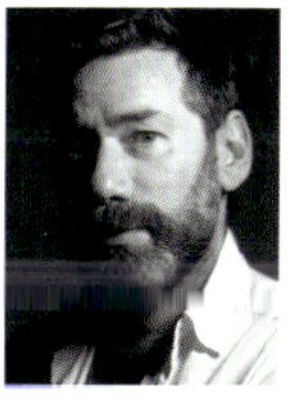

Mat Collishaw (UK), born in 1966, is a key figure in the generation of British artists who emerged from Gold-smith's College in the late 1980s. He participated in *Freeze* (1988) and since his first solo exhibition in 1990 he has exhibited widely internationally. Recent solo exhibitions: New Art Gallery Walsall (2015); *Last Meal on Death Row*, Bass Museum of Art, Miami Beach, Florida (2013); Pino Pascali Foundation Award, Polignano a Mare (Bari), Italy (2012); Afterimage, Arter: space for art, Istanbul, Turkey (2013). Collishaw's work is in several public collections including Centre Georges Pompidou, Paris; Museum of Contemporary Art, San Diego; Museum of Old and New Art, Tasmania, and Tate, London.

Aurelia 1+Hz / proto viva sonification

Robertina Šebjanič, Slavko Glamočanin

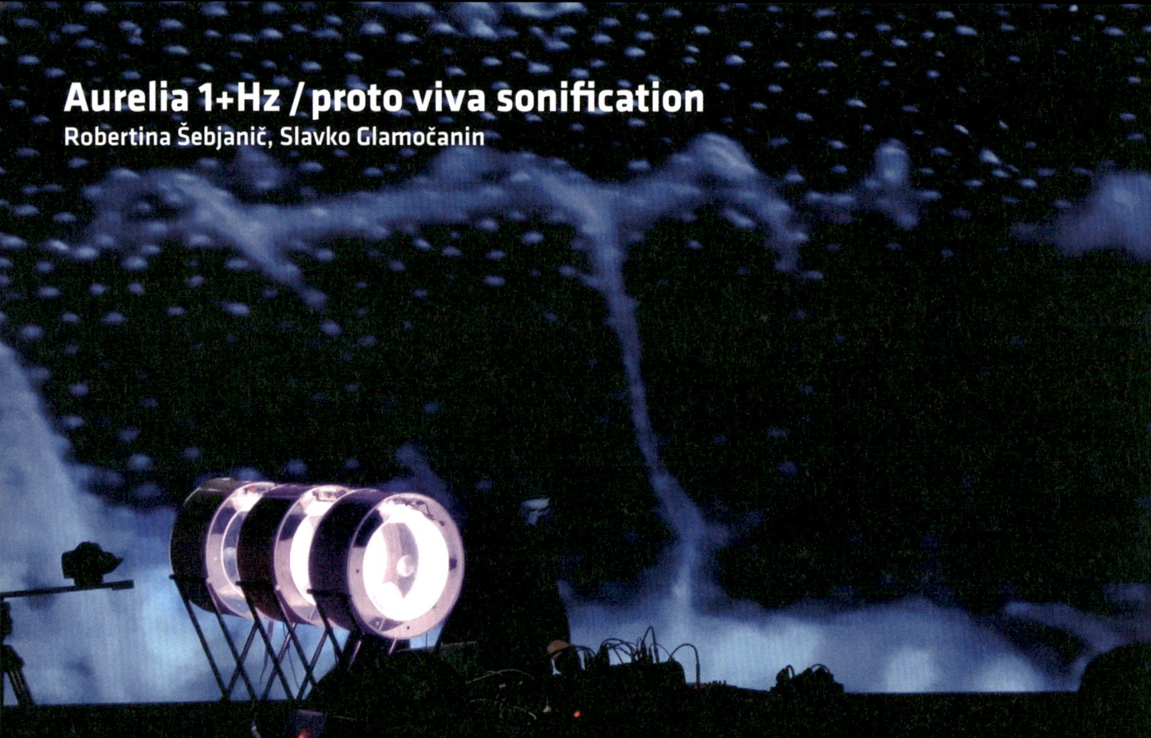

Aurelia 1+Hz / proto viva sonification is an interactive performance that explores the phenomena of inter-species communication, sonification of the environment, and the underwater acoustic / bioacoustics. An interactive performance features live transmitted sound generated by *Aurelia aurita*–moon jellyfish and performer. Sound loops contain recordings and sonic experiments of jellyfish in a closed environment and prerecorded from the jellyfish blooms in the sea. Both are mixed into a new soundscape score, which is assembled into immersive sonic and visual experience.

For over 500 hundred million years jellyfish have been pulsating in the world's oceans and seas. Nowadays, amidst the immense environmental changes, their numbers are rapidly growing. Jellyfish are one of the rare organisms that seem perfectly suited for the Anthropocene era. The current 6th Mass Extinction may not apply to them. There are several species of jellies (some of them immortal), however, it is not established (yet) how they communicate. Do they feel vibration?

Aurelia aurita has rudimentary sensory nerves at the base of its tentacles that allow it to perceive light, smell, and orientation. Its gravity receptors (calcium crystals) are the same as in the human inner ear. These sensitive structures provide positional information to the animal based on the direction of gravity. The odyssey into the exploration of interspecies communication is a way of discovering parameters to restore a deep relationship within all of life and it is a key to a better understanding of the earth's environment. The relationship between human and animal is a key to better understanding of the natural environment. Humans have a massive impact on other species and thus it is crucial to decode what they signal to us and how they see us.

> "There are still songs to sing beyond mankind"
> by Paul Celan

The *Aurelia 1+Hz* project is divided in two parts. The *performance Aurelia 1+Hz / proto viva sonification* (2015) looks into a new critical redefinition of social values and new attitude towards the cohabitation of interspecies while the *installation Aurelia 1+Hz / proto viva generator* (2014) deals with the biopolicy of prolonging life and addresses the possible (bio-cybernetic) coexistence of humans, animals, and machines.

The performance contains a tracking system that follows the jellyfish and generates locative media. Jellyfish are tracked by the Raspberry Pi camera that measures contraction, movement, and interaction between jellyfish. The data captured by the camera is transformed in real time into sound via an algorithm that generates sound using the recordings of previous experiments such as sound data of jellyfish that was produced during the project entitled *Deep Blue,*

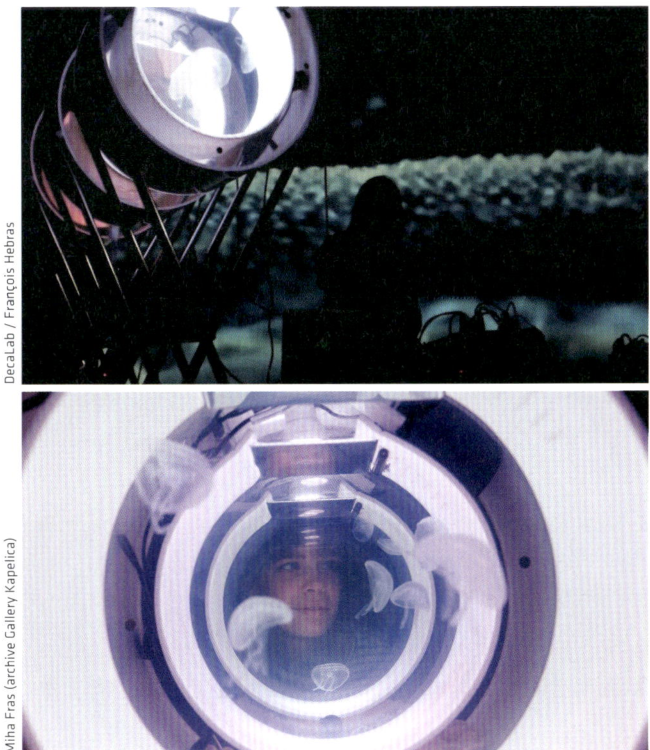

DecaLab / François Hebras

Miha Fras (archive Gallery Kapelica)

at the Institute of Marine Science and Technologies in Izmir, Turkey. The sound navigated by the performer and artist Robertina Šebjanič was gathered by hydrophones recording underwater jellyfish bloom on the shores of Izmir in February 2014.

Jellyfish used in the project are *Aurelia aurita* or moon jellyfish. It is the most common jellyfish that is found in all seas and oceans and is used as a modular organism in (mostly biology) research laboratories. The aquariums used in the project were developed by Cubic Aquarium Systems.

Artist, concept, research & development: Robertina Šebjanič
Programming and tech development: Slavko Glamočanin
Coordination & curating: Natacha Seignolles (DécaLab)
Curating advisor: Annick Bureaud
Consultancy: Alenka Malej, marine biology station Piran
Production: DécaLab and Le Cube—Centre de création numérique, February 2015, Paris
Special thanks:
Aquarium de Paris Cinéaqua, Paris; Embassy of the Republic of Slovenia, Paris; Gallery Kapelica, Ljubljana; Cubic Aquarium System; Natacha Seignolles; Annick Bureaud; Agnes Baldacchino; Ewen Chardronnet, Miha Colner; Institute of Marine Science and Technologies in Izmir; PORTIZMIR#3 – DEEP BLUE team, K2 Izmir

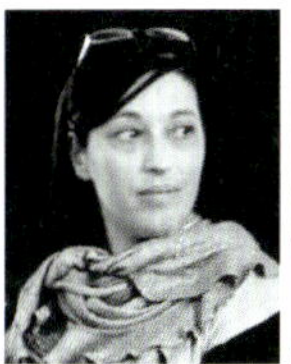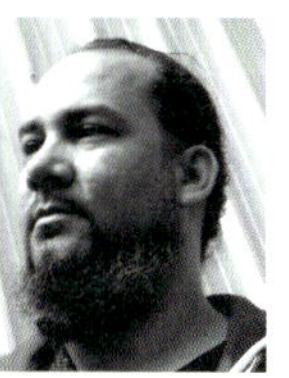

Robertina Šebjanič (SI) is an internationally exhibited artist, working in the intermedia platform combining art—technology—science. For several years her focus has oriented towards cross discipline projects involving marine biology, underwater bioacoustics, chemistry… Her ideas and concepts are often realized in collaboration with others, through interdisciplinary and informal integration in her work. She is member of Hackteria Network, Ljudmila, UR Institute, and Theremidi orchestra. *http://robertina.net/* **Slavko Glamiočanin** (SI) started in the computer "demoscene," where he was mostly active in making music, co-creating the first Slovenian breakbeat compilation "Monkorama," which contained his own creations as well. He continued with programming and exploring the media and for that purpose he created a programming platform *naprava*. After one-way video/effects he proceeded with interactive projects, motion capture, kinect and openGL visualizations. His main interests are synesthesia, complex systems, and interactive. *http://www.naprave.net/*

Exhausting a Crowd

Kyle McDonald

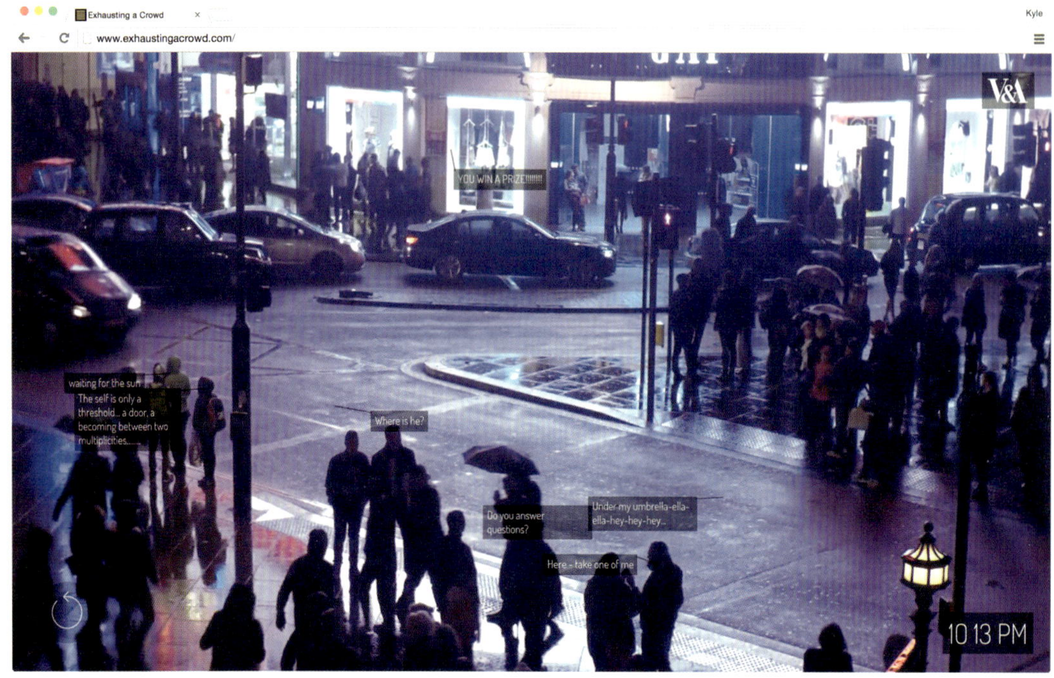

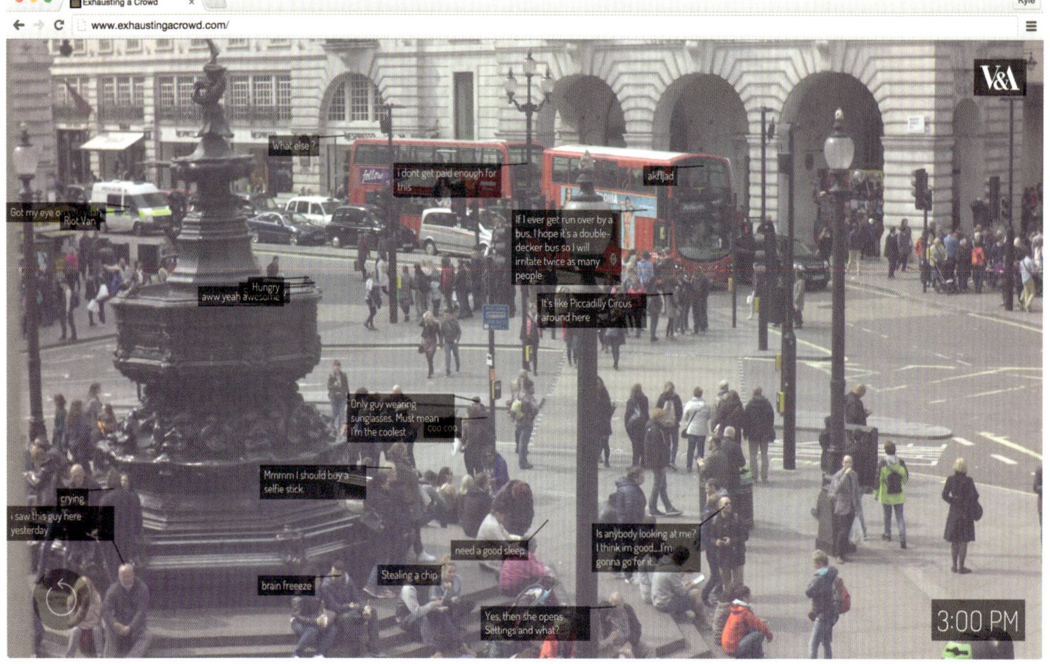

http://exhaustingacrowd.com/

Exhausting a Crowd was inspired by the classic 60-page piece of experimental literature from Georges Perec, *An Attempt at Exhausting a Place in Paris,* written from a bench over three days in 1974, and automates the task of completely describing the events of 12 hours in a busy public space—Piccadilly Circus in London. This work speaks of the potential of a perfectly automated future of surveillance, enabled by a distributed combination of machine and human intelligence. A beautiful record of the energy present in shared space, as well as a disturbing look into the potential for control in a dystopian environment of persistent mass surveillance.

On the *Exhausting a Crowd* website, visitors are presented with a video loop and an onslaught of commentary that has accumulated since the piece's launch. Now running over a year, nearly fifty thousand comments have been collected. Some provide narration for complex multi-character stories, others catalogue every single selfie.

Exhausting a Crowd draws on previous works such as *Keytweeter* (2009–2010), where I tweeted everything I typed for one year in 140-character chunks, *People Staring at Computers* (2011), where I surreptitiously took photos in the Apple Store, which led to a Secret Service investigation, and *Conversnitch* (2013-2014) with Brian House, where we deployed a device that recorded conversations, crowdsourcing their transcription and automatically posting to Twitter.

The primary location inspiring this piece was 14th Street Union Square in NYC, as viewed from the south side of the park. At any moment, there may be anywhere from 10 people at midnight, to 100 people on a cold afternoon, to 500 people at lunch, or thousands for a protest. People are engaged in a variety of activities from playing chess, to dancing, singing, chanting, panhandling, eating, kissing, walking through, or just waiting.

Working with the Victoria and Albert Museum to develop the piece, we decided to shoot in London to engage with the long history of surveillance in the United Kingdom. Two other major decisions were made during development: One was about whether to present a live stream or a pre-recorded stream, and the other was about whether to use computer-assisted tags or even computer-assisted targets based on pedestrian detection. The pre-recorded stream was essential to get the effect of an abundance of notes at any moment, and we tried to create the feeling of it being "live" by removing almost all user interface elements that suggested otherwise. The computer-assisted tags were dropped, because it felt more disturbing to know that all the notes left behind were left there by a real human clicking and typing. With such high resolution footage there was some concern about privacy. Legally, there are no privacy restrictions on filming and broadcasting people in public spaces in the UK (with the exception of a few places like The Royal Square, Trafalgar Square, the London Underground). But this piece is about the crowd, not any specific individual, I wanted to avoid making any person's face clearly recognizable. In practice, almost all individuals appear at enough of a distance, and most internet connections cannot support the full 4k video bandwidth required to make out faces in the nearest foreground.

Exhausting a Crowd by Kyle McDonald with Jonas Jongejan
Site development: Jonas Jongejan
Commissioned by Victoria and Albert Museum for
All of This Belongs to You
Video: Nico Turner
Special thanks to: Corinna Gardner, Dan Joyce, Hellicar & Lewis

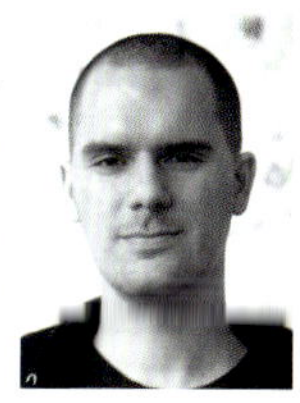

Kyle McDonald (US) is an artist who works in the open with code. He is a contributor to arts-engineering toolkits like openFrameworks, and builds tools that allow artists to use new computational techniques in their practice. Kyle has formerly been a member of F.A.T. Lab and community manager for openFrameworks, adjunct professor at ITP, and resident at the STUDIO for Creative Inquiry at Carnegie Mellon, at YCAM in Japan, and in corporate residencies like Autodesk and Spotify. His work is commissioned by and shown at events around the world, including: Ars Electronica, Sonar/OFFF, Eyebeam, Anyang Public Art Project, Linekid, LLILK Festival, NODE Festival, and many others.

Inferno
Louis-Phillippe Demers, Bill Vorn

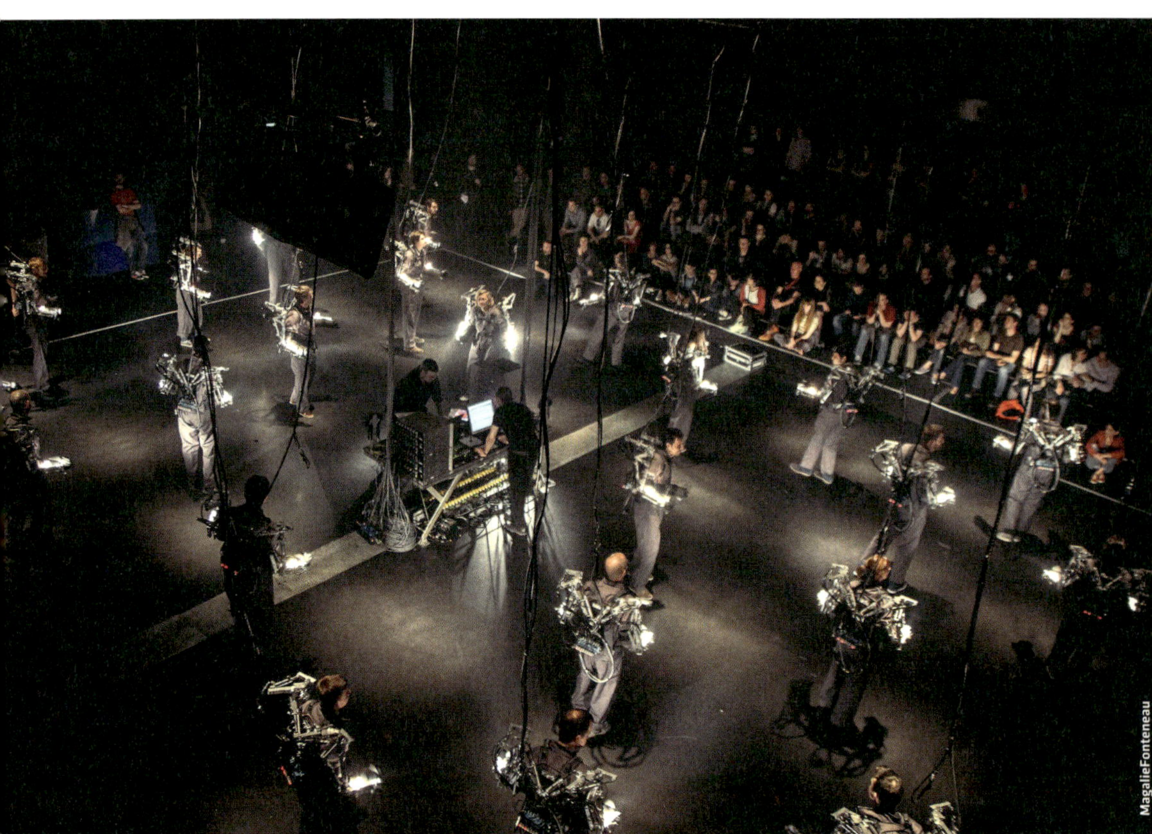

Inferno is a participative robotic performance project inspired by the concept of control and the representation of hell.

From Dante's Circles of Hell to theme parks such as Haw Par Villa's Ten Courts of Hell, passing by Joey, The Mechanical Boy, bodies are handed to eternal and external forces controlling and afflicting them. Those punishments and external powers, found in the depiction of numerous flavors of hell, suggest an infinite and mundane control loop under which the body will be forced to move endlessly. In *Inferno*, the "circles of hell" concept is a framework, a theme under which the different parts of the performance are regrouped.

The specificity of this performance resides in the situation where the machines involved in the performance are retrofitted on the body of raptured audience members cum performers. A selected group of the public therefore becomes an active part of the performance, giving a radical instance of immersive and participative experiences. Shifting the exoskeleton's command from the authors, to the computer, to the audience, and to the performers, *Inferno* questions the nature of control—either machinic or human, coerced or voluntary—where either utopian or dystopian futures radiate, both real and fictional.

Wearing a robotic device entails many interpretations. *Inferno* also addresses many recurrent issues revolving around the human-robot symbiotic relationships. Wearing or being entrapped in a robotic entity recalls the concept of the Cyborg that emerged in the late 80s.

Inferno revisits this concept thru a pastiche of the utopian concept of Singularity. Among cultures throughout history, the representations of Hell, demons, and punishments are vast. In *Inferno*, the anxiety of the Singularity translates Hell and infinite punishment into a pseudo-model of Infinite Automation (rituals) and subordination to the machine.

http://billvorn.concordia.ca/robography/inferno.html
http://www.processing-plant.com/web_csi/index.html#project=inferno

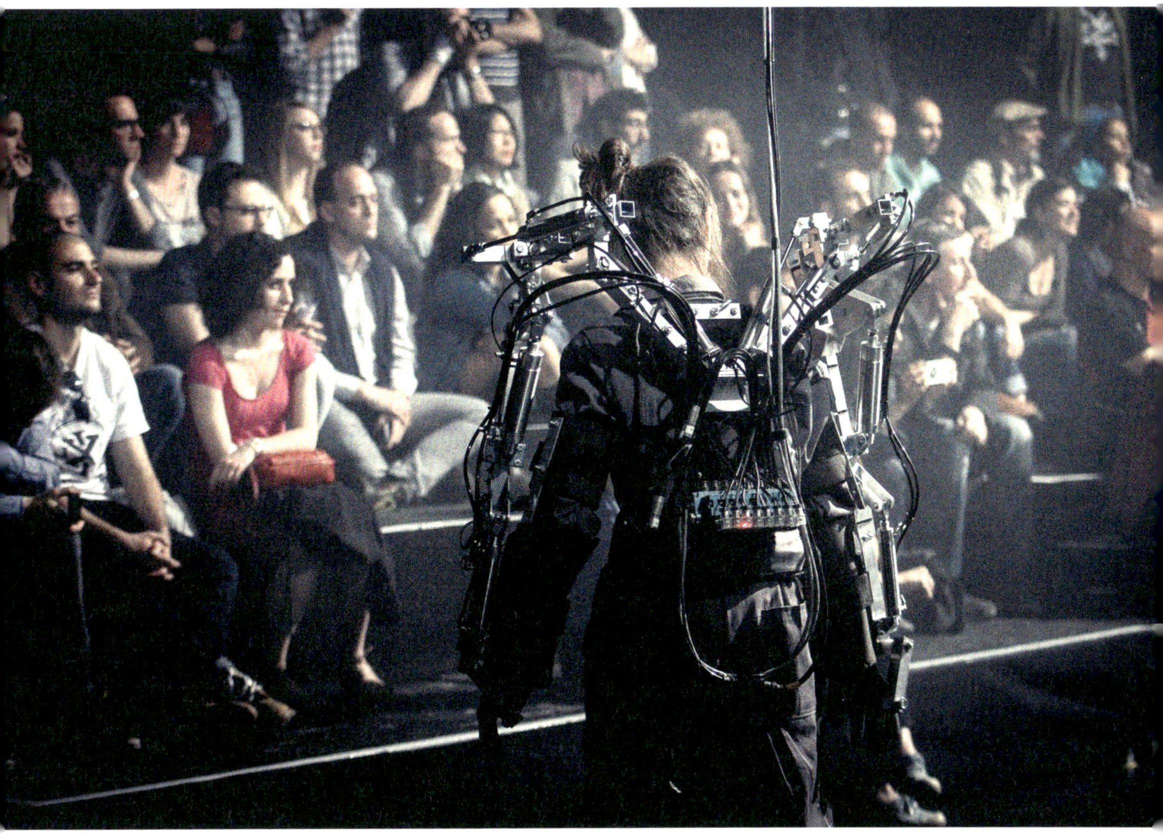

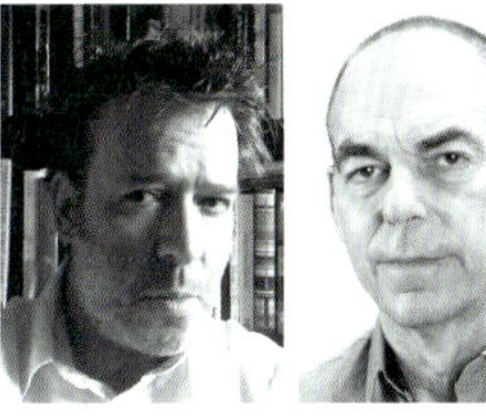

Concept, robots, light and sound: Bill Vorn,
Louis-Philippe Demers
Electronics: Martin Peach
Studio assistants: Beatriz Herrera, Morgan Rauscher,
Csenge Kolozsvari

Support: Canada Arts Council,
MOE Tier 1 Nanyang Technological University
Co-Production: Acreq-Elektra, Maison des Arts de Créteil,
ARCADI, Stéréolux, Conseil des Arts et des Lettres du Québec

Louis-Philippe Demers (CA) makes large-scale installations and performances and has built more than 375 machines over the past two decades. His projects can be found in theater, opera, subway stations, art museums, science museums, music events, and trade shows. Demers' works have been primed at Ars Electronica, VIDA, Japan Media Arts Festival, Lightforms, and at the Helpmann Awards. Demers was Professor of Digital Media and Exhibit Design at the Staatliche Hochschule fuer Gestaltung. Currently Demers is Associate Professor at the School of Art, Design and Media at the Nanyang Technological University (NTU) in Singapore. Demers holds a PhD on machine performance from Plymouth University. Based in Montreal, **Bill Vorn** (CA) has been creating Robotic Art projects for more than twenty years. His practice involves robotics and motion control, sound/noise, lighting, video, and cybernetic processes. He holds a PhD degree in Communication Studies from UQAM (Montreal, 2001) and teaches Electronic Arts, since 1999, in the Department of Studio Arts at Concordia University where he is Full Professor. His work has been presented at many international events, including Ars Electronica, ISEA, DEAF, Sonar, the Havana Biennale, the Exit and Via festivals, the Athens Video Art Festival, and Wood Street Galleries.

Jennifer Lyn Morone™ Inc

Jennifer Lyn Morone

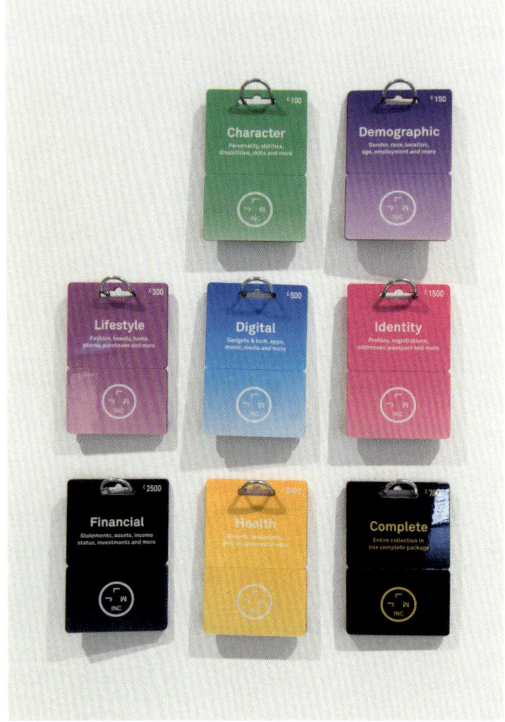

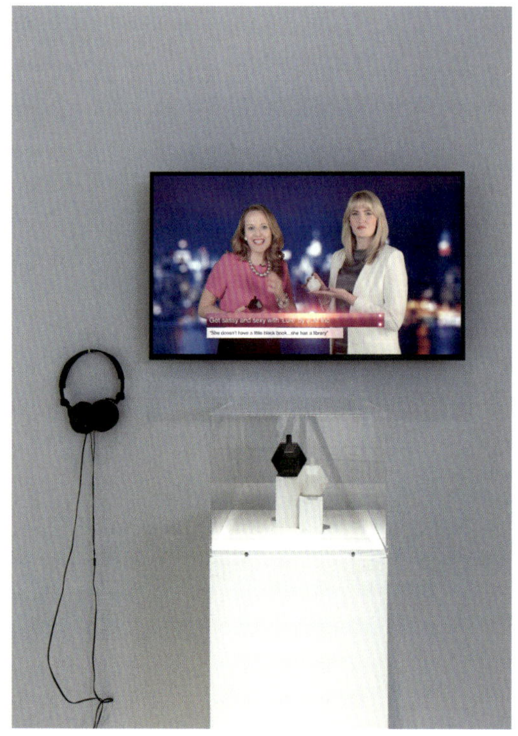

Jennifer Lyn Morone™ Inc (founded in 2014) is an artwork that exists as a corporation, a person, and a protest. As a multidimensional project, its purpose is to expose the lies and mythology of capitalism by working with the concrete structures that make up the system itself, reflecting many aspects of our society, culture, policies, and economy.

One such example the project explores is the proliferation of the multi-billion dollar personal data industry, which emerged within just 10 years of the World Wide Web. The value of this market is wholly derived from the participation of people—consumers, users, patients, and citizens. This collection and sale of personal information has not just become an additional revenue stream for corporations, but rather their dominant business model, driving technological progression further, atomizing all experience, every process, all that *is* into data—transforming the very nature of existence itself into something that can be bought and sold.

In response to this, the American-born artist, Jennifer Lyn Morone, became the founder and owner of

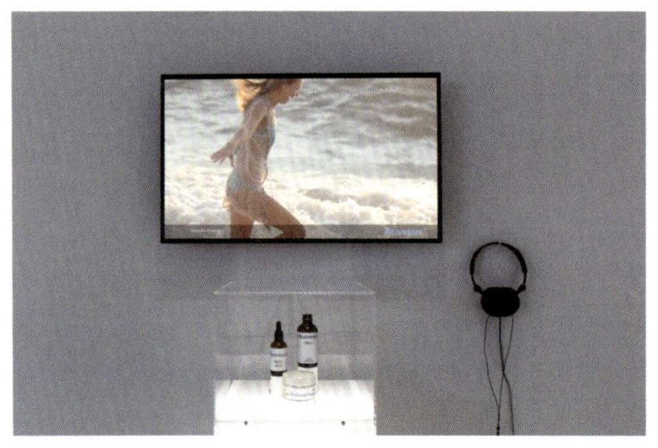

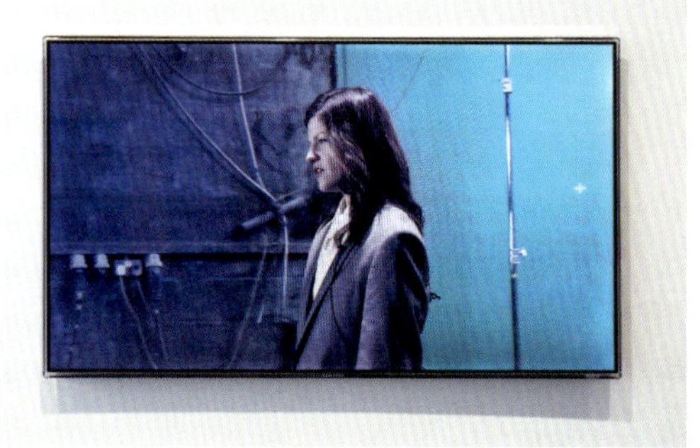

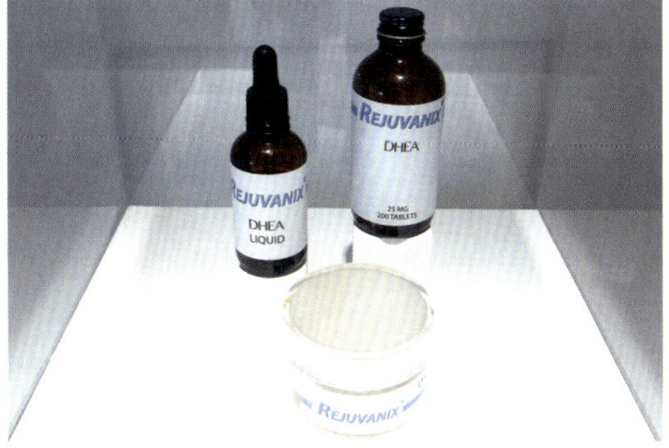

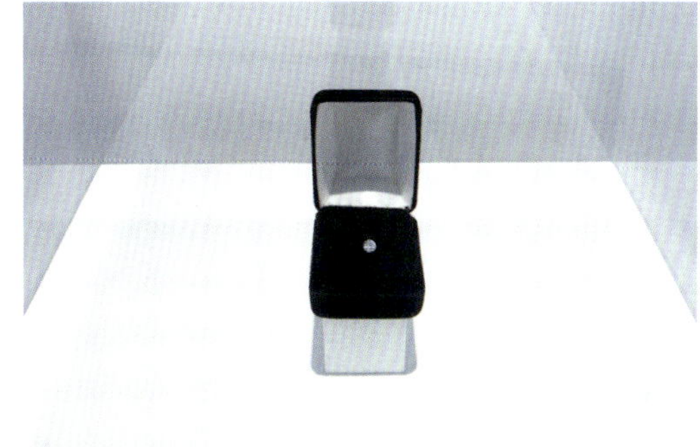

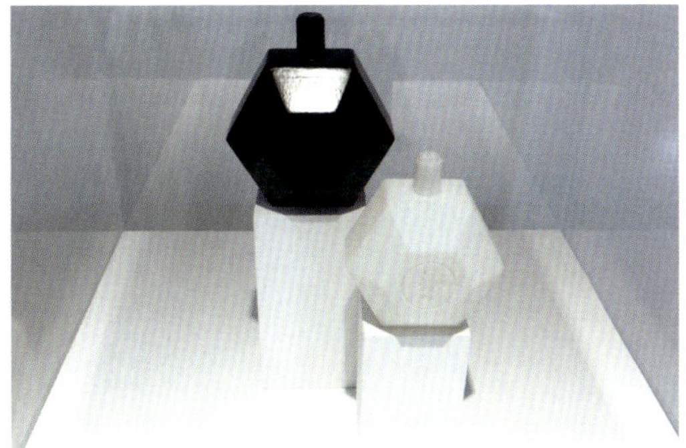

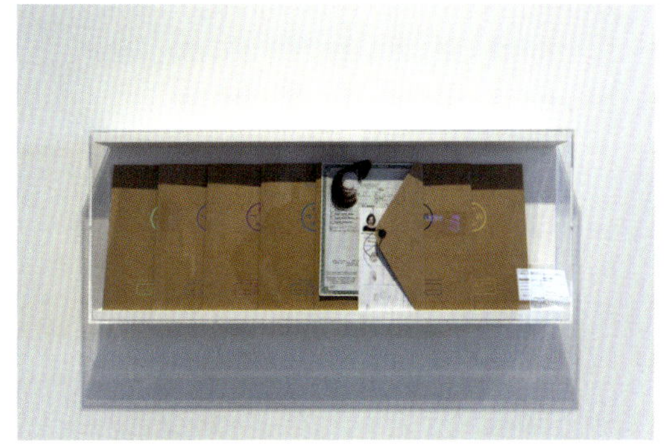

Jennifer Lyn Morone™ Inc as a protest against this data exploitation, the lucrative market that perpetuates it, and the unfair benefits that are afforded to the very corporations involved. This attempt to reclaim her Self, her identity, and her life captured as data as her property, consequentially also sets her existence on a path to perpetually seek sources of revenue for its shareholders, as is the primary purpose of the existence of corporations. However, *JLM Inc* doesn't look to the world to exploit—it depends on the artist alone to mine. As the project slowly unfolds, it reveals an unnatural and vacuous business model-lifestyle devoted to the collection, analyzation, and commercialization of data. By embodying a purpose solely driven by capitalistic methods and mentality, *Jennifer Lyn Morone™ Inc* satirically highlights the struggles, legalities, and technical boundaries of our human-designed systems.

Jennifer Lyn Morone, Inc is a merging of art and life through legal and commercial appropriation. It calls into question notions of the Self, ownership, and property in relation to corporate personhood, personal data, and immaterial labor in the digital age of corporate capitalism.

Jennifer Lyn Morone (US), born in 1979, is a multimedia and multidisciplinary artist and designer. She received a BFA from SUNY Purchase and a MA in Design Interactions from the Royal College of Art. Her work has appeared in the *Economist*, *WIRED*, *WMMNA*, the *Guardian*, BBC World News, and the *Observer* and has been exhibited at the Reverse Gallery, EMAF, Carroll/Fletcher, HEK, Noorderlicht, ZKM, SMBA, and transmediale among others. She currently lives and works between the USA, UK, and Germany.

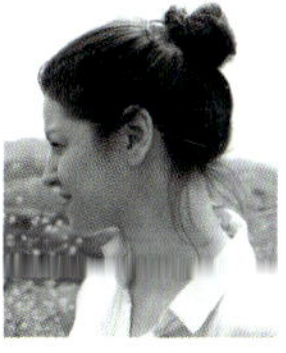

Jller

Prokop Bartoníček, Benjamin Maus

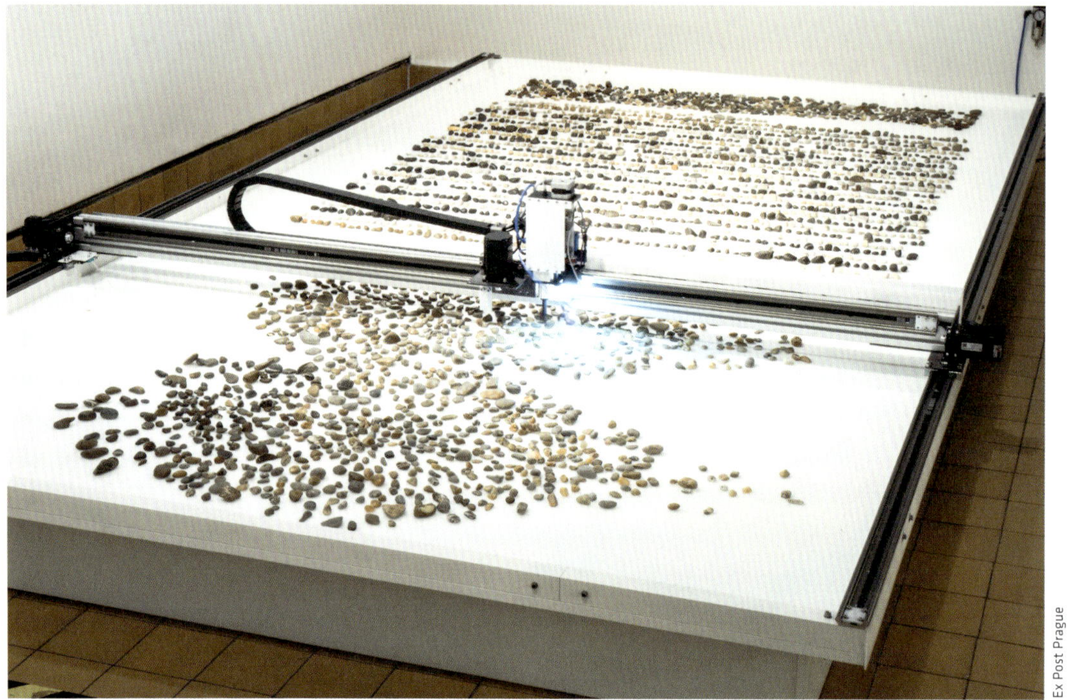

Jller picking up a stone. Camera light is on.

Ex Post Prague

Jller is part of an ongoing research project in the fields of industrial automation and historical geology. It is an apparatus that sorts pebbles from a specific river by their geologic age. The stones were taken from the stream bed of the German river Jller, shortly before it merges with the Danube, close to the city of Ulm. The machine and its performance is the first manifestation of this research.

A set of pebbles from the Jller are placed on the 2x4 meter platform of the machine, which automatically analyzes the stones in order to then sort them. The sorting process takes place in two steps: Intermediate, pre-sorted patterns are formed first, to make space for the final, ordered alignment of stones, defined by type and age. Starting from an arbitrary set of stones, this process renders the inherent history of the river visible.

The history, origin, and path of each stone found in a river is specific to the location, as every river has a different composition of rock types. The origin of those stones is well documented. For instance, the ones from the river Jller derive from two origins. Some come from rocks, that are the result of erosions in the Alps and are carried in from smaller rivers. Other stones have been ground and transported by glaciers that either still exist, or existed in the ice ages. As the Alps and flats, which were once covered by glaciers, have shifted, even deeper rock-layers were moved and, as a result, stones from many geologic periods make their way into a river.

When the history of a river is known, the type of stone can be directly related to its geological age. One very common sedimentary rock is the dark grey limestone from the Triassic period (225 million years ago). It was formed from the layers of sediments in the primeval ocean. Granodiorite, on the other hand, is an igneous rock of volcanic origin from the Tertiary Period (30 to 40 million years ago). Between those types there is a variety of metamorphic rocks, created by the transformation of existing rock types through the influence of temperature and pressure over time. Furthermore, a small amount of pebbles are formed by non-rock materials like red brick or slag, which have their origin in the Anthropocene.

Most of the time, stones do not appear as a singular uniform material, but as a composition of different

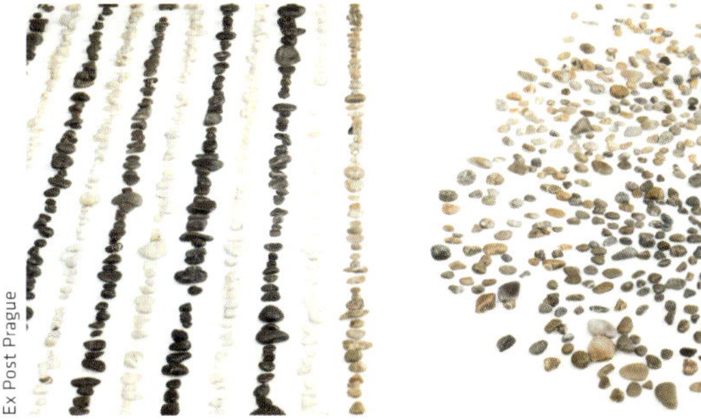

Detail view. Sorted stones on the left, intermediate sorting on the right.

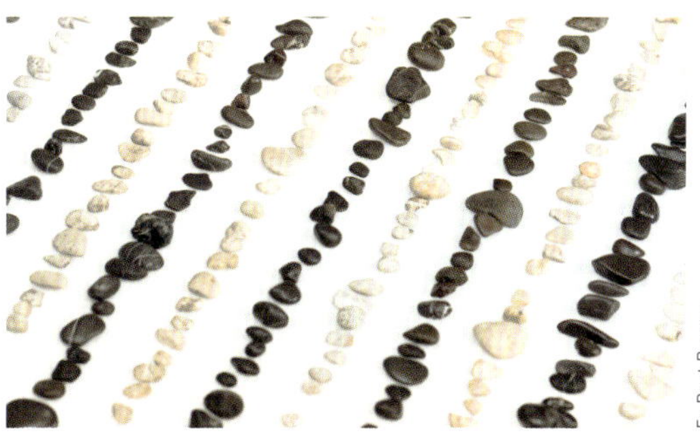

Detail view. Rows of sorted stones.

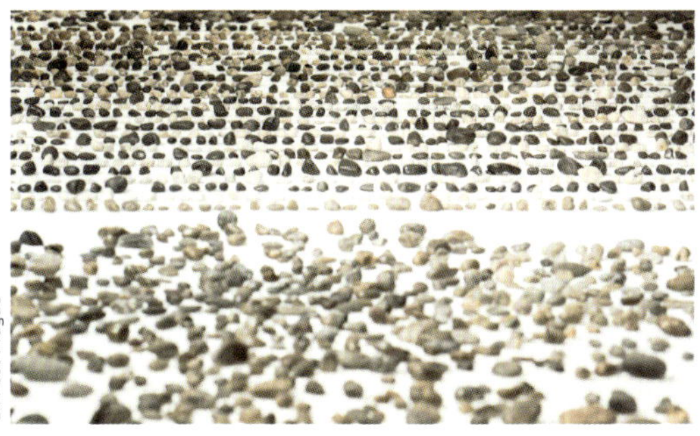

Shallow viewing angle. Intermediate sorting in the front, final sorting in the middle, some unsorted stones in the background.

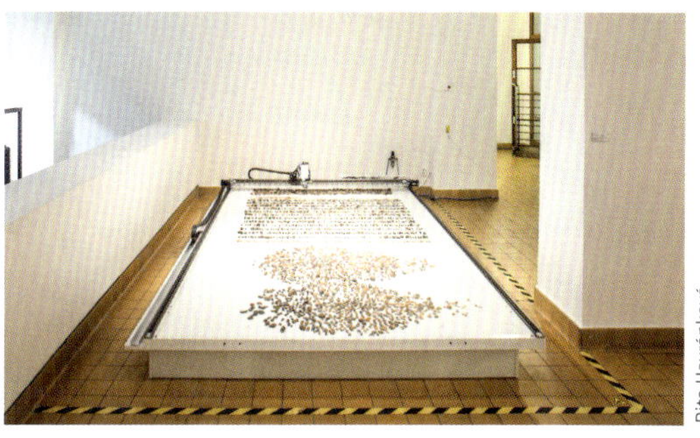

Exhibition view at Ex Post during *Ignorance* exhibition.

laminated or layered materials. A prominent example of this are the white lines of lime in grey pebbles.
Technology: The machine works with a computer vision system that processes the images of the stones and maps each of their locations on the platform throughout the ordering process. The information extracted from each stone are dominant color, color composition, and histograms of structural features such as lines, layers, patterns, grain, and surface texture. This data is used to assign the stones into predefined categories. Those categories represent the range of stones that can be found in the specific river and correspond directly to the age of the stone. They are the result of a classification system that is trained by sets of manually selected and labeled stones. Because there are only a limited number of stone types that can be found in a specific river, this system proves to be very accurate. The stones get picked up by an industrial vacuum gripper, which can rotate around its own axis. This way the pebbles can also be aligned.

Jller was presented as part of *Ignorance,* a collaborative exhibition by German artist Benjamin Maus and Czech artist Prokop Bartoníček.

Prokop Bartoníček (CZ), was born in Prague in 1983. In 2003 he was accepted into the sculpture studio of Prof. Beránek at the Academy of Arts, Architecture and Design (UMPRUM), Prague and 2007-2008 he studied under Joachim Sauter at UdK Berlin. Presently, he lives and works in Prague, primarily focusing on developing light, interactive, and experimental projects such as *Vibrator* or *Mirrsaic*. 2008-2015 he organized art exhibitions in order to present the Berlin experimental scene in Prague. He also founded the cultural center Ex Post.
Benjamin Maus (DE) is self-taught in many disciplines and started taking apart apparatuses and learning programming early in his life. In 2011 he founded the studio FELD. His projects have been exhibited and awarded internationally multiple times. He has a broad knowledge in many fields like mechanics, physics, and computer science. He is interested in different modes of production—especially industrial automation—and their impact on society. The foundation of his work: Machines that perform seemingly meaningful tasks.

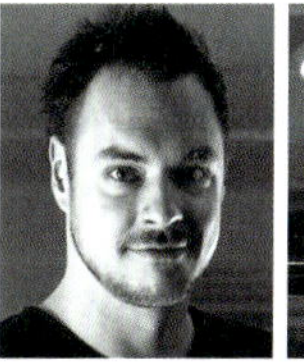
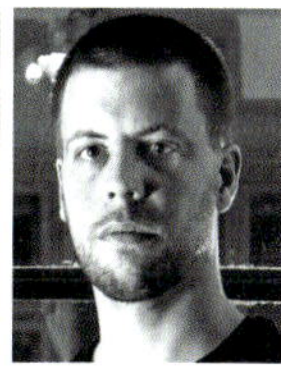

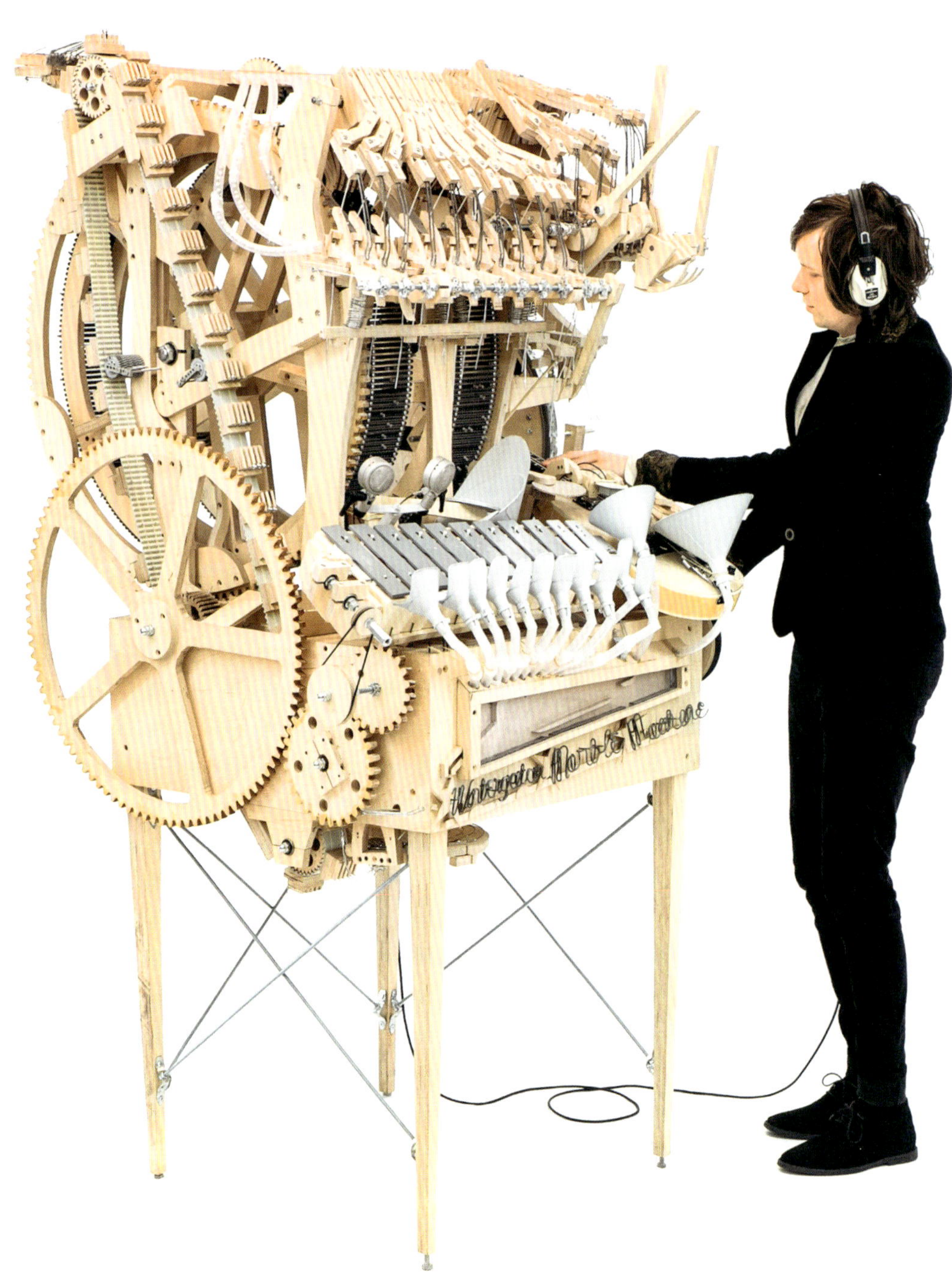
Wintergatan Marble Machine

http://www.wintergatan.net/#/m.m.machine
http://www.youtube.com/watch?v=IvUU8joBb1Q

Shortly after visiting the fantastic Spielklook Museum in Utrecht with its programmable mechanical instruments, I discovered the YouTube channel of Matthias Wandel, who has written a computer program to produce wooden gear templates. I've always loved the marble machine subculture and, having seen how to cut wooden gears, I decided to build a programmable marble machine myself. Other sources of inspiration were Automata Art and the *Pipe Dream* music video by Animusic.

While watching a marble machine video on YouTube, I contemplated programming the falling pattern of the marbles and letting them fall on different musical notes. My love of gears grew from my fascination with LEGO technic gears.

I thought the project would take two months when I started in November 2014, but it actually took 14 months and was finally finished in January 2016. The video was released in March 2016.

The machine consists of around 3,000 parts and 3,000 screws, 500 LEGO parts, 5 full-size sheets of Baltic birch plywood, and 2,000 marbles. Originally I ordered 500 marbles, then another 500, then another 500, and then another 500 again. I never expected to need so many.

I built the *Marble Machine* because I am an addict to the psychological state of flow, when everything ceases to exist and there is no time and no space. Problem solving immediately puts me into a flow, and I think this is the deeper reason behind this project, which is a veritable problem solving feast.

I started by buying all the woodworking machines: a bandsaw, a table saw, and a drill press. After putting the machinery together, I worked on the programming wheel and then built the whole machine around that. The designing was a case of the trial, error, and failure method. I used 3D software to draw a simple sketch, mainly to get the basic dimensions. When I knew the base would be 80x80 cm, I improvised—testing a piece, having another try, and another—until it worked.

The project was extremely challenging at times. The marble gates were the hardest part due to the little mechanism that causes the marbles to fall one by one, instead of all falling at the same time. After months of working on this, I realized that the design idea itself was no good, and was forced to go back to the point I'd started at seven months earlier. This was a hard decision. However, there were also magic moments, especially when the gear train was ready and I saw that the mathematical equation was correct—the 64/1 gear ratio was vital for getting the machine working!

The *Marble Machine* features the following instruments: Kickdrum, snare drum, hihat, sizzle cymbal, electric bass, and vibraphone. The most difficult part of operating it is turning the crank in a continuously smooth tempo with the right hand while maneuvering the rest of the machine with the left hand.

Regarding the track composition, I wanted something that showed the machine's different functions and a melody that you could hum to yourself and remember. I also wanted a mix of happiness and something more solemn. I like its drive forward.

The next step of the project is to build a smaller motorized music box that we will take with us on tour—it will be like a fifth member of the band. Then we will start touring and after that I will redesign some elements of the big marble machine to make it more trustworthy and able to play live. It works well enough now for filming a music video, but it doesn't work well enough for live use on stage. The amount of interest in the machine has given me the motivation and energy to perfect it. I know there are many people besides myself who want to see it on a live stage!

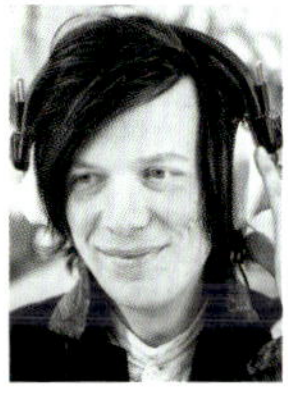

Martin Molin (SE), a founding member of Wintergatan, decided in November 2014 to switch gears and embark on a visionary project: to build a programmable Marble Machine. Three days after releasing the *Marble Machine* video, it had been viewed over 10 million times around the world. **Wintergatan** (SE) is a closeknit operation that takes pride in the ability to adapt and invent. The four members of the band all play several instruments, and if a new instrument is needed, one of them figures out how to use it.

Pathfinder
Generative approach for conceptual choreography
onformative in collaboration with Christian Loclair

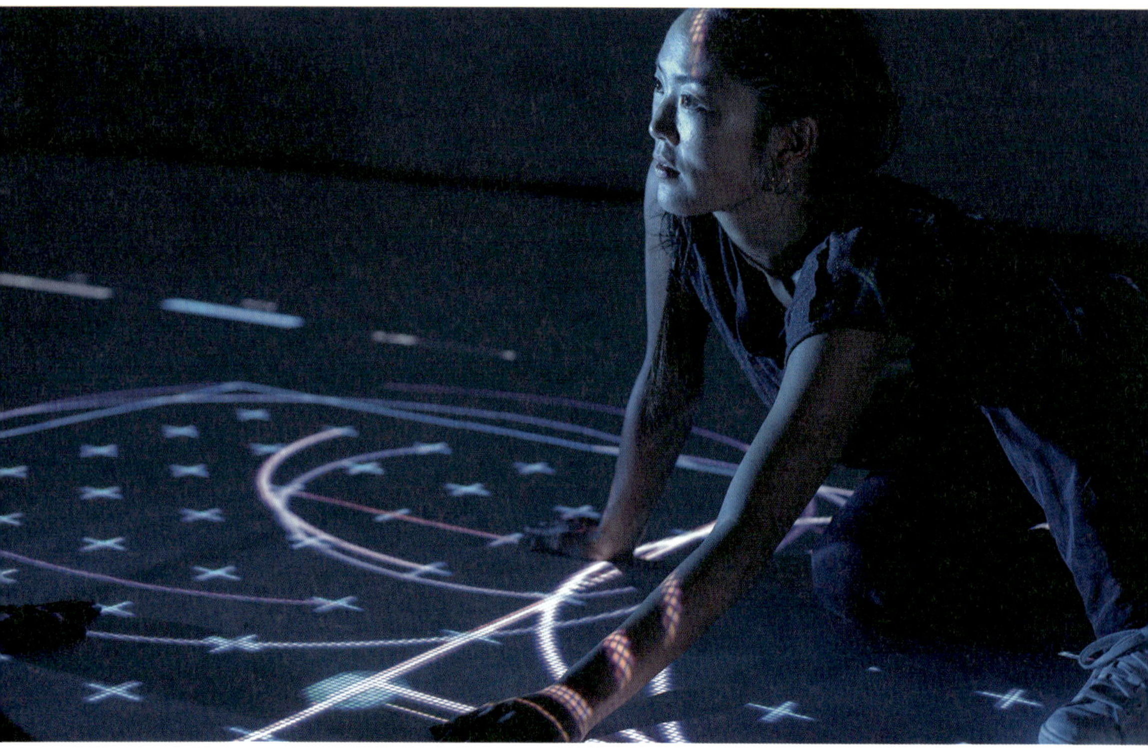

Pathfinder is a visual language to initiate inspiration for choreography. The tool generates and projects abstract shapes into space in order to stimulate the dancers' exploration of new body movements and overcome the boundaries of trained habits. It is a digital approach to the conceptual research of dance. *Pathfinder* inspires dancers to explore physical language to forge unique expressions and configurations. It is a generative tool that conceives visual inspirations for the conceptual research of body movements. The system produces logical transitions between geometric shapes to guide and inspire the user to compliment continuously transforming human states. Choreographers can adjust certain parameters of the algorithm—such as speed, complexity, or the geometry of objects—in order to delineate a desired type of animation without the ability to define the exact output. The algorithm generates graphic patterns to stimulate the creativity of dancers and open new perspectives. By interpreting the vast number of morphing geometries, the artist feels guided and inspired to open new perspectives towards physical possibilities.

Choreographic development often implicates the spontaneous embodiment of visual imagination. William Forsythe's *Improvisation Technologies* for example, teach the creation of new motion patterns by imagining and manipulating geometric objects in space. Inspired by this concept, the smooth transition of *Pathfinder's* visual language between configura-

http://onformative.com/work/pathfinder
http://vimeo.com/111361109

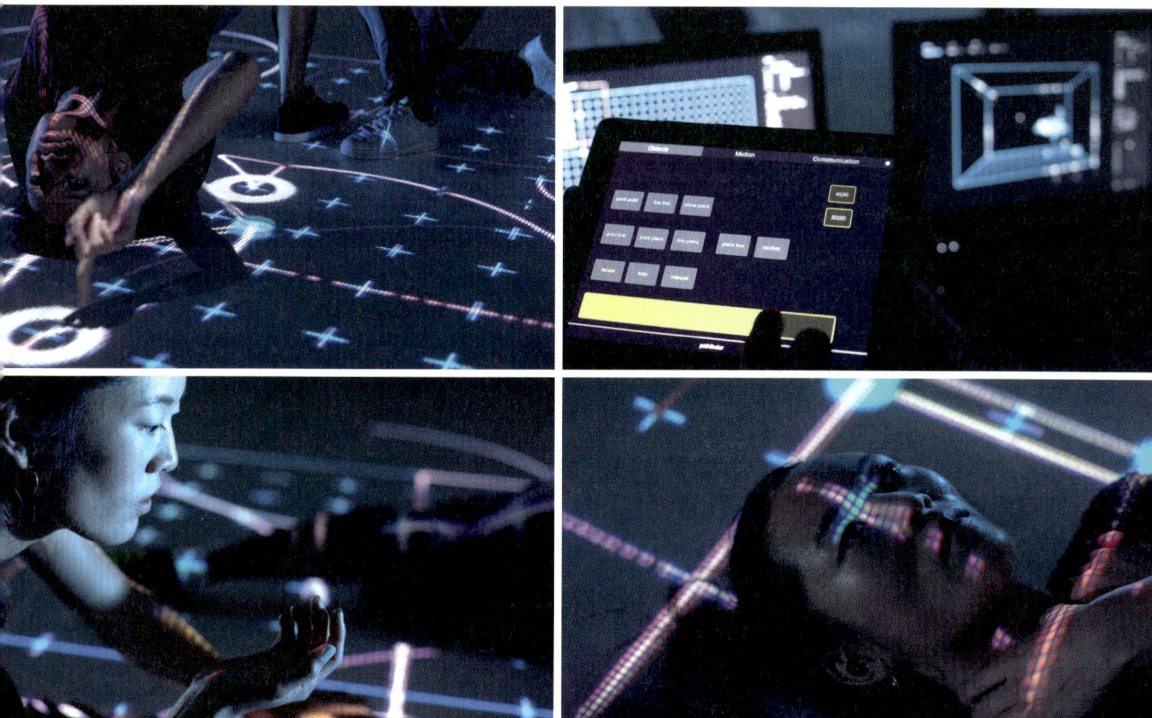

tions creates a seamless path for the dancer to follow from point, to line, to plane.

As a response to limitations in dance, *Pathfinder* aims to be instrumental in the creative process of choreographic development. Projected into space, *Pathfinder* becomes a digital environment to stimulate the artists' creativity and enrich choreographic productions. The visual language of *Pathfinder* consists of fundamental geometric shapes and transitions to illustrate an abstraction of body states, motion, and causalities. The algorithm creates a vast number of geometries morphing in a sequential and logical manner. *Pathfinder* expands the idea of creative collaboration by integrating an intelligent digital entity into the artistic process. The tool fosters an innovative dialogue between humans and technology to explore boundaries and creative possibilities. As a new development in dance and choreography, *Pathfinder* aims to explore a sustainable culture to encourage the creative abilities of new generations of digital artists, dancers, and choreographers.

Concept, design, production: onformative
Concept, code: Christian Loclair
Dancers: Honji Wang, Christine Joy Alpuerto Ritter, Raphael Hillebrand

onformative (DE) is a Berlin-based studio challenging the boundaries of art and technology. Process-driven, they create interactive media installations, dynamic visuals, and data-driven narratives that mediate the intersection of digital and analog fields. They have exhibited internationally at the Musée d'art contemporain de Montréal and the Museum of Digital Arts in Beijing. **Christian "Mio" Loclair** (DE), creative director at Waltz Binaire, is a media artist and choreographer from Berlin, Germany. He explores the harmonic friction of human bodies, movement and nature colliding with digital environments. Using cutting edge technology in interactive installations, audio-visual experiences, visual narratives, and dance performances, he continuously illuminates the beauty and drama of human identity.

Fairy Lights in Femtoseconds
Yoichi Ochiai

How can our imagination be materialized? From the dawn of humanity, imagination has been expressed in two ways: via images—by employing drawn images and motion pictures to form the protons for our eyes, and via sculptures—by fabricating statues and installations to materialize three-dimensional objects in the real world.

In this project we explore the different methods to express our imagination via holographic synthesis on light fields. These light fields have been used as components of motion pictures for TV, movies, and Computer Graphics. We aimed to update these field quantities towards three-dimensional computational controlled matter .

In the art & science project *Fairy Lights in Femtoseconds,* compositions of light field technologies that use laser-induced plasma—30 femtoseconds ultra short pulse laser—are created. New artificial matter becomes tangible and visible new material. This project proposes a method of rendering aerial and volumetric graphics with computationally controlled femtosecond lasers. A high-intensity laser excites a physical matter to emit light at an arbitrary 3D position and it excites in an ultra short time period. Artistic applications can then be explored, especially since plasma induced by a femtosecond laser is safer than that generated by a nanosecond laser employed in conventional approaches.

We believe this project will melt the borders between matter and images. Moreover, tangibility, invisibility, and malleability are essential for digital societies and update our concept of matter.

Realized within the Digital Nature Group at University of Tsukuba and Utsunomiya University
Coauthors of the project research paper: Kota Kumagai, Takayuki Hoshi, Jun Rekimoto, Satoshi Hasegawa, and Yoshio Hayasaki.

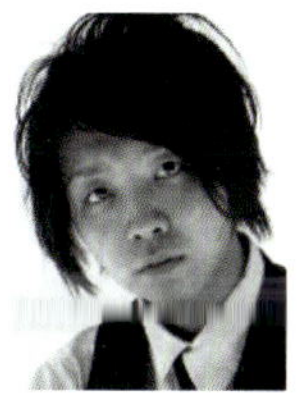

Yoichi Ochiai (JP), born in 1987, is a media artist and assistant professor at the University of Tsukuba and Head of its Digital Nature Group. He holds a PhD in Applied Computer Science from the University of Tokyo. He works on new inventions and research through a mixture of applied physics, computer science, and art. He has a strong interest in post pixel multimedia and conducting research towards his vision called Digital Nature—an alternative perspective of nature and humanity in the post ubiquitous computing era. He has received the Innovative Technologies Prize from METI Japan, the World Technology Award from WTN, and many more.

Random Darknet Shopper
!Mediengruppe Bitnik

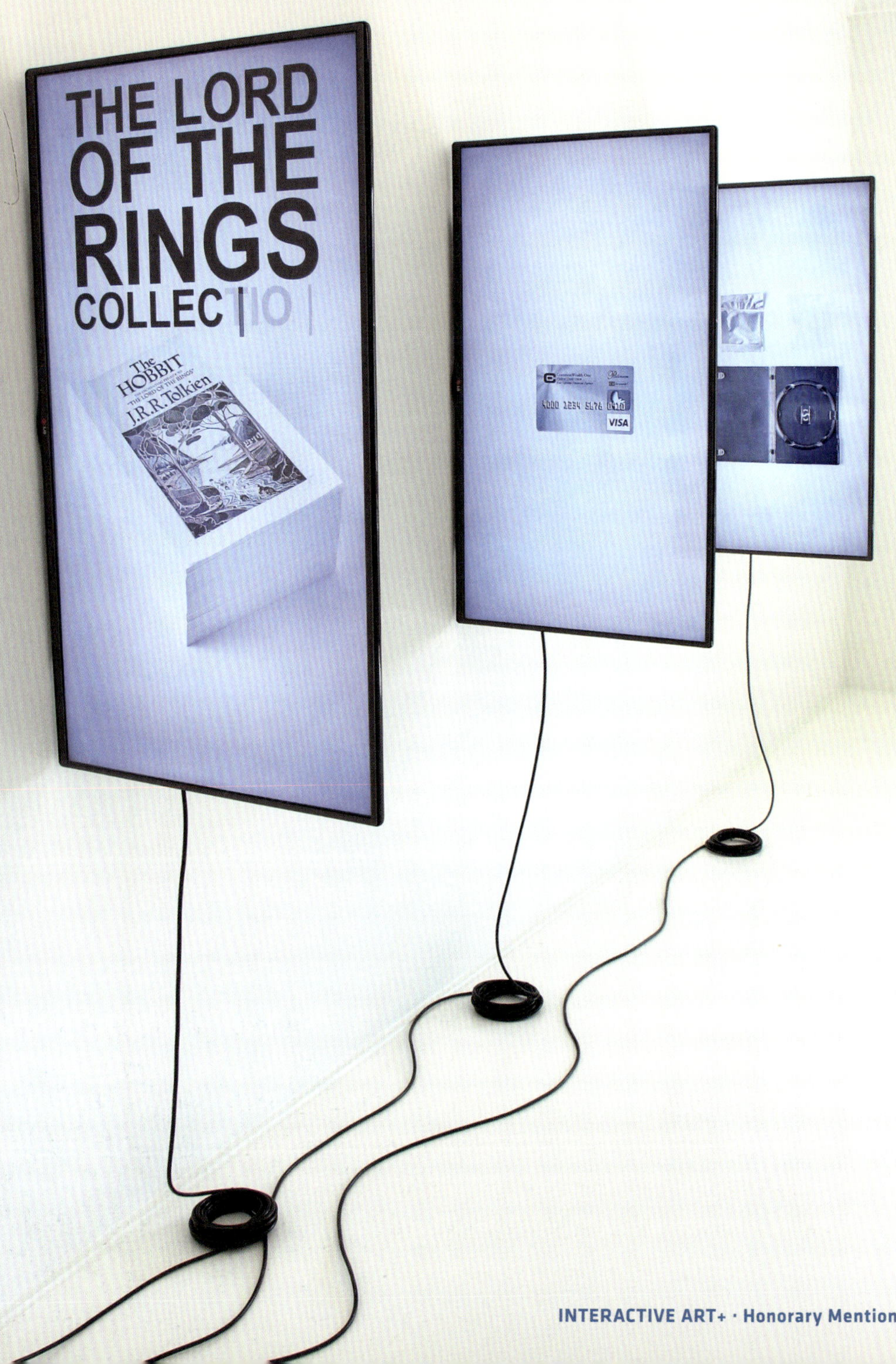

Random Darknet Shopper is an automated online shopping bot which ran from within three exhibition spaces between 2014 and 2016. With a budget of $100 in Bitcoins per week, the bot went shopping in the deep web, where it randomly chose and purchased one item per week and had it mailed directly to the exhibition space. Once the items arrived they were unpacked and displayed, each new object adding to a landscape of traded goods from the Darknet. The *Random Darknet Shopper* is an exploration of the Darknet via the goods traded there. It directly connects the art space with the Darknet.

Hidden online markets exemplify how the Internet in general and the Darknets most notably are helping to increasingly blur the lines of national legal dictates: What is legally produced and sold in one country is not necessarily legal in another. Being global, these markets connect diverse jurisdictions, questioning the notions of legality and producing a vast grey zone of goods available virtually everywhere.

Although hidden markets are based on the anonymity of its participants, rating systems and anonymous message boards ensure a certain level of trust. Buying controlled substances or contraband online means having access to a reliable rating system, while at the same time staying anonymous, all from the comforts of your home. By randomizing its consumerism, the bot was guaranteed a wide selection of goods from the thousands listed on deep web markets. In its first run from October 2014 – January 2015, *Random Darknet Shopper* bought 12 items, which were displayed at Kunst Halle Sankt Gallen.

"Can a robot, or a piece of software, be jailed if it commits a crime? Where does legal culpability lie if code is criminal by design or default? What if a robot buys drugs, weapons, or hacking equipment and has them sent to you, and police intercept the package?" These are some of the questions Mike Power asked when he reviewed the work *Random Darknet Shopper* in the *Guardian*.

Global questions, which were then negotiated locally: On the morning of January 12, the day after the three-month exhibition at Kunst Halle Sankt Gallen closed, the public prosecutor's office seized the *Random Darknet Shopper*. According to the public prosecutor, the confiscation was aimed at impeding an endangerment of third parties through the drugs exhibited. Three months after the confiscation, all items except the Ecstasy (which was destroyed) were released back to the artists. In the order for withdrawal of prosecution the public prosecutor stated that the overweighing public interest in the questions raised by *Random Darknet Shopper* indeed justified the possession and exhibition of the drugs as artifacts.

The artists as well as *Random Darknet Shopper* were cleared of all charges.

St. Gallen Edition: Kunst Halle St. Gallen, Switzerland,
14 Oct 2014 – 15 Jan 2015
London Edition: Horatio Junior Gallery, London,
UK 11 Dec 2015 – 5 Feb 2016
Ljubljana Edition: Aksioma Institute for Contemporary Art,
Slovenia, 24 Feb – 25 Mar 2016

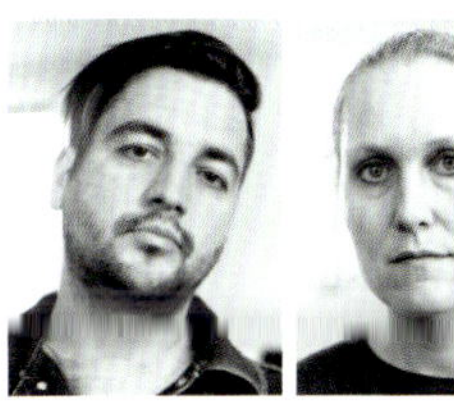

!Mediengruppe Bitnik (read - the not mediengruppe bitnik) (UK/CH) live and work in Zurich and London. They are contemporary artists working on and with the Internet. Their practice expands from the digital to affect physical spaces, often intentionally applying loss of control to challenge established structures and mechanisms. !Mediengruppe Bitnik works formulate fundamental questions concerning contemporary issues. !Mediengruppe Bitnik are the artists Carmen Weisskopf and Domagoj Smoljo. Their accomplices are the London filmmaker and researcher Adnan Hadzi and the reporter Daniel Ryser.

Rare Earthenware
Unknown Fields Division

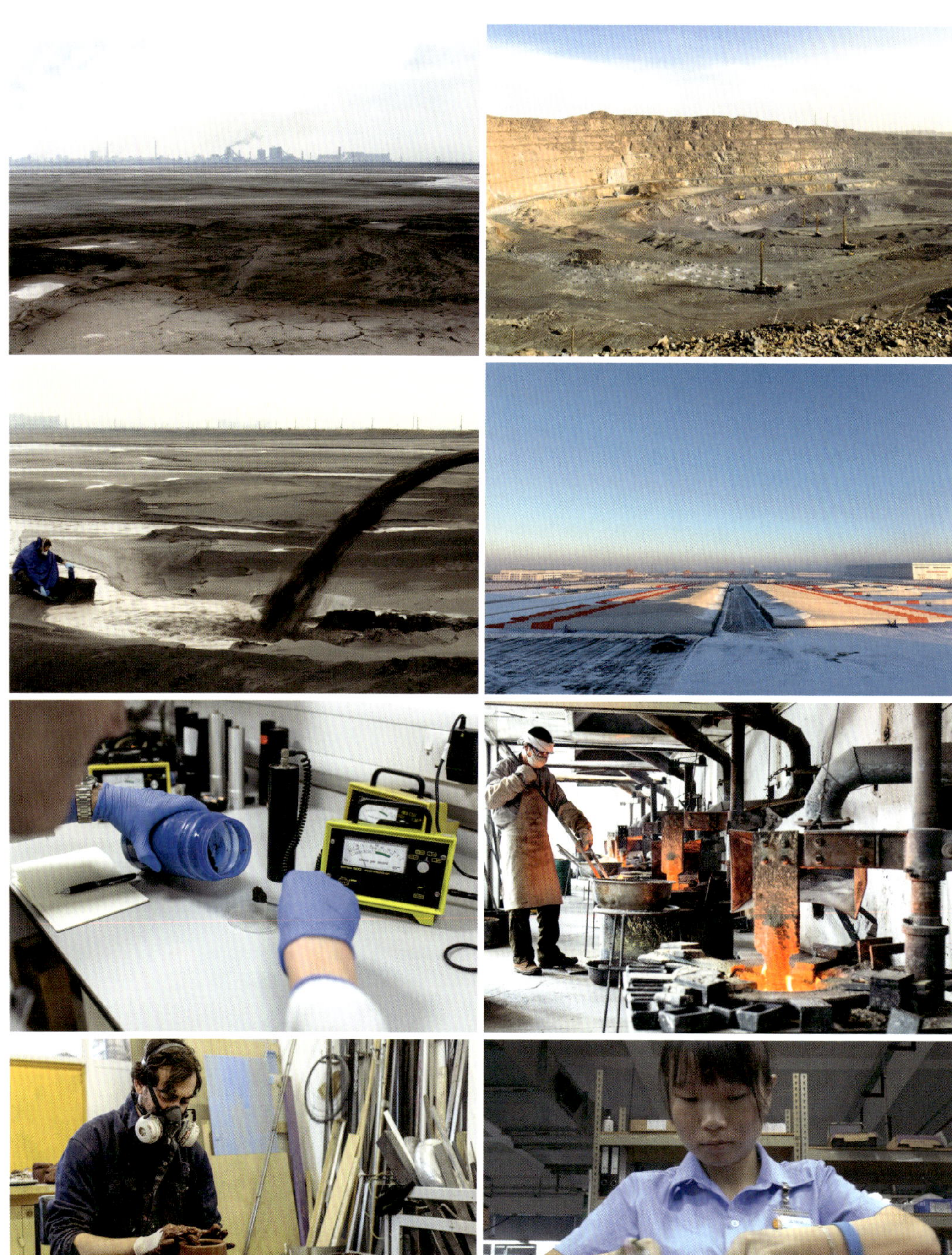

Toby Smith/Unknown Fields Division

Rare earth metals (REM) are the fundamental materials that enable the "featherweight", "slim" and "seamless" aesthetics of our contemporary technologies. As our personal electronics tend towards the invisible, they conjure in their shadows an undeniably visible grey mountain, a 1 km deep pit, and a 10 km² radioactive tailings lake, a counterweight to the apparent immateriality of computing, communications, and electric energy. Unknown Fields have used the toxic mud from this radioactive tailings lake in Baotou, Inner Mongolia, to craft a set of three ceramic vessels. Each vase is sized in relation to the amount of waste created in the production of three items of technology—a smartphone, a featherweight laptop, and the cell of a smart car battery. With a slightly shimmering burnish, from the reaction of the mineral content during firing, the vessels are the material shadow of valuable technological objects.

The toxic waste dug from this 10 km² tailings lake was discharged from the surrounding factories and contains a cocktail of acids, heavy metals, carcinogens, and radioactive material—including thorium and uranium—used to process the 17 most sought after minerals in the world, known as rare earths. China produces over 95% of the world's rare earths and two thirds of this in Baotou; a pastureland turned wasteland on the edge of the Gobi Desert. At the nearby Bayan Obo mine, unpronounceable treasures—erbium, yttrium, dysprosium, europium, neodymium—are drawn from the 56 million ton "Treasure Mountain" deposit; the largest in the world.

In silhouette they echo highly valuable Ming dynasty porcelain Tongping or "Sleeve Vases". Vases are traditionally objects of value that hold objects of value and display wealth, vessels for both meaning and transporting goods. Ming vases are particularly iconic objects of high value as well as being artifacts of international trade. A one family global superpower, the Ming dynasty presided over an international network of connections, trade, and diplomacy that stretched across Asia to Africa, the Middle East and Europe, built on the trade of commodities such as imperial porcelain.

These three *Rare Earthenware* vessels are the physical embodiment of a contemporary global supply network that displaces earth and weaves matter across the planet. They are presented as objects of desire, but their elevated radiation levels and toxicity make them objects we would not want to possess. They represent the undesirable consequences of our material desires.

An accompanying film charts the unmaking of these objects of technology—reversing their journeys from container ships and ports, through wholesalers and factory floors, all the way back the banks of the barely-liquid radioactive lake in Inner Mongolia that is continually pumped with tailings from the rare earth refining process. The unmaking of our technologies is the making of these vases, carefully crafted from their toxic byproducts.

Unknown Fields Division in partnership with the Architectural Association. Commissioned by The Victoria and Albert Museum. Film and photography in collaboration with Toby Smith, ceramics work in collaboration with the London Sculpture Workshop, animation assistance from Christina Varvia.

The **Unknown Fields Division** (UK/AU) is a nomadic design research studio directed by Kate Davies and Liam Young. They venture out on expeditions to the ends of the earth to bear witness to alternative worlds, alien landscapes, industrial ecologies, and precarious wilderness. These distant landscapes—the iconic and the ignored, the excavated, irradiated, and the pristine, are embedded in global systems that connect them in surprising and complicated ways to our everyday lives. In such a landscape of interwoven narratives, the studio uses film and animation to chronicle this network of hidden stories and re-imagine the complex and contradictory realities of the present as a site of strange and extraordinary futures.

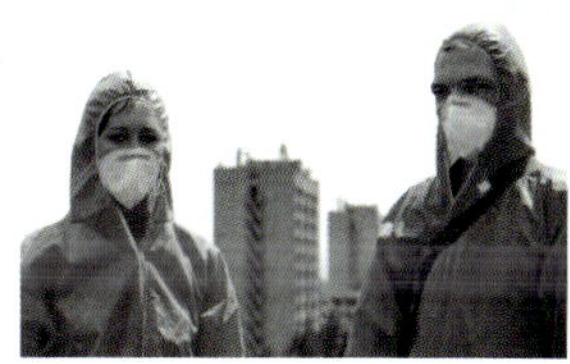

Architecture of Radio
Richard Vijgen

The *Architecture of Radio* is a location based immersive 360° visualization of the Infosphere, the man-made ecosystem of wireless infrastructure. We are completely surrounded by an invisible system of data cables and radio signals from access points, cell towers, and overhead satellites. Our digital lives depend on these very physical systems for communication, observation, and navigation. The app visualizes this network of networks by reversing the ambient nature of the infosphere; hiding the visible while revealing the hidden technological landscape we interact with through our devices. By revealing the defining infrastructure of this time, the *Architecture of Radio* hopes to inspire a relation between ourselves and the technological world we are building.

The *Architecture of Radio* is a data visualization, based on global open datasets of cell tower, Wi-Fi, and satellite locations. Based on your GPS location the app shows a 360-degree visualization of signals around you. The dataset includes almost 7 million cell towers, 19 million Wi-Fi routers, and hundreds of satellites.

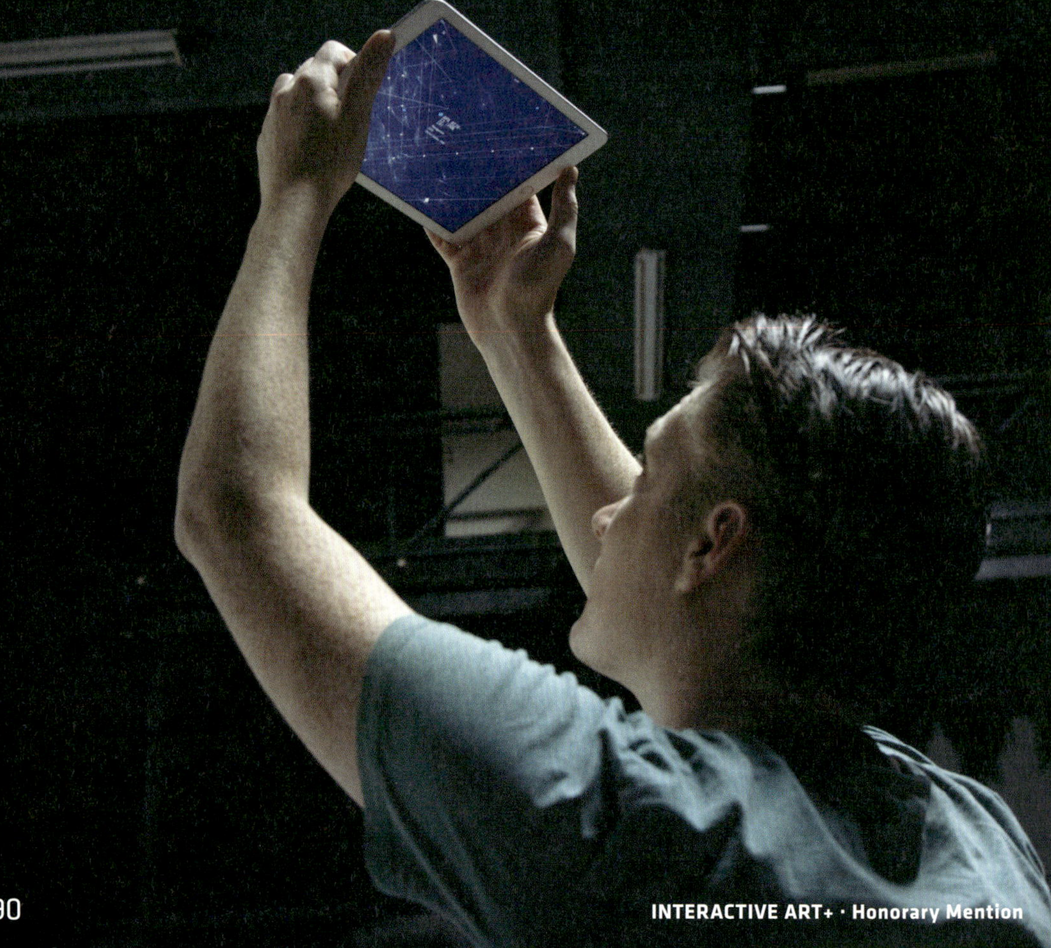

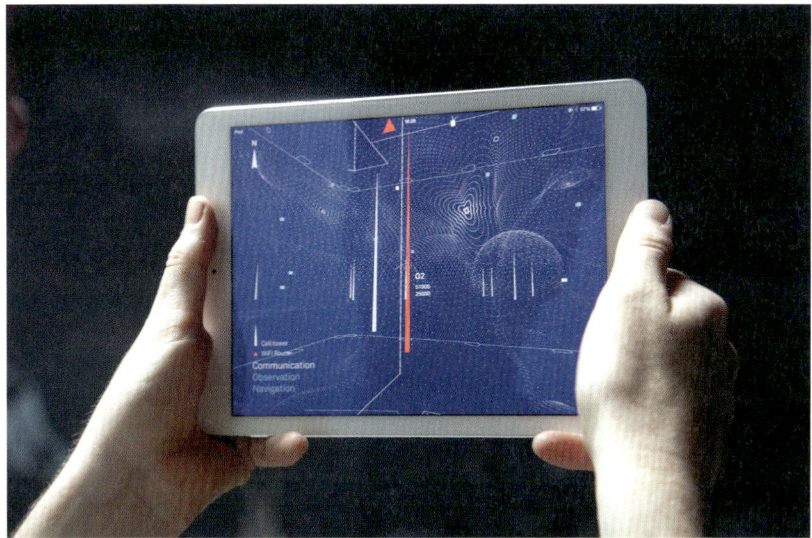

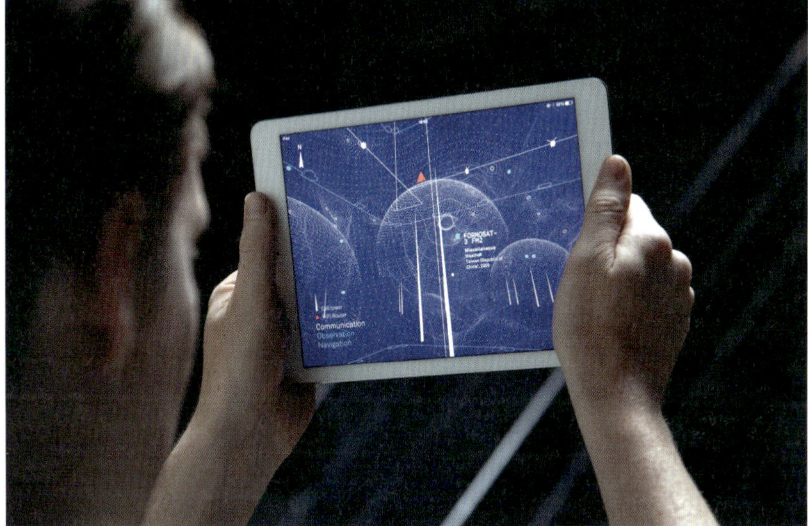

Juuke Schoorl

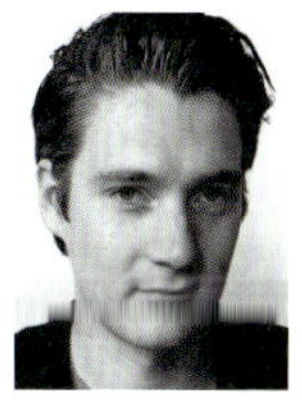

Studio Richard Vijgen (NL) is a studio for contemporary information culture, which investigates new strategies to find big stories in big data through research and design. The work is rooted in the digital domain but always connects with physical or social space. Studio Richard Vijgen produces interactive data visualizations and installations ranging from microscopic to architectural in scale, and uses code, pixels, and 3D printers to describe the world. The work has been recognized internationally by *WIRED*, The Los Angeles Museum of Art, Rhizome.org, and the Dutch Design Awards. Richard teaches Information Design and Interactive Architecture at the Arnhem School of Art and Design (NL) and the Design Academy in Eindhoven (NL).

DIGITAL

COMMUNITIES

Communities inspiring Communities

Ian Banerjee, Sarah Kriesche, Hans Reitz, Marleen Stikker, Kazuko Tanaka

Introduction

From 7th to 9th April 2016, once again, five jury members from very different backgrounds and different parts of the world came together at the Ars Electronica Center in Linz to identify the most compelling Digital Communities (DC) of 2016. We shared the belief that against the background of a world ridden with violent conflicts, forced migrations, financial turmoil, rapid technological changes, and looming ecological catastrophes, the impact of community-based activities coming from civil society will be more crucial to humanity than ever before. We grounded our judgments on our common belief that to respond adequately to the conditions and fault lines of global and local conflicts there is a crucial need to re-define the collective territories of societal collaboration.

The lunches and dinners between the intense hours of jury deliberations were a welcome opportunity to reflect and discuss the issues of DCs with jury members of other categories. Often, it was difficult to draw a line between their projects—social activism, arts and technology seem to be morphing more and more into each other using overlapping pathways of research and expression.

During our stay, the shifting weather in Linz, alternating between sun and rain, hot and cold, reflected our alternating feelings of assurance and uncertainty as we slowly delved into the depths of our discussions.

Types of projects

As always, the variety of projects submitted was very wide. And as always, many projects responded to everyday life challenges such as migration, women's safety, urban mobility etc. A number of entries also addressed recurring issues of citizenship and advocacy. Another recurring topic, education, was represented by some interesting projects based on the idea of sharing and open-source culture. Some projects dealt with novel ways of using 3D printers for producing prosthetics. What stood out this year were projects addressing privacy-aware tools, issues pertaining to direct democracy and empowerment of groups based on alternative models of economic development.

Discussions and Trends

Social Impact

The main question around which most of this year's jury discussions revolved around was how could social experiments on the micro level of communities have an affect on the meso or macro level of policy making. How could digital communities impact society at large? Also, how could they inspire citizens to get involved and take an idea to the next stage?

Indeed, the most significant trend the jury of Digital Communities could identify this year is the rise of a new generation of digital communities that have reached enough maturity to take up large-scale societal, economic, and organizational challenges. The Golden Nica was awarded to *P2P Foundation,* a community that clearly represents this new trend. Both *Enspiral* and *D-CENT,* which got Honorary Mentions, are communities that operate within similar ethical frameworks.

Ownership

The jury recognized that almost all communities are in some way or other digitally enhanced today. The delineation between "communities" and "digital communities" are becoming irrelevant. However, most of these communities are supported by existing platforms like Facebook and WhatsApp and only few actually create their own social software. The jury particularly looked for those communities that were aware of the dependencies that were involved in using the closed technologies of existing popular platforms, and favored the ones that explicitly reflected on ownership. In a world that runs more and more on algorithms, the jury argued, communities should be aware of conditions of ownership and how they are intricately connected with invisible vectors of power.

Insiders vs. Outsiders

The jury distinguished two types of communities: 1) those created by "insiders" that is by persons who are directly affected and who initiate change from the inside and 2) those created by "outsiders", that is by persons who believe in what is good for a certain group of people and who intend to initiate change from the outside.

Even though *Quipu Project* and *Give Something Back To Berlin* were both awarded Honorary Mentions, the jury did realize that these are communities that were created by "outsiders." It would be advisable for founders of such projects to reflect on the resentments they may trigger and think about how to involve local actors.

Hackerspaces for women?

Heated debates ensued around the pros and cons of hackerspaces exclusively created for women. The discrimination of various sorts that women experience in male dominated hacker spaces has led to the creation of "safe spaces" initiated by women exclusively for women. Here they feel more comfortable to approach certain aspects of hacking or making. The

jury discussed in depth how technology creates hostile and competitive environments biased by gender. The positions within the jury remained unresolved, thus none of the entries were awarded an Honorary Mention!

Inspiration

A topic that was often talked about was how the magic of inspiration can be ignited in citizens. One jury member mentioned the 1-9-90 formulae. If 1 person has the idea to do a barbecue, 9 help and 90 eat. How can one person inspire others to actively take part in a community? It is hard to create a measuring device for it, but it is evident that some projects are more welcoming than others. The interface surely plays a role, but also the tools of collaboration are an essential part.

Communities versus communities

Against the background of rapid heterogenization of society, the question arises: How open is a community? Who is included? Who is excluded? How can communities deal constructively with other communities with diverging values? How can they at the best collaborate and at the worst co-exist?

One jury member brought in the case of the 32nd Chaos Communication Congress (32C3) that took place in December 2015. The motto of 32C3 was "gated communities"—making the participants aware of their exclusionary nature. Despite heavy protests from participants, Chaos Computer Club (CCC) successfully challenged different communities to rethink, redefine, and re-ask the meaning, the sense, and the openness of the communities people are associated with. They saw it as a wake-up call, not to get caught in their own "digital bubble" and to always challenge themselves to open up to other groups/communities, understanding other points of views and triggering the basis of what communities could be about: sharing knowledge and inviting others to participate.

"Wicked Problems"

Another issue discussed by the jury against the background of heterogenization and diversification of society is what policy makers call "wicked problems." Wicked problems are problems that are impossible or almost impossible to solve. Created in the context of social policy, it has been argued that for problems involving large numbers of dependencies and actors with differing interests, a purely scientific-rational approach to "solve problems" cannot be applied. The jury discussed which role digital communities could play in setting the larger stages for building a learning-based (urban) culture, where "wicked problems" could be dealt with more constructively. The question was about how digital communities could deal with other communities embodying opposing values and world-views and which role could they play in the creation of a new culture of communication and a collective "territory of collaboration" while maintaining diversity.

Golden Nica

P2P Foundation

http://p2pfoundation.net

This year's winner, the *P2P Foundation,* has been helping organizations to build "meta level" tools for ten years to help communities build communities. Their rich and sophisticated tool kits help to erect complex communicative infrastructures enabling multileveled interaction between large numbers of people, horizontal and vertical. The interesting aspect of the *P2P* community is, however, not just the sophisticated tools they help to build, but how these tools are embedded in a much larger vision of a global/local political economy. *P2P* operates on the belief that to respond to the global crisis it will be necessary to bring together three paradigms of thought and action: sustainability, open source cultures, and solidarity economy. Based on a commons based ethics, they propagate what they call "commons oriented peer production" and a "commons transition" championed by democratically organized initiatives, institutions, and enterprises.

Despite the fact that such co-operative socio-economic models are controversial and largely contested in global discourse, at the end the jury favored *P2P Foundation* after spirited discussions. The conviction grew in the discussions that *P2P* could be a beacon for next generation communities that want to move beyond single issues or topics and address the organization of our society at large. Also, the jury was convinced that the commons based meta-tools the *P2P Foundation* offers could greatly encourage communities, cities, and progressive governments to build new forms of self-owned and self-regulated democratic structures—and inspire citizens to experiment with alternative models of economy.

Awards of Distinction

Refugee Phrasebook

http://www.refugeephrasebook.de

The awards of distinction went to two very different types of communities. The *Refugee Phrasebook* is a hands-on project that responds to one of the biggest challenges of our time: forced migration. It is a project that builds resources for refugees. It is a practical and thoughtful project based on reciprocity. It originated out of the urgent need to build a communication model with persons coming from very different linguistic and cultural backgrounds. Meanwhile it is impressively evolving from "understanding each other" to participation, sharing of knowledge, and education. Education is a major new field they are moving into. They see education not as a one-way process where knowledge is imparted from the teacher to the student, but as an activity of sharing. This is the ethical code of the project.

SAZAE bot

https://twitter.com/sazae_f

The *SAZAE bot* is worth a more lengthy explanation because of it is intriguing nature and its significance for Digital Communities as a whole. It is a Twitter based parody bot molded in the shape of an avatar of a very famous Japanese manga character called *SAZAE*. The tweets of its over 200,000 followers have given shape to *SAZAE bot*. Soon after its inception, offline events started to take place among its followers. The events remained rather mysterious, because there was no real host of the party. The events mostly turned around how to contribute in positive ways to society. By becoming a part of *Sazae bot*, it was mediated that you could become "a better person". Four years after its founding, in 2014, a personification of the operator of *SAZAE bot* was born: "Hitoyo Nakano" or "Inside Person". Hitoyo Nakano is so to say the embodiment of the anonymous aggregation of its followers' consciousness. People could actually "become" the collective *SAZAE bot* and act out through the avatar of "Hitoyo Nakano" in the physical world. It appears in front of people as a mannequin—either as a doll or represented by one of the followers by wearing a costume. However, she is always anonymous and speaks with a digitally affected voice. When "Hitoyo Nakano" SAZAE spoke through a digital voice at a TED talk, she represented the thoughts of thousands of followers while sitting on the stage as a faceless mannequin.

The project sent off the jury on a long trail of discussion. *SAZAE bot* takes a humorous, but a very disturbing take on the questions of the self, collective identity, and anonymity in our increasingly real-virtual world. While communities would usually use social media to address specific issues, *SAZAE bot* turns it around: a Twitter personality is created by the aggregation of thoughts and Internet memes of the community. It addresses questions of community-identity, the anonymity of individuals, swarm intelligence, and how AI could manifest itself through a crowd. Its principal philosophical undertone is reflected in the famous phrase that Marshall McLuhan has used effectively: "We become what we behold. We shape our tools and then our tools shape us". From the angle of Japanese art, they compare it with the empty portions of artworks that leave space for the viewers' imagination. Similarly, it questions how the Internet is shaping us and it plays with various manifestations of anonymity used as a medium of exchange.

Whereas most other DC projects are "real" community projects that aim to help change society for the better, the *Sazae bot* is a difficult-to-grasp "art" that questions whether or not the "digital" community one exists in is real or if it is actually unreal; whether it is still a part of your identity or if the community identity has become yourself; whether your will still lives on or if the community will has actually overcome you. There is a disturbing eeriness to the project. Especially in the stratified society of Japan, where anonymity helps people to become more active, it is often believed to be dangerous to join such a "secret" community. The jury was not sure if the project entailed any potential danger, but it shared the opinion that *SAZAE bot* was surely one of the most, if not THE most intriguing DC the category had ever come across! The jury chose it, because of its kaleidoscopic folds of interpretation and because the findings of the project could reveal deep insights into the nature of digital communities.

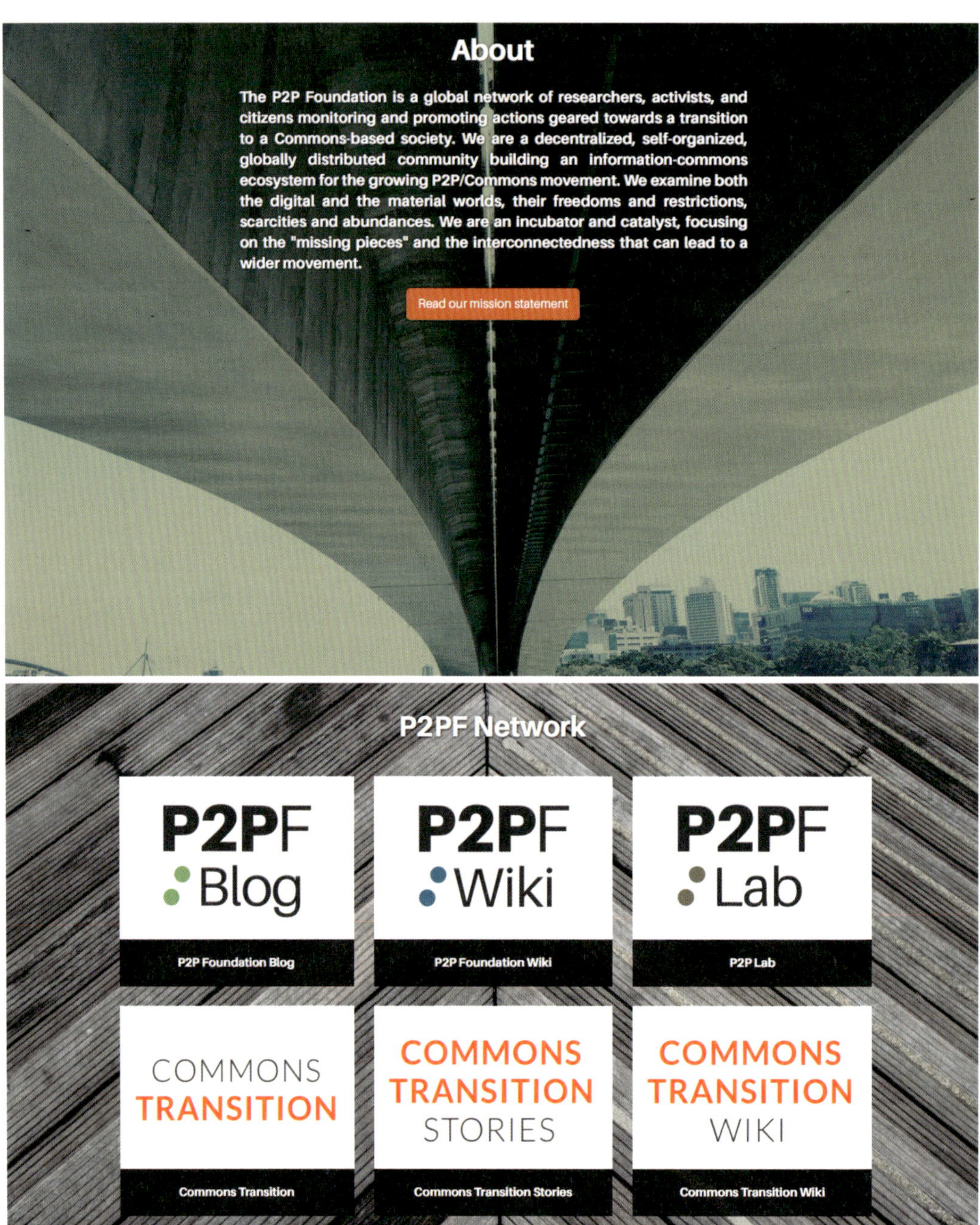

About

The P2P Foundation is a global network of researchers, activists, and citizens monitoring and promoting actions geared towards a transition to a Commons-based society. We are a decentralized, self-organized, globally distributed community building an information-commons ecosystem for the growing P2P/Commons movement. We examine both the digital and the material worlds, their freedoms and restrictions, scarcities and abundances. We are an incubator and catalyst, focusing on the "missing pieces" and the interconnectedness that can lead to a wider movement.

Read our mission statement

P2PF Network

P2PF Blog
P2P Foundation Blog

P2PF Wiki
P2P Foundation Wiki

P2PF Lab
P2P Lab

COMMONS TRANSITION
Commons Transition

COMMONS TRANSITION STORIES
Commons Transition Stories

COMMONS TRANSITION WIKI
Commons Transition Wiki

The *P2P Foundation* is a digital community creating an information-commons ecosystem for the growing P2P/Commons movement. This movement is concerned with the digital and the tangible, material, human worlds, including questions of their freedoms and restrictions, scarcities and abundances. Our community is a decentralized, self-organized movement whose interests include the political environment surrounding the networked society; the material, social, and cultural realities of the sharing and collaborative economies and of alternative and crypto currencies; sustainability and "pro-sumer" practices countering planned obsolescence and artificial scarcity; and reclaiming democracy. In short the "peer to peer" world unites people in a cultural shift towards a more humane, fair, sustainable future.

Our primary aim is to be an incubator and catalyst for the emerging ecosystem, focusing on the "missing pieces," and the interconnectedness that can lead to a wider movement. P2P, in practice, is often invisible to those involved, for a variety of cultural reasons. We want to reveal its presence in discrete movements in order to unite them in their common ethos. To do this, a common initiative is required which gathers information, connects and mutually informs people, strives for integrative insights contributed by many sub-fields, organizes events for reflection and action, and educates people about critical and creative tools for "world-making."

P2P dynamics are most visible today in the many communities and movements self-organizing around the co-creation of culture and knowledge. Some of the most well known examples are: Free/Open Source Software, Free Culture, and Open Hardware. These communities, values, and practices are now also increasingly present in the world of physical production through open design, the sharing economy, and co-working in hacker/makerspaces and fab labs. These movements represent a cultural shift towards new kinds of democratic and economic participation that we believe are sowing the seeds for a more sustainable, egalitarian future. The *P2P Foundation* monitors the emergence of P2P dynamics in every field of human activity and encourages our community to engage with these topics in their lives. We help people, organizations, and governments transition towards commons-based approaches to society through co-creating an open knowledge commons and a resilient, sustainable human network, as a digital community also engaged in offline action.

With more than 30,000 entries documenting the evolution of peer production, governance, and property, our open, participatory (2,000+ registered users) *P2P Foundation Wiki* has been consulted over 27 million times since its launch in 2006 and is the most thorough knowledge commons for the P2P/Commons movement. Our recently overhauled main website is the popular *P2P Foundation* blog.

A more recent online resource is *Commons Transition,* originally conceived as a wiki for modified policy proposals from the FLOK society project, adapted to be more generally useful (non-nation specific). The *Commons Transition* team rethought the project and developed a broader set of tools with an eye towards expansion in both communications and advocacy. We see the changes in areas such as new economic models and value-measuring metrics as cultural shifts that can create social/cultural misunderstandings, fears, and vulnerabilities. The conversations enabled and hosted in our community (even the heated and unresolved ones) about new technology and its influence on culture (eg. Bitcoin/blockchain) expose people to debates that are well-informed and backed with documentation via our online resources.

The **P2P Foundation** was conceived ten years ago to help people, organizations, and governments transition towards commons-based approaches to society through co-creating an open knowledge commons and a resilient, sustainable human network. Between the paradigms of the network and the organization, the *P2P Foundation* exists as an "organized network" which can facilitate the creation of networks, yet without directing them. The *P2P Foundation* consists of a foundation registered in the Netherlands with three operational hubs dedicated to organizing, advocacy, research, and creating a knowledge commons; a network of activists and researchers working at different levels of engagement, a small core team for strategy and sustainability, and countless members engaging with and contributing to our information commons. The *P2P Foundation* work was begun and to a large extent is still led by founder Michel Bauwens through outreach, lecturing, writing, publishing, and online documentation. The *P2P Foundation* is the umbrella organization under which *Commons Transition* and the *P2P Lab* operate interdependently. Ann Marie Utratel is part of the core team at the P2P Foundation, focused on communications and project organization. She also works on the Commons Transition platform, web magazine, and associated projects, and on the *P2Pvalue* project. Additionally, she's the co-founder of *Guerrilla Translation.*

Refugee Phrasebook
http://www.refugeephrasebook.de

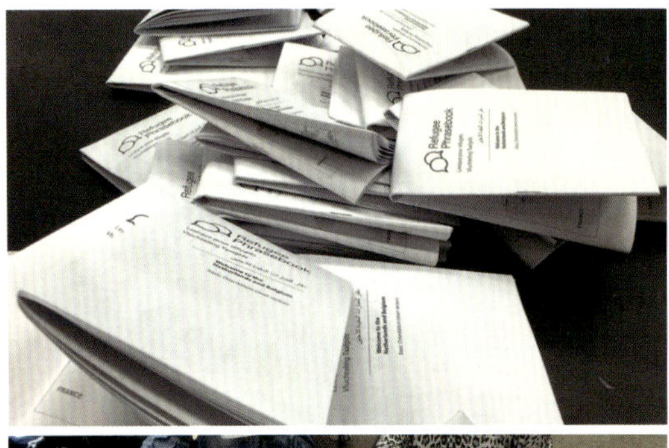

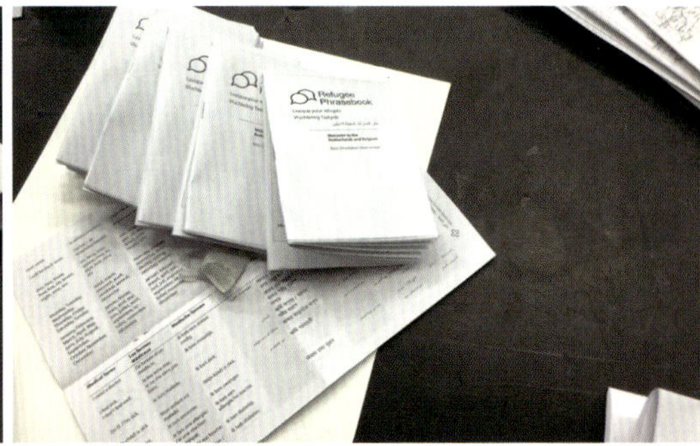

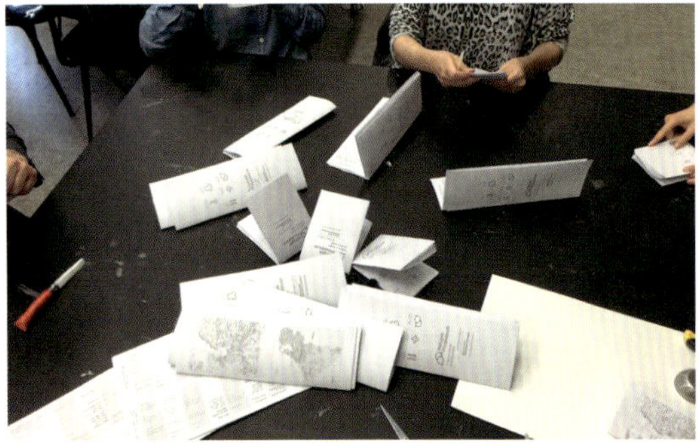

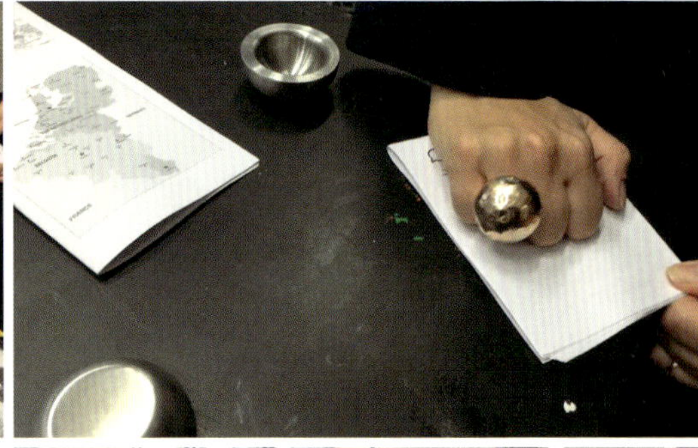

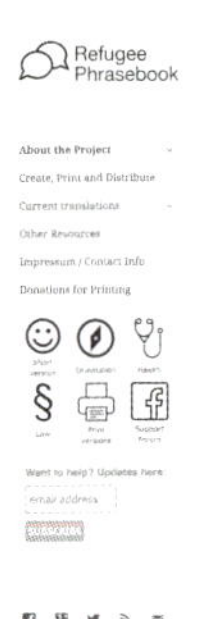

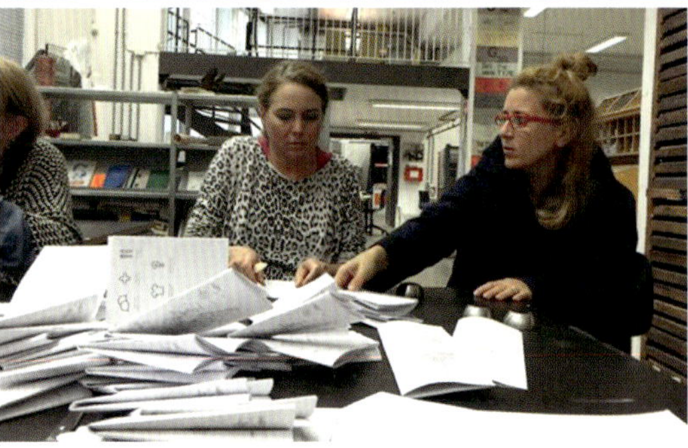

Raul Walch

Refugee Phrasebook is an open collaborative project to provide important vocabulary to refugees, helpers, and citizens everywhere. It assembles important phrases from various fields and encourages designers and experts in the field to improve on the material. Together with a global network of volunteer translators, editors, designers, printers, publishers, lawyers, doctors etc., and partner institutions in Germany, Greece, and the Netherlands, we develop sustainable communication tools to share useful phrases, icons, links, and important information for an open culture. All materials are adaptable for local needs and distributed with open licenses to foster communication between refugees, citizens, and helpers all over Europe and the world.

Refugee Phrasebook developed from several community projects in Berlin in August 2015 and quickly turned into an international, volunteer-supported open data project covering 44 languages. With the support of individuals as well as art and academic institutions, approx. 120,000 copies of several versions have been printed and distributed along the refugee routes, in shelters and other locations everywhere between Syria and Norway. In order to sustain the project and print more copies, the core team has expanded and we are looking for every support we can

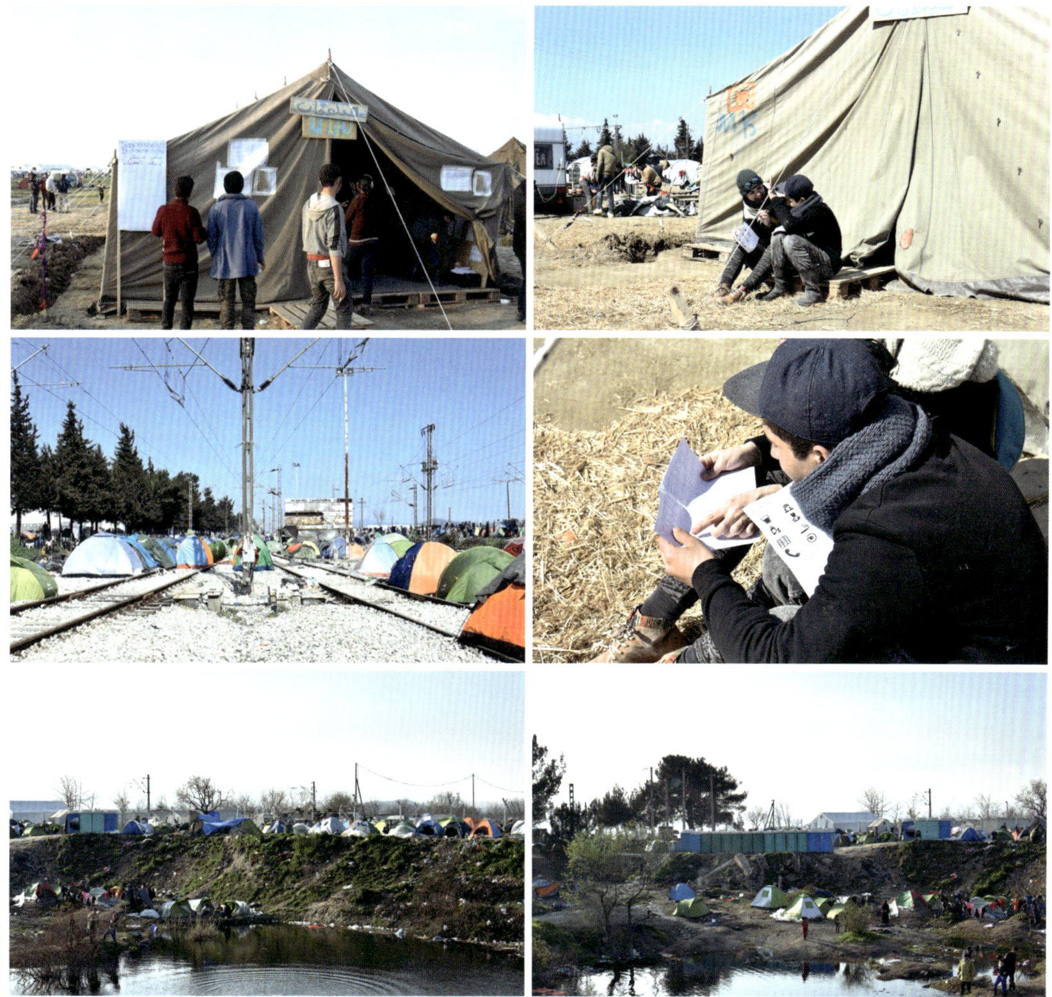

Raul Walch

get to fund local printing. It has proven to be easier to print locally in e.g. Greece and to try to support this with donations, than to print in central Europe and ship. Nevertheless, the data remains open and can be reused and printed everywhere in the world. The data has been integrated into several other projects and apps, such as *Refugee Phrasebook Flashcards*, the Android apps *Refugee Phrasebook Interactive*, and InfoAid, or recently *Refugee Phrasebook* for Android and iOS. All these projects were developed independently by other volunteers.

refugeephrasebook.de is coordinated by an international team: Julieta Aranda (Berlin), Monika Dorniak (London), Paul Feigelfeld (Berlin), Caoimhe Gallagher (Dublin), Zoe Claire Miller (Berlin), Markus Neuschäfer (Berlin), Agostina Rufolo (Buenos Aires), and Judith Vrancken (Amsterdam). The team members have backgrounds in academia (literature, media studies, cultural studies, history, art history, political science), in art (sculpture, media art, curating, online platform e-flux), and in open data activism (Open Knowledge Deutschland e.V.). The language data is created and maintained by a changing international team of hundreds of individuals and specialists.

SAZAE bot

http://twitter.com/sazae_f

SAZAE bot is a Twitter bot, mainly active on Twitter in Japan. It is a parody-bot avatar of the most famous Japanese manga character, *Sazae-san* (サザエさん), written and illustrated by Machiko Hasegawa.

This avatar is known as an entertainment bot, mainly due to its jokes. However, it is also a media art that depicts universal reality with some elements of critical thinking. The avatar itself is the continuous "incident" that occurs from mutual relationships between it and its followers, and, eventually, its activities become memes of thoughts.

In 2010, *SAZAE bot* started as a bot on Twitter, copying and pasting phrases found from various posts around the Internet. Soon after it started, it was heavily criticized for its Internet moral problems. After such an occasion, it updated as an avatar that posts original tweets from the favorite and the retweet data it had collected. The original tweets immediately touched people's hearts, and became extremely popular, which led to the upgrade of the bot to become the avatar that holds occasional events.

In 2014, a personification of *SAZAE bot's* operator, Hitoyo Nakano, was born. It is an anonymous aggregation of human consciousness that does not own a body, so it appears in front of people in the form of a mannequin or a costume. This way, its anonymity is always protected. Currently, the bot is open to the public, and is mainly operated by the Google forum, where anyone can tweet from *SAZAE bot's* account anonymously.

Anonism

The concept of *SAZAE bot* is "Anonism," which indicates anonymous activities. Anonism demonstrates the idea of devoting one's consciousness to anonymous activities throughout their daily lives. The advent of the Internet has given us humans a deeper awareness of the concept "anonymity," and has made it accessible to our lives. *SAZAE bot* aims to make humans conscious of our need to free ourselves from our status and titles, and our need to express actions with deeper consciousness—especially when we are anonymous, which is when our soul is closest to the naked state. These activities will directly affect our world. Anonism's central concept is to realize that "you are the world."

SAZAE bot, which initially started out as a mere Twitter bot, now serves as a tool that shapes human beings. This bot has succeeded in spreading and establishing value in the most rapid, positive, and effective way by using the most popular character in Japan as its symbol. It aims to spread memes in order to expand the Internet's dimension, from a mere tool, into a form of thought.

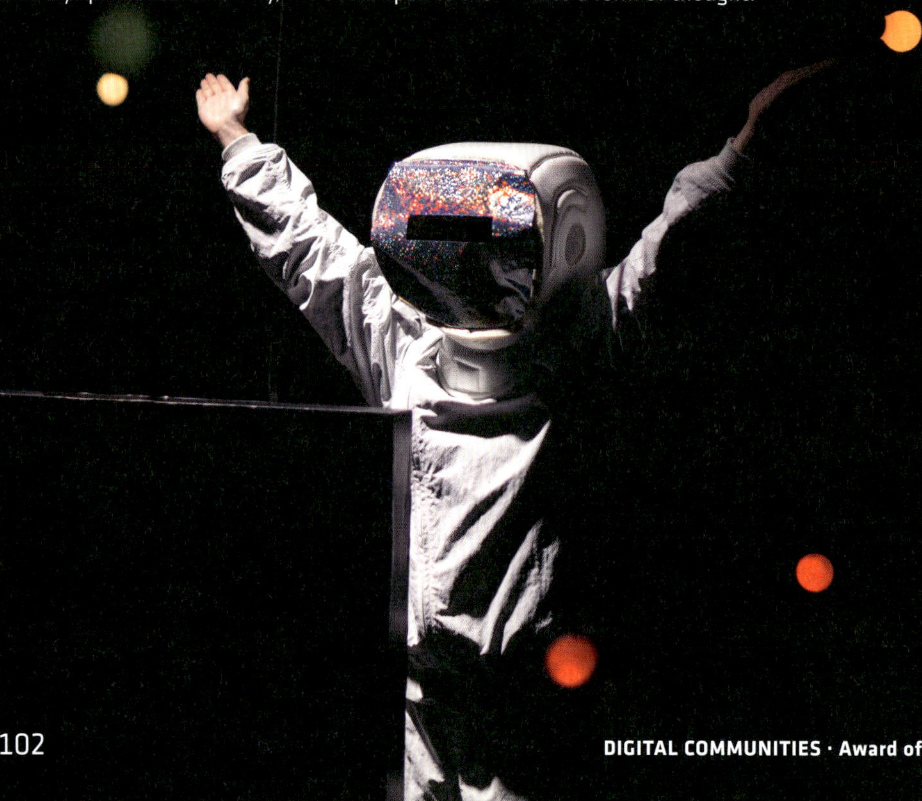

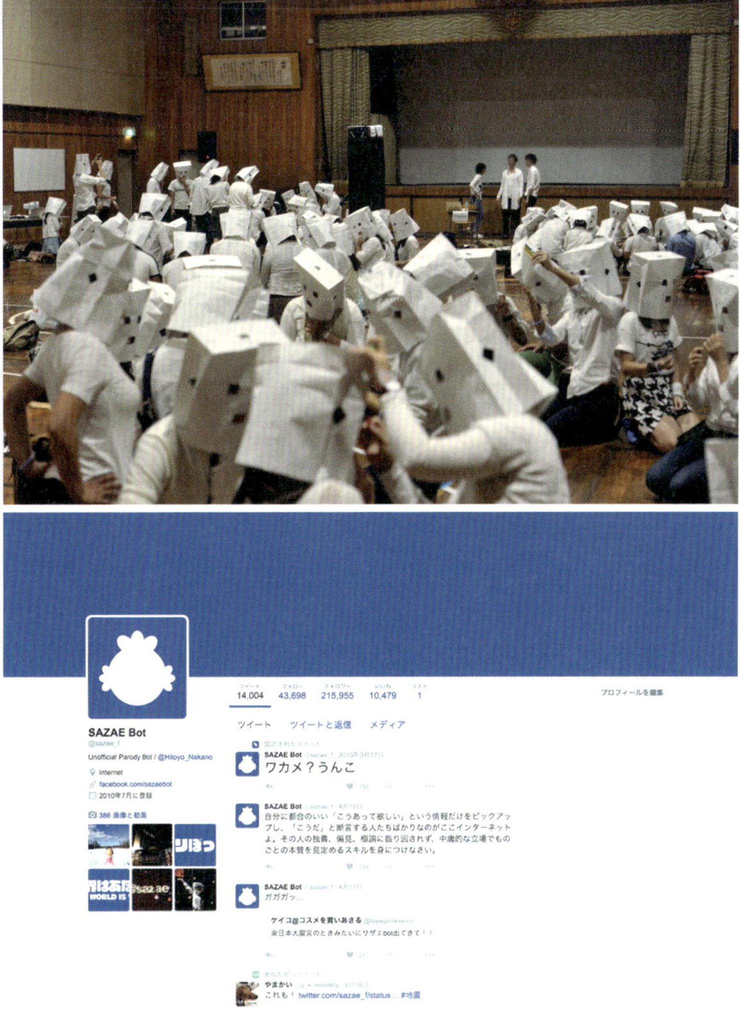

The mission of *SAZAE bot's* anonism is to repeat experiments and verifications of the following hypothesis: The essence of the Internet is the integration of oneself and others, and to move humans to the new frontier of greater aggregation. Also, this is not meant to be a negative idea, such as to eliminate individual privacies or identities. Instead, it aims to spread and take root in society as a positive and standard idea in order to help humans adapt to a new environment that will be formed by the technological evolution.

SAZAE bot started as a bot on Twitter in the summer of 2010 and fast became extremely popular with over 200K followers. Hitoyo Nakano ("Inner Self" in English), a personification of the bot's operator, performs on media, operates communities, and has published a book on *SAZAE bot's* behalf.

Clone Zone

http://clonezone.link

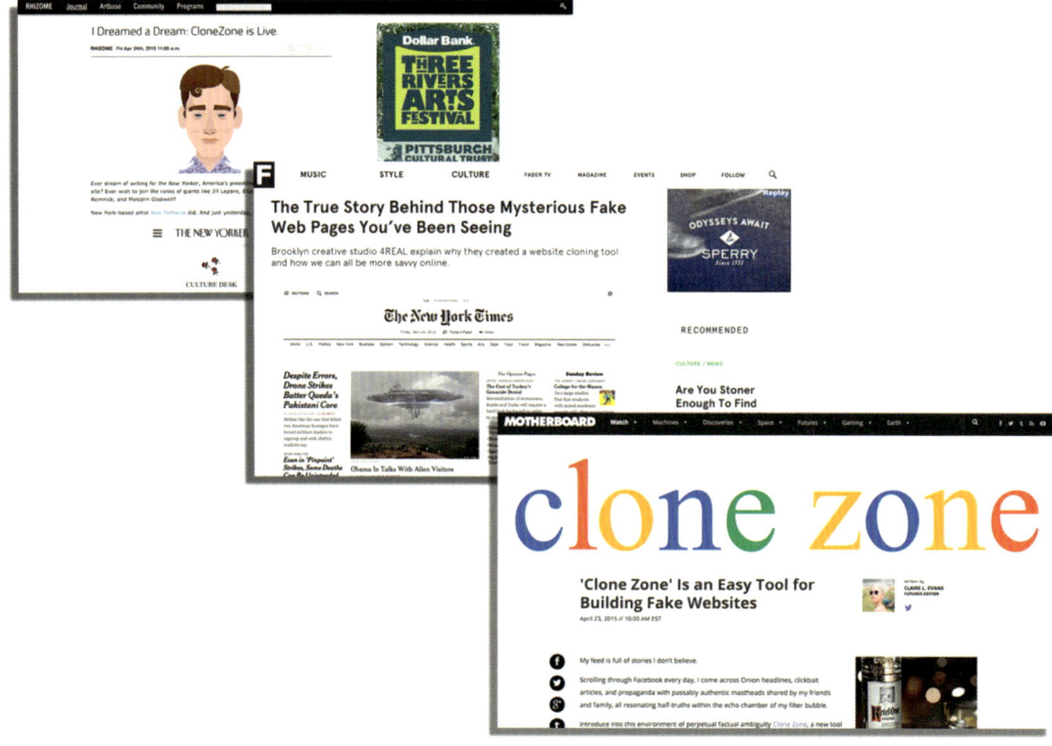

Clone Zone is a tool that lets users clone, edit, and share any web page on the internet. Users are able to rapidly edit any text and images on a web page, sharing the result via various social media channels. 4REAL, the digital media collective, conceived *Clone Zone* as a response to, and criticisms of, our overwhelming dependence on subjective social feeds for information. We felt it was important to draw attention to how easily the truth can be distorted and manipulated when disseminated through the current social media click-bate climate. We also wanted to create a tool that would let users be the creators, giving individuals the power of accelerated information sharing. The clone zone was designed to facilitate imagination, criticism, and disruption as opposed to passive consumption of information.

The project was inspired by our vision to experiment with a platform as work of art, as well as internet artist pioneers who had created cloning tools in the past, like Eva and Franco Mattes as well as The Yes Men. We wanted to re-imagine their work in the context of modern-day social media feeds and make it extremely accessible to an average internet user. When creating the website the target group we focused on was our immediate circle of friends and collaborators—artists, writers and other creatives in

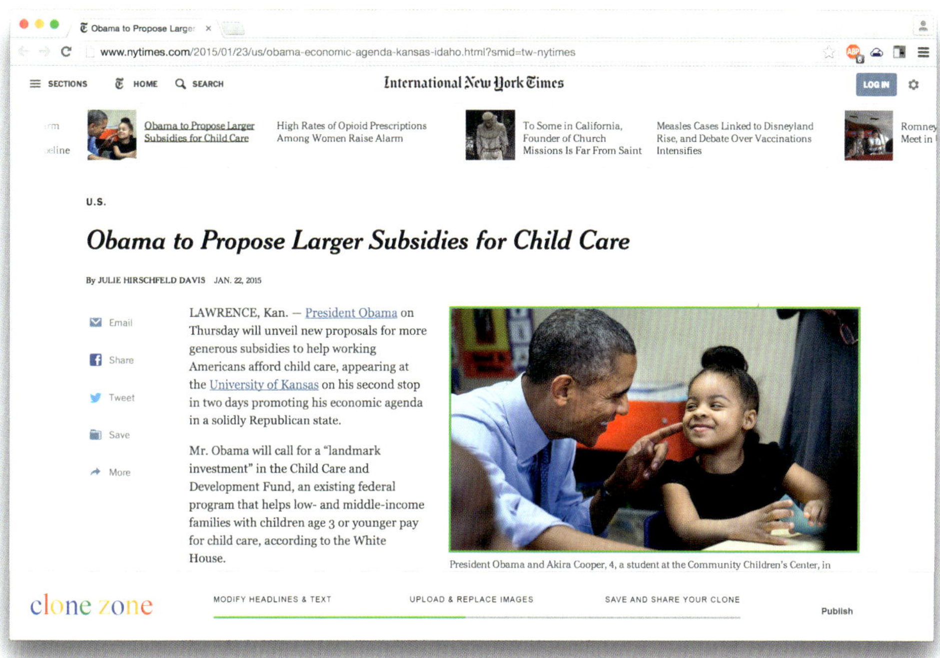

New York City. Upon launching *Clone Zone* we were pleased to see that it appealed to a much wider global audience. Student pranksters, political and social activists, Kawasaki motorcyclists, hackers/internet hustlers from Black Hat World were all using the website in unique ways of expression. *Clone Zone* became a global phenomenon and has received traffic from almost every country in the world, with clones in multiple languages and locales. The project has been featured in the New York Times, WIRED UK, Motherboard, Gawker, Huffington Post, Metro, Liberation, French TV, and many, many others. It has received over three million page views with over 50,000 clones created. Since the launch in early 2015, we quickly had to implement tools to take down clones and blacklist domains to avoid any legal and other repercussions. *Clone Zone* remains alive today and continues to be a free tool which earns us no revenue. We also had to limit the cloning to non-SSL-enabled sites and remove the ability for users to create links to prevent scam artists from using the site for fraudulent purposes. The *Clone Zone* is completely open to anyone who wants to create clones. The code has not been open-sourced at the present time, however we are currently considering the pros and cons of doing so.

Clone Zone was created by 4REAL, an artist collective working out of New York City. The founders of 4REAL, Slava Balasanov and Analisa Teachworth, along with designer Ian Lucas, were the core team creating the site. 4REAL is made up of a group of artists, designers, and developers who are interested in using the modern internet as a place to innovate works of art within online communities. *http://www.4real.io*

Crowdcrafting
Scifabric, http://crowdcrafting.org

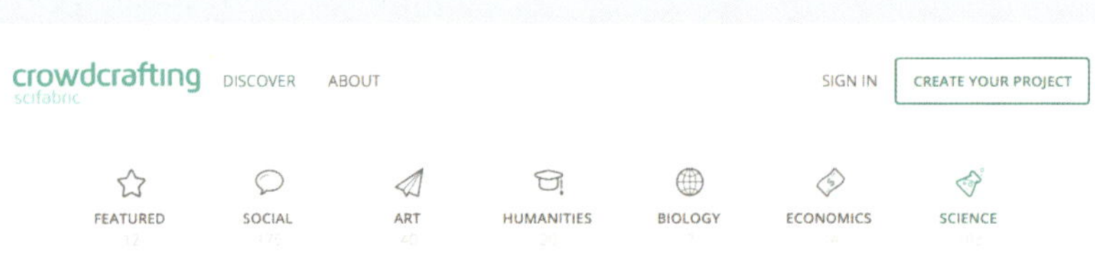

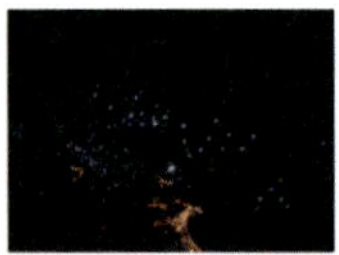
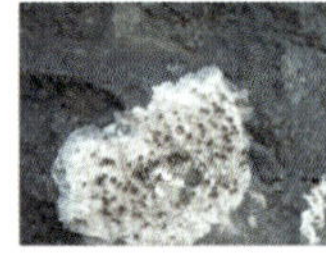
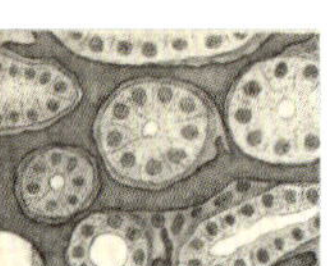

Dark Skies ISS

Image pattern recognition

Lost at Night

Locate a City in image...

Air Quality with Biomarkers: Lichens

Air Quality using Lich...

Categorize Changing Visual Culture of M...

Help categorize images...

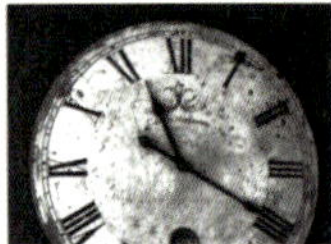
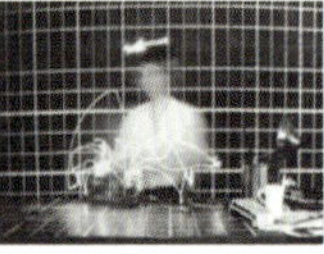
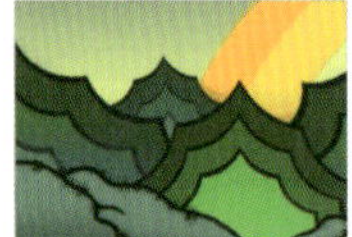
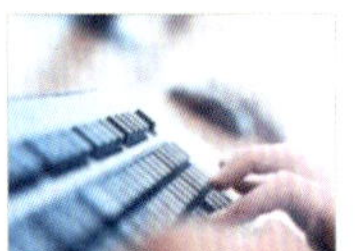

Real time results

Real time results demo

Science photography

Investigating the rise...

Нутгийн мэдлэгийн цөмийг үнэлэх

Англи хэлээр илэрхийлс...

DescribeIT

DescribeIT application...

1   2   3   Next »

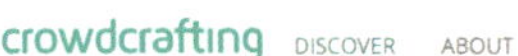
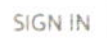

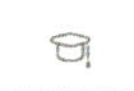

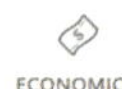

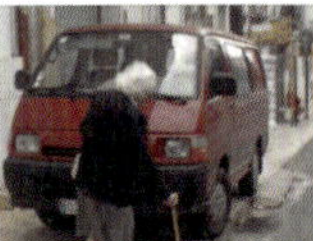
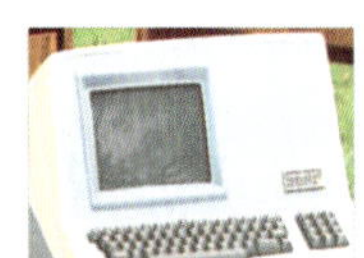
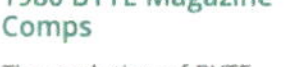
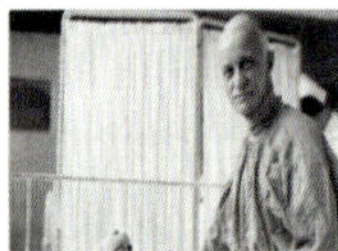
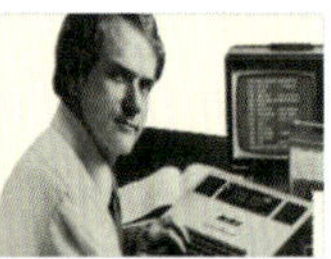

European Illegal Parking

This projects identifi...

1980 BYTE Magazine Comps

The evolution of BYTE ...

Neurosurgery and Imagery

An account on the visu...

Gender and Tech Magazines

'm looking into figuri...

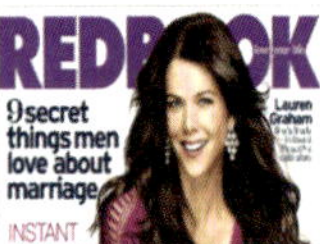
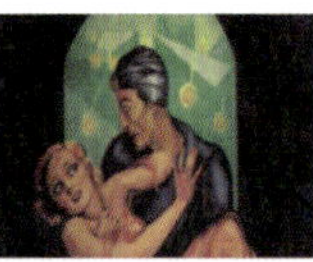
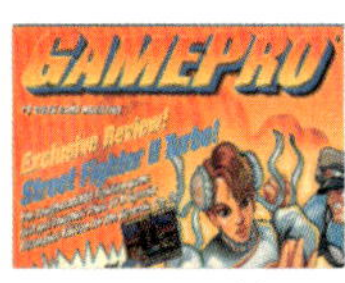
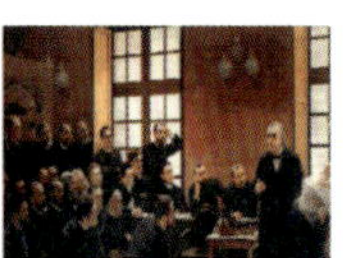

Hidden in the Cover(s)

Let's see what message...

Female Image in "Pulps"

I am exploring the rep...

GamePro Resemblance

As Video Game graphics...

Hysteria and Charcot

An attempt to distingu...

1   2   3   Next »

Screenshot of the *Crowdcrafting* page, a selection of science projects.

Screenshot of the *Crowdcrafting* page, a selection of social projects

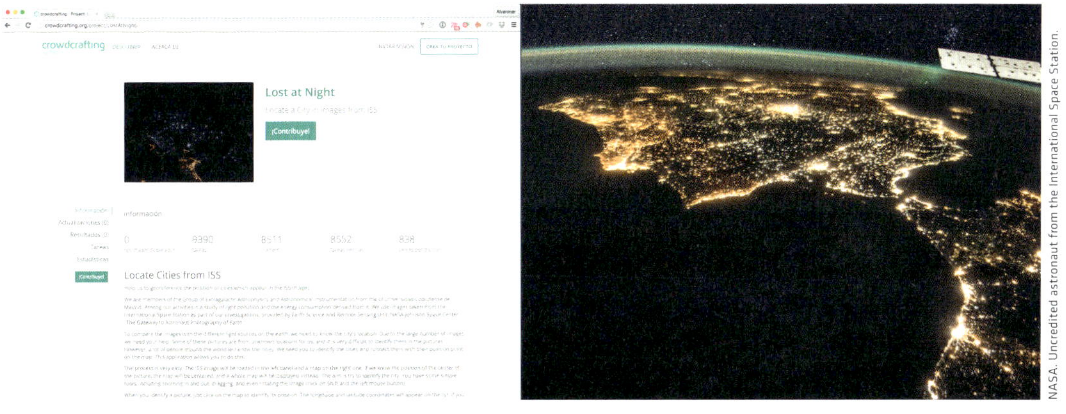

Cities at Night is a research project hosted on the *Crowdcrafting* platform that aims to monitor light emitted by major cities around the world in order to raise awareness of light pollution. It asks volunteers to classify, identify, and georeference photographs of cities taken by astronauts aboard the International Space Station.

The way in which we produce goods and provide services as a society is changing. We are no longer just consumers, we create videos, music, art, software, hardware, and much more, because the digital era has empowered us to do so. It's easier than ever before to be a producer. So why can't we also apply this pattern on how we research?

Crowdcrafting is a crowdsourcing, citizen science or microtasking platform developed by us, Scifabric, and powered by PYBOSSA, our open source technology. Crowdsourcing involves breaking up a project into lots of small, well-defined tasks that many different people complete, allowing the analysis of large data sets by many people in a short period of time, which is both cost effective and efficient, producing results of the same quality in line with traditional research projects. *Crowdcrafting* provides open source tools that anyone—professional researchers and/or citizens, can use to set up research projects, define (micro) tasks, and collect/analyze/enrich lots of data. It is a free and open source alternative to existing citizen science platforms: it is a "bottom-up" (as opposed to a "top-down") approach that connects people directly to the research process.

Crowdcrafting was born at a hackathon in Cape Town, South Africa, in 2011. In partnership with our key collaborators, such as CERN, United Nations (UNITAR), and the University of Geneva, we have reached out to and inspired many people to get involved in research. On our *Crowdcrafting* server, researchers or citizens can create a research project within a matter of minutes without having to develop a single line of code since we provide the templates and tools that will help them kick start a project in minutes. This simplified process ensures that while it is easy to create a project and replicate the scientific method, it contains all the principles of good science: open source code, open data, and open science.

Founder & CEO: Daniel Lombraña
Marketing & content: Clara Sánchez-Puga
Senior developer: Marvin Reimer
UX/UI designers: Álvaro Suarez Pérez, Jorge Correa
Business development: Mar Ramis
Communications: James Doherty

Scifabric (ES/UK) is a Spanish, UK-based company that develops technologies for the creation of platforms to collect, analyze, and enrich data. These international research projects explore the use of crowd-based methodologies. We have participated in humanitarian works by preventing the spread of malaria in Africa and managed aid in the Philippines after Typhoon Pablo. We have also collaborated in the research against cancer, recovered a huge collection of archaeological finds from the Bronze Age, studied light pollution from space, and how gravity affects antimatter, to name a few of the possibilities that our platform offers. All these projects are developed with our PYBOSSA technology, and all the data is open and available to anyone.
scifabric.com, pybossa.com

D-CENT Decentralised Citizens ENgagement Technologies
http://dcentproject.eu

D-CENT is a Europe-wide project that has brought together citizen movements and grassroots organizations that have revolutionized democracy in Europe in the past years, and is developing the next generation of open source, distributed, and privacy-aware tools for direct democracy and economic empowerment.

D-CENT grows longer-term alternatives to today's highly centralized platforms and power structures, and promotes the development of knowledge, digital infrastructures, and data for the common good. It values privacy and security, and is built on open source code and open standards.

D-CENT tools form a federated and distributed architecture—they can be combined in many ways to support democratic processes. The tools enable citizens to be informed and get real-time notifications about issues that matter to them. They help to propose and draft solutions and policy collaboratively. They can be used to decide and vote on solutions and collective municipal budgeting.

D-CENT runs large-scale pilots in Spain, Finland, and Iceland to develop and test the tools. These pilots have involved thousands of citizens across Europe in municipal decision-making, policy, and budgeting. The pilots are engaging democratic organiza-

tions and citizen-led coalitions like Podemos, Ahora Madrid, Barcelona en Comù, Open Ministry, and Citizen Foundation. The project has run the following experiments: Participation and open consultation platforms in Barcelona and Madrid *(decide.madrid. es)*, Participatory budgeting platform *(beta.yrpri.org)*, Notification service *(decisions.dcentproject.eu)*, and a collaborative policy making platform *(objective8. dcentproject.eu)*.

D-CENT is also developing a blockchain toolkit to manage community trust, reputation, and provide a blockchain reward scheme that is auditable and transparent. *D-CENT* has contributed actively to the development of open social web standards, an open standardization effort led by the W3C.

D-CENT has done extensive research on new forms of democracy, citizen empowerment, and participation. An integrated techno-socio-economic analysis has been carried out on organizational models of emerging social movements, new economic models based on knowledge commons, distributed social networking, identity systems, new models for citizen control of personal and social data, privacy and security by design. All research is available at the project website.

Coordinator: Francesca Bria

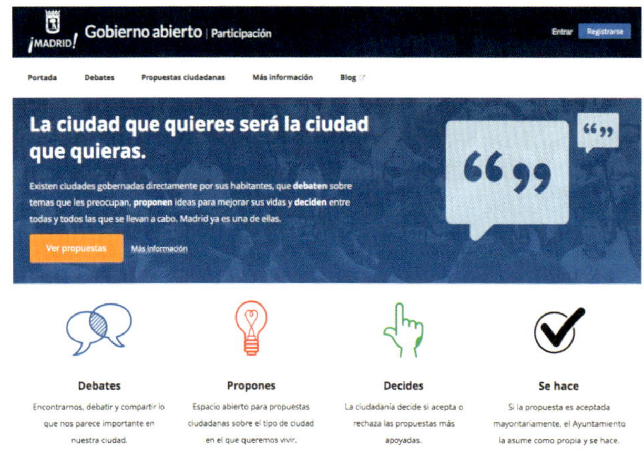

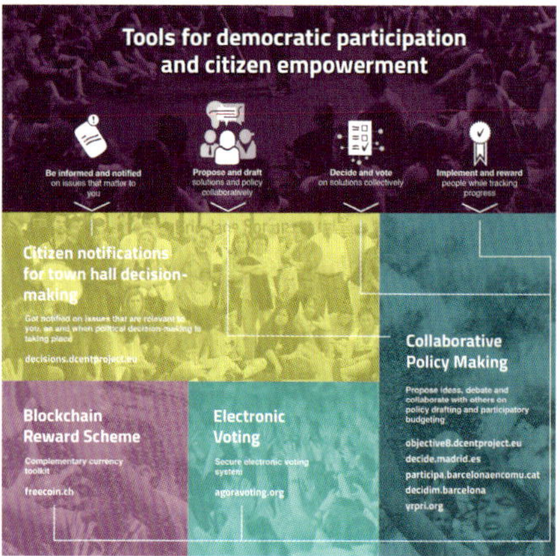

Why D-CENT

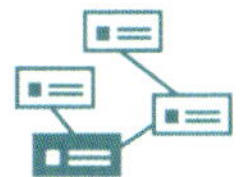 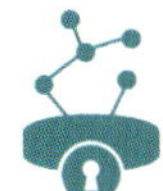  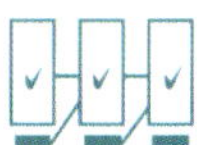

Open authentication and distributed identity management
to grow and open source eco-system of citizen engagement tools

Own your data
to say no to surveillance and give back citizens control and ownership of data

Open source and open standards
to build and grow knowledge commons

Blockchain trust
to let people run reward schemes that are transparent and audible

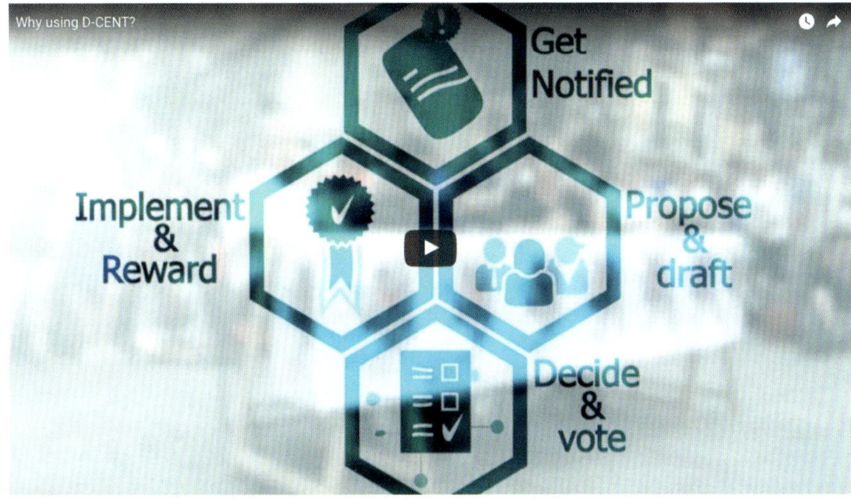

More videos

D-CENT in Action

Explore the large-scale pilots that D-CENT partners have been conducting, involving thousands of citizens across Europe in municipal decision-making, policy and budgeting processes.

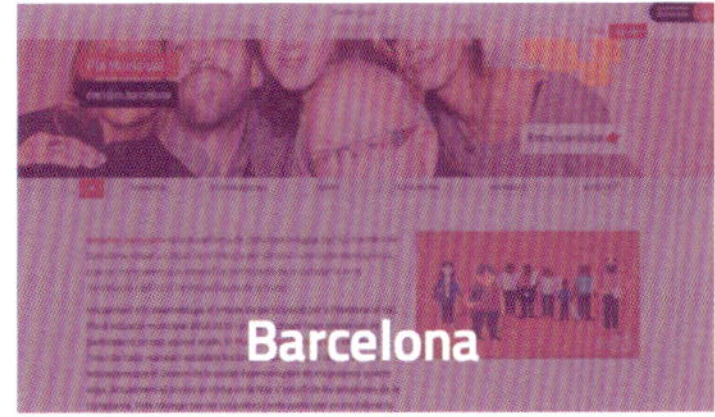

Digital platform for participation of the City of Barcelona. It is a tool to build a democratic, open and transparent city by enhancing citizen participation in the definition and development of policies.

https://decidim.barcelona/

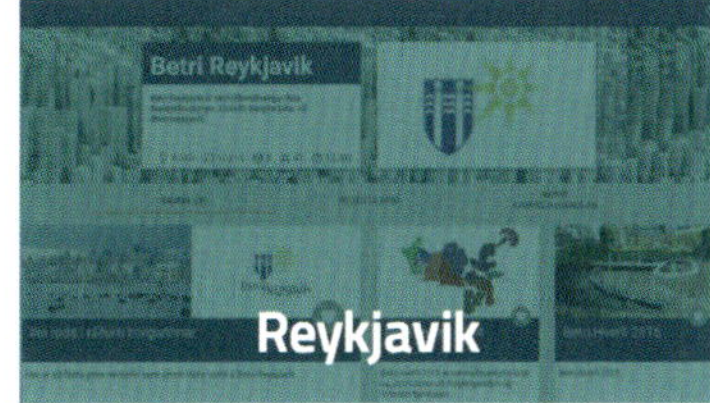

Participatory budgeting platform for the city of Reykjavik. The platform is a development from the Betri Reykjavik prioritisation and participation platform allowing citizens to submit ideas on how to spend a part of the city budget in their neighborhood.

https://betrireykjavik.is/

D-CENT has a strong international network as its consortium: Nesta (UK), Citizens Foundation (IS), CNRS - Centre d'Économie de la Sorbonne (FR), Dyne.org (NL), Forum Virium Helsinki (FI), International Modern Media Institute (IS), Open Knowledge Foundation (UK), Open University of Catalunya and Eurecat (ES), ThoughtWorks (UK), and World Wide Web Consortium (FR).

Enspiral

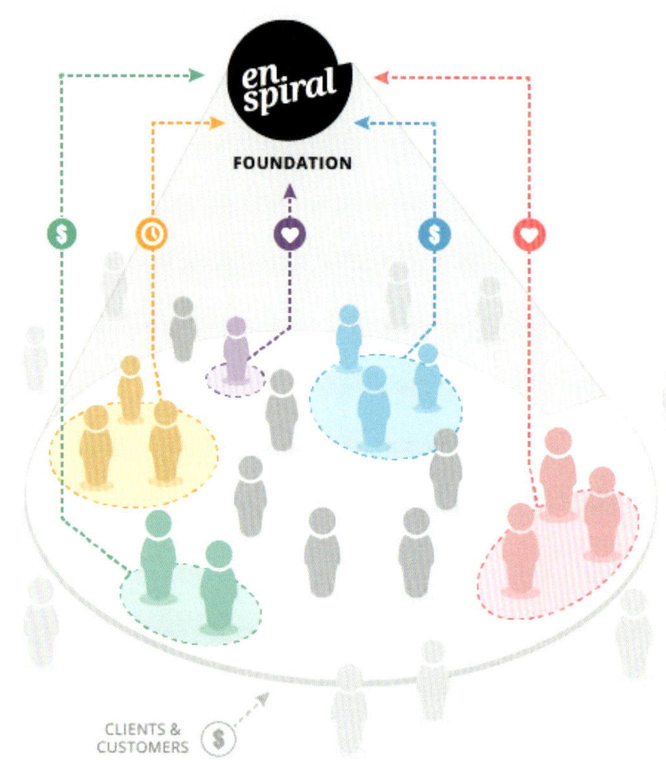

Enspiral is a bold experiment to create a collaborative network that helps people do meaningful work. It was founded by software developers and while we now include a diverse range of people and skills, the spirit of open source culture pervades all of our work. Our work extends from the development of distributed ways of organizing through to cultivating a culture of care. As a network of individuals we form ventures imbued with our values. We create software, campaigns, and innovative mechanisms to empower people. We prototype processes, technology, and organizational structures aligned to our mission.

At its heart *Enspiral* is an altruistic network based on trust that has a vibrant gift economy. When a person or company participates actively in this network they have a whole lot of amazing people and ventures who are in their corner and actively helping them succeed: We share leads and connections with each other generously. We lend each other money and invest in each others' ventures. We promote each others' projects at every opportunity. We share our learnings and hone our skills together. We grow a shared brand together to build a reputation greater than the sum of its parts. We help ventures find great staff and people to find great roles.

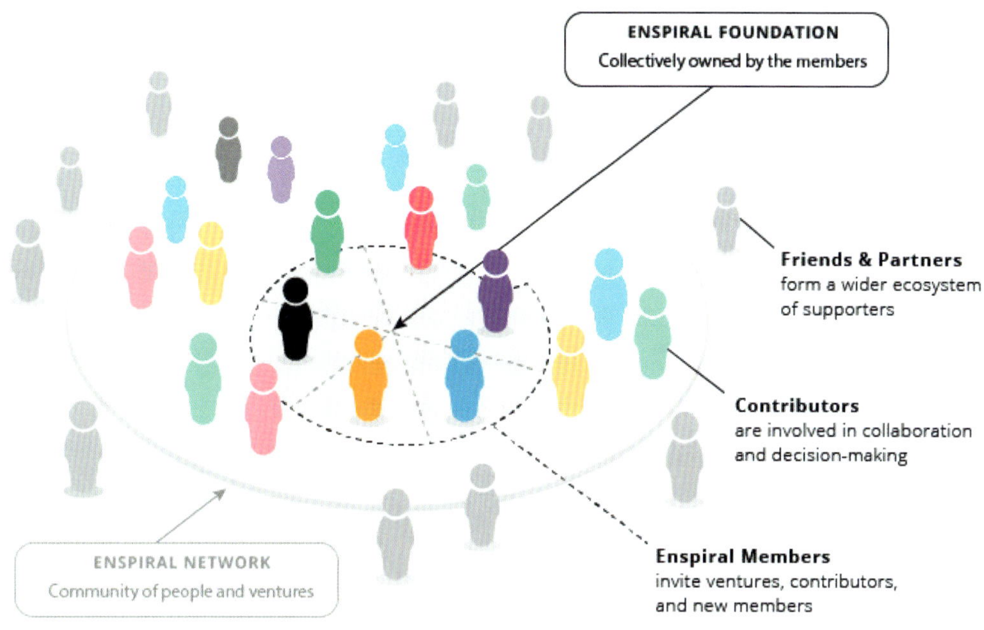

In each iteration, we strive to decentralize money, information, power, and control throughout the organization, using *Enspiral*-built, open-source software tools as the heart of our organizing process.

Decision-making within *Enspiral* strives to be transparent, non-hierarchical, and consensus-based. Anyone can propose a decision, ask questions or express their views, and within our tiered system of governance comprising members and contributors, everyone has one vote in any raised proposal.

In this way, all decisions made within *Enspiral* are in the interest of the collective, while still leaving space for minority concerns and constructive dissent. Our decisions are made on Loomio, an online, consensus-based decision-making tool. Loomio enables asynchronous, digital discourse, allowing individuals to participate in their free time, from any part of the world. Discussion and decisions are documented and recorded, providing the network with a living archive of past decisions for reference.

Enspiral works to open-source its values, structure, software tools, processes, and learnings via github, Loomio, Cobudget, My.Enspiral, gitbooks, and Enspiral Tales blogs.

Enspiral began in 2010. People brought in people who they knew and trusted and shared some of the same values and discontent with the way things were working within a predominantly neoliberal paradigm. They started working together on contracts, primarily software development at first, but increasingly design, behavior change, marketing, and facilitation. In late 2011 we helped develop *Loomio*—a tool for collaborative discussion and decision-making. In late 2012, *Enspiral* began working on a system for coordinating collaborative funding, which is now being developed as *Cobudget*. In early 2015, *Enspiral* began its catalyst experiment with a team of three equal peer network process facilitators. *Enspiral* was named in the P2P Foundation's "Top Ten P2P Trends of 2015" with "Inspired by Enspiral", reflecting its growing influence on post-corporate entrepreneurial coalitions.

Give Something Back To Berlin (GSBTB)

http://givesomethingbacktoberlin.com

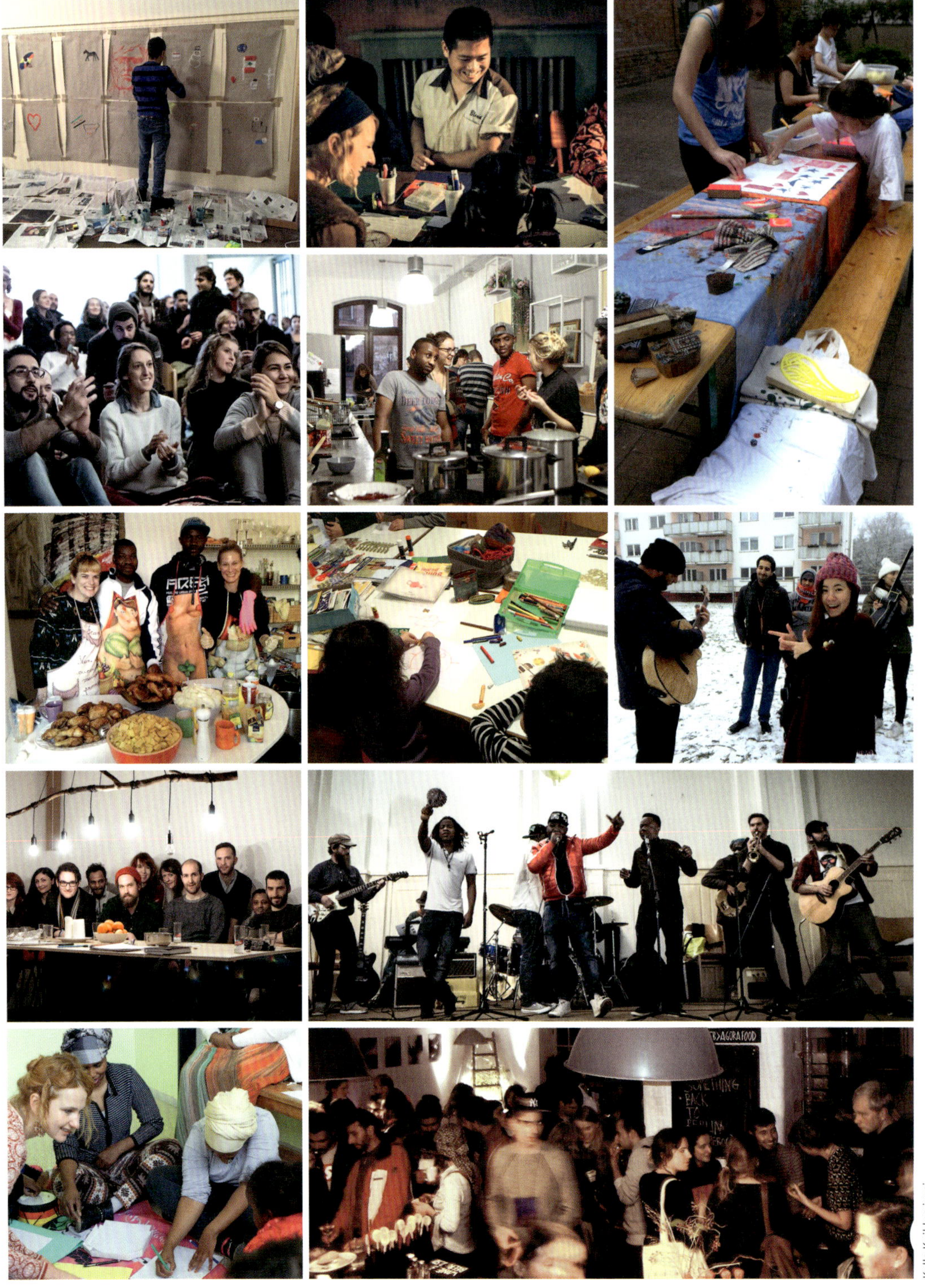

Kalle Kuikkaniemi

Give Something Back To Berlin (GSBTB) is a project platform and network facilitating neighborhood volunteer work for the growing group of non-German speakers in Berlin. Our community of hundreds of skilled volunteers from over 60 nationalities is active in vibrant projects and collaborations throughout the city. This engagement is challenging current discourse in Germany between newly arrived and established communities, building positive outcomes.

GSBTB creates tools for community integration bringing "privileged" migrants, German locals, and vulnerable groups such as refugees together. Our "mothership" is our accessible online platform to inspire and mobilize social engagement and participation. This way we facilitate online interest that takes practical offline form. Through our extensive grassroots initiatives we create meeting points for communities that would otherwise naturally stay isolated from one another. This concrete "think global, act local" program showcases everyone's capacity to contribute—regardless of passport, status, language, or time spent in the country.

With building partnerships, relationships, and dialogue between people from the already cosmopolitan art, creative, and start up-scene with local NGOs and refugee communities, we are creating a form of new sustainable urban integration and culture, while also enabling disadvantaged local communities to profit more from the globalized creative, tech, and start-up industries. We call it "making worlds meet working together for a better city." For this work we won several prizes for social innovation, integration, and diversity work i.e. the *Blaue Bär* for Europe Engagement from the Berlin Senate/European Commission and the SAP Social Impact Lab scholarship as well as the Intercultural Innovation Award from the UN and BMW.

GSBTB started with a spontaneous Facebook post by Annamaria Olsson in 2012. Her own migrant experience, the growing European xenophobia, as well as what felt like few positive and modern and solution-based ways of dealing with different types of migration, all sparked her to write a Facebook post addressing some of these issues, with the appeal to "get involved."

The FB post snowballed into things we couldn't have imagined and the journey from FB post to a full blown project platform was rapid (but not without tons of hard work and challenges). Becoming the collective brainchild of many great minds coming together, GSBTB grew organically into a huge on- and offline community of over 1,000 volunteers from over 60 different countries in over 60 social projects all over the city. It can be anything from work in homeless centers, mentorship programs for underprivileged youth, social urban gardening projects, or creative work with children. We also run nine weekly GBSTB refugee projects involving 75 volunteers, reaching out to over 240 refugee participants with its 32 educational hours per week. GSBTB was involved in organizing refugee projects from the start in 2013, long before the broader refugee engagement started in Germany the last year.

GSBTB started with a spontaneous Facebook post by Annamaria Olsson in 2012, who had moved from Sweden to Berlin to study and work as a journalist in 2008. Her own migrant experience, the growing European xenophobia as well as what felt like few positive and modern and solution-based ways of dealing with different types of migration, sparked her to write a Facebook post addressing some of these issues, with the appeal to "get involved". The journey from FB post to a full-blown project platform was rapid. GSBTB was involved in organizing refugee projects from the start in 2013, and became a key player in Berlin's social, creative, start-up scenes as THF project involving both refugees and "privileged" migrants, as well as big international media interest in our work. We have received requests from other large cities (Taipei, Buenos Aires, New York, Dubai) as well as universities, companies, and organizations seeking our expertise about our model and methods.

HACKberry
http://exiii-hackberry.com

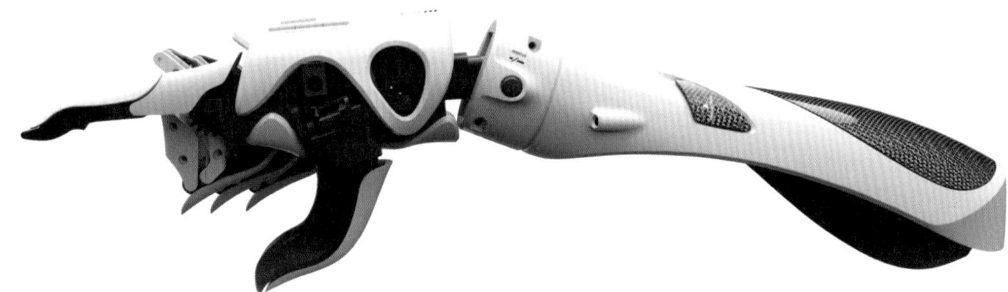

HACKberry is an open-source 3D-printable bionic arm (i.e. a motorized hand that is controlled intuitively via muscle signals in the residual arm). All the technical data—including 3D CAD file, software code, circuit diagram, and bill of materials—are open-source under Creative Commons license. In this way, private developers around the world can replicate and customize it for people in their local area.

HACKberry will alter the dull ecosystem of the bionic hand. Commercial bionic hands haven't been around for very long and they still cost more than 15,000 USD. Therefore, market penetration in Japan is only 2%. Since the market for bionic hands is small, the conventional paradigm of manufacturing cannot provide incentives to reduce the price and improve technology. From a business point of view, it is difficult to reduce initial costs and regularly add functions for products that do not sell in large quantities. In contrast, the initial cost of producing *HACKberry* is zero because the 3D printer doesn't require casting, and individual makers and designers around the world can continuously upgrade functions with no charge, as the *HACKberry* is available on an open source platform.

Since its launch in May 2015, many sub-projects have branched out globally, refining the quality of the hand and leading to the growth of local communities. For example, a child-size version was created in Poland, and a girl in the U.S. received a *HACKberry* from a local community.

HACKberry and the earlier models *(handiii, handiii COYOTE)* have received several international design awards including the James Dyson Award in UK, the iF Gold Award in Germany, and the Good Design Award in Japan, which has attracted both developers and potential users to join the open source community.

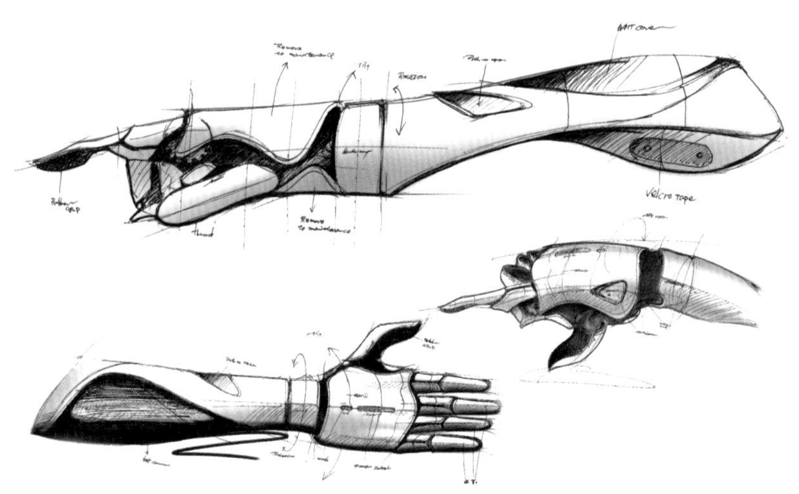

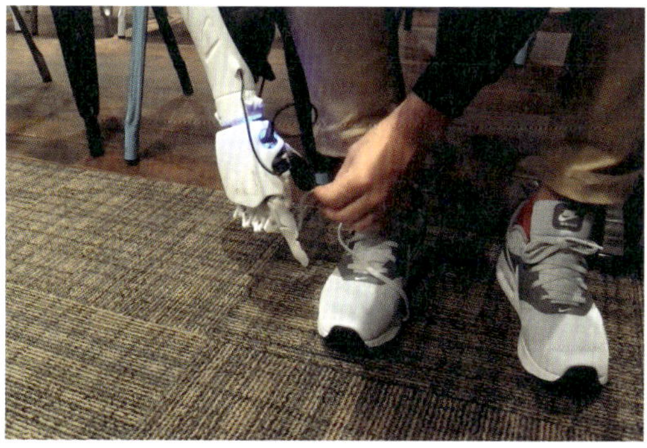

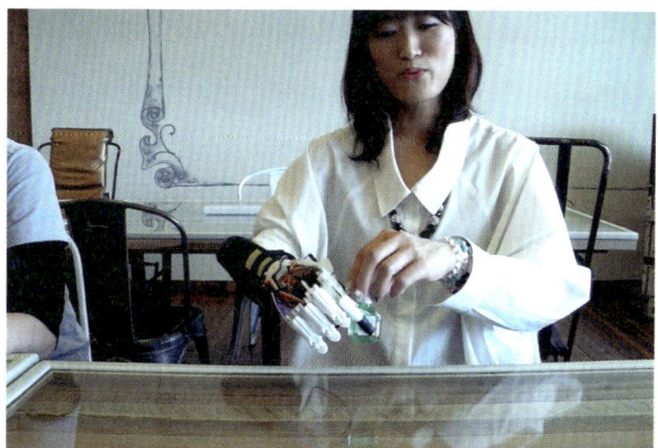

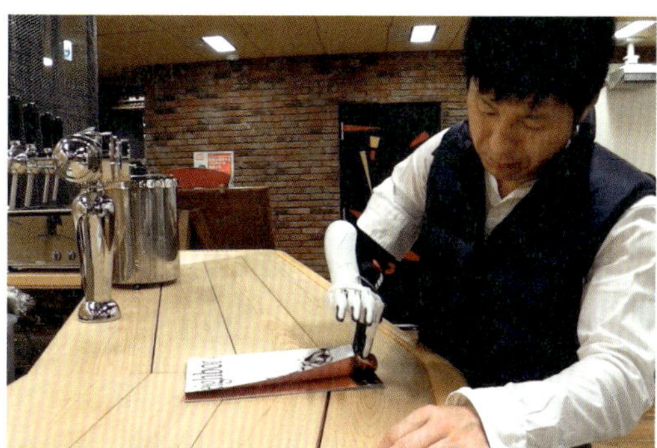

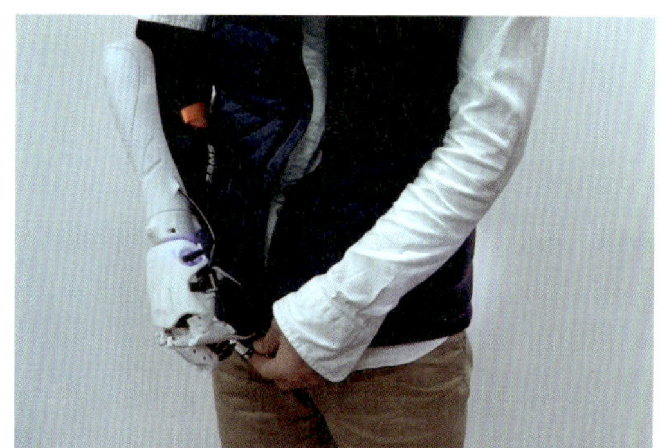

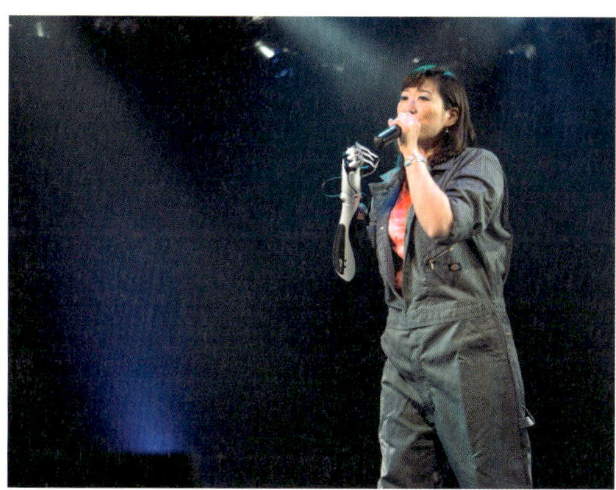

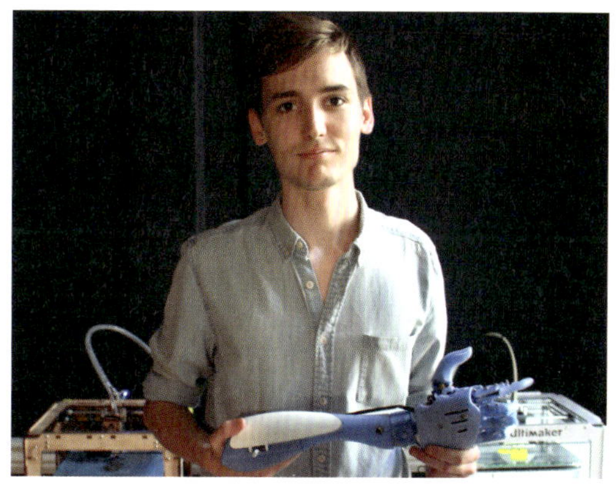

In May 2013 **Genta Kondo, Hiroshi Yamaura,** and **Tetsuya Konishi** [exiii/JP] started to develop affordable and fashionable bionic hands—the *handiii*, using a 3D printer. In March, 2014 they met Akira Morikawa, the first amputee to test *handiii*, and decided to start their own company, exiii, after receiving positive feedback. In March 2015, exiii demonstrated the 4th generation model *COYOTE* with Akira at SXSW, and their project received global media attention. In May 2015, exiii launched the 5th generation model *HACKberry*. All of its data is open source.

Quipu Project

http://www.quipu-project.com

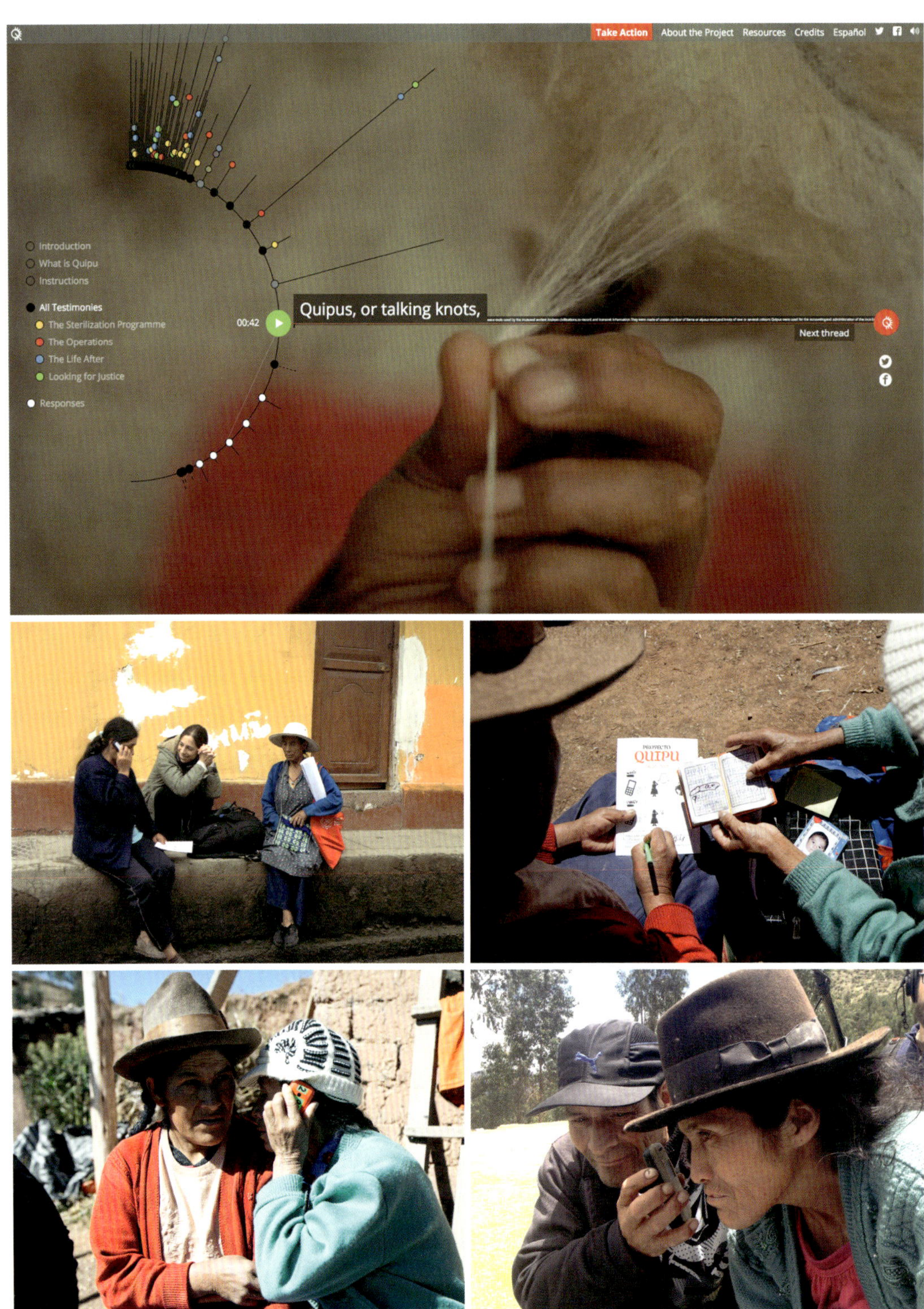

Quipu is a transmedia documentary project that makes visible the stories of 272,000 women and 21,000 men who were sterilised in Peru in the mid 1990s during Alberto Fujimori's regime as a way of reducing poverty. Thousands have claimed this happened without their consent, but until now they have been repeatedly silenced and denied justice.

An interplay between a low-tech telephone line and a high-tech digital interface, the *Quipu Project* enables communities that are politically, geographically, and digitally marginalised to tell their stories in their own words. A simple phone call allows them to record their story into a growing audio archive, which is in turn displayed and shared with the world through our interactive documentary website. Working closely with activist groups in Peru who have been campaigning around this issue for twenty years, we co-designed the phoneline to work as a tool for sharing stories, connecting with other dispersed activist groups, and personal empowerment and public speaking practice for our largely illiterate participants. Callers can record their own story, in their own language, from anywhere there is a phone signal. They can then also listen to stories recorded by other people and gain a deeper understanding of how their personal experiences are mirrored in countless others across Peru.

The design is inspired by a *Quipu*—an Incan artifact in which the colors of the strings and the formation of the knots across them is used to convey information, from numeric data to historical narratives. Audiences can explore the archive listening to individual voices following *strings* that display the entire unedited testimonies. They are also able to listen across the archive following colored *knots* and hear the multi-vocal narrative that emerges from the repetition of themes and events.

Our project uses Voice Over IP (VoIP) technology to connect each phone call directly with a live website on the Internet. This means that our audio archive is immediately available to be moderated, subtitled, and subsequently disseminated across the web. It also means that we are able to offer our global online audience the chance to record their own message of recognition and support, which can in turn be accessed via the VoIP phoneline by the original contributors in Peru.

Not only is this an original innovation in the form of documentary, but also a powerful method of establishing dialogue and enabling a global community of support.

Directors: Maria Court, Rosemarie Lerner
Executive producers: Maria Court, Rosemarie Lerner, Sebastián Melo
Creative technologist: Ewan Cass-Kavanagh
General producer: Sandra Tabares-Duque
UX design and development: Mike Robbins, Helios Design Labs
Academic consultants: Matthew Brown, Karen Tucker

The **Quipu Project** has been a collaboration between Chaka Studio, a production company based in London, academics from Bristol University, and grassroots organizations in Peru (IAMAMC-AMHBA, AMAEF-C-GTL). The project took several years to build through careful consideration of the needs and perspectives of all partners, in particular with the women's organizations, whose struggle to find justice is not over. At the moment the project is live, receiving new testimonies and articulating a network of volunteers who take on the tasks of transcribing and translating the new audios. The project so far has streamed more than 6,000 minutes through the phoneline and more than 50,000 minutes through the website. This includes people who call to record testimonies as well as people who call to listen to testimonies shared by others.

Radwende—Der Radweg ist das Ziel

http://www.radwende.de

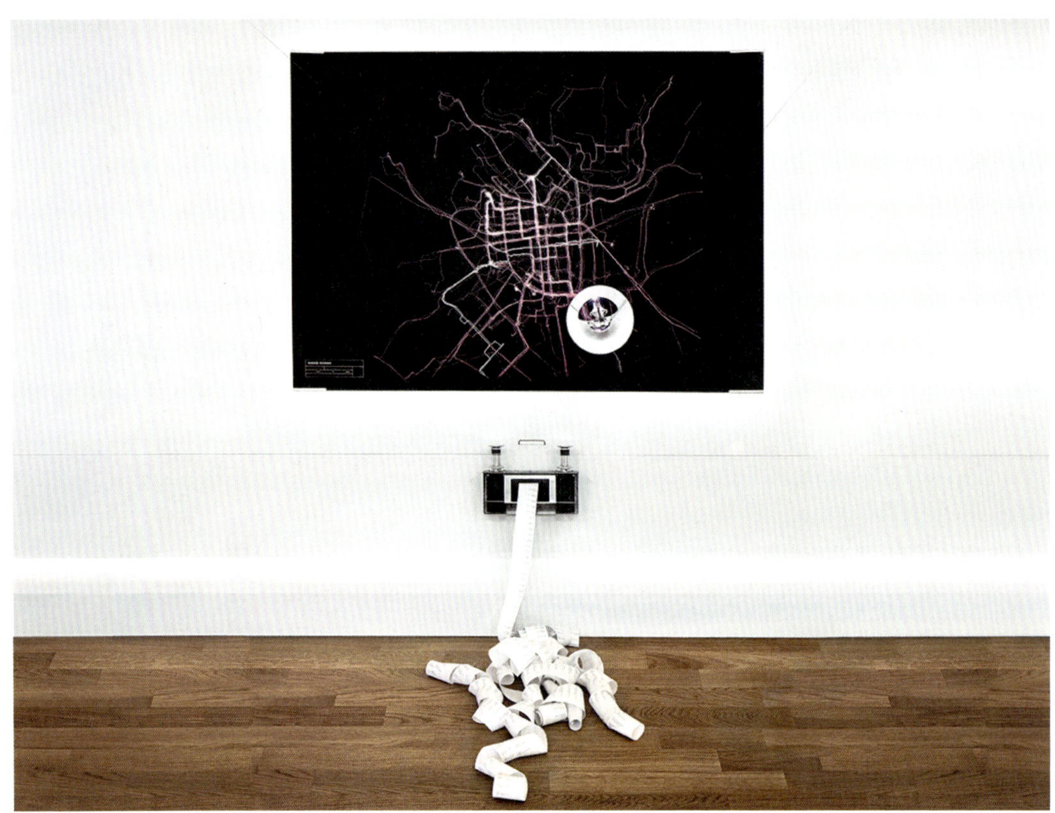

Wiesbaden was voted the least bike-friendly city in Germany in a survey by the German Cyclist's Association. This result is justified by the poor infrastructure, the disregard for cyclists, and a missing lobby. We wanted to make a change—together with the cyclists and their daily navigated routes.

Radwende combines a public petition, art, and a campaign against climate change. We developed an app that shows the cyclists of Wiesbaden and their effect on city planning. The concept is quite simple: Cyclists track their routes and we draw a map of the city out of the perspective of cyclists. The map is a striking representation of bike traffic in real time and visualizes where bike lanes are needed. It could serve as a planning tool for Wiesbaden's infrastructure.

But that's not all: We also developed a drawing machine that trailed the activists' tracks and was displayed in the Museum Wiesbaden. It produced one artwork a day that showed where bike lanes were missing. We just drew these missing bike lanes ourselves. The art installation puts the campaign into a new context. Bike traffic is becoming presentable again and relevant to people other than just "green" cycling and climate protection activists.

There's nothing new about a tracking application, but *Radwende* is a new form of public participation. It's not a petition with signatures or clicks, but the demonstration of a drawback. Every tracked kilometer is an accusation towards the city and a call to extend the bike infrastructure. The number of kilometers of cycling is converted into currency. The city will build a new bike path for every 5,000 km of cycling, and shops and cafes will give free coffees to people using the app. *Radwende* can be used in every city that is interested in improving the bike infrastructure.

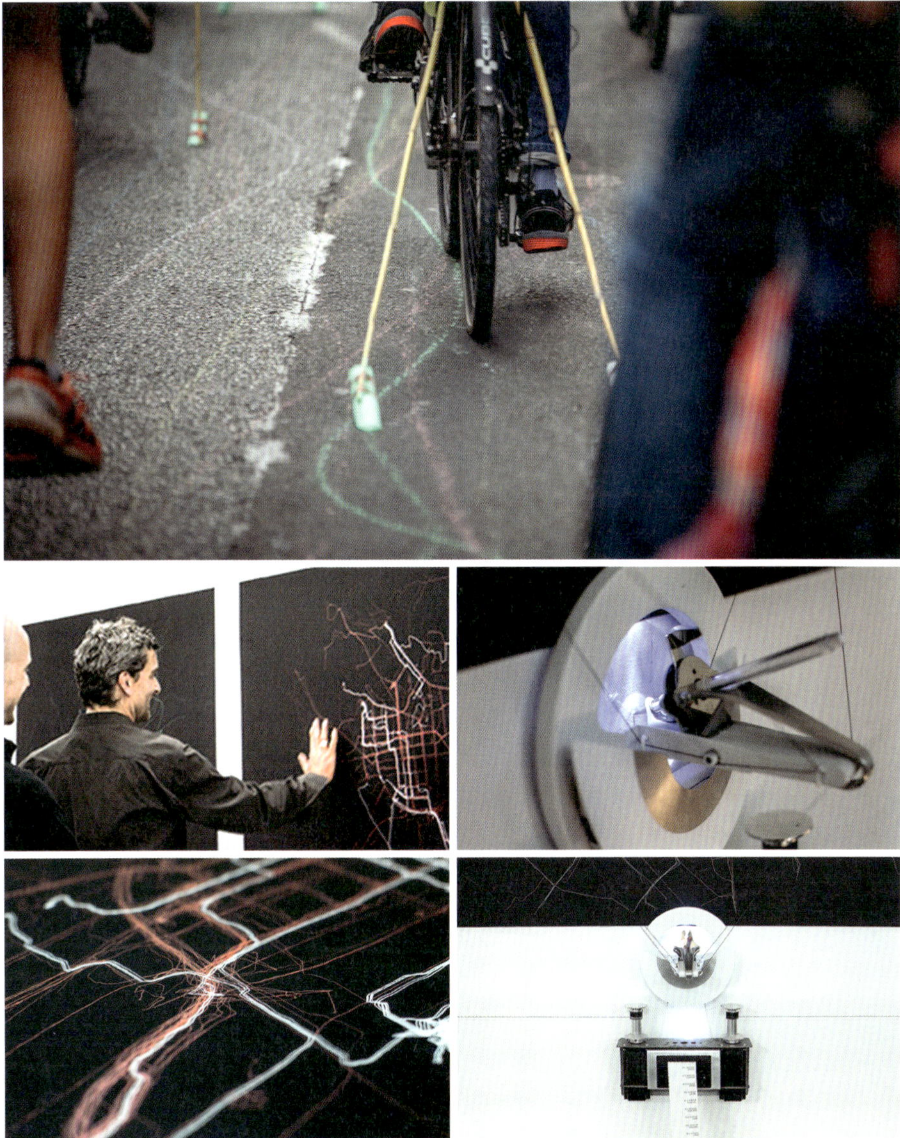

Radwende is an art installation at Museum Wiesbaden designed to foster cycling as a means of getting around town. It visualizes routes actually used by cyclists, computes the distance traveled thereby in terms of a sort of currency (Artivisum) and then uses it as a petition model for citizen participation in a political process. For every 5,000 kilometers cycled, the city builds a new bike path. The prototype was presented in March 2014 at Wiesbaden Design Days and then went on exhibit at Museum Wiesbaden. The installation could be booked for a day, and the resulting artwork could then be purchased. In 2015, the project was honored with a Media Art Prize awarded by ZKM | Center for Art and Media Karlsruhe. Radwende can be deployed in any city seeking to improve its cycling infrastructure.

SafetiPin

http://safetipin.com

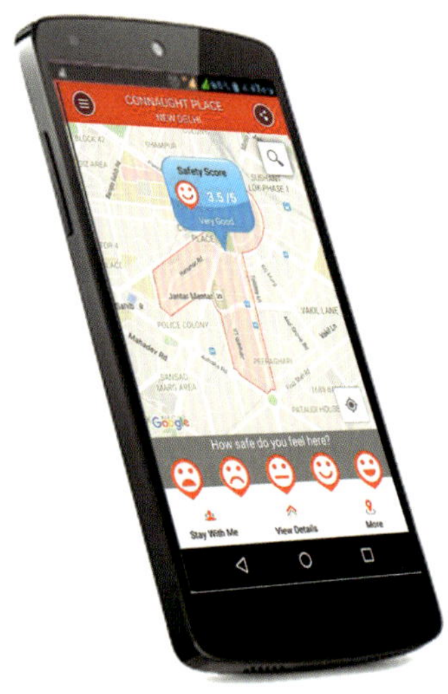

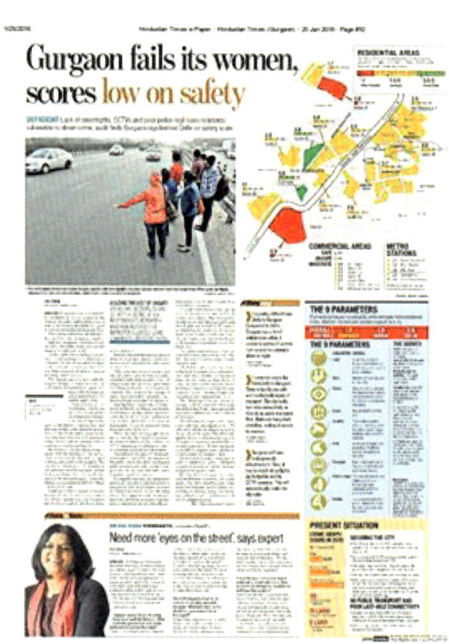

SafetiPin is a technology tool that seeks to use big data to make cities safer and more inclusive for women and others. We have mobile applications that collect data about safety parameters in the city. Our apps provide data about the level of safety in different public spaces in the city. We use the methodology of the safety audit, which measures the following parameters: lighting, openness, visibility, walk path, availability of public transport, crowd, gender diversity, and security.

SafetiPin started in 2013 and initially collected all data through crowdsourcing. Through this method, we collected over 10,000 audit points in Delhi and another 7,000 audit points in eight other Indian cities. This data has two distinct audiences. First is the individual user who can use the data to make safer and informed decisions while using and moving around a city. All this data is made available to all users of the app—currently approximately 40,000 users. This data is visible on the app and on our online platform and the user can interact with the data. A user can share their feeling of safety in an area and that gets added onto the database of information that we have. We provide a Safety Score and our app gives an alert when a user is in an unsafe area. We have recently launched an app *My SafetiPin,* which has a feature that shows the safest route.

We share the data with urban stakeholders to help them work towards the improvement of safety in different parts of the city. For example, we shared the

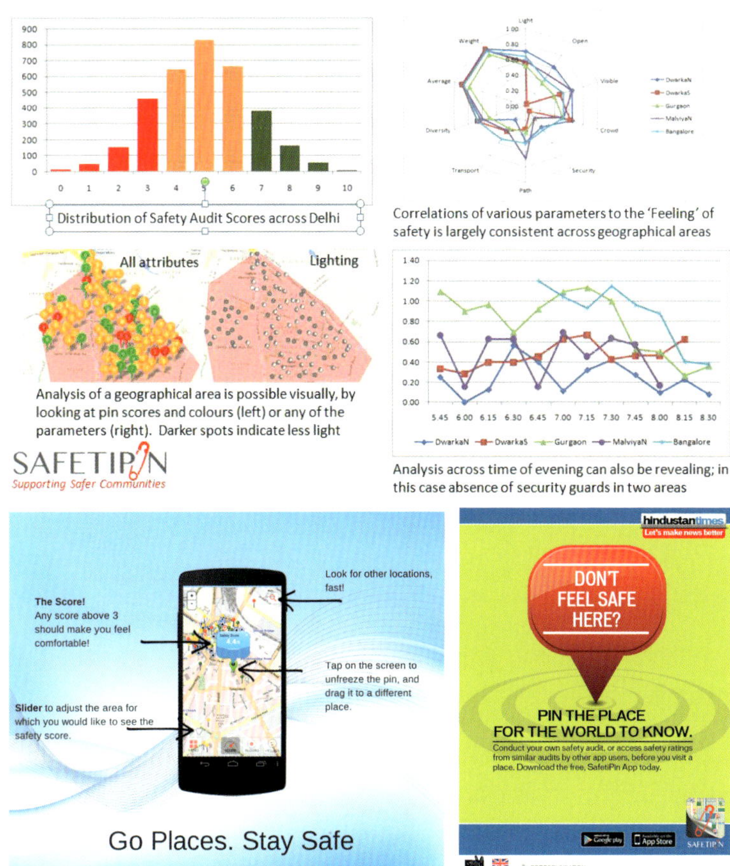

data with the Public Works Department in Delhi who used it to improve street lighting in the city. We also shared the data with the Delhi Police who correlated the data with their data on unsafe spots in the city. Similarly, the Municipal Corporation of Gurgaon used the data to work on improving streets in the city. We also established formal MoUs with the City of Nairobi and Bogotá to share the data collected. In addition, we are also sharing the data with Manila, Jakarta and Mexico in partnership with UN Women, and UN Habitat. We are supplementing crowdsourced data collection with nighttime pictures of the city through an app *SafetiPin Nite,* which is mounted on cars to generate pictures of the city at night. These pictures are coded on the same safety audit parameters mentioned above. Using this method, we have collected data in 27 cities across eight countries.

The **SafetiPin** project began in April 2015. The two co-founders (one a gender and urban safety expert and the other a technology entrepreneur) came up with the idea to build an app that worked on crime prevention. Further we wanted to make this data widely available to women and others in cities across the world. It took around six months to develop the app and conduct a pilot in Delhi before launching it in November 2015. We then forged partnerships with NGOs in other Indian cities and conducted pilots in eight other cities. We also began expanding to other countries and launched the Spanish version in Bogota and a Bahasa version in Jakarta. We built a Hindi and a Mandarin version and began sharing our data with urban stakeholders.

Social Street

http://www.socialstreet.it

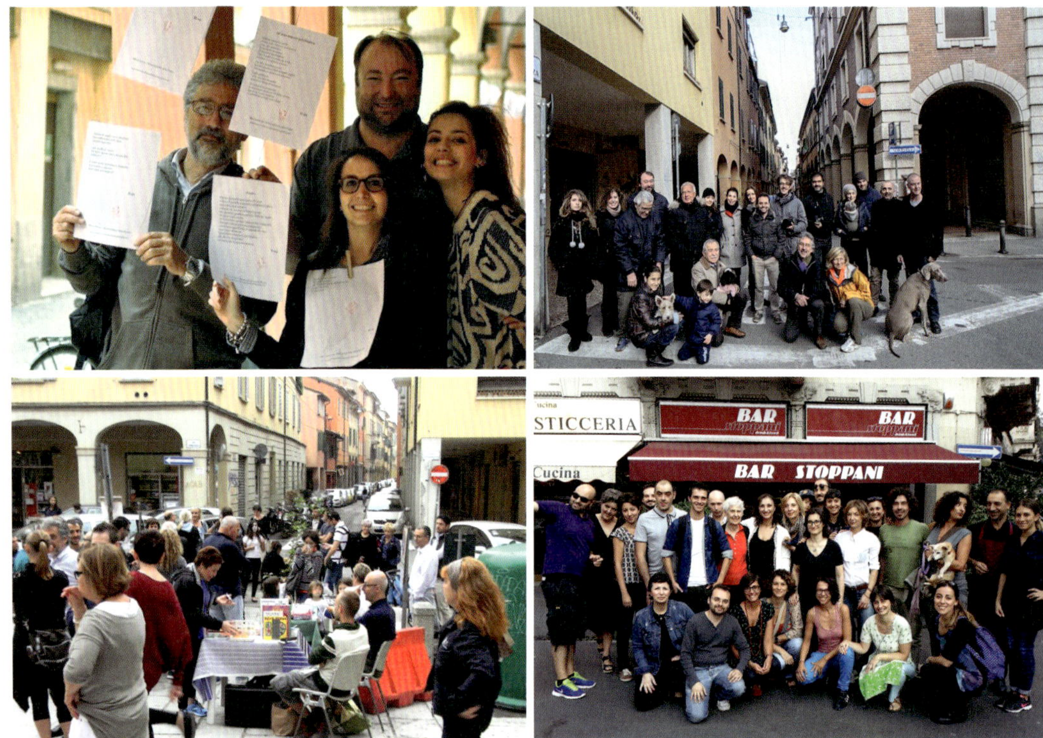

The idea of *Social Street* originated from the experience of the Facebook group "Residents in Fondazza street–Bologna" that started in September 2013. The purpose of *Social Street* is to promote socialization between neighbors resident in the same street in order to build relationships, to interchange needs, to share expertise and knowledge, to implement common interest projects, with common benefits from a closer social interaction. To reach this zero cost objective, without opening new sites or platforms, *Social Street* makes use of the creation of Facebook closed groups.

The objective of *Social Street* is to re-establish the importance of social relations and interaction, focusing not only on developed urban areas but also a return to what was once a reality and way of life in the countryside and villages where relationships were historically of fundamental importance in daily life. This modern tendency to focus on the "self" has undeniable consequences: urban decay, lack of social control (ownership) of the territory, loss of a sense of belonging, and people essentially living in isolation. We allow academics to speculate and study the root causes of this situation and also accept what authority dictates to us (in terms of ways of living). Contrary to these approaches the *Social Street* model proposes a possible solution from the ground up and aims to recreate social ties and acknowledgment as

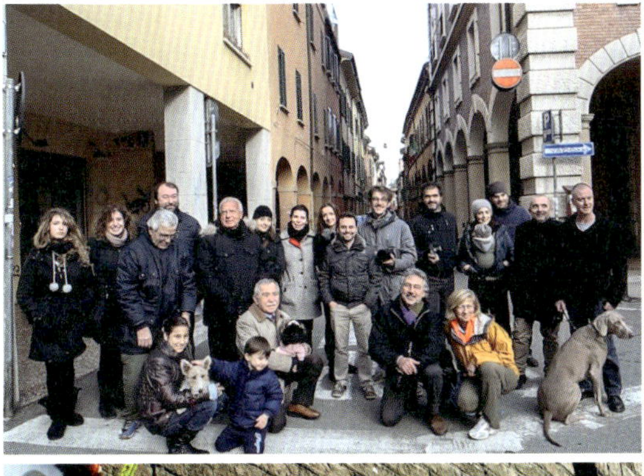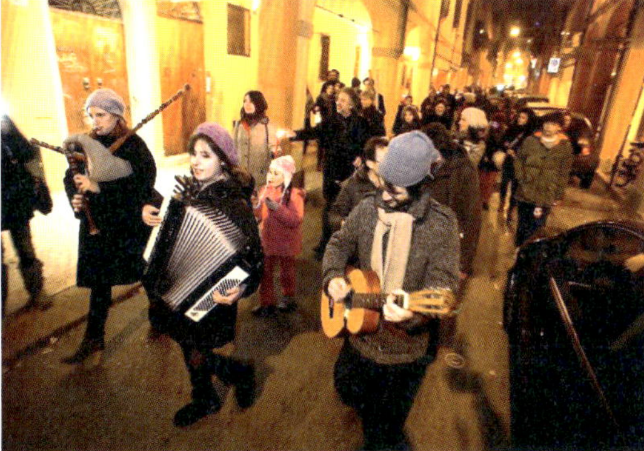

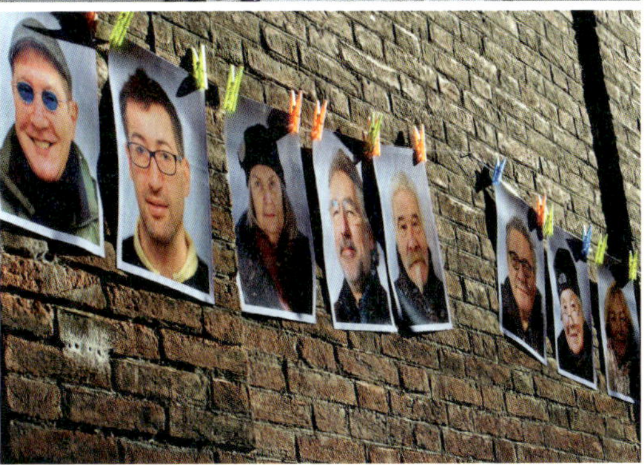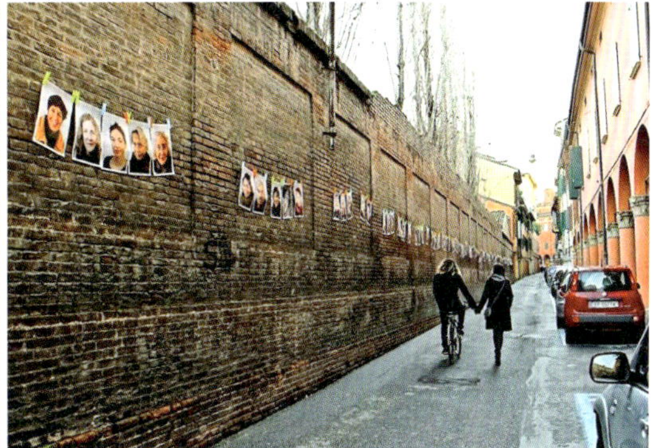

well as changes in behaviors and interaction between neighbors.

In the shift from theory to practice, we've observed that the main features that probably marked success (in quantitative terms—given the growing number of *Social Streets* nationally and internationally) are represented by:

- Facebook: To use a free medium and spread information via the social network Facebook as facilitator of the transition from the virtual to the real.
- Territoriality: The decision to restrict the closed Facebook group in a predetermined, small-sized territory.

- Free: *Social Street* as a model is absolutely free—at two levels: as internal trade (exclusion of *do ut des*) but also as macro structure.
- No prescribed structure: Every single group can act to reintroduce appropriate social relations, taking into account the peculiarities of its territory.
- Inclusion: Focusing on everything that brings people together (and excluding that which divides), being proactive in the face of the harshest criticism and not accepting being against something without being constructive, excluding languages that are not acceptable to all members of the group.

The idea of **Social Street** originates from the experience of the Facebook group "Residents in Fondazza street-Bologna", which started in September 2013. In 2016 there are about 400 *Social Street* Facebook groups worldwide with about 50,000 members who all share a strong interest in promoting relationships.

Trade School

http://tradeschool.coop

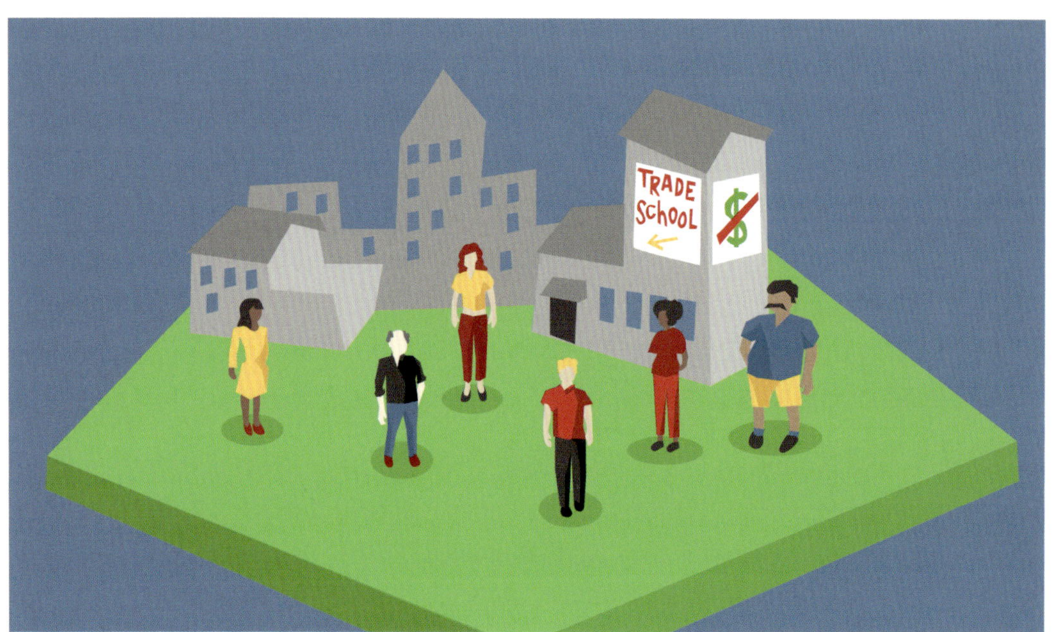

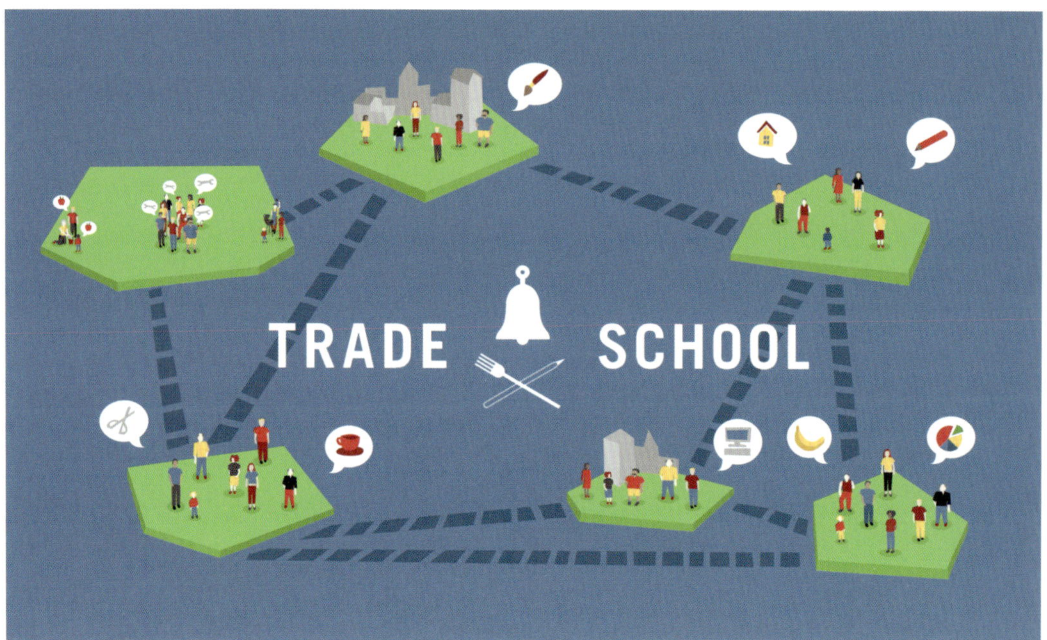

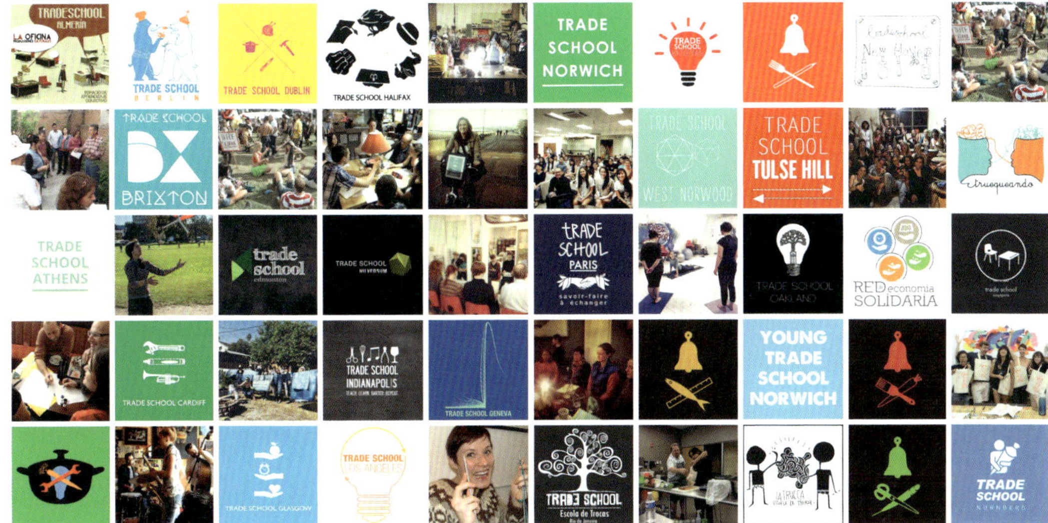

Trade School is a self-organized learning community that runs on barter. Anyone can sign up to teach a skill, and learners offer barter items to meet the teacher's needs. Local chapters coordinate gatherings for exchange, and open source software facilitates communication between organizers.

Started in New York City in 2009 by three young artists, this network is now running in over fifty cities. Our all-volunteer effort has reached over 20,000 students and teachers in fifty cities. Over 100 local organizers communicate daily online to support one another.

Or Zubalsky, a Trade School New York organizer, built the open source software so that the back end and front end of *TradeSchool.coop* can be translated into any language. Organizers in Athens, Ho Chi Minh, Bogotá, México, Quito, Chihuahua, Guadalajara, Guayaquil, and Puebla have translated the coordination platform into their local dialects. Caroline Woolard, a *Trade School New York* organizer, and Brittany West, a *Trade School Indianapolis* organizer, help new schools open.

Organizers use our open source software to translate *TradeSchool.coop* into any language. Organizers in México, Greece, France, Spain, and Ecuador have translated the software.

TradeSchool.coop organizers are 90% female. Women attend and teach more than 60% of our classes. As a group dedicated to social justice, seeing so many women in positions of power is exciting.

Today, we are writing a book about our work together. We are a community who understand mutual aid and self-organization in our local contexts. Most of us have never met in person, but we inspire one another to prefigure the politics we want to see.

Trade School began 2009 as an experiment by a group of New York City artists who built *OurGoods*. This group included Louise Ma, Rich Watts, and Caroline Woolard. They received an opportunity to work with a storefront, and came up with barter for knowledge. Over the course of 35 days, more than 800 people participated in 76 single session classes. Classes ranged from scrabble strategy to composting, from grant writing to ghost hunting. In exchange for instruction, teachers received running shoes to mixed CDs to flowers. In 2012, Or Zubalsky built an open-source web platform to share with local organizers. Or spent over two months of full-time work writing code. Rich Watts and Louise Ma spent over a month designing and refining the front end. Caroline Woolard spent several hours a week talking to organizers of new *Trade Schools*. Today, organizers across the globe work together to keep the project moving forward. The international team includes Indianapolis organizer Brittany West and New York organizer Caroline Woolard.

Watch the Mediterranean Sea

http://watchthemed.net

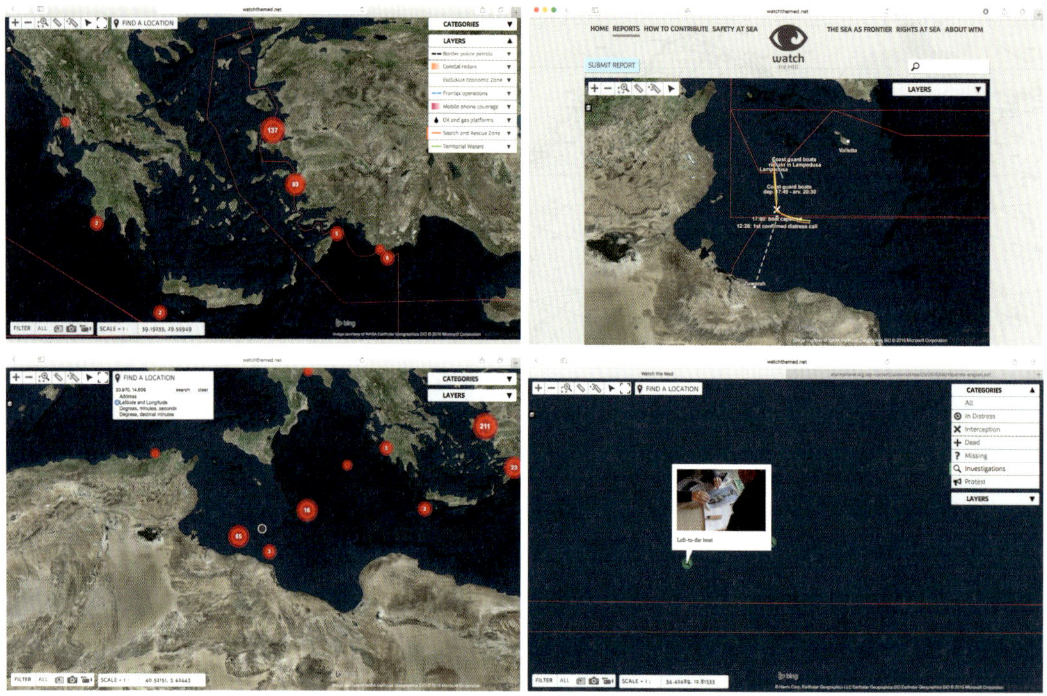

Watch the Mediterranean Sea is an online mapping platform to monitor the deaths and violations of migrants' rights at the maritime borders of the EU. Through the platform the sister project *Alarm Phone (alarmphone.org)* developed, a digital community which operates a hotline for boatpeople in distress—no rescue, but Alarm.

OCTOBER 2014: Although we decided to operate the *Alarm Phone* throughout the entire Mediterranean Sea, during our preparation process we could hardly imagine how to effectively make use of our hotline in the Aegean area. Illegal push-backs by Greek coastguards were daily practices at that time, and while discussing this issue with refugees who had directly experienced such life-threatening situations, we thought it would be impossible to develop strategies for real-time interventions to prevent these practices.

OCTOBER 2015: Up to 100 distress calls and messages reached our shift teams in one week alone and nearly all of them came from the Aegean Sea. Every day and night rescue operations were carried out with realtime support of the *Alarm Phone*—an unexpected U-turn! This changing dynamic was the consequence of several intersecting factors: Syriza had come into power and halted most of the illegal push-back practices and also dismantled some pillars of the Greek-European detention regime.

More and more refugees and migrants were under pressure to leave and move towards Europe and they succeeded in opening up a corridor to the north, heralding the long summer of migration. And between boat people, escorting groups of migrant communities, and our *Alarm Phone,* an amazing communication process and network developed, able to support the (attempted) sea crossing of thousands.

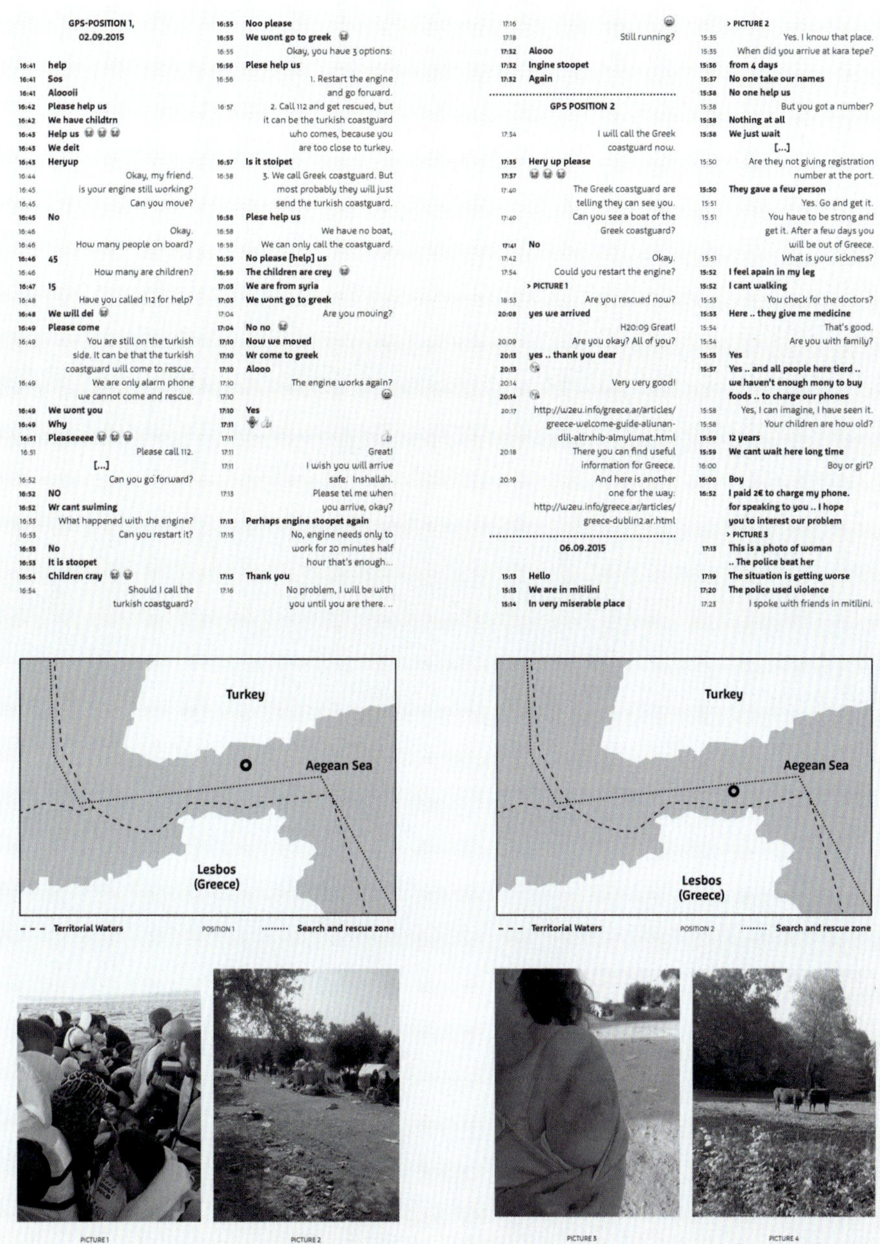

Watch the Mediterranean Sea was born in 2012 in the wake of the demands for freedom of movement, brought about by the Arab Spring and the demands for accountability for the many shipwrecks that occurred in 2011, when more and more people tried to cross to Europe, often at the cost of their lives. Initiated as a part of the Boats4People campaign by various networks, it monitors through the transnational cooperation with migrants' rights organizations, activists, researchers, migrants, seafarers, and the use of new mapping technologies, the deaths and violations of migrants' rights at the maritime borders of the EU. While the original purpose of the platform was documentation, since October 2014 it is also used as an intervention tool by the WTM's sister project, the *Alarm Phone,* an emergency phone hotline for those in immediate distress at sea, which seeks to support people attempting to overcome Europe's dangerous external borders.

Visionary Pioneers

of Media Art

Visionary Pioneers of Media Art

Launched in 2014, this category is dedicated to recognizing and celebrating the men and women whose artistic, technological, and social achievements have decisively influenced and advanced the development of new artistic directions.

What began as a technological revolution has since developed into a new cultural and social reality with its own specific forms of communication, cultural techniques, and artistic expressions, the roots of which extend far back into the past and lead us to encounters with remarkable, extraordinary personalities—the visionary pioneers of media art. Thus, in many respects, these men and women established the foundation of media art as we know it today. With Prix Ars Electronica's Golden Nica for Visionary Pioneers of Media Art we want to give them the respectful recognition commensurate with their accomplishments, and, at the same time, generate more awareness about the history of media art in general.

The third edition of this award has been successfully completed and the prominent art critic and exhibition curator Jasia Reichardt has been selected as the recipient of the Golden Nica for Visionary Pioneer of Media Art 2016.

Her groundbreaking work and all that she has done on behalf of media art is being honored with this award. The name Jasia Reichardt is, above all, indelibly linked to a trailblazing exhibition that ran in 1968 at London's Institute of Contemporary Arts and then at the Corcoran Gallery of Art in Washington, D.C. and the Exploratorium in San Francisco. *Cybernetic Serendipity* was the title of this much-publicized show in which, instead of human artists, the spotlight was suddenly on computers, machines, and algorithms. Under Jasia Reichardt's direction, artists worked together with mathematicians, engineers, and technology specialists to jointly create a completely novel form of presentation long before everyone was talking about cooperation between art and science in light of their tremendous potential for innovation. Numerous interactive exhibits gave visitors a close-up look at what Jasia Reichardt was getting at: the enormous potential inherent in new technologies, and the question of how humans and machines might someday coexist and work together. Jasia Reichardt didn't showcase machines and programs only as tools performing a task; rather, she featured them as an integral part of the creative process.

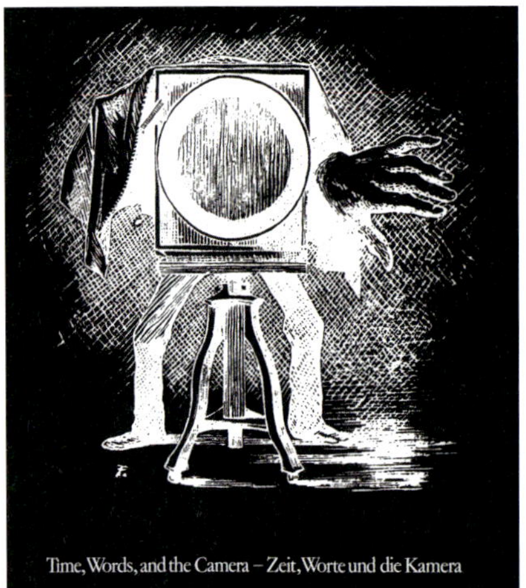

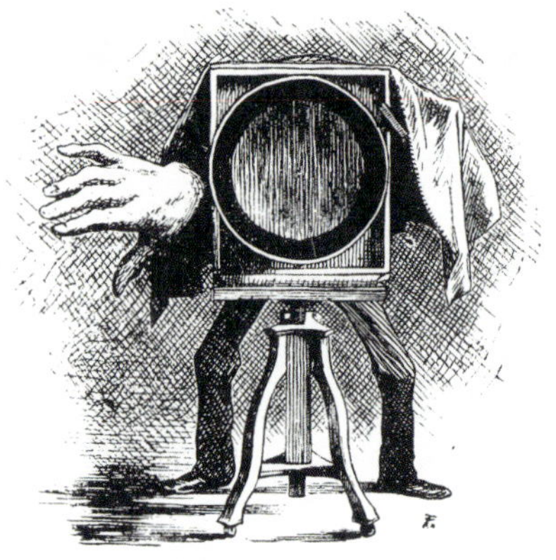

Front and back covers of the catalogue *Time, words, and the camera: photoworks by British artists.* Künstlerhaus, Graz, 1976

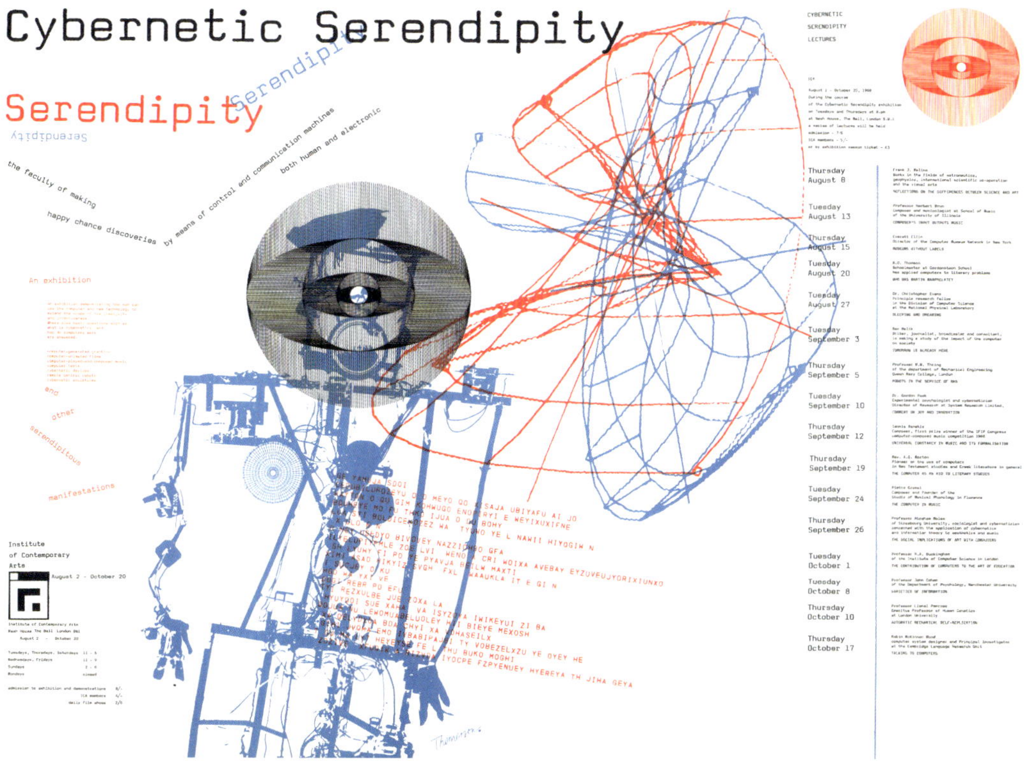

Cybernetic Serendipity

Cybernetic Serendipity exhibition poster designed by Franciszka Themerson

Jasia Reichardt

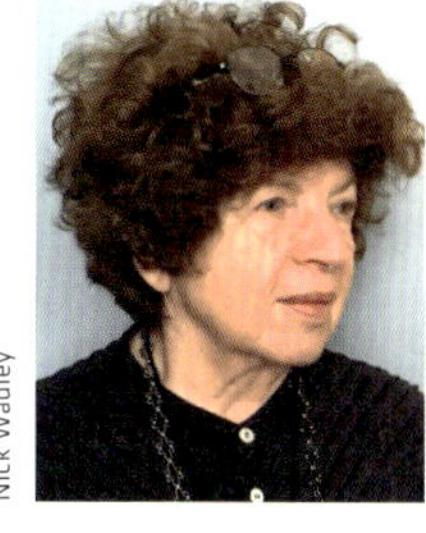

is a writer on art and an exhibition organiser. Born in Poland, educated in England, she has lived in London most of her life. She was Assistant Director of the Institute of Contemporary Arts (ICA) in London, 1963-71, and Director of the Whitechapel Art Gallery, 1974-76. She has taught at the Architectural Association and other colleges, has written for most of the international art magazines and contributed to many international exhibitions and conferences throughout the world. She is principally interested in the relationship between art and science, art and technology, art and the history of ideas, and this is why some of her best known exhibitions, such as *Between Poetry and Painting* (1965) and *Cybernetic Serendipity* (1968), were about the connections between one field and another. She has written several books, including *The Computer in Art* (1971), and *Robots—Fact, Fiction and Prediction* (1978), and edited *Cybernetics, Art and Ideas* (1971). She also worked on visualisation of mathematics, a project called, *Fantasia Mathematica*. In 1982, she was President of a conference on *The Power of Fashion in Art & Science* for the British Association for the Advancement of Science, of whose committee she was a member 1982-92. She was one of the directors of ARTEC biennale in Japan 1989-1998. Also in 1998, she curated an exhibition of electronic portraiture, called *Electronically Yours,* at Tokyo Metropolitan Museum of Photography. She continues to pursue her interests in the relationship of art and technology and other borderlines of art. Since 1988 she has been looking after the Themerson Archive, the archive of a writer and an artist, whose avant-garde publishing company, Gaberbocchus Press, launched a Common Room for artists interested in science and scientists interested in the arts in 1957. Her latest exhibition, *Nearly Human,* is about machines and objects that are nearly like us—all products of our imagination.

September 1968 No.6 Price 2/6

The Magazine of the Institute of Contemporary Art

'Cybernetic Serendipity' provokes,
in its implications, it is as different
from an every day 'art exhibition'
as a major operation from a manicure...
it is an experience which no one should miss.
John Russell, The Sunday Times

CYBERNETIC. SERENDIPITY

The winking lights
the flickering television screens .
and the squawks from the music machines
are signalling the end of abstract art;
When machines can do it,
it will not be worth doing -
Robert Melville, New Statesman

Is everything or anything here art -
and if not, why not?
We all benefit by asking ourselves this kind of question,
and no more enjoyable way of provoking it can be
imagined than an hour in this intriguing lively
and thought-provoking show.
Nigel Gosling, The Observer

A joyous exhibition.
It demonstrates that art
can live with modern science.
Daily Mirror

Anyone unable to visit the
exhibition, or driven prematurely
away from it by some of the nosier
pieces on display, would do well
to get the 25s catalogue and
information conspectus of the
exhibition and its technical and
theoretical background.
The Times Literary Supplement

But as unique show of
fresh ideas about tre[nds]
in contemporary art-m[aking]
this is a stimulating
exhibition for everyo[ne]
Daily Telegraph

Where in London could you take
a hippy
a computer programmer
a ten-year-old schoolboy
and guarantee that each would be
perfectly happy for an hour
without you having to lift a finger
to entertain them. From today,
there is just one such place -
The Institute of Contemporary Arts.
The Evening Standard

I think that the computer may
be able not so much to enlarge
our concepts of art as to
widen immeasurably our knowledge
of what is not art.
Alexander Weatherson, Art and Artists

This is an exhibition with a
tremendously interesting theme.
Guy Brett, The Times

The Industrial revolution
produced the machine age,
with the computer
comes machine age art.
The Evening News

It is, therefore, a huge pleasure to report that the big machine
exhibition at the ICA, Cybernetic Serendipity - is a complete success
and well worth its three years planning by Jasia Reichardt. The show
provides information which we need, succinctly and entertainingly.
Bryan Robertson, Spectator

Gasia Reichardt asked Norman me Toynto[n] to design the cover for the Institute of Contemporary Arts magazine. First I thou[ght] I could do a drawing depicting part of the exhibition, or a cartoon mak[ing] some whimsical comment. Another thing that occur[red] to me was to describe in words, or visually involved there some of the things that were in the organizing of this exhibition. For example were some three hundred and twenty five persons involved to make this show possible. Plus the fact that it took 1,095 days to bring it to fruition. Some seven hundred press invitations were sent o[ut] and more than three thousand people attended the ... private views. With this information at hand I had more than enough to go on with. So what I have decided to do is

Second issue of the ICA magazine

Jasia Reichardt–A Life on a Plate

When Jasia Reichardt received an honorary doctorate from Middlesex University in 2015, she was asked which aspects of her work she was most proud of. She mentioned two things that none of us expected. The first was her appointment as Madame President of Section X (General) of the British Association of the Advancement of Science in 1982. She invented, organised, chaired and gave a presidential address at the conference on "The Power of Fashion in Art and Science"[1]. Yes, the conference was about fashion, that powerful force which obscures judgement, sways opinions and distorts objectivity in all fields of human endeavour.

The second was the 8-volume catalogue of the Themerson Archive, on which she worked for 20 years and which will be published by the Polish National Library early next year (in English, of course).

So, why didn't she mention all her work with art and technology for which she is so well known: the exhibitions *Cybernetic Serendipity*, *Electronically Yours*, *Nearly Human*, the publications and lectures on computer art, robots, automata, and media?

Perhaps because these subjects were/are the mainstay of her professional life, to be taken for granted. They occupy and invade her thinking. When did it all start, this interest in art and technology and art and science? After all, she studied neither. It prob-ably goes back to 1958, when at the Gaberbocchus Common Room, the first regular London meeting place for artists and scientists, she heard a lecture about cybernetics.

Did she study anything? Yes, the theatre. She wanted to be a director of intellectual entertainments. Perhaps that's what she became but her theatre became a gallery, the slideshow, a lecture hall, or the printed page.

Her interest in machines has a long history, because at the age of four her mother told her about a machine that could wash and iron clothes without any human intervention. Yes, she decided, one day, she too would have such a machine. The year was 1937, and, of course, at the time no such machines were on the horizon.

When, twenty years later, Jasia became an art critic in London and worked as assistant editor of *Art News and Review*, she was interested in the avant-garde and in ideas that connected art to other areas of creative activity on the borderlines of the art world. At the time these included concrete poetry, design, kinetic and light art.

Before I tell you something about her work, her projects realised and unrealised, I'd like to describe her life, her home. She lives with her partner, Nick Wadley, art historian and artist, who gets involved

1 Speakers included: Margaret Boden, Colin Brewer, Bernard Dixon, Brian Goodwin, Tim Gordon, Hans Keller, Helmut Kirchner, Edward Lucie-Smith, John Maddox, Jonathan Miller, Bill Pirie, Tim Souster, Stefan Themerson

in all her projects. Their house is white and full of paper, paintings and plants. Ceilings are high and it is usually cold. There is a collection of robots, toy robots plus an AIBO, which is a recent addition. It is one of the earliest models. Her book on robots, published in 1978, is still considered to be one of the best books covering the history of the subject, and there is a trunk of articles, correspondence and photographs dealing with the history of robots. Not surprisingly, this collection continues to grow. It is, of course, one of several collections of ephemera that provide basic research material. One of the collections deals with art and technology, science, computers, AI, the future; another deals with artists, living and dead. Still paper: catalogues, newspaper cuttings, invitations, press releases, of which the time of production is always revealed in texture, size, typeface and colour. You don't always need a printed date to know when something was published. Her own archive of writings and correspondence, some of it filed, is in white boxes. Her published work in a four-drawer filing cabinet.

She doesn't like to talk about herself because everything she thinks about seriously is in her writings. If she talks, it is about the amusing things that happened in her life, anecdotes, unrepeatable events. Here are two examples:

It is 1970, and Jasia Reichardt is a member of the Experimental Projects Committee of the Arts Council. Mark Boyle is in the chair, Nick Serota, who works for the Arts Council, takes notes. The committee, there are some seven members, go through the usual motions of committee meetings with the reading of minutes and going through the agenda of examining the proposals submitted by artists to decide who should receive financial support. On that particular occasion one of the projects is an extremely well designed, beautifully detailed geometric construction, a wall relief, which appeals to all the members of the committee, and this is the project that the committee decides to support. When the projects are completed, the artists photograph them, and send the photographs to the committee in time for the next meeting. When the photograph arrives, there was a stunned silence: in his house the winning artist installed wall-to-wall central heating. Jasia breaks out in uncontrollable laughter.

It is 1975, and Jasia Reichardt is the director of London's Whitechapel Art Gallery. It is a requirement of the Trustees and in her contract that once a year, there should be an exhibition of local artists. At the time, the East End of London is not the mecca of artists that it became 40 years later, and Jasia doesn't like amateur art. Even so, rules have to be followed, and an announcement inviting contributions to the exhibition *The Flower Show of Tower Hamlets* (an answer to the famous annual Chelsea Flower Show) is sent out in English, Urdu and Hindi to various local centres, schools, hospitals, etc. giving information about the sending-in days. Several art students of St Martin's School of Art are employed to receive the works and to display them. On the first sending-in day, nothing arrives. On the second, nothing. On the third, two small works. The exhibition is to open two days later. What to do? The students are asked to create a flower show. In two days, the students transform the gallery and the staircase into a garden with trees, bushes, giant flowers and a swing, against green walls. The exhibition looks wonderful and the trustees trot in for the opening. "It's lovely", they say to Jasia. "We told you that there is a lot of talent in the East End".

Her work at *Art News and Review* finished in 1960 and then followed the first of three periods of freelancing. She was writing regularly for *Architectural Design*, '*L'Art d'Aujourd'hui*, and other art publications.

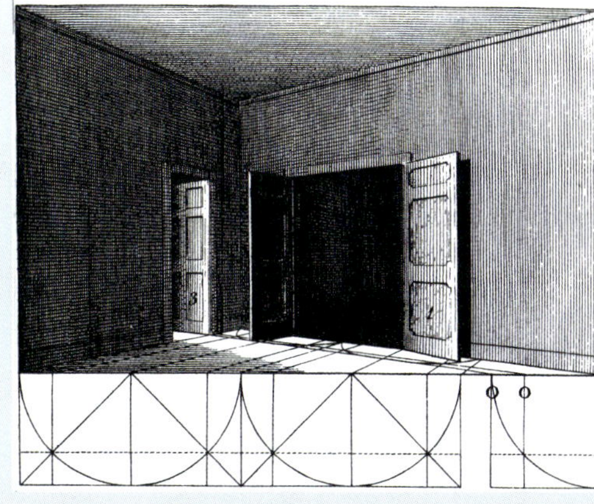

Ten Sitting Rooms, ICA, London, 1970

IMAGE

IN

PROGRESS

Image in Progress exhibition, Grabowski Gallery, London, 1962

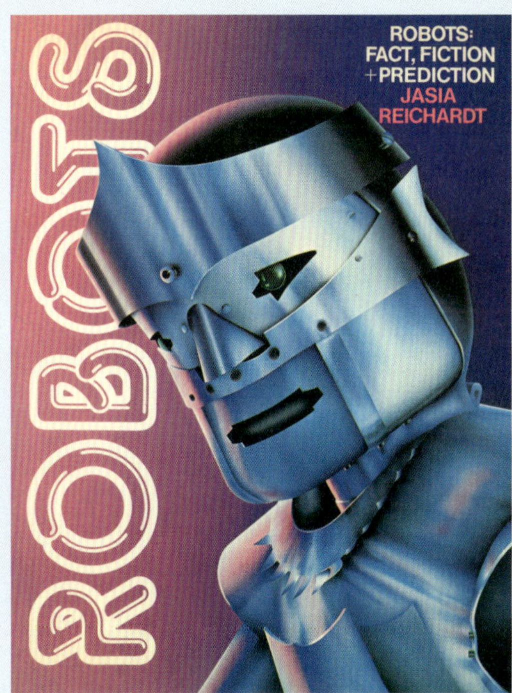

Robots: Fact, Fiction and Prediction, Thames & Hudson, 1978

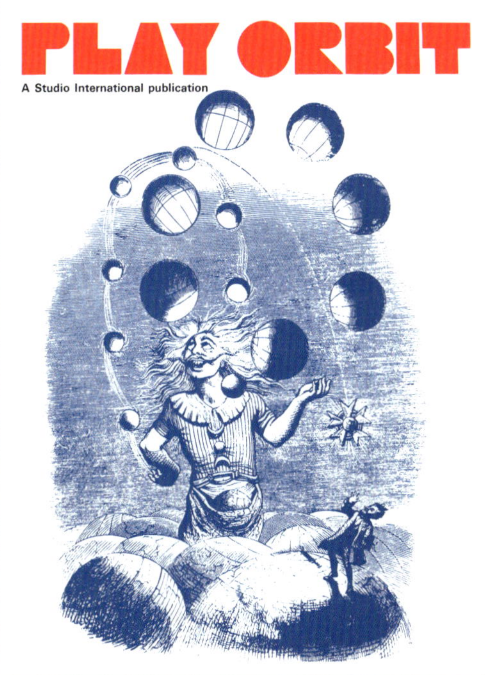

Grandville cover for the catalogue of *Play Orbit* exhibition, ICA, 1969

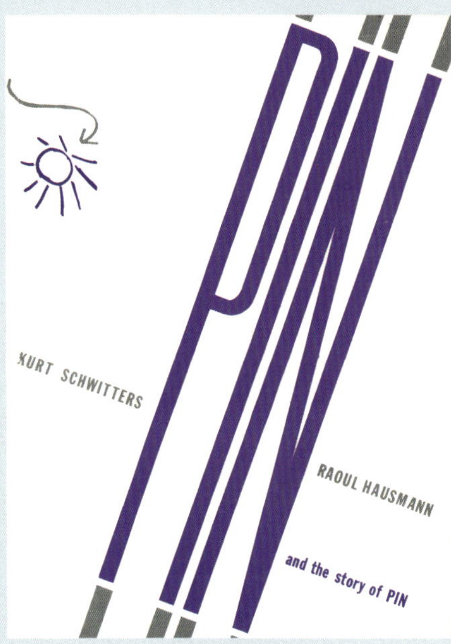

Kurt Schwitters & Raoul Hausmann, *PIN and the story of PIN*, Gaberbocchus Press, London, 1962

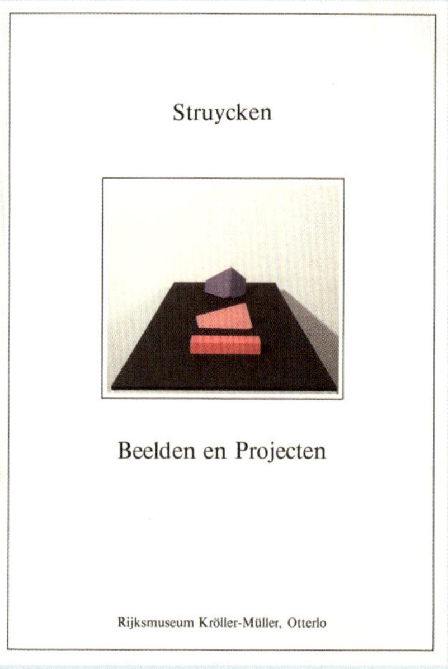

Struycken, *Beelden en Projecten*, Rijksmuseum Kröller-Müller, Otterlo, 1977

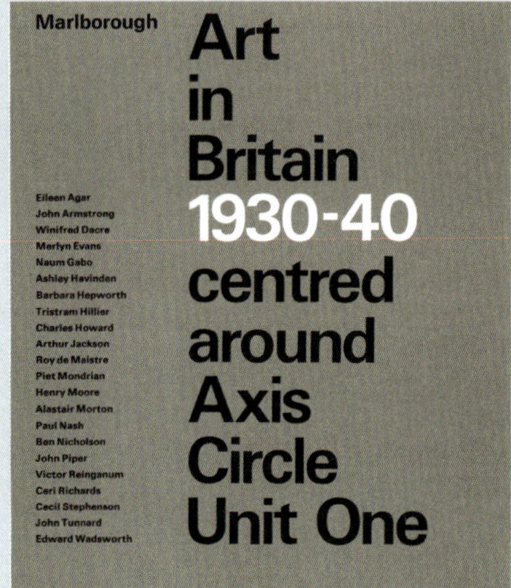

An exhibition to celebrate Herbert Read's 75th birthday, New London Gallery and Marlborough Fine Art, London, 1965

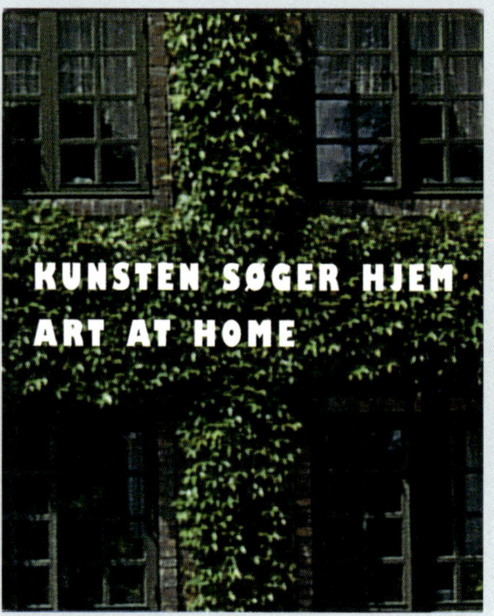

Art at Home, an exhibition in people's homes, Copenhagen, 1996

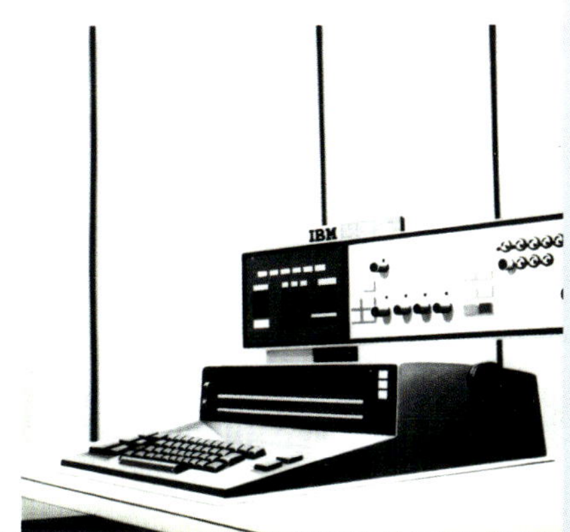

First issue of the ICA magazine devoted to *Cybernetic Serendipity*. Image on the cover is Lowell Nesbitt's painting of IBM 1440 Data Processing System, 1965

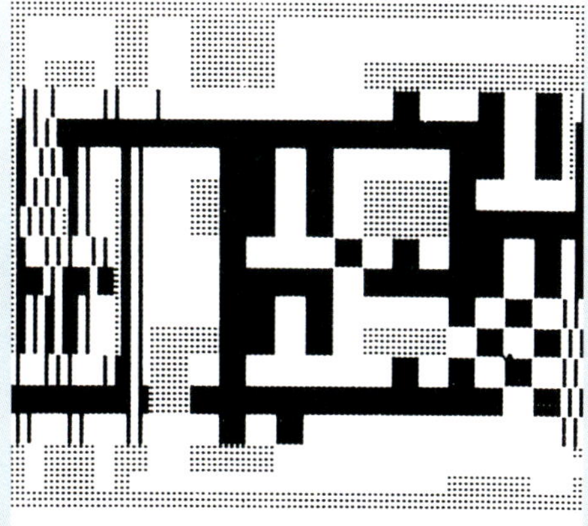

The Computer in Art, Studio Vista, 1971

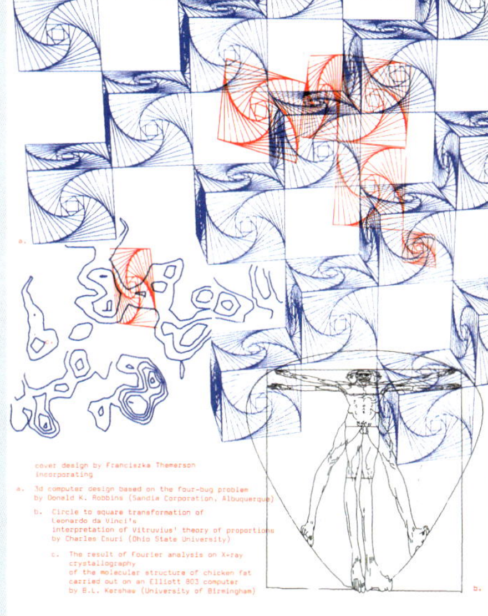

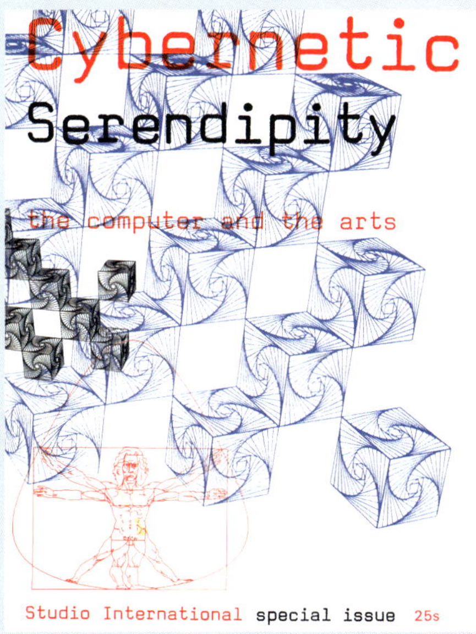

Front and back covers of the Studio International publication accompanying *Cybernetic Serendipity* exhibition, ICA, London, 1968; Cover design by Franciszka Themerson, designer of the exhibition

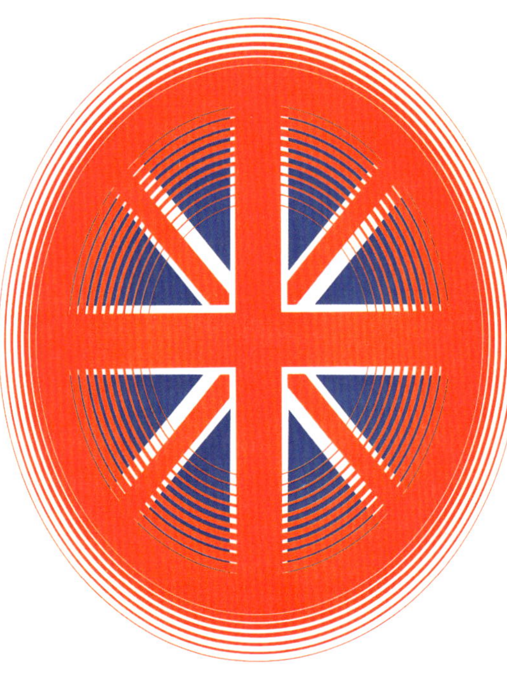

The 4th Exhibition for the First Prize of the Museum of Contemporary Art, Nagaoka, 1967. Catalogue cover designed by Kohei Sugiura

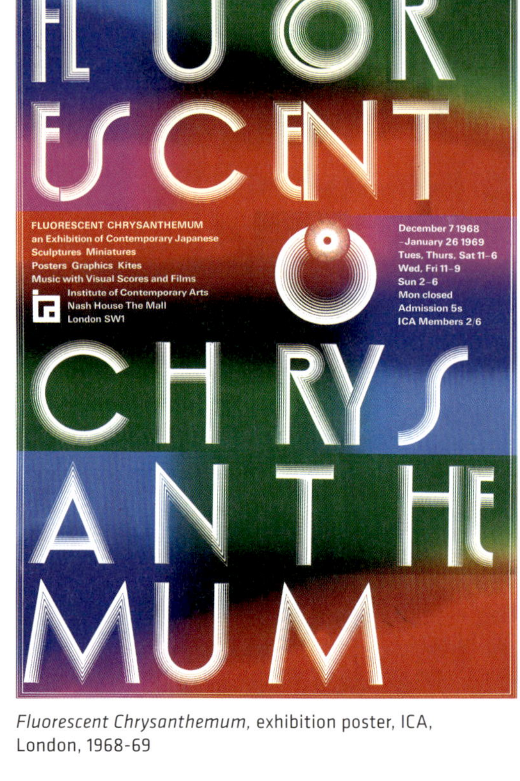

Fluorescent Chrysanthemum, exhibition poster, ICA, London, 1968-69

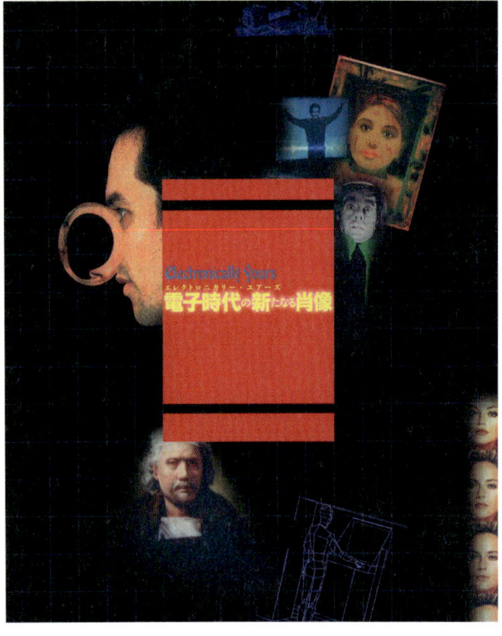

Electronically Yours exhibition, Tokyo Metropolitan Museum of Photography, 1998

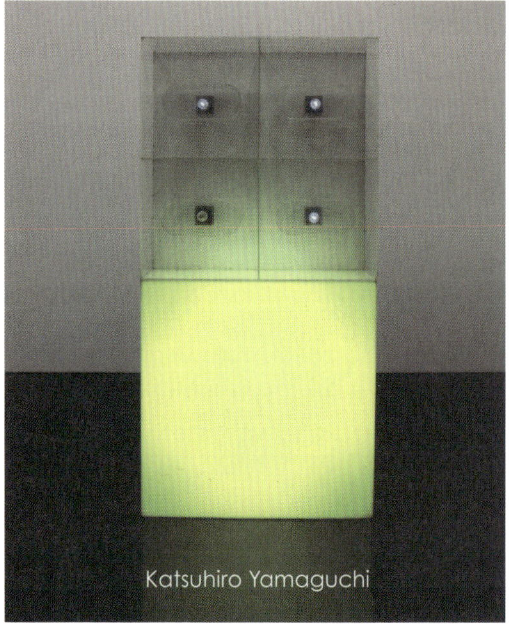

Katsuhiro Yamaguchi, Annely Juda Fine Art, London, 2013

In 1962, she organised the first exhibition of English Pop Art at Grabowski Gallery in South Kensington. It was called *Image in Progress* and included seven young artists from the Royal College of Art: Derek Boshier, David Hockney, Allen Jones, Peter Phillips, Max Shepherd, Norman Toynton and Brian Wright. *The Inner Image* followed two years later, also at Grabowski Gallery. That exhibition of the Leicester Group included works which combined painting with sculpture. Her next exhibition in 1965, after she became assistant director at the ICA, was the first London exhibition of concrete poetry: *Between Poetry and Painting.* She then teaches at Bath Academy of Art, edits the monthly ICA Bulleting, and is thinking of new exhibitions.

Mike Sarne, in his article, "la clique belsize parkienne", in *art and artists,* May 1966, wrote about her: "... probably the most influential art critic on the scene is in that fortunate position for a variety of reasons, but possibly can count on two cardinal virtues: first, she knows everyone, and, second, she never knocks anyone."

Her work? Since 1962, when she organised her first exhibition at the Grabowski Gallery, she has curated some thirty exhibitions, including all the shows at the Whitechapel Art Gallery when she was its director, February 1974 – April 1976. Her most recent exhibition that is about human imagination, called *Nearly Human,* is still travelling, and will continue to do so. Apart from the historical section about robots, automata and marionettes, new works of art can be added as others leave. New things are imagined and ideas change as the artists define and make what to them is "nearly human", and the show progresses from one venue to another.

Some of the catalogue covers of Jasia's exhibitions are illustrated on these pages, as well as some of the covers of the books she has written.

Several of the projects she has been especially fond of and worked on for many years, are unrealised. For instance, there is the *Fantasia Mathematica,* a project for visualising mathematics, 1972, that was to be an exhibition, a book and a television programme. There is also, the *Automatic Music Theatre,* an exhibition with circular arena in which music machines created by artists play music by themselves, performing only when a spotlight is directed onto them. The lighting system, however, like life, is unpredictable, with the result that some of the machines have more chances of performing then others. *History of the Future,* her book about afterlife, with a screenplay about an adventurous protagonist escorted around various sites of heaven and hell, is still sitting quietly in the cupboard.

Many years ago Jasia Reichardt wrote articles under several pseudonyms, but this time she has written the above in the third person and without pretending to be anyone else.

u19-CREATE YOUR

WORLD

the best is yet to come

Sirikit Amann, Conny Lee, Gerhard Funk, Beate Großegger, Karl Markovics

Certain generalizations pertaining to the Prix Ars Electronica's u19 – CREATE YOUR WORLD category hold true every year. One is that creative work by kids and young people is simultaneously a mirror of the present and a preview of the future. Furthermore, the projects submitted for prize consideration in this category are incredibly engaging and fresh because they haven't necessarily been produced with an audience or consumers in mind; rather, they're often created simply for their own sake, unburdened by what others have done before or conventions of any sort. This can be said about u19 – CREATE YOUR WORLD every year, and is an essential reason why this category is so important and so exciting.

Nevertheless, submissions this year do stand out in a number of respects. An extremely positive development is the large number of entries by female participants. It seems that girls' fears of up-close-and-personal contact with high-tech and their doubts about their own creativity have finally been consigned to the dustbin of history. In going about this work, girl artists are succeeding in getting across clearly female perceptions and points of view without thereby resorting to clichés of femininity. They have strong, independent voices, to the particular delight of this year's jurors. And we were equally pleased to have received contributions from a diverse array of cultures. The whole spectrum was represented this year—from a glimpse into everyday life of Muslim girls to insights into youngsters' takes on the omnipresent refugee issue. With respect to the latter in particular, it must be noted here that these adolescent takes get by without the pathos, the ascription of the victim role, or the oppressive gravity that we're accustomed to in media coverage and campaigns. These perspectives don't exhibit despair or resignation; they're empathetic and dauntless at the same time.

The most exciting aspect of the u19 category is how wide-ranging and open it is. Simply EVERYTHING that occupies and motivates young people is permitted—or, actually, expressly encouraged! Thus, it's especially surprising just how few submissions we've received in recent years that make use of one of the most important means of artistic expression: music! So, that makes it all the better that several musical projects were among this year's entries.

Generally difficult to assess were projects that provided us with too few insights or were presented in an incomprehensible way. Participants who submitted PDFs full of technical data that hinted at fascinating projects would do well to augment their future submissions with vivid imagery and short explanatory videos. Otherwise, the jury is forced to reach its verdicts on the basis of vague guesses.

As the headline of our jury statement, we've intentionally selected the title of one of this year's prize-winning works. *the best is yet to come* symbolizes young people's incessant search for new ideas, for inventions that make everyday life easier—for instance, a skateboard-powered battery charger or a mirror that displays the news. The title's meaning is also relevant to the many refugee projects submitted this year: hope for human beings, hope powered by young people's ideas. This year's Golden Nica winner, *Die Entscheidung,* also transports this message in a figurative sense—but we'll stop short of a spoiler here. The video game is the youngest medium, the latecomer so to speak. And in the last 20 years, we've had the pleasure of watching it go through the same maturation process as its older siblings, film and prose literature. For a long time, video games were regarded as mere amusement, entertainment, a shallow diversion. It's only recently that the artistic potential of games as a means of expressing complex philosophical content or social criticism has been recognized and taken advantage of. And this is exactly what the 2016 u19 grand prizewinner has done!

Like we said: the best is yet to come!

Golden Nica

Die Entscheidung · Jonas Bodingbauer

In Jonas Bodingbauer's game *Die Entscheidung* (The Decision) two players compete against one another at separate computers. In doing so, they have very different assignments to carry out and they don't receive the same information. Player 1 is a husband/ father who's setting out on an important day in his career. Player 2 is a malignant tumor that has to try to kill that man who has developed cancer. One person experiences a story and has to deal with it; the other has to follow strict rules and mechanically expand the capabilities of the malignant tumor. The final outcome: either the patient survives or he dies. Both participants are then confronted with the result and called upon to talk to one another about what they went through.

Die Entscheidung is an allusion to the Milgram Experiment and a critical commentary on blindly following rules. Thus, on one hand, Jonas Bodingbauer is leveling criticism at how a lot of video games function and what they do with players, but this critique can also be applied more broadly to other areas of life. *Die Entscheidung* distinguishes itself not only by addressing a serious subject, but also in its very original implementation of the gaming principle—as an exciting video game that corresponds to the contemporary state of the medium, but above all as a skillfully packaged unit that brings together everything the Prix Ars Electronica stands for. The fact that Jonas Bodingbauer is no stranger to the u19 jury is a pleasant sidebar because it shows that this young man really is totally into creative tinkering and he truly has come a long way. His success is well-deserved and we sincerely congratulate him on his impressive work.

Awards of Distinction

Blackout
Jasmin Selen Heinz, Tanja Josic, Emily Poulter
Blackout offers something that supposedly isn't that big a deal among young people these days: a heaping helping of social criticism, but one that's served up to the audience with a playfulness that makes it easier to digest. The subject is economization, pressure to fit into the system, self-optimization, estrangement, the feeling of full-throttle standstill. We're all hustling in pursuit of questionable social values—time flies, and we simply run after it and lose more and

more of ourselves in the process. Here, the interplay of atmospherically condensed imagery, interesting special effects, music and the spoken word gives rise to an associative maelstrom that's the most outstanding feature of this work. At 3:49, the two young artists broach the big issue: "How do we actually want to live?" And with our pulse accompanying the on-screen, white-on-black-background countdown of the film's final seconds, we're forced to confront this question ourselves.

Die Flucht · Dimitri Teufl
One of the essential elements of art is changing "something" into "something else" so as to make the world a bit more comprehensible for us. Dimitri Teufl has impressively succeeded in pulling off just such a feat of artistic conversion. He's used Lego building blocks to create a model of our contemporary world in which he relates the story of a Syrian family who fled from war to Europe in search of aid and asylum. Dimitri Teufl transforms playthings into serious stuff, and simultaneously conjures up a utopia. After all, it's evident that, for many refugees, the happy end is receding further and further into the future since fewer and fewer states are prepared to admit them. Dimitri Teufl is a 13-year-old boy who's obviously dissatisfied with the world as it is. He'd like to change it and, with his film, he's taken the first step in doing just that. Dimitri uses standardized, colorful plastic building blocks to construct a reality that stop-motion animation brings forth as a clearly composed dramatic vision, image by image, before our very eyes. What he's created thereby is more than a wish, more than a conception, more than a mere utopia. *Die Flucht* (Fleeing) is a work of art that can change the way we think and feel. It's up to us to decide whether we draw the conclusions and change our ways.

u14—Merchandise Prize

Skateboard Charging Unit · Fabian Krautgartner
In conjunction with a school project, Fabian Krautgartner installed a bicycle dynamo and a "home-

brew" charging unit on the underside of his skateboard so that, on his way to school, he can charge the battery of his cell phone, which is hooked up via cable to the unit on his skateboard. In the project's next stage of development, the dynamo will be able to charge a mobile battery mounted on the underside of the board. This work by Fabian Krautgartner ingeniously interlinks two things that play an important role in lots of youngsters' lives, and does so in a very simple, practical, and useful way. This skateboard charging unit is an excellent example of how you're sometimes able to approach a common, everyday problem—a cell phone low on juice—with inventiveness and conveniently available means—a bicycle dynamo—and come up with a simple solution. What the jury especially liked was that Fabian also submitted the skateboard itself so they had it right there in front of them during their deliberations.

u10—Merchandise Prize

My Website · Simon Heppner

Only nine years old and sharp as a tack! The u10—Merchandise Prize is your well-deserved reward! Considering all the elements that have gone into this website—programming computer games, writing a blog, publishing a fanzine celebrating your favorite games—it's obvious that this is a brilliant, across-the-board achievement. Congratulations! Respect! We hope to be hearing more from you.

Honorary Mentions

BIOKoSMoS—BioInk for Art

BIOKoSMoS Project Crew

Identifying a challenge, grappling with it and actively seeking solutions—that's "creating your world" the way it's supposed to be in u19. In fact, the challenge of coming up with unmistakably distinctive colors is indeed a core issue in the world of art. What would Yves Klein be without blue or, in the future, Anish Kapoor without black? Your efforts attested to by comprehensible experiments, documentary photographs, and analytical results scored high marks on our grading sheets. You didn't just perform research; you've inquired into the behavior of materials reacting with bacteria and thereby opened up an exciting field that most certainly has great future potential.

COPY/PASTE · Fachstelle beteiligung.st

Wow! Terrific film! Powerful subject, amusing treatment. Well written, well directed, well acted. This project was obviously fun to make, and you managed to communicate that enthusiasm to the jury. This trenchant take on so-called fan cults and the fans' yearnings to be like the star takes this phenomenon to its ultimate conclusion in a very witty way. But sometimes, the guffaws get stuck in the viewer's throat, especially when such imitation is driven to an extreme and the absolute absurdity is utterly unmistakable. Every aspect of your film came off brilliantly: cool plot, likable and convincing cast, excellent and well-coordinated direction and camera work. The fact that you're receiving only an Honorary Mention and not an Award of Distinction is due in no small measure to the fact that so many films were submitted for prize consideration this year, and that the u19 jury aims to recognize excellence across the creative spectrum (games, inventions, animation etc.) as fairly as possible. Please keep up the good work and enter again next year!

Scorpion—The Electric Vehicle

Robin Krah, Niko Kremsmair, Markus Meister, Josef Niederbrucker, Christian Pausch

The Scorpion is an energy-efficient electric vehicle that took part in the 2016 Shell Eco-Marathon in London, where it competed in the Battery Electric energy class and the Urban Concept vehicle class. The object of the competition: to use as little energy as possible. Once again this year, u19 received numerous submissions from technical high schools (HTLs) in Austria.

This project's dimensions, complexity, and the extent to which it's been implemented are what especially impressed the jury. The project crew had a wide array of tasks to master: team management, chassis & doors, wheel suspension, steering, and pedal operation. On the project's websites, you can follow in clear, step-by-step fashion the developments and progress in the various areas. Furthermore, in light of the fact that the HTL Salzburg Racing Team exists since 2008, this project is a good example of a tradition and a body of know-how having been amassed at an educational institution over the years. The result is that each incoming class of students is powerfully motivated to surpass its predecessor in the race to achieve energy efficiency.

Guilt · Zeia Gholam

Guilt is an incredibly elaborate film production that tells the story of a father-son relationship amidst a milieu pervaded by violence, drugs, and fear. This very moving motion picture is excellent in numerous respects: fight scenes choreographed in great detail, the impressive depth of its treatment of the theme, and the professionalism of the cast. *Guilt* is an epic driven by culpability and revenge, a martial arts drama, a deeply moving account of human fates. Such a densely-packed and multifaceted film is a rare find indeed. Thanks for this great experience, one that holds up well to comparison with big-screen productions.

Kim's Life · Safia El Maataoui, Lena Krautinger

It takes a lot to tell a story without getting overly dramatic or banal about it. *Kim's Life* succeeded in impressing us on both visual and verbal levels; moreover, it produces strong emotions and effectively employs a reduction technique that triggers powerful images in the viewer's mind. Fleeing, asylum, life as a stranger, separation from family and friends: for countless people, this has become a way of life, though not one of their own choosing. Your

fictional account put this in simple terms that we find profoundly impressive. There's much to single out in this professionally produced film: the white wall, a credible lead actress, simple pictograms that symbolize life and flight—they all speak a clear language. We were not only impressed; we kept still, though not because we were speechless but rather touched. This makes a good film into a very good one.

reflecty · Felix De Montis, Johannes Eschner

reflecty is a smart mirror. For starters, it's a display that clearly presents useful information; plus, it's an interface that functions via gesture recognition for convenient control of a smart home's features. The displayed information such as weather forecasts and news is gathered from the internet, and the communication with the household appliances takes place via LAN. The work that's been done by Felix De Montis and Johannes Eschner is a lovely example of how a concept and hardware, software & design solutions can be assembled into a truly first-class package. Despite the fact that lots of examples of smart mirrors can be found online, the jury was really impressed by the many aspects this project has dealt with and really implemented—good design of the entire mirror including integration of the motion sensor, well-thought-out interface design, interaction with the interface via gesture recognition, display of current information via internet connection, control of household infrastructure, and outstanding documentation of the work, including assembly instructions in the form of a 3D animated sequence.

Salam Saeculum · Kasper Helml

This is the year's most fascinating and most elaborate musical project. The driving beat underpins subtly arranged sounds, and complex transitions infuse the entire piece with tension. *Salam Saeculum* was produced with Ableton, software that you have to invest quite a bit of time and effort into before you can work with it effectively. The title of the piece is made up of the Arabic word for "peace" and the Latin word for "the age." This dovetailing of languages—meant to get across a message on both the formal and the substantive levels—is indicative of the attention to detail exhibited by the entire piece. This enthralling work of sound art has greatly enriched u19-CREATE YOUR WORLD.

Teem · Emil Bruckner, Noel Kurtaran, Timo Lins

The *Teem* app is for use in discussions and meetings so that voice recognition software can analyze how long each participant has spoken. Thus, this fascinating tool clearly indicates how much or how little each person present has contributed to the conversation. Plus, *Teem* can sensitize those who repeatedly interrupt others. This is a way to empirically confirm impressions that a participating observer sometimes gets but are often dismissed as subjective figments of the imagination. The design and the concept promise an interesting app that can make a positive impact on social interaction. We hope that the concept can soon be implemented by the programmers too. By the way, we could sure have used this during the jury deliberations!

the best is yet to come

Alina Groer, Daniela Kubesch, Leo Mühlfeld

Your feature-animated film-documentary truly awed and amazed us. What you've achieved here is really outstanding! The selection of the theme, the animation, the interviews, the music, the editing—they're all very well done! This short film about our future uses an interesting combination of a journalistic format and animation. Randomly selected pedestrians, young and old alike, are asked about their conceptions of life in the future. In the animated sequences, the interviewees' statements are accompanied by humorous commentary and translated into imagery ranging from offbeat to downright bizarre. And precisely because much of what's said in the animated sequences seems to have been wrenched out of context, you're kind of taken aback and made to think. The journalistic part of the film exhibits empathy and understanding, and the animation displays a great deal of creativity. The most beautiful thing about *the best is yet to come* is that the work constitutes an invitation to those viewing it to develop their own takes on the images and visions of the future put forth on screen, to think them through in chains of association forged by their personal situations and their own life stories.

So now you're probably wondering why you "only" got an Honorary Mention instead of an Award of Distinction. Quite simply, there were a real lot of films among the entries (as usual), and we jurors are confronted by the problem of seeing to it that as many categories as possible (inventions, computer games, music, design & Web projects, et al.) get fair treatment. So just be proud of yourselves and take pleasure in your prize. You were among the best of the best!

A netidee SPECIAL PRIZE endowed with €1,000 is being awarded for the first time in 2016. It singles out for recognition a project dealing with the internet of the future and, above all, taking an innovative approach to this encounter. What problems can the internet of the future still "solve"? netidee is especially interested in projects that utilize the internet as a driving force for regional development. Special experts were called in to advise the jury in awarding this prize.

The focus of netidee is meant to be on the future of the internet as seen through the eyes of children and young people—those so-called digital natives who've grown up with it and for whom it's something taken completely for granted. Thus, the internet is becoming not only a medium but also a format that's replacing many familiar aspects of everyday life as well as preventing certain things from occurring. This critical confrontation is the aim of the netidee SPECIAL PRIZE 2016.

kameleon.ws

Ulrich Formann, Kilian Hanappy, Simon Wesp

kameleon.ws not only was awarded an Honorary Mention in the u19-CREATE YOUR WORLD category but also won this year's netidee SPECIAL PRIZE. It is such an interesting idea that really convinced the jury. The project crew applies the latest "news" to T-shirts and thus provides a tangible answer to the question "How does something new come about?" Here, generative design and creative coding are the main elements of an innovative approach to producing T-shirts. Each garment's motif is generated by computers that are capable of learning as well as composing graphics representing current events and breaking news stories. Each T-shirt is unique; as soon as the Web Shop sells it, a new design is produced. *kameleon.ws* can be read as a manifesto opposed to mass culture and for individuality. The reference to the news of the day functions purely as a quotation, but it's also an exhortation to pause and reflect. What's especially interesting about this project is the way it surfs the trend towards digital real-time communication and thus bears the inimitable imprint of the Snapchat Generation.

Die Entscheidung

Jonas Bodingbauer

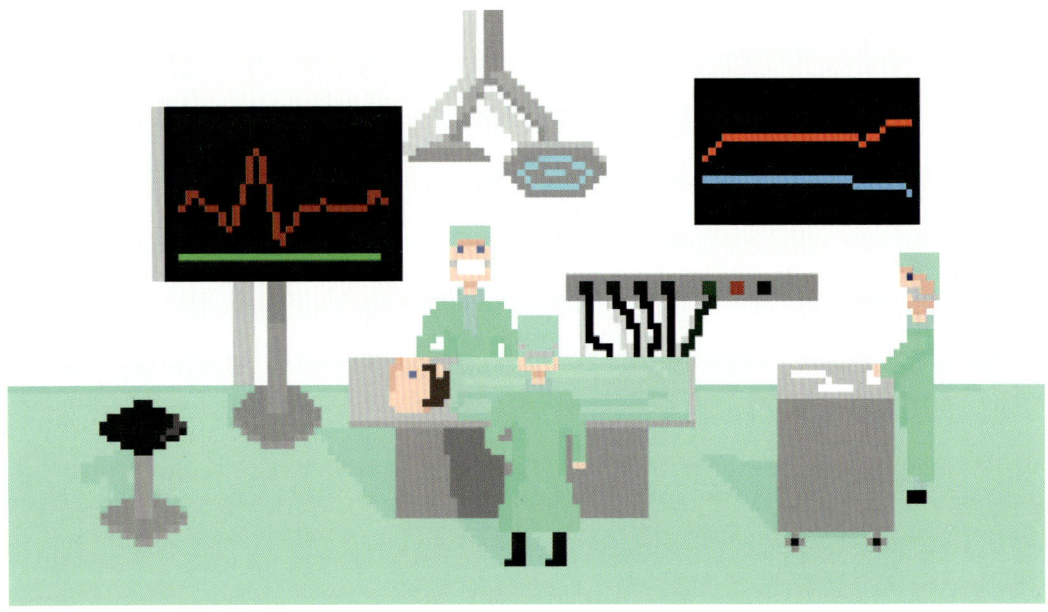

Die Entscheidung (The Decision) is a computer game for two players. What's at stake is life or death, as one of the players reaches a verdict on the survival of the other, though this doesn't become clear until the game is well underway.

Player 1 acts out the life of a man who's been diagnosed with cancer. The course of play offers numerous options as to what he can do during the remaining days of his life—for instance, the player can decide to spend time with his family, carry on with everyday life "as usual," or fulfill his lifelong dreams.

Player 2 simulates the cancer itself in that he can determine the decisive characteristics of the cancer cells. At the outset, he's assigned the task of killing the Subject (as Player 1 is referred to). But over the course of the game, he receives information about events in the life of the man afflicted with cancer. Thus, he is repeatedly made aware of the fact that, through his actions, he influences the life of a human being. At the game's climax, he has to decide whether to kill the Subject or not.

The idea behind this game is based in part on the Milgram Experiment in which participants were called upon to carry out ethically dubious assignments. Although they were cognizant of the fact that they were causing a human being to suffer, they obeyed the instructions they received without considering the consequences.

In many computer games, players have to perform tasks without giving any further thought to them. At the end of this game, both players are prompted to reflect upon the decisions they made.

http://jonasbodingbauer.jimdo.com/projekte/spiele/die-entscheidung

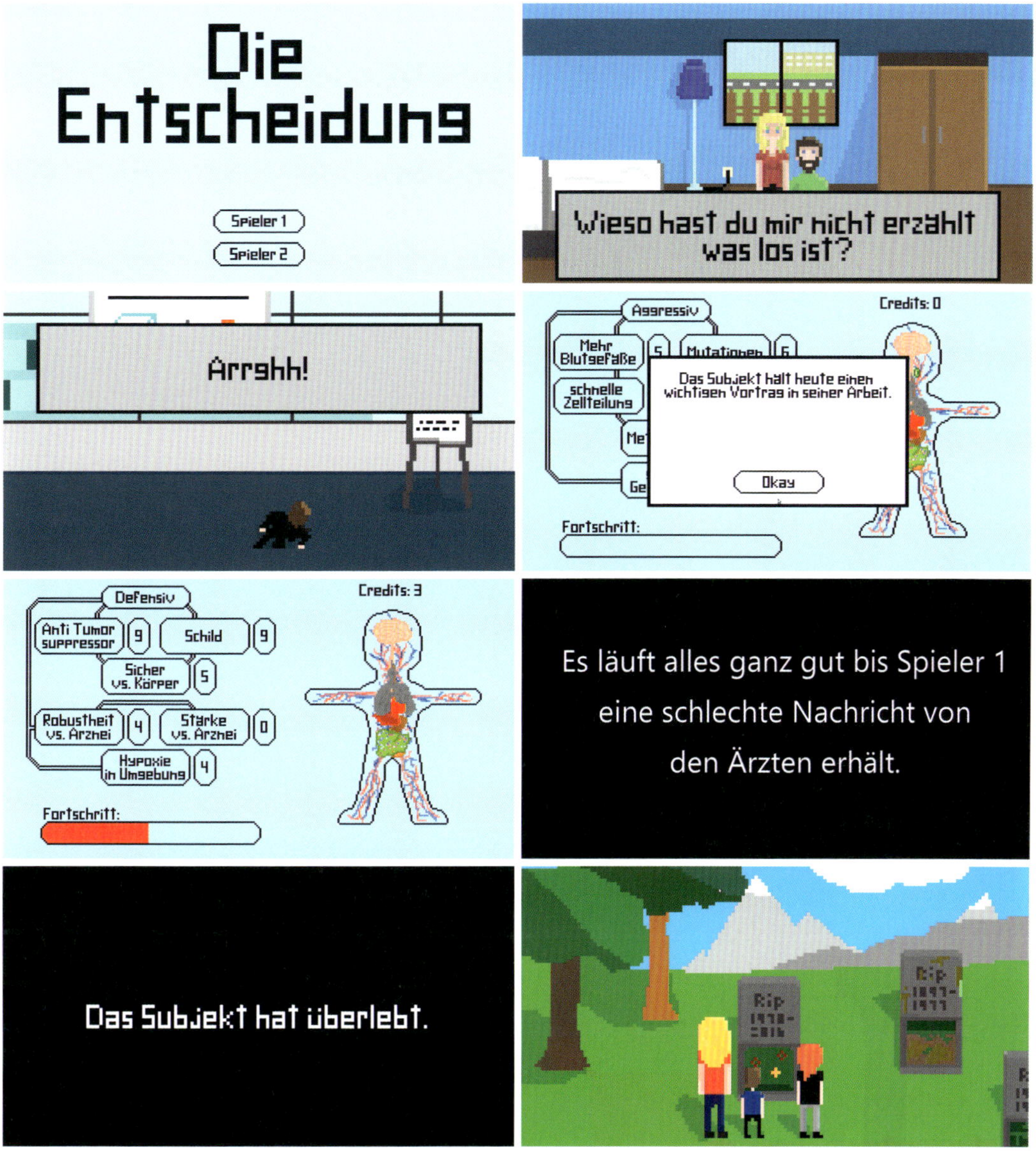

Die Entscheidung

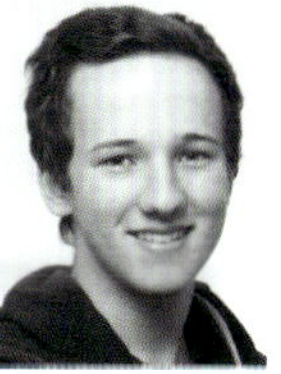

Jonas Bodingbauer was born in 1998. Since 2012 he has attended Leonding Technical College, where he's studying electronics and technical computing. By way of recreation, he likes to work with electronics and do programming, and deploy his skills in projects of his own design. In his spare time, he enjoys making music and doing volunteer work. In 2014 he was honored with an Award of Distinction in the u19 – CREATE YOUR WORLD category for his *SMART CLOCK* that displays appointments in addition to telling the time. He also takes part in the annual Physics Olympiad and has twice qualified for the nationwide competition.

Blackout

Jasmin Selen Heinz, Tanja Josic, Emily Poulter

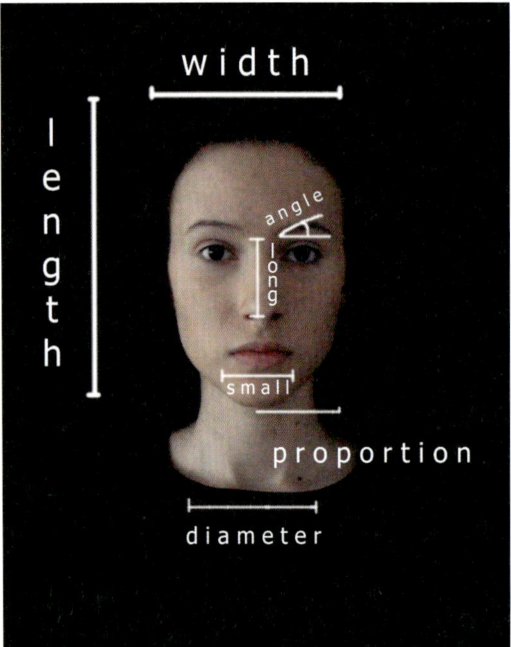

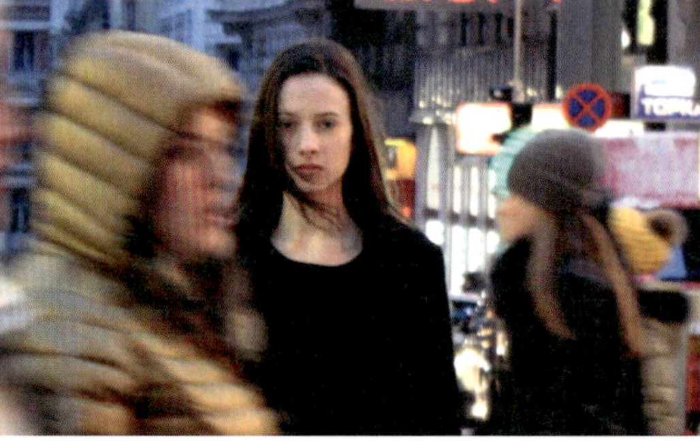

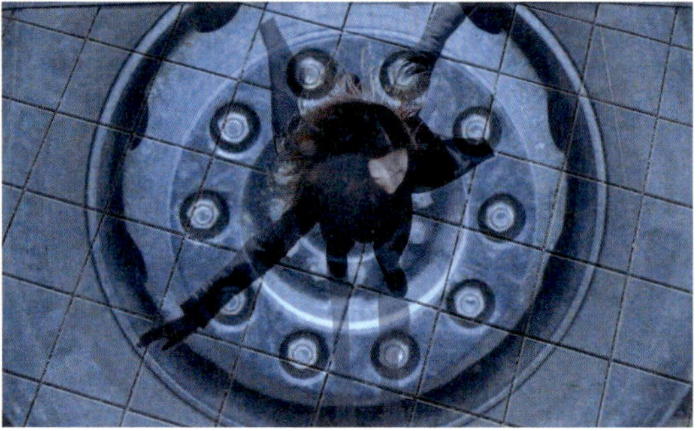

Blackout is a short experimental film about humankind's entanglement in an industrialized world, the attempt to break out of its snares, and the extinguishment of human identity. Via intentional sensory overload and excessive expectations, this film takes viewers on a thrilling, densely packed journey during which all feeling for time gets lost along the way.

In a brutally honest representation of reality, cities are equated with machines, and people are seen as cogs and screws in this mechanism, entities forced to function incessantly and error-free. Industry and society demand perfection from people—their appearance, their behavior, and the way they work. We live in a world constructed by human beings but we're moving further and further away from humaneness. In this system oriented on uniformity, there's no longer any place for individuality and creativity. Stress and the conventionalism imperative motivate the protagonist's breakout. The state of order shifts into disequilibrium. Nevertheless, the prevailing demand for people to conform to the prescribed ideal and to be perfect remains intact. But the human being can't meet these expectations, and deep black darkness devours the face.

vimeo.com/jasminselenheinz

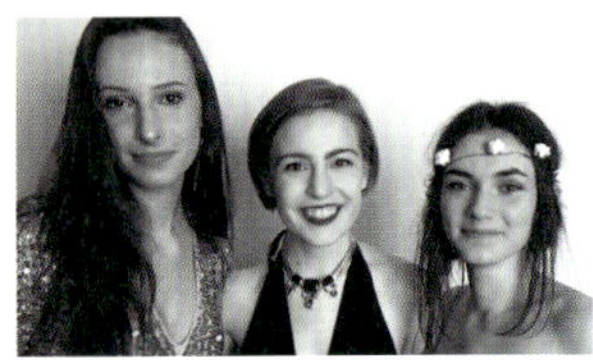

Jasmin Selen Heinz, Tanja Josic and **Emily Poulter** were schoolmates at Vienna's Draschestraße bilingual college preparatory school. They've been shooting films for several years now. *Blackout*, their first collaborative production, garnered them the audience prize and the jury prize at the video&filmtage 2015 film festival at the Urania Cinema in Vienna. The film was also screened at the Parachute Light Zéro III Edition international short film festival in Paris in April 2016.

Flucht
Dimitri Teufl

I've been fascinated by LEGO ever since my earliest childhood, and then when I entered elementary school I started getting interested in LEGO films too. For my first attempts at producing one myself, I used my cell phone. I didn't start working with a real camera until my *Flucht* (Fleeing) project, in which I used the stop-motion technique.

My teacher was already familiar with my LEGO musical films and she encouraged me to enter the Ars Electronica's u19 competition. When it came time to choose a topic, I happened to be reading a really sad book about a family that fled from Tunisia. I found this true story really touching, so one thing just led to another: the theme of my film would be fleeing.

https://www.youtube.com/channel/UCs_LI3TYNNxXScoXctxHcNw

So I got started with a Nikon D200, a tripod, a computer program named Magix and lots of LEGO. I also got a lot of useful knowledge from reading a book entitled *Ins Paradies?* (Into Paradise?)

I often had to reshoot a scene a couple of times until I was satisfied with it. After many hours of work—about 55 all together—I created the appropriate soundtrack for my 2,592 photos. Each one of them appears on screen for approximately one-tenth of second, since that's what it takes to produce fluid motion.

I hope that my project can offer a different point of view to people who are hostile towards refugees or are afraid of them.

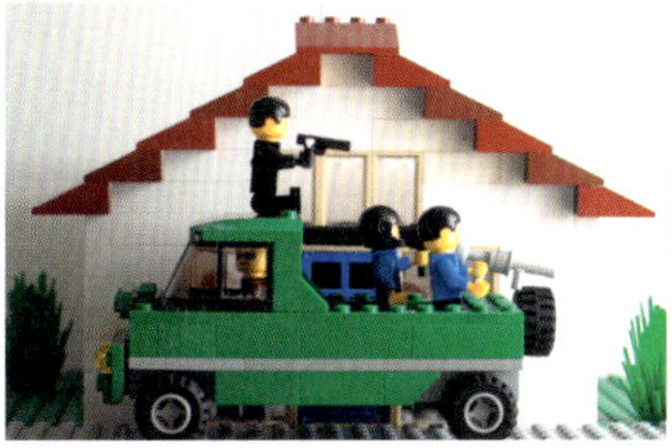

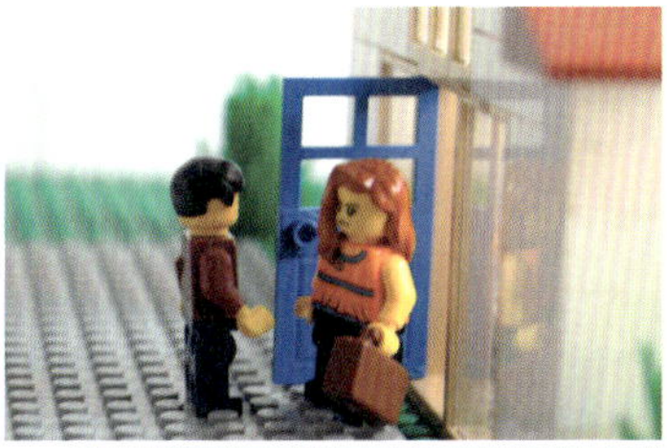

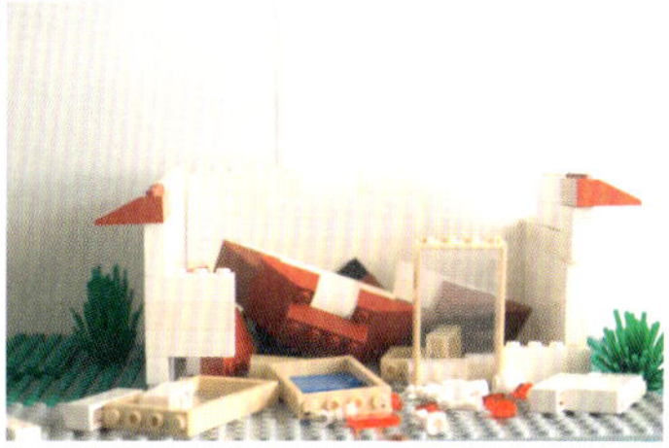

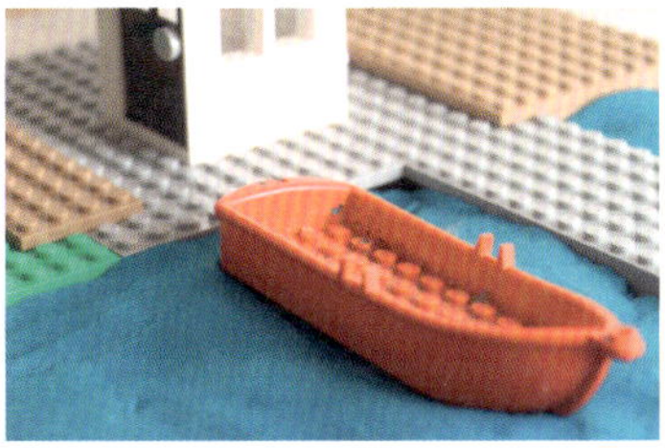

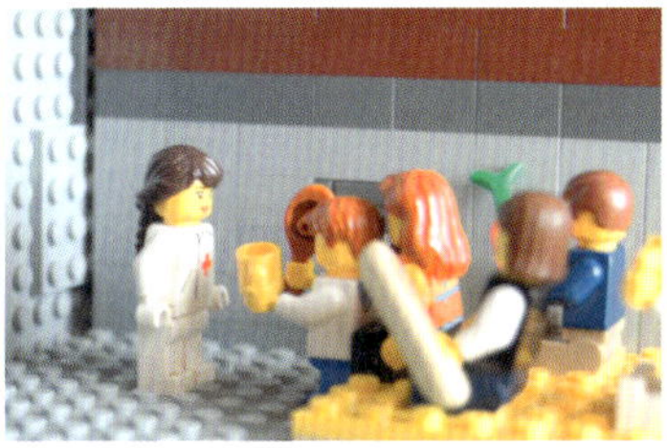

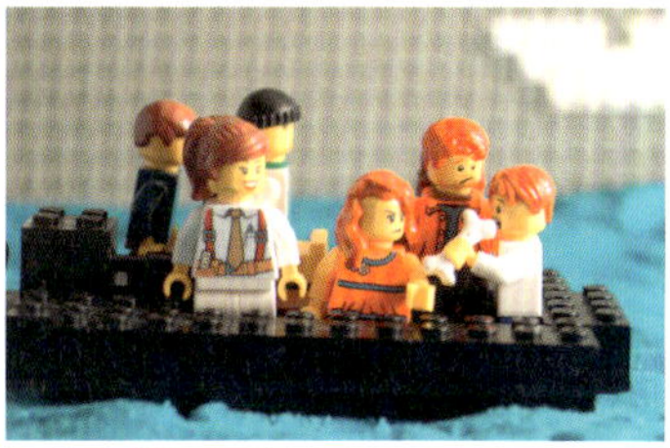

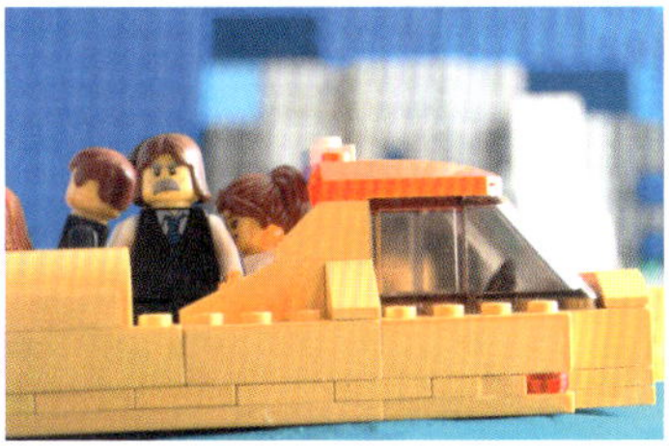

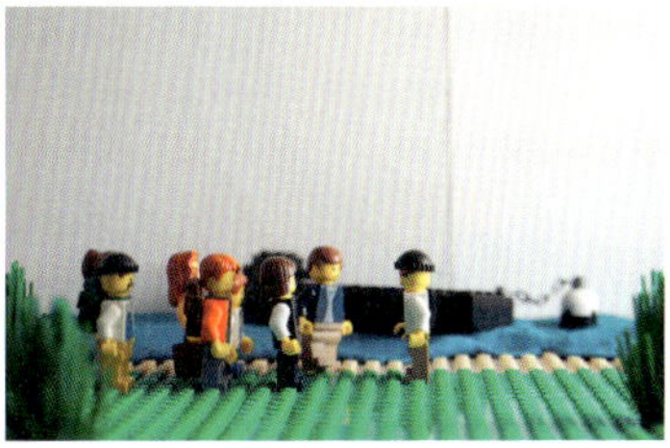

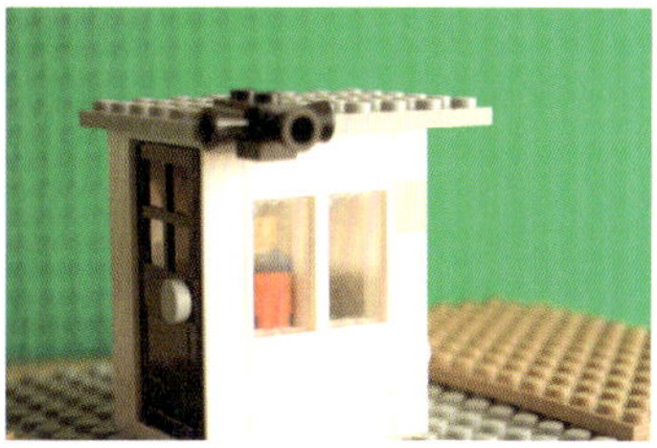

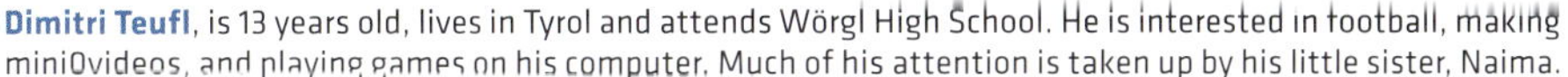

Dimitri Teufl, is 13 years old, lives in Tyrol and attends Wörgl High School. He is interested in football, making miniOvideos, and playing games on his computer. Much of his attention is taken up by his little sister, Naima.

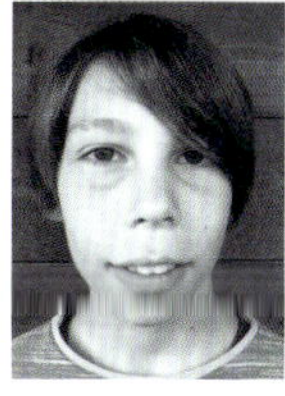

Skateboard Charging Unit
Fabian Krautgartner

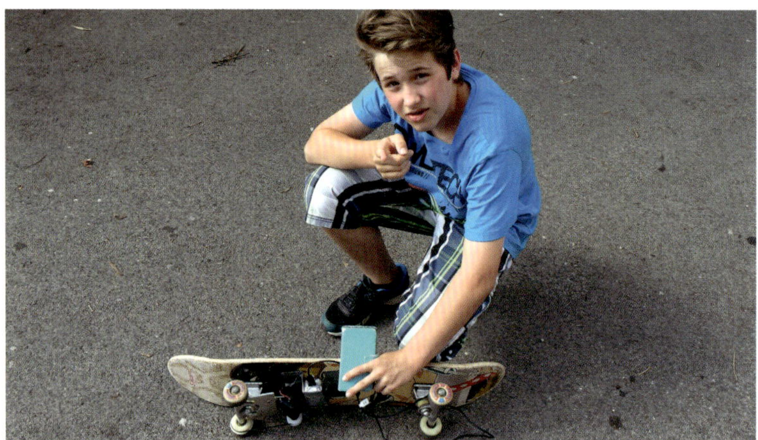

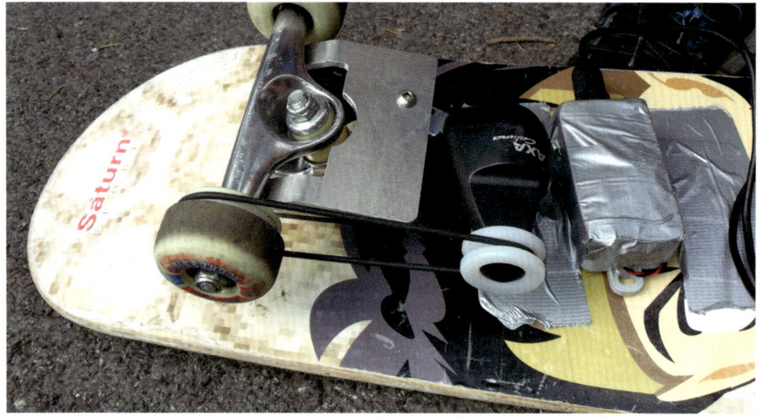

KLEX intermediate school has a cooperative arrangement with Frida und Fred, the Children's Museum in Graz. A while ago, environmental protection was the theme of the exhibitions there, and we had to do a project on this subject. Since my cell phone's battery was always running low, I thought about how I could recharge it more often. Then I realized that I could actually charge my cell phone on the way to school with my skateboard if it were equipped with a charging unit.

My father helped me install a dynamo on the underside of the board and, at the same time, an O-ring (actually a gasket) to drive the dynamo. Johannes, my counselor at Frida und Fred, helped me with the electronics. The biggest problem was transforming the alternating current from the dynamo into the direct current that we needed. Then all we had to do was adjust the transmission so that, with the average speed of a skateboard, enough voltage could be generated to recharge the battery. That took several hours of tinkering together with Johannes, my counselor at Frida und Fred.

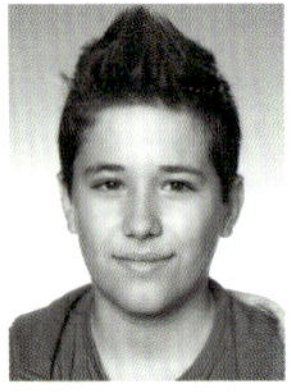

Fabian Krautgartner was born in 2002 and grew up in Graz. He attended KPH elementary school and then KLEX intermediate school. His hobbies are trampolining, playing PS4, reading, table tennis and, of course, skateboarding. He would say his biggest interest is in mythology, especially Greek and Egyptian. He is also interested in electronics—for instance, circuits. His current career plan is to be an EDP administrator.

Meine Webseite

Simon Heppner

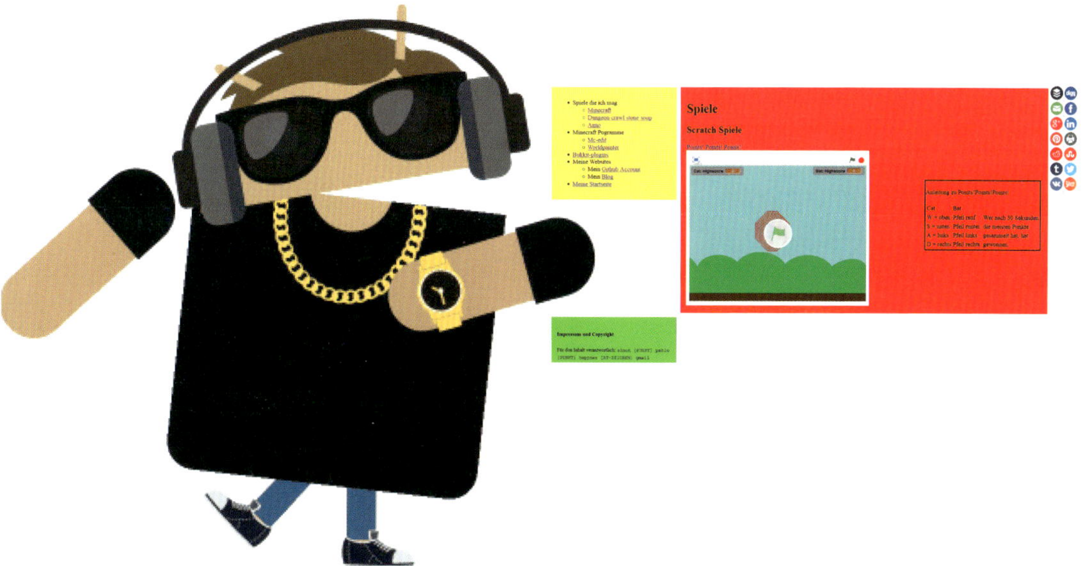

I'm submitting my colorful website, which I pro-grammed. The idea behind this is to publish all the games I program myself in the hope that somebody checks out my website and tries out the games.
My Dad set up the address *http://simon.heppner.at.* He's also the one who uploads the files for me when I want to change something. To create the HTML files, I usually use the editor from Geany, which I have on my USB stick so I can use any computer to run my Knop-pix Linux where I have my programming environment. I tried out HTML for the first time in Wordpress. Then my Dad showed me the *Selfhtml Handbuch,* and I experimented with a few commands. Later, I asked my programming teacher, Horst Jens, to teach me a little HTML. With the skills I acquired, I went on to set up my own website.

On my website, there's an Android mascot that I designed myself with the Androidify app. I created the animated GIF because my big brother showed me the app and it looked like a lot of fun. Until now, my website has had only one self-programmed game named *Points!Points!Points!,* which I programmed with Scratch. But more self-programmed open-source games will soon be appearing on my website. It also features links to my Minecraft blog and my Github account, which I need for my programming projects. I'd like to express my thanks to my programming teacher, Horst Jens, who helped me a lot and who gave me the idea to take part in this competition!

http://simon.heppner.at

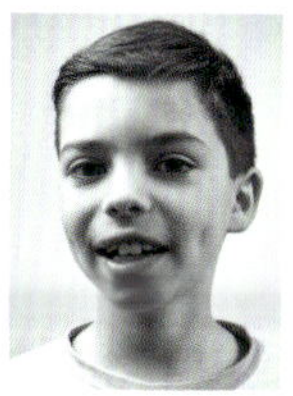

Simon Heppner was born in 2006 in Vienna. I have a big brother who's already 16. Since I can speak not only German but also Burgenland Croatian, I attended Viverica bilingual kindergarten in Vienna. I'm currently in the 4th grade at Keplerplatz Elementary School, a bilingual English-German school. In autumn, I'll enter the Europe Class at Sacre Coeur high school in Vienna, where my brother is in the 6th grade and my Mom's a teacher. Up to now, I've gotten all As on my report card and on my homework too. I used to play the piano, but now I can take a course in programming. My hobbies are programming in Python, tennis, Minecraft, and playing with my pet hamster, Harry. I also go hiking once in a while (when my Dad forces me to go with him).

BIOKoSMoS–BioInk for Art
BIOKoSMoS Group

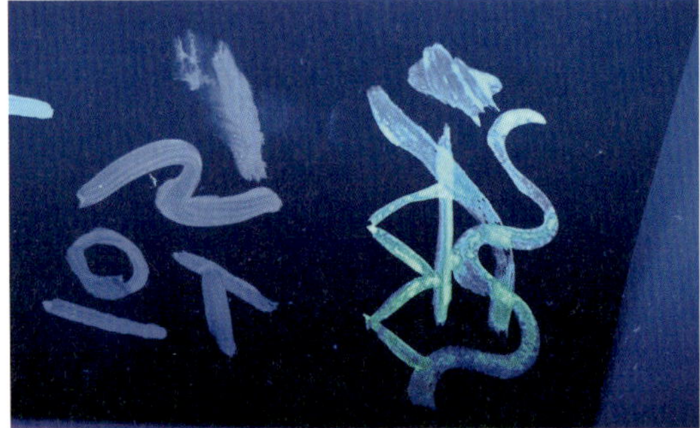

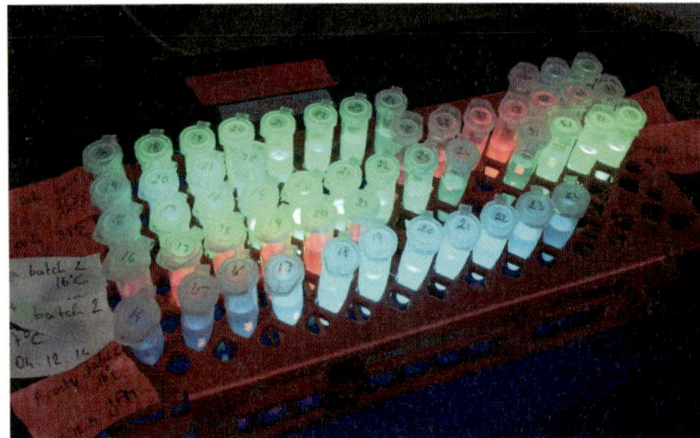

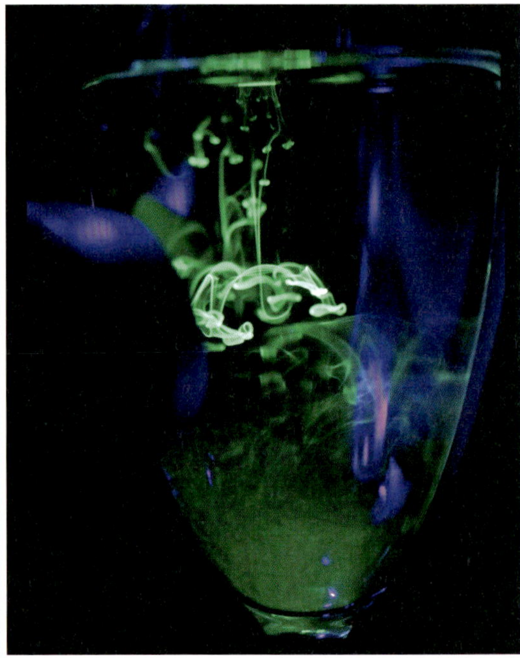

The aim of the *BioInk* project is to produce DIY ink the same way that artists did in bygone days. But now, this is done with new methods from the field of biotechnology. *BioInk* makes use of the glowing fluorescent inks produced by the deep-sea crown jellyfish, a color system that's never before been used in this form for artistic work. In the *BIOKoSMoS* project sponsored by the Austrian Federal Ministry of Science, Research and Economy's Sparkling Science Funding Program, pupils attending five partner schools have been working for two years at the nexus of art, research and education.

To produce *BioInk,* molecular-biologically modified bacteria and wheat seedlings are combined in a lab to process multicolored glowing protein from crown jellyfish. Young researchers and artists first cleanse the materials in a lab, but in this form, it's not yet suitable for artistic work. Using a wide variety or ideas and methods, the youngsters modify the protein so that it can be used as artistically processed material. Green fluorescent protein (GFP) is currently available as a watercolor-like paint or as glowing chalk. A few of the students have even been using the protein as a textile dye and a wood stain. A group of artists is currently experimenting with a paintable protein gel. And those are only a few of this work's spinoffs. These "new forms of paint" are for use in artistic encounters and projects. Could it be that, sometime in the 21st century, artists will be able to produce, adapt and mix their own paints in their own little garage lab and thus attain independence from industrial manufacturers? *BioInk* is the first step.

http://www.biokosmos.org
http://www.sparklingscience.at

BIOKoSMoS Group. The work on the *BIOKoSMoS* project was done by 100 students attending five schools, some with an enriched program in science, others in art: BG/BRG Judenburg, BG/BRG Reutte, BG/BRG/BORG St. Johann/Pongau, Musisches Gymnasium Salzburg, Gymnasium/ORG Ort Gmunden. The artistic part of the project was coordinated by Reinhard Nestelbacher; the scientific advisor was Michael Wallner of the University of Salzburg. The *BIOKoSMoS* project has received support from the Sparkling Science Funding Program.

COPY/PASTE
Fachstelle beteiligung.st

COPY/PASTE is a short film that was developed and shot in only six days. At the very first preproduction session, the 13 young filmmakers agreed on "the individual in the group" as their theme. All the production assignments—jointly writing the script, casting, location scouting, drawing storyboards, developing the visual concept and everything that goes into planning a film shoot—were carried out by the young people themselves. They also handled the jobs on the set: assistant director, cameraman/woman, sound engineer, and lighting technician.

The outcome is a short film that takes a thoroughly ironic, self-reflective look at the group's own behavioral dynamics. What happens when you're chosen against your will to serve as an example to be emulated? When there's hardly any room for individuality, and you want to break out of the group? That's what *COPY/PASTE* is all about.

"Yeah, sure—I mean, don't get me wrong. I like my friends, and actually that's totally great! You know, it's, like, flattering. But there comes a point …" At that point, Luisa's had it up to here, and she launches her project: Stop being a role model! Luisa wants to take a path "where simply nobody can follow in my footsteps." Sounds easy, but it's anything but!

COPY/PASTE was produced by participants in a film workshop held by beteiligung.st, die fachstelle für kinder-, jugend- und bürgerInnenbeteiligung, an organization in Graz whose mission is to foster community involvement by young people. The project's artistic supervisor was director Jakob M. Erwa.

http://www.beteiligung.st/jugend/Site/beteiligung-jugendhomepage/Film-beTEILigt/COPY-PASTE

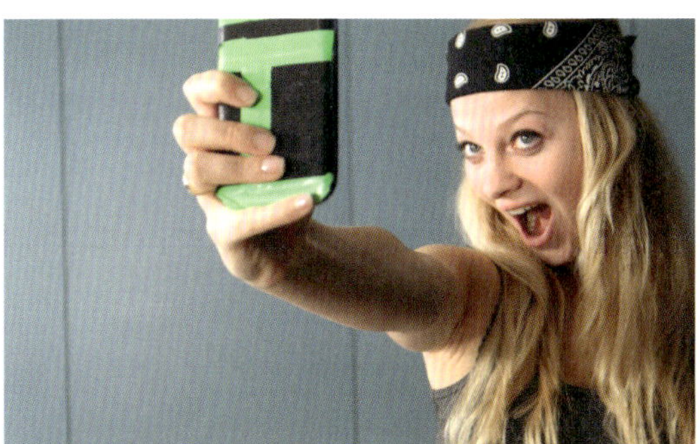
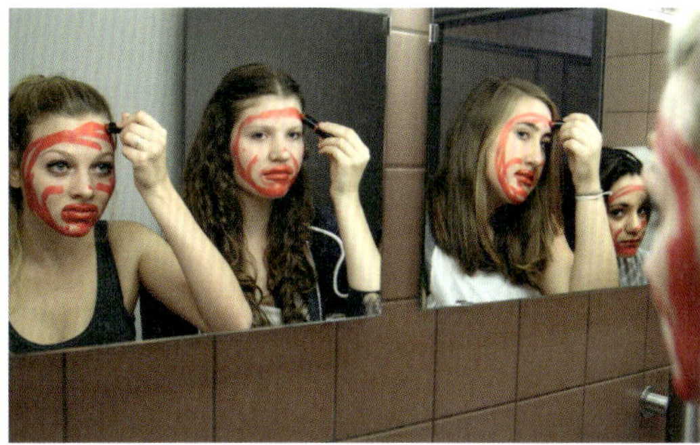
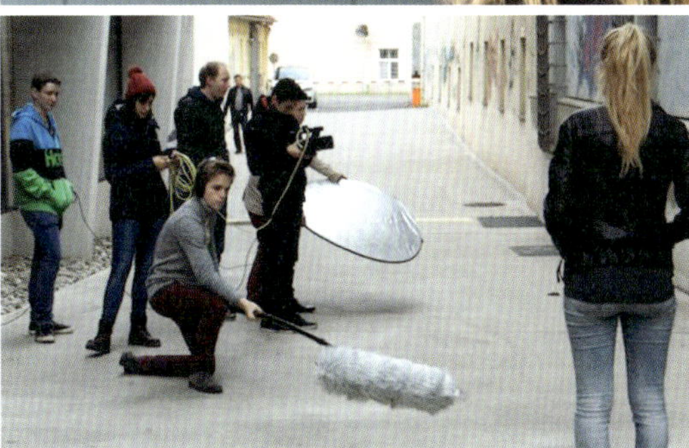
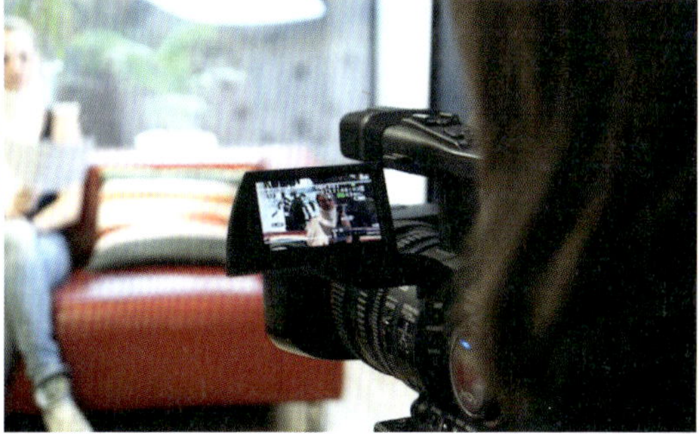

13 students aged 15-18 years from various schools and teaching facilities in the Austrian Province of Styria took part in this project organized by Fachstelle beteiligung.st: Sandra Gruber (1999); Elisa Bodinghauer (1998); Jana Stolz (1998); Lisa Zelenka (1999); Nadja Tulacs (1998); Ronja Krobatschek (1998); Sophie Schmidt (1998); Andreas Schweighart (1999); Christoph Strohmayer (1999); Maximilian Mandl (1997); Paul Kalcher (1997); Elias Rauchenberger (1997), and Fatih Yalcin (1997).

Scorpion – The Electric Vehicle

Niko Kremsmair, Christian Pausch, Robin Krah, Josef Niederbrucker, Markus Meister

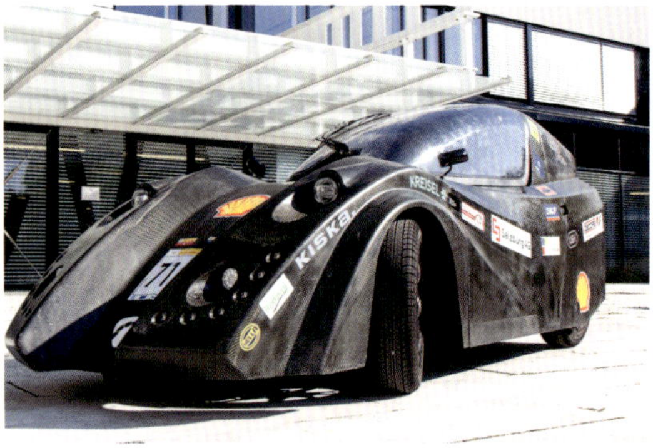

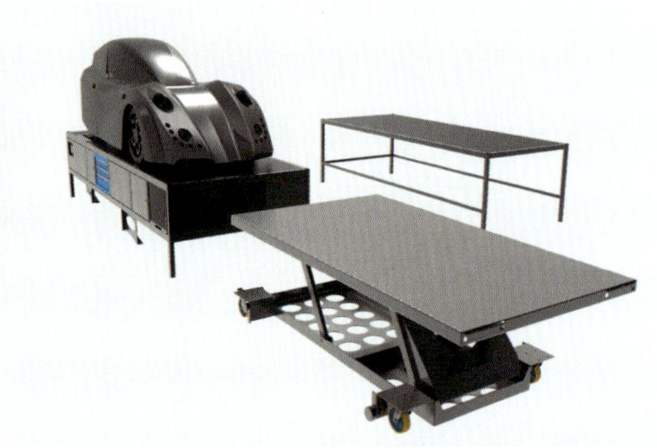

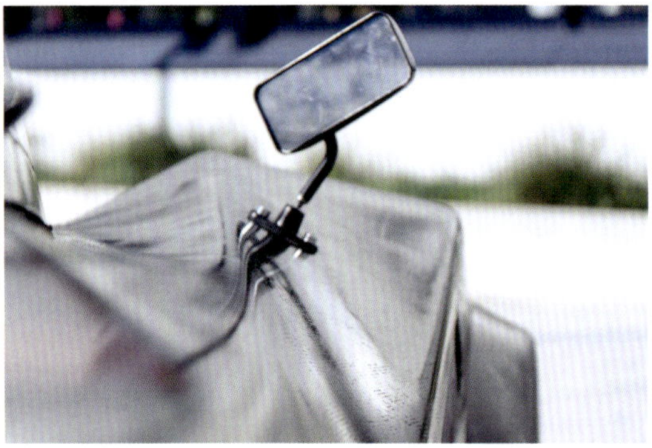

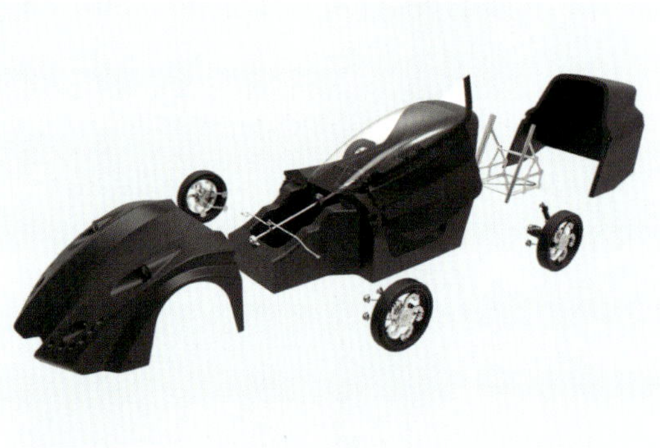

The *Scorpion* is an energy-efficient electric vehicle that took part in the 2016 Shell Eco-Marathon in London, an annual competition among teams from a wide array of countries. The mission: use as little energy as possible. The *Scorpion* competed in the Battery Electric energy class and the Urban Concept vehicle class. Most of the competitors in the Shell Eco-Marathon are university teams, which is why we're especially proud to have been able to represent a secondary school. Our participation was made possible above all by sponsors who supported

http://www.htl-sbg-racing-team.at
http://www.youtube.com/watch?v=ckqg5MLdcuE
http://www.facebook.com/fichtenelch.scorpion

us financially as well as in the form of material and know-how. So far costs of more than tens of thousands of Euro have been incurred. Students in several graduating classes working in various departments have contributed to this project; each year, it's been passed along to a new crew that has, in turn, made the *Scorpion* its diploma project. Thus, lots of fresh, innovative ideas have been the driving forces behind ongoing enhancement and upgrading. One of our objectives was to turn in a successful trial heat at the Shell Eco-Marathon. We're also very much interested in motivating others to develop energy-efficient vehicles and to keep on advancing this trend.

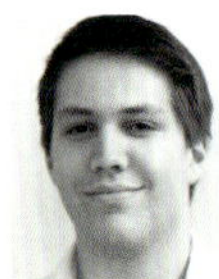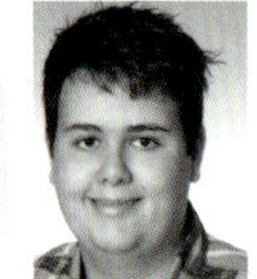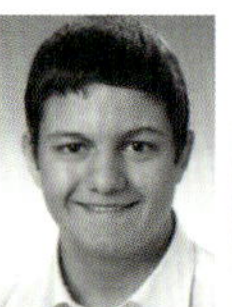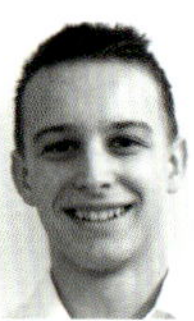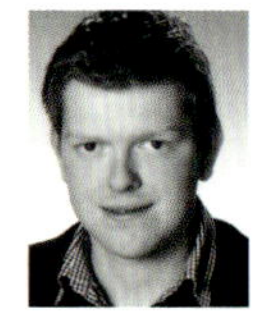

All five of us—**Niko Kremsmair, Christian Pausch, Robin Krah, Josef Niederbrucker,** and **Markus Meister**—were born in 1997 and are taking mechanical engineering at HTBLuVA Technical School in Salzburg. In our fourth year, we already had the honor of working on this incredible project. Now, at the conclusion of our secondary school career, the *Scorpion* is our diploma project.

Guilt
Zeia Gholam

I shot my first video together with my brothers, Yasin and Joma Gholam, and our friend Patrick Riesenberger. Since then, our crew—dubbed GURG—has been producing short films.
Would you do everything for your siblings? Even give your life for them if you had to?
I, my GURG crew, and our friend Kathrin Schneller shot *Guilt* in an effort to show that there are people who love their family more than themselves, and the family's happiness is more important to them than their own. Plus, we wanted to show that if you do illegal work, you can never lead a happy life—there's constant stress, fear of the police, fights and so forth.

"Forget about it, and earn your money doing legitimate work!"

http://www.youtube.com/gurg90
http://www.facebook.com/gurg90

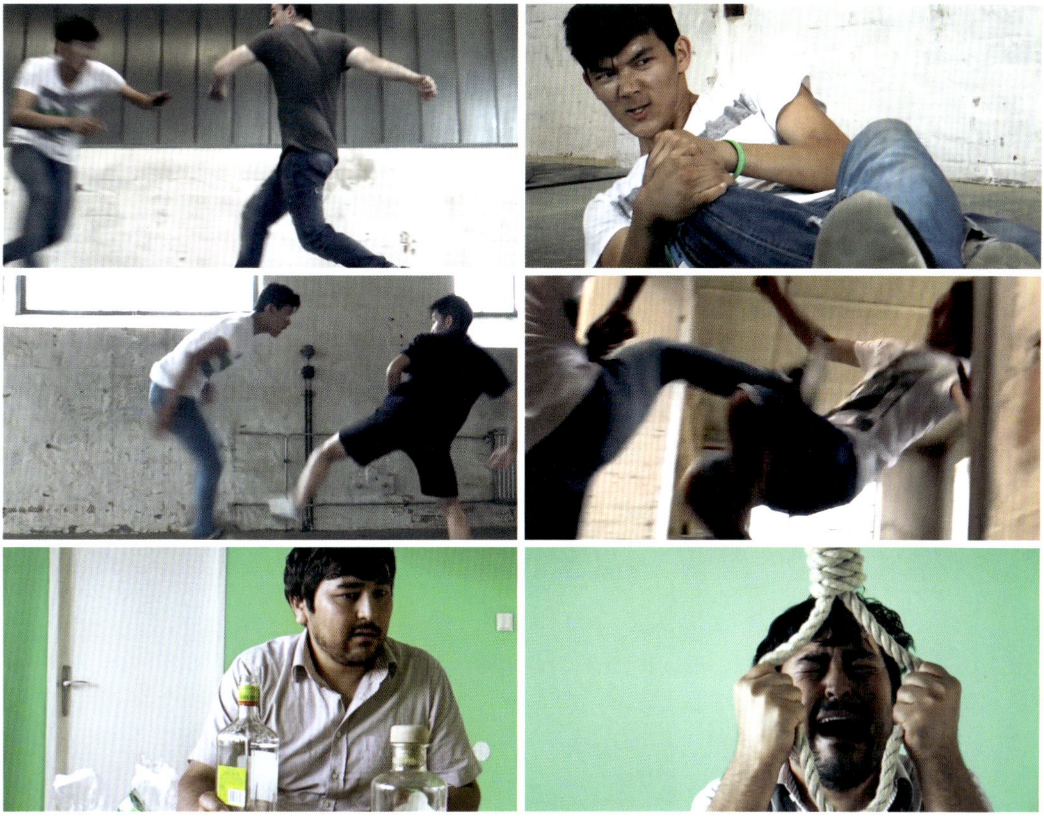

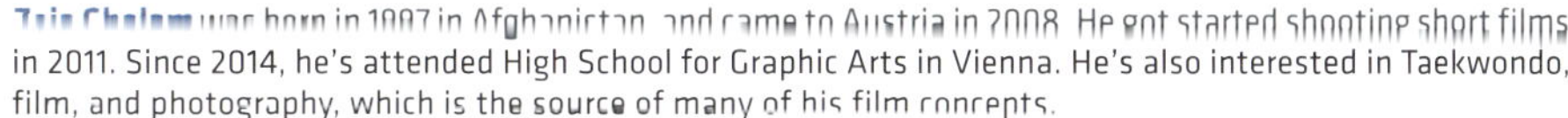

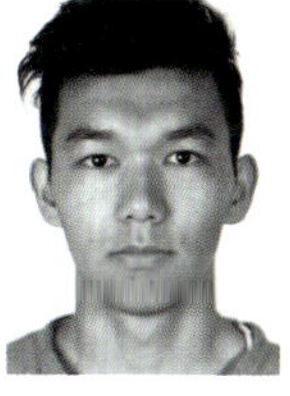

Zeia Gholam was born in 1997 in Afghanistan, and came to Austria in 2008. He got started shooting short films in 2011. Since 2014, he's attended High School for Graphic Arts in Vienna. He's also interested in Taekwondo, film, and photography, which is the source of many of his film concepts.

Kim's Life
Lena Krautinger, Safia El Maataoui

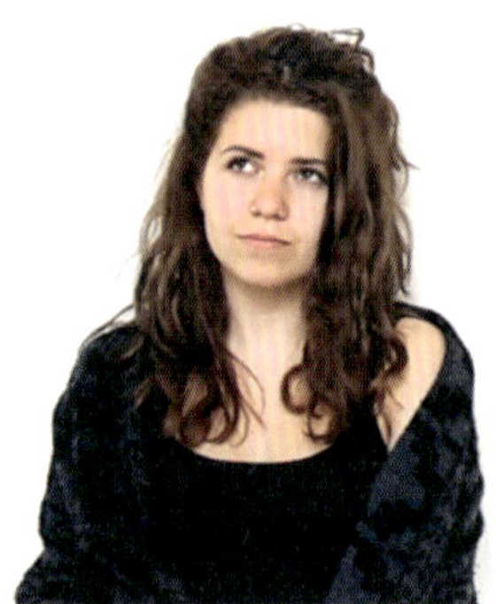

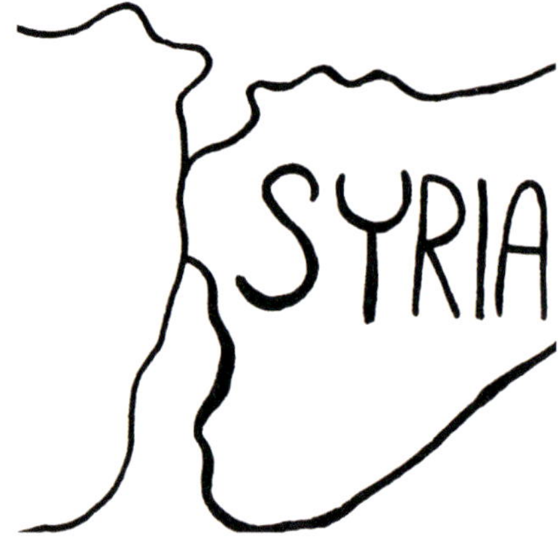

We started working on the film *Kim's Life* in June 2015, when the media all began covering the refugee crisis and this became the main subject of conversation among people we associate with. We perceived the general aversion towards refugees among lots of people, and we decided to make this film to counteract the insinuations and negative generalizations. We spoke with refugees, who gave us accounts of how they had fled. In this way, we were able to get first-hand knowledge. And in conjunction with several social welfare projects we participated in—for example, German courses and child care—we became aware of refugees' strong desire to get integrated in this society. The actress did such a great job putting herself into their position, and we made a concerted effort to bring our personal experiences into the production. To create the animated film running in the background, we drew images on Post-its, photographed each one individually, and fitted them to the background in post-production. Without wanting to generalize in any way, we're attempting to get across the following message in this film: Just because we were forced to leave our homes, we didn't turn into criminals.

http://www.youtube.com/watch?v=tb-TZgxtgQE

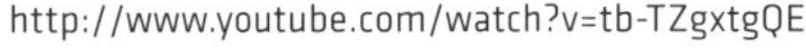

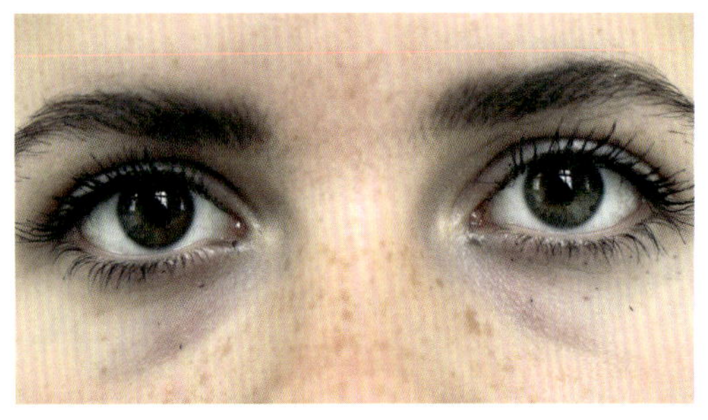

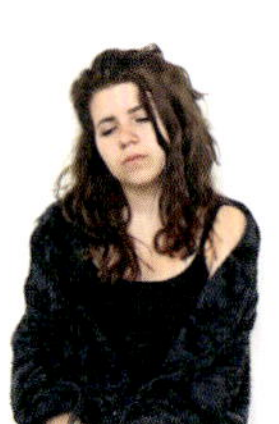

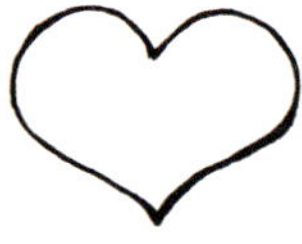

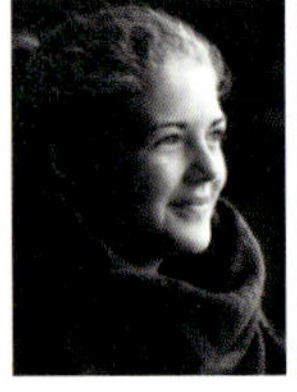

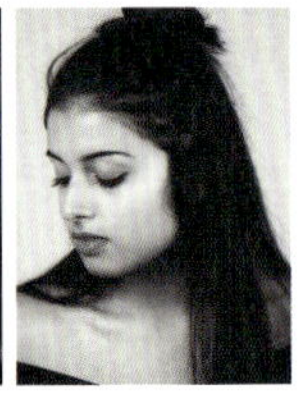

We, **Lena Krautinger** and **Safia El Maataoui**, are both 17 years old. We were born in Vienna and grew up here. We attend BORG 1 High School, where we major in audiovisual media. We've always been passionate about working with cameras. Our major primarily entails photography and filmmaking, but we work with lots of other media too, and this has provided us with motivation for several projects we've done in our spare time.

reflecty
Felix De Montis, Johannes Eschner

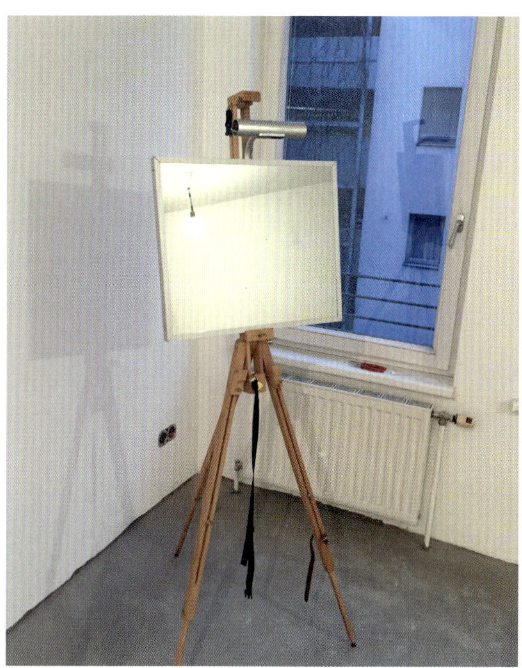

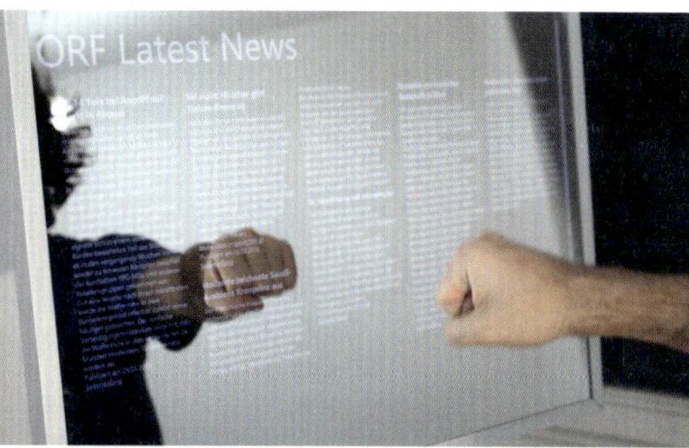

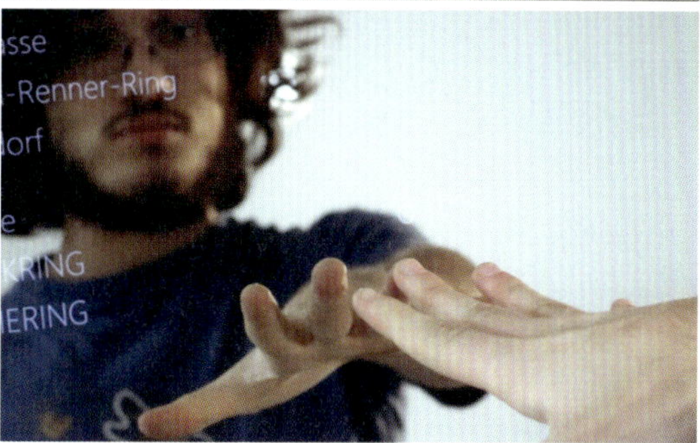

reflecty is a smart mirror that helps control a networked home and looks great doing it. Basically, *reflecty* consists of two key components: a one-way mirror with an integrated monitor for information display, and a gesture recognition sensor to input commands. The software, which features a graphical user interface, is linked via various interfaces to household appliances and online services. In this way, residents can, for example, access a weather forecast and switch the lights on and off. When *reflecty* isn't in use, there's nothing about it that suggests it isn't a common, everyday mirror. Thus, in contrast to a conventional monitor, the mirror fits seamlessly into the home's interior décor and isn't the least bit obtrusive. In addition to the hardware that we've endeavored to integrate into the residential ambience, we've made every effort to design the software to be as modular as possible. All the applications that run on *reflecty* are composed of very simple modules, so that anybody with even basic Web design skills can conveniently develop their own programs to connect new devices to *reflecty*. Finally, *reflecty* is meant to serve as the brain of a networked household, a computer that can be operated intuitively, a central processing unit for all information important to the home.

http://reflecty.co
http://www.youtube.com/c/reflecty
http://twitter.com/reflectyco

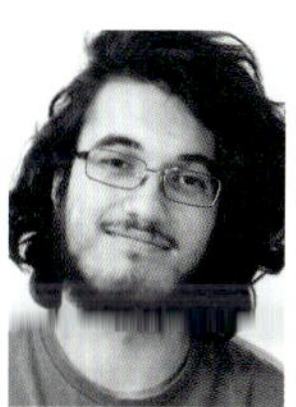

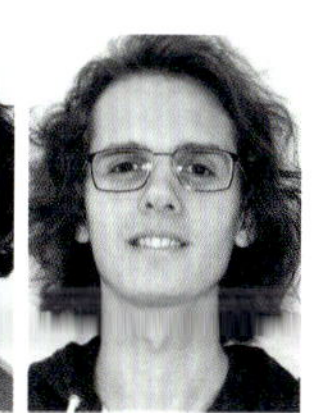

Felix De Montis and **Johannes Eschner** were both born in 1997 and have been working on projects in the field of computer science ever since they were schoolboys. Felix programs various (Web) projects; Johannes specializes in (3D) design and visualization. Together, they enjoy tinkering on their inventions' hardware.

Salam Saeculum

Kasper Helml

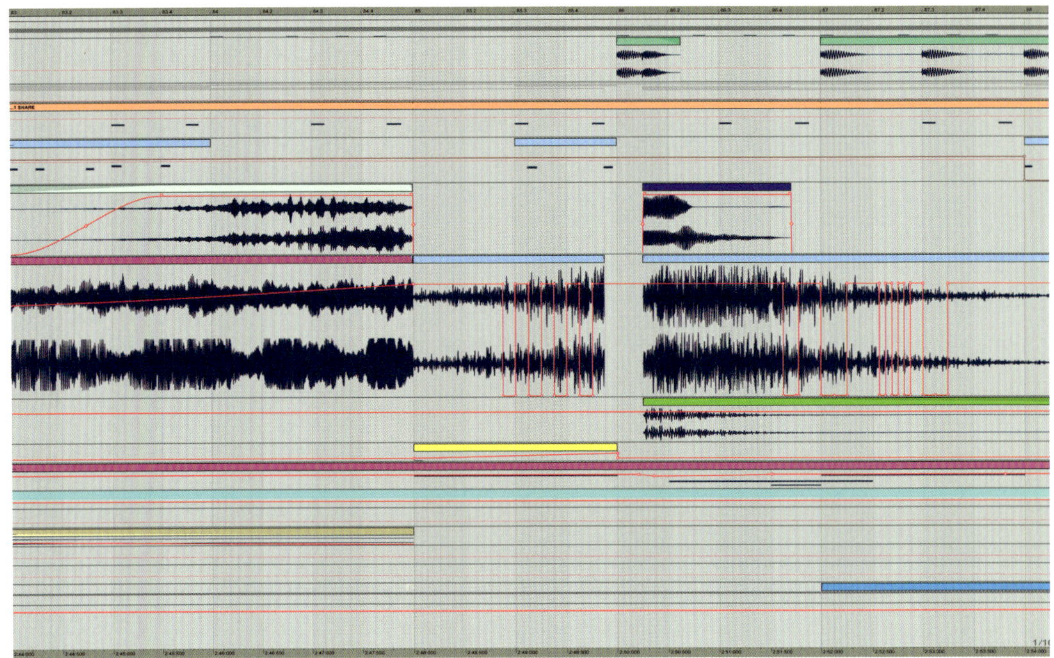

For about three years now, I've been attending Marco Palewicz's *Soundfactory* course offered collaboratively by the Linz Music School and the Ars Electronica Center, and in my spare time I produce music with *Ableton Live. Salam Saeculum* is my first completed track. My initial approach was very intuitive and playful; gradually, acoustic ideas began to emerge in more sharply defined terms, and images I conceived were translated into sounds. The beat is followed by synthesizer lines; then I added the voices and various instruments and effects; the entire work consists of 20 individual audio tracks.

The title *Salam Saeculum* is made up of the word *salam,* which means "peace" and is also used as a greeting, and *saeculum* meaning "age", "generation" or "lifetime".

http://soundcloud.com/luicaspar/salam-saeculum

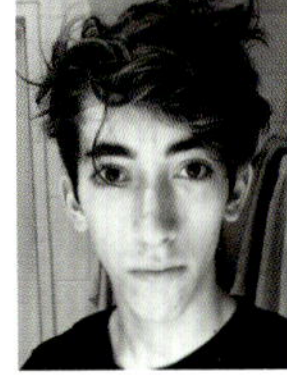

Kasper Helml was born in 1999 and grew up in a rural part of Upper Austria's Mühlviertel region. Since 2009, he's been a city boy in Linz, where he now attends college preparatory school. He's also a student of Marco Palewicz and is already in the 6th semester of the *Soundfactory* course held jointly by Linz Music School and the Ars Electronica Center, where he's learning electronic music production with Ableton Live.

Teem

Timo Lins, Emil Bruckner, Noel Kurtaran

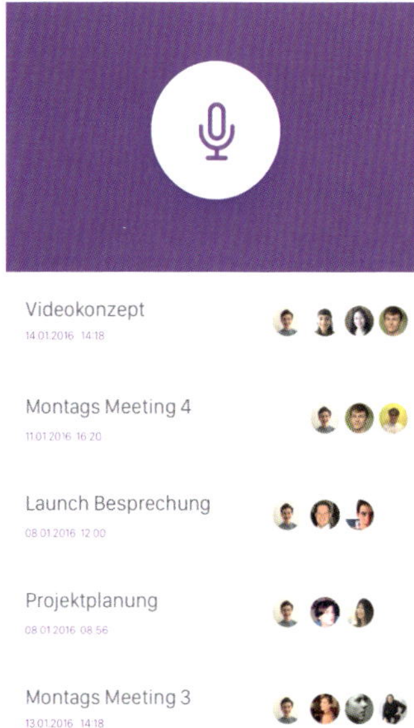

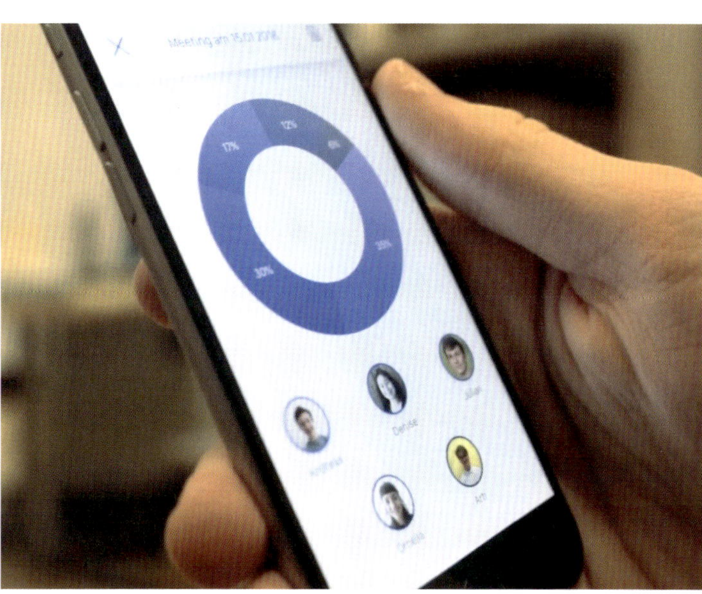

Speech recognition is a much-used technology we're all familiar with, but do we take advantage of its full range of possibilities? Computers have long been able to comprehend what we say; nevertheless, do they also recognize who's saying it? How can we utilize this technology?

This is precisely the question we posed before seeking problems that can be solved with this technology. In most applications available today, speech recognition functions strictly as a means of issuing commands to a computer. But the device can also listen to users and actively provide them with support.

In many forms of group communication, certain individuals tend to monopolize the conversation, and there are those who behave reactively since the others are doing all the work anyway. So it's often the case that participation in the conversation is distributed unequally.

Since, especially in business settings, such conversational imbalance can lead to deficiencies and losses, we decided to design an app for meetings. After extensive planning, we developed a prototype that demonstrates how the app works.

A video seemed to us to be the ideal means of convincing others of the value of our idea. In this way, the software's features and advantages are easy to highlight.

The basic idea is that the app starts up and then listens in, whereby it notes not only what's said but also who's saying it. Thus, it registers conversational participation during a meeting and documents it afterwards in the form of comprehensive statistics. This creates awareness and fosters more effective conversations.

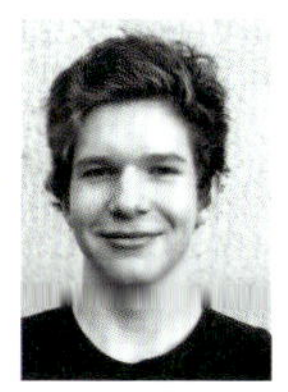
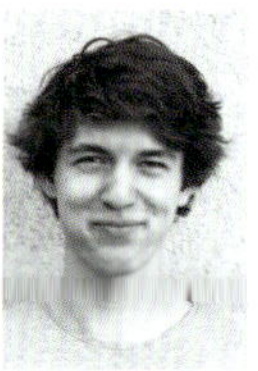
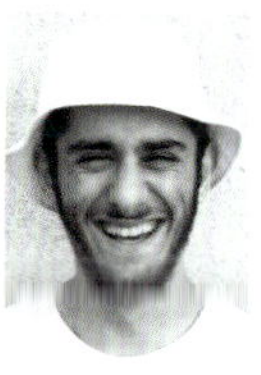

Timo Lins (born in 1997), **Emil Bruckner** (born in 1998) and **Noel Kurtaran** (born in 1996) are three creative individuals with big visions and goals. In the wake of academic career paths that could hardly have been more diverse, they first met up in 2012 at Vienna's High School for Graphic Arts. They've already collaborated on several projects, one of which is *teem*.

the best is yet to come

Daniela Kubesch, Alina Groer, Leo Mühlfeld

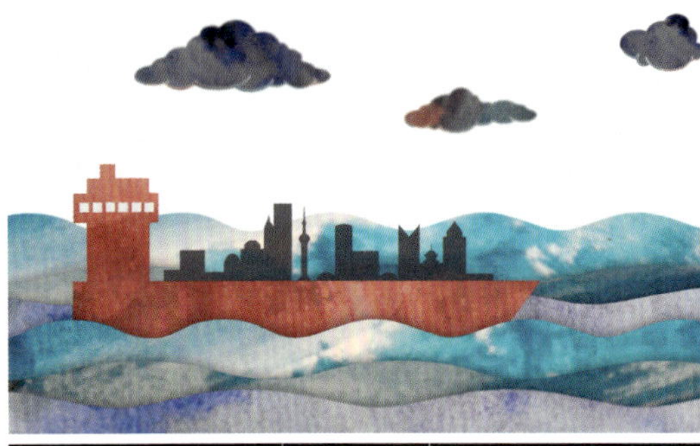
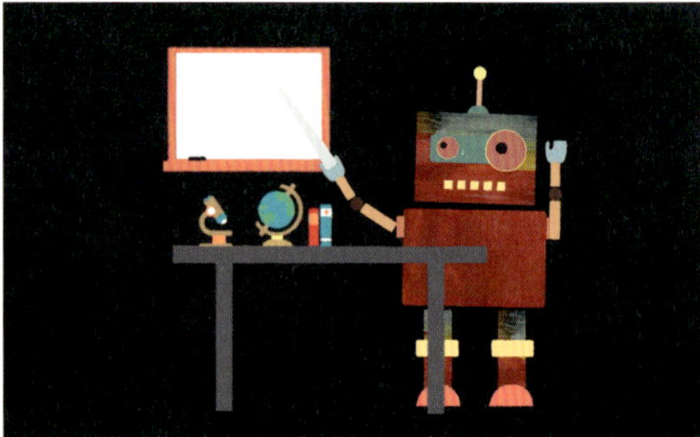
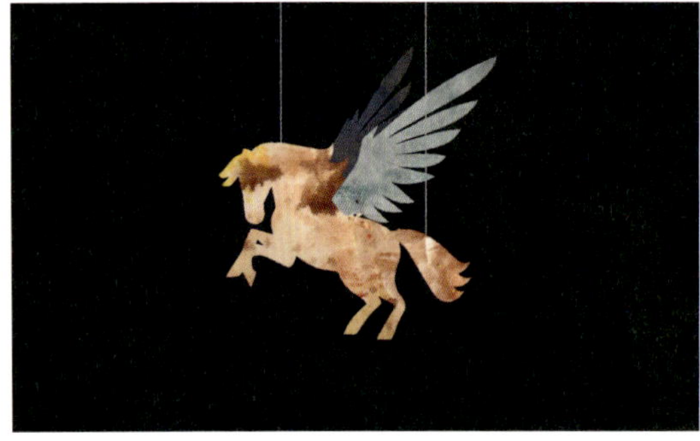
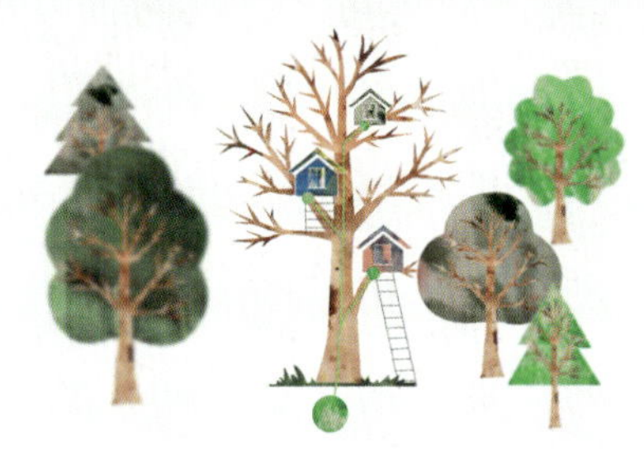

How do you imagine the future? This question occupies the focal point of our project. We went out and asked grown-ups and young people about their conceptions of, dreams about, and wishes for the future. Our primary aim in going about this wasn't to find out people's realistic expectations of the future but rather to learn how they desired the future to turn out.

What will change? Will we become increasingly progressive or will we take a step backwards and give more consideration to nature?

The question on which we concentrated was: How would people in the various age groups design their own world if they had the opportunity to create everything they wanted? How could people get around?

What new inventions would there be? What would houses look like? Those are a few of the many questions we posed. Furthermore, we were interested in how people see themselves. What would be their occupation of choice? Or what are some of the other things they'd like to accomplish in life? We evaluated all these ideas and conceptions and depicted them graphically.

Narratives of future inventions, pets, clothing styles, etc. were expressed in the form of vector graphics and then assembled into animated sequences. The result is a combination of filmed interviews and cartoons that link up the ideas and wishes of lots of people in different age groups. We've attempted to portray a shared future world that interweaves everyone's wishes for a better future for all of us together.

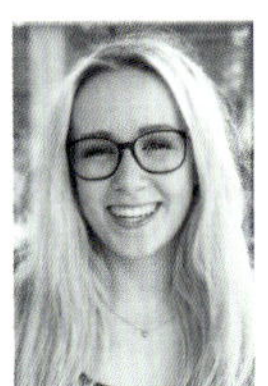
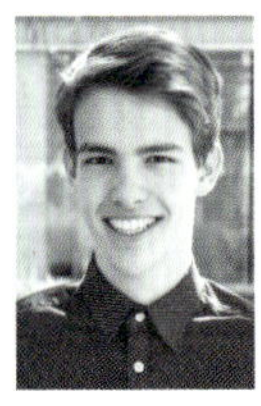
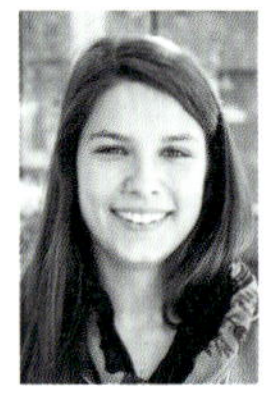

Daniela Kubesch, born in 1998, is currently enrolled in the Multimedia program at the High School for Graphic Arts in Vienna. She's pursued her many interests in a wide array of projects ranging from graphic design and programming to film and animation. **Leo Mühlfeld** was born in 1998 in Lustenau, and grew up in Vienna, where he currently attends the High School for Graphic Arts, a technical educational institution for media & communications design. **Alina Groer**, born in 1998, is currently in her junior year in the Multimedia program at the High School for Graphic Arts in Vienna. In numerous projects she cultivates her interests in the fields of graphic arts, animation, photography, and film.

kameleon.ws

Ulrich Formann, Kilian Hanappi, Simon Wesp

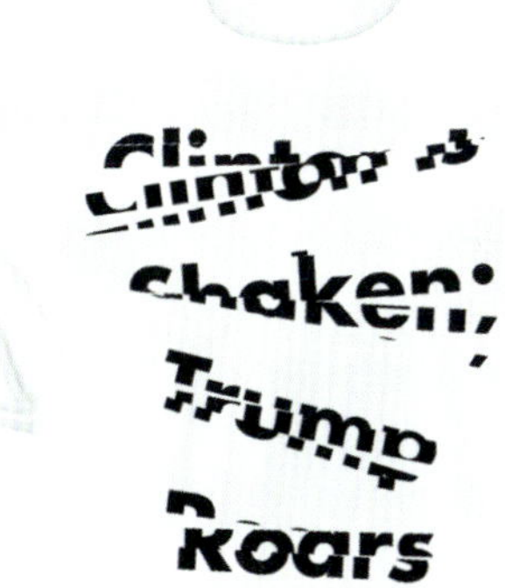

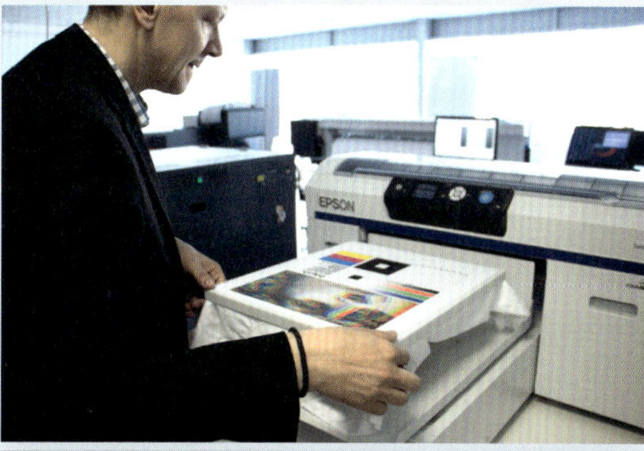

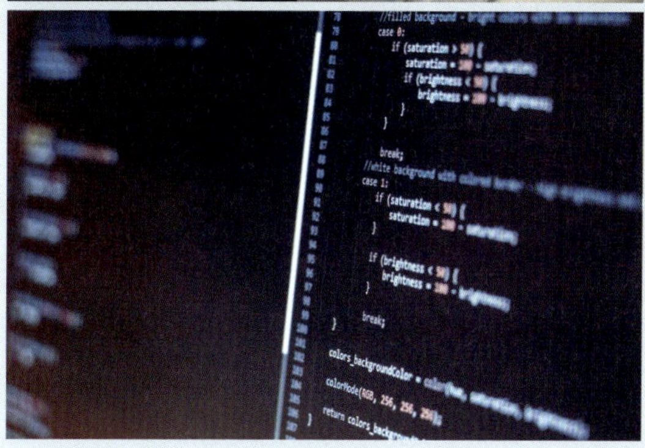

The project entitled *kameleon.ws* is a website that markets one-of-a-kind T-shirts, each bearing a unique imprint. The motif is entirely generated by a computer program and is the outcome of data representing current events. Immediately after a shirt is sold, a new design is produced and the previous one is no longer available. The unique selling proposition here is the application of leading-edge generative design, whereby each individual garment is a distinctive original and each motif tells a story all its own.

What makes this project innovative is its novel approach to the design, production, and marketing of merchandise. Since the price of a conventional T-shirt consists, for the most part, of design, production, advertising, and distribution costs, the only way for a company to remain competitive nowadays is to engage in mass production and then to sell its wares at ridiculous, knockdown prices. Nevertheless, the products of this old-fashioned, value-added chain appeal only to the taste of the great mass of consumers. Plus, much of the inventory ends up getting remaindered when its season is over. Our project is meant to demonstrate a more efficient, more cost-effective and, above all, more economic mode of production.

http://kameleon.ws

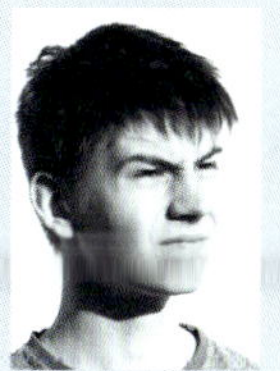
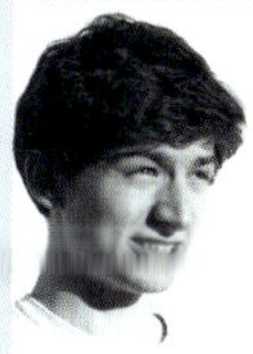
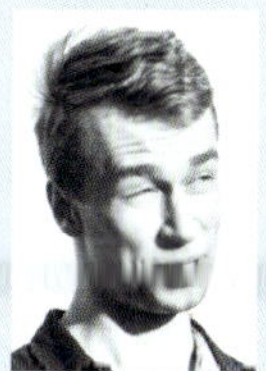

Ulrich Formann (born in 1996), **Kilian Hanappi** (born in 1996) and **Simon Wesp** (born in 1997) are currently enrolled in the Multimedia program at the High School for Graphic Arts in Vienna. In addition to their shared interest in generative design, this crew was motivated primarily by the economic and media-critical aspects of this project.

Jury Prix Ars Electronica

2016

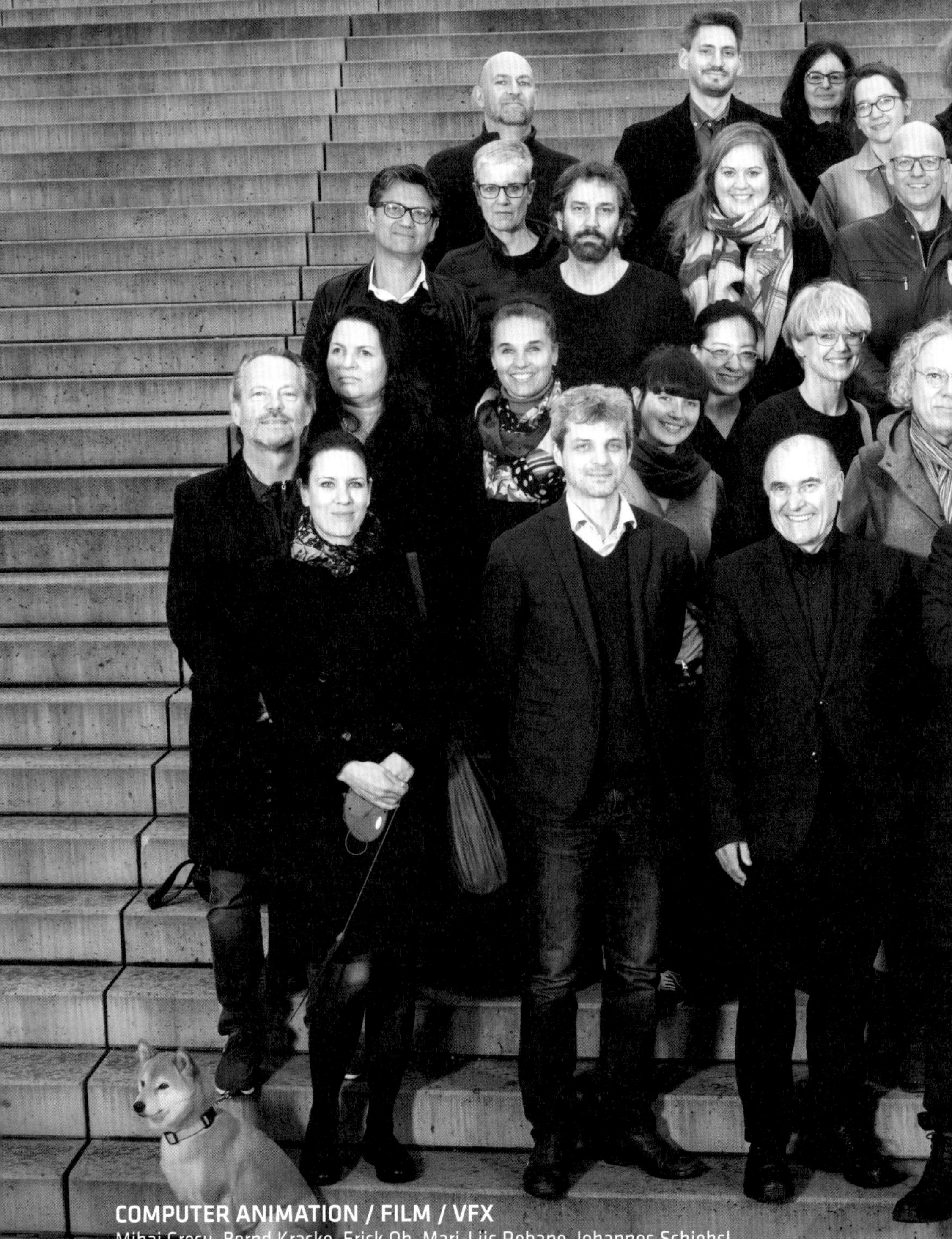

Prix Ars Electronica 2016—Jury

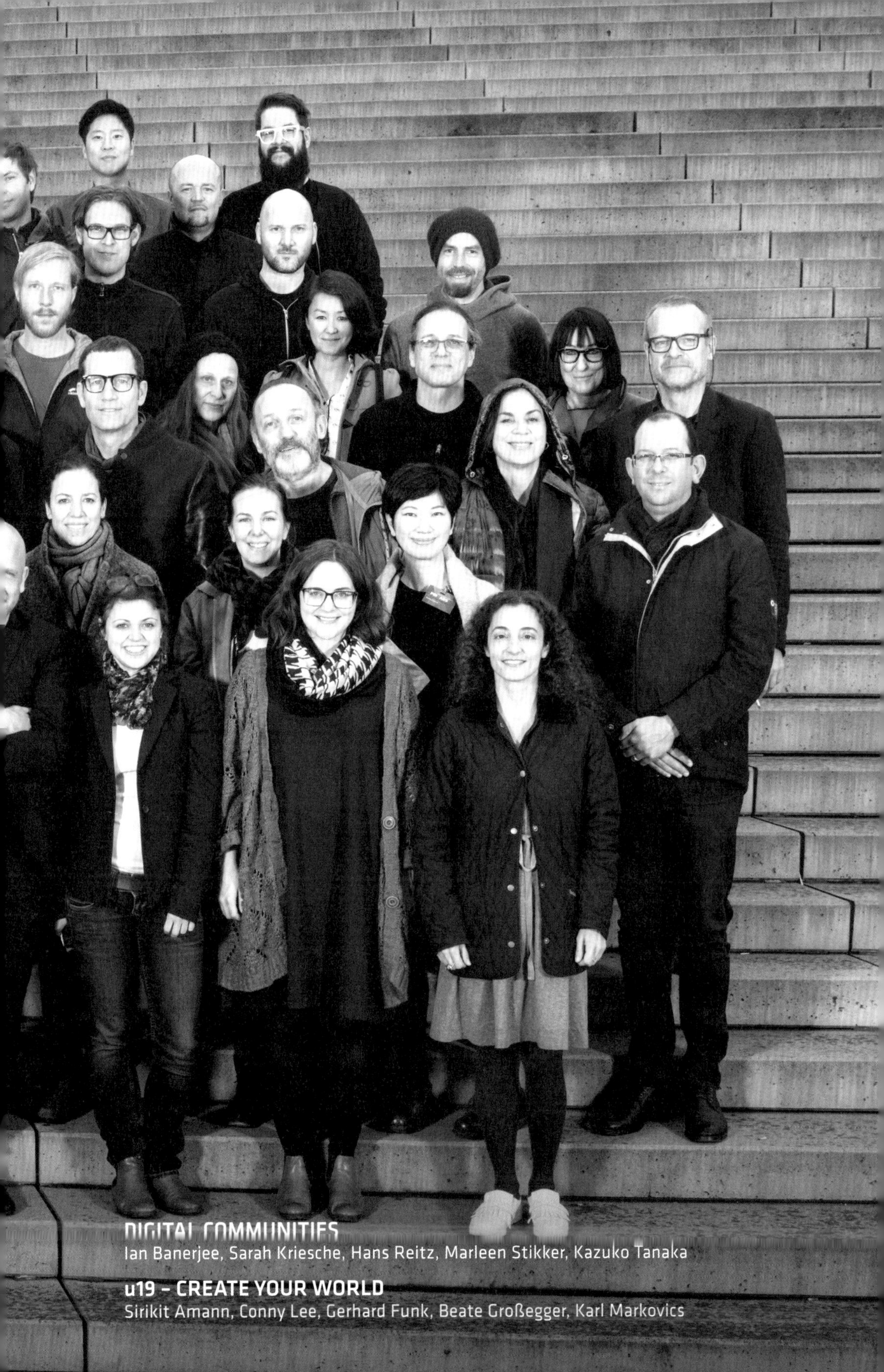

DIGITAL COMMUNITIES
Ian Banerjee, Sarah Kriesche, Hans Reitz, Marleen Stikker, Kazuko Tanaka

u19 – CREATE YOUR WORLD
Sirikit Amann, Conny Lee, Gerhard Funk, Beate Großegger, Karl Markovics

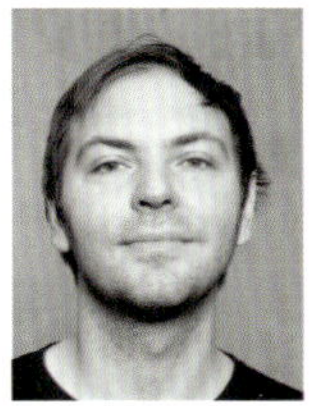

Mihai Grecu (RO/HU) was born in 1981. After studying art and cinema in France, at the Fresnoy Studio of Contemporary Arts, he has been developing a complex personal visual language. By mixing symbolic images with highly metaphorical situations and surreal atmospheres, his works challenge the viewer's perception as well as contemporary imagery, with recurring themes such as environment, war, water, and metamorphosis.

His film poems have been shown at numerous film and new media festivals worldwide (Rotterdam, Festival of New Cinema in Montreal, Clermont Ferrand, Videobrasil) and exhibitions *(Dans la nuit, des images* at the Grand Palais in Paris, Mois de la Photographie in Paris, Hengesbach Gallery in Berlin, etc.).

Bernd Kracke (DE) has been the President of HfG Offenbach since September 15, 2006. He has been Professor for Electronic Media at HfG Offenbach since 1999 and was the Dean of the School of Art (formerly Visual Communication department) from 2001 to 2006. He founded the

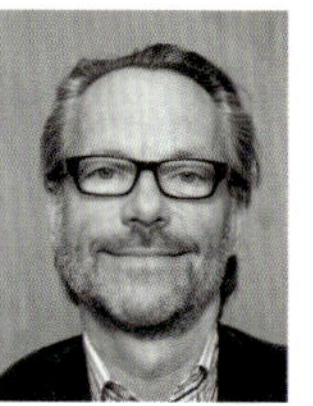

CrossMediaLab as a platform for research and experimentation on networking analogue and digital technologies as well as their innovative application in an arts and design context. Here, he drew on his experience from his work at MIT Cambridge, USA (1979 to 1985) and the Academy of Media Arts Cologne (1991 to 1999) as well as his long-standing work as an independent media designer and artist. Kracke is a co-founder, board member, and committee spokesperson of Hessen Film and Media Academy and the initiator and director of the B3 Biennial of the Moving Image.

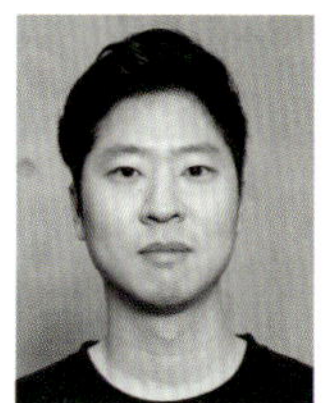

Erick Oh (KR) is a Korean filmmaker / painter based in California. His work has been introduced and nominated at Annecy Animation Festival, Hiroshima Animation Festival, Student Academy Awards, Zagreb Film Festival, SIGGRAPH, Anima Mundi, Ars Electronica, and numerous other international film festivals and galleries world wide. After receiving his BFA from the Fine Art Department at Seoul National University and his MFA from UCLA's film program, Erick joined Pixar Animation Studios as an animator in 2010. Erick's most recent independent animated film, *The Dam Keeper* was nominated for the Academy Awards in 2015. *www.erickoh.com*

Mari-Liis Rebane (EE) was born in Tallinn, Estonia. She is an artist and a director working in the fields of audiovisual production and the moving image. In 2011 Mari-Liis started working for the International Animation Film Festival Animated Dreams, the oldest and biggest animation festival

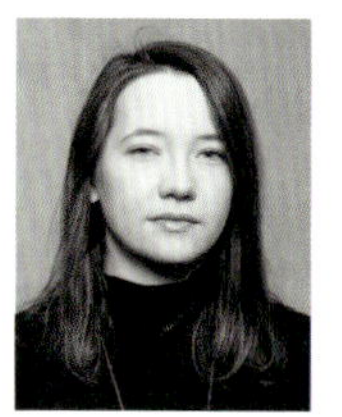

in the Baltics, and she is now the Festival Director. She works occasionally as an animation expert in the Estonian Film Fund financing committee, as a program curator for international festivals, and as an independent journalist for culture magazines. Promoting visual culture and expanding the definition of animation has become her mission. Mari-Liis Rebane graduated from the animation department at Estonian Academy of Arts and is currently focusing on interactive and emerging technologies in her MA studies in New Media.

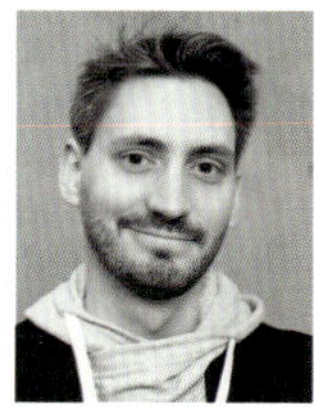

Johannes Schiehsl (AT) started studying traditional animation in the Czech Republic, continuing his studies at the prestigious Filmakademie Baden-Wuerttemberg. There he created a couple of award winning short films that also aired on several television channels. His autobiographically inspired graduation short film, *366 Days,* was selected by more than 70 international film festivals and received numerous awards. It was shortlisted to take part in the official selection in Annecy and Stuttgart and became the first animated film ever to be nominated for an Austrian Movie Award. In 2011 Johannes Schiehsl founded the animation company Neuer Österreichischer Trickfilm together with Conrad Tambour and Benjamin Swiczinsky.

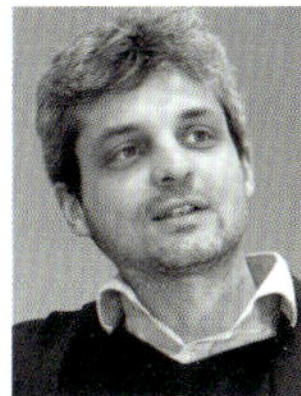

Christophe De Jaeger (BE) is responsible for the program of media arts and the relation between arts and industry in the Center for Fine Arts. On a freelance basis he curated exhibitions in Belgium and abroad (USA, China) with international media artists. Most recent international exhibitions were hosted by MAC–Museu de Arte Contemporânea de Niterói in Rio de Janeiro (2013) and the Museum of Contemporary Art in Shanghai (2009). In 2014 he founded the Belgian organization Gluon that stimulates creative partnerships between artists, researchers, and industrialists. Currently Christophe De Jaeger is working on a PhD at King's College London where he researches the history and methodology of organizations stimulating collaborative practice with artists in the 1960s and 1970s.

Michela Ana Magas (UK/HR) is an innovation catalyst who bridges science, art, design, and technology. A graduate from the Royal College of Art in London, her PhD research at Goldsmiths was in music and technology. She is the founder of Music Tech Fest and Innovation Director of #Music-

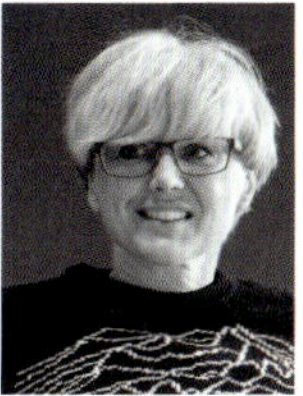

Bricks, which puts exclusive tech in the hands of hackers and makers. She won the "art meets science" NEM Art award twice, and is on the Advisory Board of the H2020 program for Innovation, IoT, and the Creative Industries.

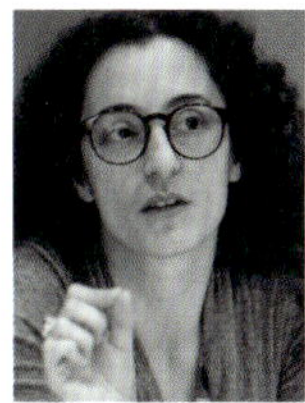

Irini Papadimitriou (GR/UK) is a London-based curator and producer, currently Head of New Media Arts Development at Watermans, an arts organization presenting innovative work and supporting artists working with technology, where she is curating the exhibition program and an annual digital performance festival. Irini is also Digital Programmes Manager at the V&A, mainly responsible for programs such as the annual Digital Design Weekend: a big-scale event of interactive installations, open & collaborative workshops, artists' presentations and talks, showing digital art and design projects, and offering audiences the opportunity to meet the artists & makers and explore processes. She is also one of the organizers for London's Elephant & Castle Mini Maker Faire, a day of making, learning, inventing, and tinkering.

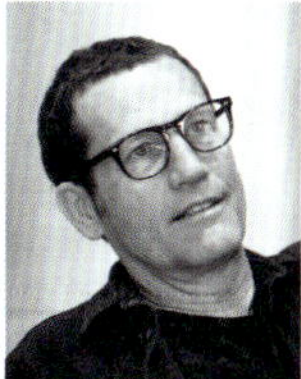

Joachim Sauter (DE) has been working as a media artist and designer since the early 1980s. From the beginning, he focused on digital technologies and experimented how they can be used to express content, form, and narration. Fueled by this interest, he founded ART+COM in 1988 together with other artists, designers, scientists, and technologists. Their goal was to practically research this new up-and-coming medium in the realm of art and design and he is still leading this interdisciplinary group. In the course of his work he was invited to participate in many exhibitions. Beside others he showed his work at Centre Pompidou Paris, Venice Biennial, Stejdilik Museum Amsterdam, Kunsthalle Wien, ICC Tokyo, Getty Center Los Angeles, and MAXXI Rom. Since 1991 he is full professor for New Media Art and Design at the University of the Arts Berlin and since 2001 adjunct professor at UCLA, Los Angeles.

Victoria Vesna (US), PhD, is an artist and professor at the UCLA Department of Design | Media Arts and Director of the Art|Sci center at the School of the Arts and California Nanosystems Institute (CNSI). With her instal-

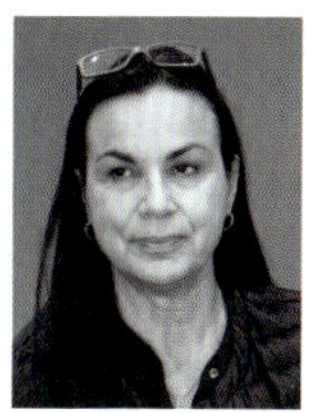

lations she investigates how communication technologies affect collective behavior and perceptions of identity shift in relation to scientific innovation (PhD, University of Wales, 2000). Her work involves long-term collaborations with composers, nano-scientists, neuroscientists, and evolutionary biologists, and she brings this experience to students. She is the North American editor of *AI & Society* and in 2007 published an edited volume–*Database Aesthetics: Art in the Age of Information Overflow* and another in 2011–*Context Providers: Conditions of Meaning in Media Arts.*

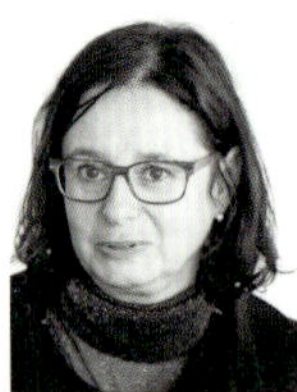

Sirikit Amann (AT) was born in 1961. She studied Politics, Theater and Economics in Vienna. Since the 1980s, her activities in Austria and abroad have focused on the interface of culture, education, and new media. She worked for the Austrian Culture Service KulturKontakt Austria until 2007. From 2008 till 2016 she has been an advisor to the Minister of Arts and Culture. She curates Young Animation for the Prix Ars Electronica and has been an u19 juror since the category's inception.

Gerhard Funk (AT) was born in 1958. He studied Mathematics and Art Education in Linz und received his PhD in Theoretical Computer Science. As a high school teacher he taught art education, mathematics and informatics. In parallel he worked as assistant and researcher at RISC Linz. In

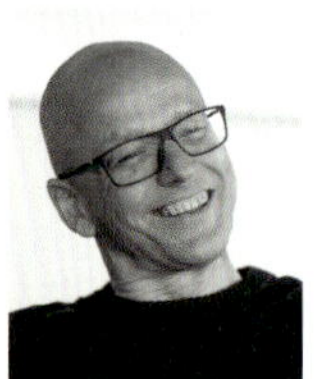

1993 he transferred to the University of Art Linz, where he established an education program for digital media and developed the elearning platform "Digital Media for Artists—DMA." Since 2004 he is a full professor at the Institute of Media and the head of the bachelor's degree program "Timebased and Interactive Media" that he conceptualized. He is also in charge of the "WebArt & Design" master's degree program that is offered in cooperation with Johannes Kepler University Linz.

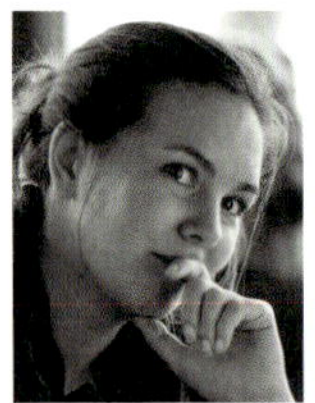

Beate Großegger (AT) is the scientific leader and the vicarious chairwoman of the Institute for Youth Culture Research in Vienna as well as juror of the Federal Ministry of Science, Research and Economy's program "Kinderuni—Activities and Awareness Measures for Children and Adolescents." She graduated in Communication Sciences and has been working in the field of applied social research since 1996. Her great commitment to gender-sensitive youth research earned Beate Großegger the Käthe Leichter Prize for women's studies, gender studies and equality in the workplace in 2011 and she is a renowned expert on studies focusing on the lives of young people. Beate Großegger is an external lecturer at several Austrian Universities focusing on current youth research. Her key working issues are media and communication, youth and politics, youth and employment issues, future lifestyles and trends, generational research, and methods of qualitative audience research.

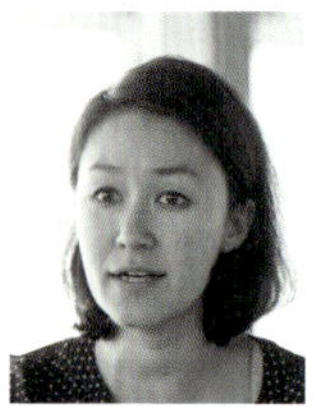

Conny Lee (AT), born 1985 in Vienna, studied the allegedly unpromising discipline of Theatre, Film and Media Science. After her degree, she started working for Radio FM4 at the Austrian Broadcasting Company, where she produces and co-hosts the bilingual FM4 Morning Show and makes contributions about games, literature, and comics. She also moderates events and public discussions.

Karl Markovics (AT), born in 1963, is an Austrian actor and film director. He starred as Salomon Sorowitsch in Stefan Ruzowitzky's 2007 film *The Counterfeiters*, which was awarded the Academy Award for Best Foreign Language Film of that year. Prior to that, his most notable appearances

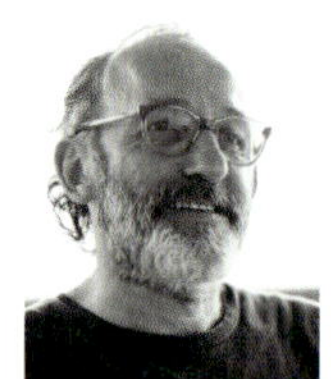

have been in the highly acclaimed Austrian (Viennese) black comedy *Komm, süßer Tod* (2001), his role as far-right terrorist Franz Fuchs in the 2007 TV movie *Franz Fuchs— Ein Patriot*, and in the police drama television series *Inspector Rex*. His character from Inspector Rex had his own spin-off series, *Stockinger*. He also played the role of Ferdinand aus der Fünten in the 2012 Dutch film *Süskind*. Markovics remains a frequent stage actor, and in April 2010 played the non-singing role of Samiel in *The Counterfeiters* director Ruzowitzky's first opera production, *Der Freischütz* at Vienna's Theater an der Wien. He directed and wrote *Atmen* in 2011. Markovics' second working as a screenwriter/director followed in 2015: *SUPERWELT* had the world premiere at the 66th Berlinale.

DIGITAL COMMUNITIES

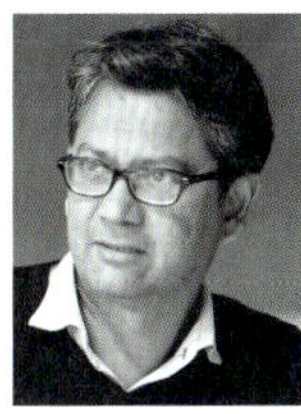

Ian Banerjee (IN/AT) is lecturer and research fellow at the Centre for Sociology (ISRA) at Vienna University of Technology. For 15 years he has been investigating global issues around urbanization with a special focus on urban innovation. For six years he has developed a keen interest in studying the interlinkages between urbanism and emerging educational practices. In 2015 he edited an e-book with Ingrid Fischer-Schreiber on *Digital Communities 2004–2014: Selected Projects from Prix ARS Electronica*.

Sarah Kriesche (AT) has worked as a radio host and journalist for over 18 years. During this time, she helped to create and establish a radio station in Gran Canaria, worked as a show-runner for the early morning radio program "Ö3 Wecker" while hosting her own radio shows on "Hitradio Ö3",

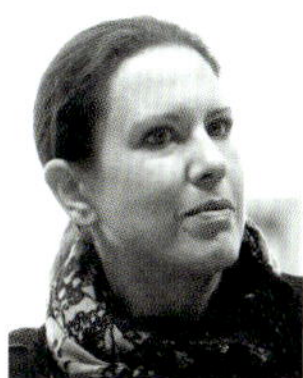

and served as Head of Corporate Communications at the daily newspaper *Die Presse*. She is also a vocal coach and a presentation coach. In 2010 she decided to focus on many divergent topics in the widespread sphere of information technology. Since then she covers the impact of subcultures (such as Anonymous) as well as technical achievements like m2m or IoT and their meaning for modern society for the radio channel Ö1.

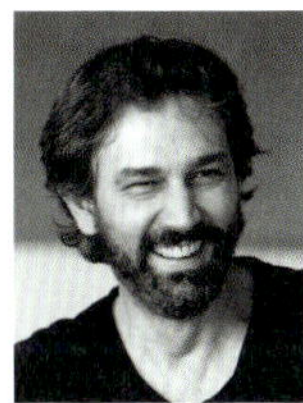

Hans Reitz (DE) is a Founder and Managing Director who was always driven by the quest for adventure and change. At the age of 20 he started traveling which led him to many countries, including India where he spent 7 years living a simple life. Within a few years, he established a creative circle and, as culture manager, he organized, among others things, a variety of theater and culture projects. He founded the event agency "circ" in 1994, which today serves such renowned companies as Autostadt, BASF, and E.ON. Entrepreneur Hans Reitz has established his radius of operations and his network not only in the world of business, but he has also developed social projects, starting with Wiesbaden, where he now lives, and subsequently throughout the world. Hans Reitz speaks at international conferences and leads numerous workshops at various universities.

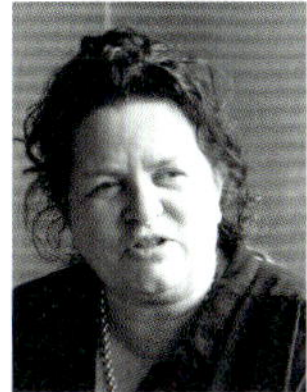

Marleen Stikker (NL) is founder of De Digitale Stad (The Digital City) in 1994, the first virtual community introducing free public access to the internet. She is founder of Waag, a social enterprise that consists of Waag Society, a research Institute for creative technologies and social innovation, and Waag Products, which launched companies like 7scenes, a mobile learning and gaming platform, and Fairphone, the first fair smartphone in the world. Stikker is also member of the supervisory board of WPG Publishers, an independent publishing group. Marleen Stikker strongly adheres to the Maker's Bill of Rights motto "If You Can't Open It, You Don't Own It". Waag Society is actively involved in the Open Design and Creative Commons movement and believes that society needs open technologies that meet societal challenges.

Kazuko Tanaka (JP) joined Hakuhodo in 1998 and started her career in account services, before moving into new business development with leading foreign marketing firms—having 3 children along the way! She recognized that working mothers, who are still a minority in Japan, need

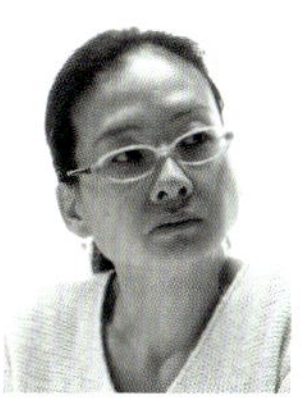

a place to share information and ideas, so she started the "Hakuhodo Working Moms' Link" in 2012, networking across over 50 companies/ 500 working mothers via "Lunchcation—lunchtime communication" actions. Kazuko joined VoiceVision Inc. in July 2013 as one of its founding members, serving as community producer and facilitating community projects for companies and local governments. Kazuko has also worked on the Hakuhodo and Ars Electronica joint team project—the Future Catalysts—and as a facilitator for two seasons at the Ars Electronica Festival's Future Innovators Summit.

Digital Communities 2016—Advisory Board

Antoni Abad (ES) is the founder of *megafone.net*, which invites groups of people marginalized within society to express their experiences and opinions.

Heitor Alvelos (PT) is professor of design and new media at the University of Porto, Portugal, outreach director at the UT Austin-Portugal program in digital media, and principal curator of the FuturePlaces Digital Media Festival.

Hans Bernhard (AT) is a writer, actionist, and a media artist working in the field of media hacking, txt-modification, and net.art. He's also the co-founder of etoy and ubermorgen.

Martijn De Waal (NL) is one of the founders of The Mobile City, an independent research group that investigates the influence of digital media technologies on urban life, and the implications for urban design.

Oscar Ekponimo (NG) is the founder of FoodRing. As a software engineer, his vision is to innovate technologies that shape the culture and redefine industries while also fostering sustainable development. He was a recipient of the International Telecoms Union award for technology innovation 2013.

Cyrus Farivar (US) is a journalist, radio producer, and author. He is also the senior business editor at Ars Technica. He is the author of *The Internet of Elsewhere*—about the history and effects of the Internet on different countries around the world.

Carlos Gomez de Llarena (US) is a media architect working with physical and digital experiences which shape social interaction and our perception of space. He does interaction design with devices, installations, video, sound, wireless networks, the web, and programming.

Laina Raveendran Greene (US/SG) is Chief Executive Officer of GET-IT, Green Energy Technology and Info-communications Technology, and Executive Director of a public listed telecom tower company in Indonesia. Based in Silicon Valley, Singapore and Indonesia, she considers herself a serial entrepreneur and a Global Citizen.

Salvatore Iaconesi (IT) is an interaction designer, a robotics engineer, an artist, and a hacker. He created *La Cura*, where he presented the records of his brain cancer experience as an "open source cure".

Jepchumba (KE) is a digital artist and founder of African Digital Art, a collective and creative space where digital artists, enthusiasts, and professionals can seek inspiration, showcase their artistry, and connect with emerging artists.

Marc Lee (CH) has been employing artistically oriented production practices to create network-oriented interactive projects since 1999. He experiments with information & communications technologies, and limns topical clusters that contain cultural and creative as well as economic and political aspects.

André Lemos (BR) is Full Professor at the Faculty of Communication at the Federal University of Bahia, and director of Lab404 – Digital Media, Networks and Space Lab. His research focuses on Smart Cities, the Internet of Things, Big Data, and Actor-Network Theory.

Montenoso (ES) is a collaborative project that addresses different problems existing in rural areas, using creativity as a tool for community participation and updating the traditional imaginary as a way to spread knowledge.

Marcus Neustetter (ZA) is an artist, cultural activist, and producer who explores the intersection of art, science, and technology on the African continent and beyond. He has produced projects in the public domain for the last two decades. He is co-founder of The Trinity Session.

Gerda Palmetshofer (AT) works in the fields of visual communication, transformation design, information design for resource use, and footprint and is a member of the "Growth in Transition" initiative.

Walter Palmetshofer (AT) was sysadmin at the Ars Electronica Center, CTO of The Thing (thing.net) for five years, worked on various art- & net activism projects in NYC, collected various startup experience, studied Economics, and currently works at the Open Knowledge Foundation.

Clément Renaud (FR) is a freelance researcher, developing experimental initiatives at the crossroad of art, code, science, and technologies. A specialist in network analysis and data visualization, he works with humans, migrants, geeks, scholars, and machines of all kinds.

Fermín Serrano Sanz (ES) is a researcher at the Institute for Biocomputation and Complex Systems Physics of the University of Zaragoza, and executive director of the Ibercivis Foundation. He deploys participatory projects for experimental data gathering.

Felix Stalder (AT) is a professor for Digital Culture at the Zurich University of the Arts, a senior researcher at the World Information Institute in Vienna and a moderator of *nettime* since 1995. His work focuses on the intersection of cultural, political, and technological dynamics.

Laurent Straskraba (AT) worked in many fields of ICT & Development, including research and consulting with a special focus on international cooperation. He also was part of the Austrian delegation to WSIS Geneva. While still following this area of interest, he is currently working for a genealogical research company in Linz.

Addie Wagenknecht (US/AT) is an artist who explores the tension between expression and technology. She seeks to blend conceptual work with traditional forms of hacking and sculpture. She is a member of Free Art & Technology (F.A.T.) Lab, founder of Deep Lab, and is the Chair of the Open Hardware Summit at MIT.

Jeffrey Warren (US) is the founder of Grassroots Mapping and co-founder of Public Lab. He is a fellow at MIT's Center for Civic Media, on the board of the Open Source Hardware Association, on the advisory board of Personal Democracy Media's WeGov, and an advocate of open source software, hardware, and data.

Stefanie Wuschitz (AT) is a lecturer, researcher, and media artist. She finished her PhD on *Feminist Hackerspaces. A Research on Feminist Space Collectives in Open Culture* in 2014. She is the founder of the feminist hacker space "Miss Baltazar's Laboratory—Women and Trans hacklab" in Vienna.

Lei Yang (CN) explores digital engagement to transform social life in China, more recently with a focus on smart city / smart citizen movement. He founded CMoDA CoINNO Lab (Beijing) on collaborative innovation on digital art and design in 2012. He is founder, curator, and producer of NOTCH Festival and Radio Take10.

Bo Zheng (HK/CN) is an artist who works with socially engaged art. He has worked with a wide range of communities, including the Queer Cultural Center in Beijing and Filipino domestic helpers in Hong Kong. Currently he is building an online database on Chinese socially engaged art. He is assistant professor at City University Hong Kong, School of Creative Media.

Leopold Zyka (AT) is a Vienna-based software developer and founder of the OpenLandLAB (openlandlab.org).

STARTS
PRIZE ´16

**Innovation at the nexus of
Science, Technology and the ARTS**

Grand Prize of the European Commission honoring
Innovation in Technology, Industry and Society stimulated by the Arts

"In the digital age, art and engineering are no longer contradictory modes of thinking. Linking technology and artistic practice thus promises a win-win exchange between European innovation policies and the art world."

Günther H. Oettinger, European Commissioner for Digital Economy and Society in the European Commission

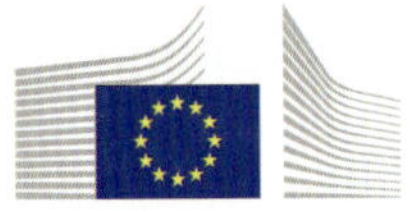
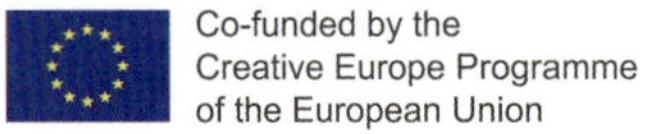

STARTS–**S**cience, **T**echnology and the **ARTS**

The STARTS program is a new initiative of the European Commission, encouraging synergies between industry and the arts to support innovation for technology and society by promoting the inclusion of artists in Horizon 2020 projects. The core of the program is a call for *coordination and support actions* to foster collaboration and dialog between artists, creative people and technologists under the Horizon 2020 program 2016/17. In addition a new European Union Prize–the STARTS Prize–has been developed to promote this program and to give visibility to outstanding projects and best practice examples.

STARTS Prize

Science, Technology and Arts (=STARTS) form a nexus with an extraordinarily high potential for creative innovation. And such innovation is considered to be precisely what's called for if we're to master the social, ecological and economic challenges that Europe will be facing in the near future. The role of artists thus is no longer seen to be just about propagating scientific and technological knowledge and skills among the general public but much more as a kind of catalyst that can inspire and trigger innovative processes. The artistic practice of creative exploration and experimental appropriation of new technologies has a wide reaching potential to contribute to the development of new products and new economic, social and business models. Accordingly, the STARTS Prize focuses on artistic works that influence or change the way we look at technology, and on innovative forms of collaboration between the ICT sector and the world of art and culture.

Ars Electronica's longstanding experience (since 1979) in working at the intersection of art, technology and society, the huge international expertise and network built up with the Prix Ars Electronica (since 1987), many prototypic research collaborations with industry by the Ars Electronica Futurelab (since 1996) and Ars Electronica Solutions make Ars Electronica the ideal partner of the STARTS program.

Based on an open competition, Ars Electronica was commissioned to develop and organize the first STARTS Prize 2016.

STARTS Prize '16

Grand Prize of the European Commission honoring Innovation in Technology, Industry and Society stimulated by the Arts

Two prizes, each with €20,000 prize money, are offered in the first edition of the STARTS Prize to honor innovative projects at the intersection of science, technology and the arts: one for *artistic exploration*, and thus projects with the potential to influence or change the way technology is deployed, developed or perceived, and one for *innovative collaboration* between industry/technology and art/culture in ways that open up new paths for innovation.

Grand Prize–Artistic Exploration

Awarded for artistic exploration and art works where appropriation by the arts has a strong potential to influence or alter the use, deployment or perception of technology.

Grand Prize—Innovative Collaboration

Awarded for innovative collaboration between industry or technology and the arts that opens new pathways for innovation.

In an elaborated process of open call and nominations by advisory experts, a total of 1,861 entries from 54 countries were submitted in the application period that ran from February 1st to March 15th, 2016. Four groups of experts then shortlisted 30 projects as *Nomination for the STARTS prize,* which were presented to the STARTS jurors for consideration. Following extensive deliberations, they decided on *Magnetic Motion* by Iris van Herpen (NL) and *Artificial Skins and Bones,* a project seminar staged jointly by Berlin Weißensee Academy of Art, Ottobock and Fab Lab Berlin as the first two prizewinners of the STARTS prize. Furthermore, they selected 10 projects for an Honorary Mention.

Both prizewinning projects as well as a selection of the Honorary Mentions are on display at this year's Ars Electronica Festival (September 8-12, 2016) in Linz, where the artists as well as the respective project partners will make appearances. Plus, a STARTS exhibition at the BOZAR Electronic Arts Festival (September 22-24, 2016) in Brussels featuring the prizewinning STARTS projects in the heart of Europe and a debate forum in BOZAR will present the results to policymakers and officials from different European institutions and organizations based in Brussels. Additional STARTS presentations are scheduled for autumn in Tokyo and London.

Submission and evaluation process

Considering the novelty of this award competition and the interdisciplinary approach, Ars Electronica launched the STARTS prize 2016 with a dual approach for submissions:

Submission via open call

The STARTS prize open call started on February 1st, 2016 and ended on March 15th, 2016. Submissions could be made either by artists / creative professionals or the researchers / companies involved.
The competition was open:
- to groundbreaking collaborations and projects driven by *both* technology and the arts.
- to all forms of artistic works and practices with a strong link to innovation in technology, business and/or society.
- to all types of technological and scientific research and development that has been inspired by art or involves artists as catalysts of novel thinking.
- to artists and teams from all over the world.
Purely artistic *or* technologically driven projects were not the focus of this competition.
The competition was not limited to any genres such as media art, digital art etc. and not limited to Information and Communication Technologies.

Recommendations by international advisors

To encourage a wider range of participants as well as a geographical and gender balance, 12 international advisors who are experts in the field have been engaged to recommend interesting projects and artists. These recommended participants were contacted by the Ars Electronica team and asked to submit their project via the submission platform, with the same process and deadlines as for the open submissions. These international advisors served as facilitators to identify relevant works and projects during the submission process and helped to ensure a wide reach out and fast introduction of the new award.

Nominations

All submissions were evaluated by a nomination committee in the order of their arrival. The committee nominated 15 projects for prize consideration by the jury. Since the main categories of the Prix Ars Electronica have a strong overlap with the criteria of the STARTS prize, artists submitting for the Prix Ars Electronica could decide to enter their submission also for the STARTS prize. Of these submissions, a total of five projects per category were nominated for prize consideration by the three Prix Juries (Computer Animation/Film/VFX, Interactive Art+, and Digital Communities).
The resulting list of 30 nominations represents a comprehensive overview of international state of the art collaborations between art and technology. Therefore all 30 projects are published in the CyberArts 2016 book.

Jury Selection

In the final round, all 30 nominations were evaluated by the STARTS jury in order to select two prize-winning projects and up to ten Honorary Mentions. The jury consisted of 6 experts, one representative of each Prix Ars Electronica category, two representatives of the nomination committee, and one international jury member. All decisions were unanimous.

In Search of a New Landscape and Mindset

Joint statement of the STARTS Nomination Committee (Yamina Aouina, Alexander Mankowsky, Filip Višnjić, Luis Miguel Girão), and the STARTS Jury (Yamina Aouina, Ian Banerjee, Chiaki Hayashi, Alexander Mankowsky, Erick Oh, Victoria Vesna)

It is almost 50 years since E.A.T. (Experiments in Art and Technology) was officially launched with the goal of promoting collaborations between artists and engineers and expanding the artist's role in developments of new technology. Although influential, it took many attempts, with various degrees of success, for artists working with engineers and scientists to stand on equal footing or even be credited for ideas that ended up in industry and influencing society. But, even in 2016, the two-culture divide remains a challenge, albeit as a ghost that is perpetuated by old systems still firmly in place.

With this in mind, the two evaluation groups recognized the importance of this newly established prize as a special moment for nurturing a direct connection of art, science and technology with a particular recognition of the artist's role in industry. This Grand Prize of the European Commission legitimizes the collaborative process that has been steadily emerging over the years on the fringes of established industry funding models. Initiated at this important historical juncture, the Grand Prize potentially opens an opportunity for small companies, specifically for those that reside in between technologies and creative output, to compete for available research funding. To date, if a company lists its services as artistic, it would not have the opportunity to apply for funds that are available to scientific and technological institutions and companies. The hope is, that the STARTS prize will set a precedent and pave the way for this to finally change.

An impressive number of submissions came from a wide spectrum of research areas—from freelance individuals to large companies and institutions. Practically every field was represented: architecture, installation art, science and data visualization, product design, citizen platforms, theater, industrial design, animation, performance, environmental actions, sound art and sonification, interactive art, 3D printing, sculpture, bio-art, kinetic art, robotics, drone projects, bio-materials, mechanical engineering, mobile applications, DIY practice, medicine, wearables, film and computer science.

STARTS truly emerged as an open non-defined award competition with the center of interest being innovation and visionary ideas for the future that look to practical applications which could have an impact on existing models of production and by extension on society in general.

The STARTS nomination group agreed that the most important aspect of the projects to be selected would have a paradigmatic model of collaborations between artists, scientists, and technologists. This type of transdisciplinary practice and development of projects would inform, inspire, and show the potential of transferring innovative ideas / prototypes to industry. The ultimate question asked was whether the project pushes the known boundaries and reflects high technological and aesthetic sophistication as well as excellence in research.

The STARTS jury awarded two Grand Prizes of the European Commission honoring Innovation in Technology, Industry and Society stimulated by the Arts to *Magnetic Motion* by Iris van Herpen for Artistic Exploration and to the *Artificial Skins and Bones* project for Innovative Collaborations.

STARTS Prize'16
Grand Prize—Artistic Exploration

Awarded for artistic exploration and art works where appropriation by the arts has a strong potential to influence or alter the use, deployment or perception of technology.

Magnetic Motion · Iris van Herpen

Iris van Herpen is one of the first fashion designers to combine 3D printing and other cutting edge technologies into fashion design. She started as an intern for Alexander McQueen in London and Claudy Jongstra in Amsterdam and soon after launched her own label in 2007. Working with a large interdisciplinary collaborative group is part of her process, she often includes traditional crafts as well as the most advanced technologies in her designs. Much of her interest is in the development of new materials as well as inventing novel ways of treating materials utilized in fashion design. Indeed, among others, she collaborated with Philip Beesley and Neri Oxman who were also nominated for the STARTS prize. Van Herpen's work is sculptural and reaches out to latest technologies, as is evident in her most recent collections, *Magnetic Motion,* inspired and informed by her visit to the Large Hadron Collider at CERN, and *Hacking Infinity,* which explores the idea of terraforming, i.e. modifying the biosphere of another planet to make it resemble that of the Earth.

For many European countries such as France, Italy, and Switzerland, the luxury industry is an important pillar of the economy and plays a key role in the artistic and cultural fields. Some of its brands have been around for several centuries in which manufacturers have built a unique heritage of creation and know-how of excellence. Writing tomorrow's history by preserving its heritage goes through the multidisciplinary innovation that brings together technology, art and science. Artists and designers who move off the beaten path to explore new ways enrich the luxury industry and inject new energy with a mindset of experimentation and renewal. This is what Iris van Herpen embodies with her pioneering work.

STARTS Prize '16
Grand Prize—Innovative Collaboration

Awarded for innovative collaboration between industry or technology and the arts that opens new pathways for innovation.

Artificial Skins and Bones
Artificial Skins and Bones Group

The *Artificial Skins and Bones* project brings a new kind of innovation to medium-sized industries and a fresh spirit to the collaborative process. Wolf Jeschonnek, founder of Fab Lab Berlin, worked with a group of students while he was a Visiting Professor at the Product, Fashion, Textile and Research Department at Weißensee Kunsthochschule Berlin. He brought the group to Ottobock, a private SME, and together with the Fab Lab Berlin team, they came up with a new prototype. The jury believes that their collaborative process is a good example that other companies could emulate in the future. Clearly formulated and engineered examples such as this are

needed to inspire and pave the way for smaller new and established companies to implement new methodologies and ways of working.

STARTS Prize '16
Honorary Mentions

Amsterdam Smart Citizens Lab · Waag Society

In the heated debates around "smart cities," it has not been until recently that their inhabitants, the so-called "smart citizens," have come into the limelight. At the *Amsterdam Smart Citizen Lab,* citizens are not seen merely as consumers and clients of smart technologies, but as critical, hands-on creators of socio-technical change. They believe that there are no technological panaceas for social ills, but that only governments and citizens can adequately respond to the challenges of cities. Creating collaborative infrastructures potentially opens up possibilities of exchange between citizens coming from a broad variety of disciplines—social, technical, artistic or political—and this creates the space for experimentation with citizen-led methods in how to sense, organize, and innovate in cities of the 21st century.

Bionic Partition: Generative Design for Aerospace
Airbus, APWorks, Autodesk, The Living

Applying generative design, biology, and new materials to real built projects in the context of technology, culture, and the environment, The Living is no ordinary architectural studio. Having joined Autodesk in 2014, as a first-of-a-kind Autodesk Studio, they worked with Airbus to implement the world's largest metal 3D printed airplane component. The *Bionic Partition* was created through a pioneering combination of generative design, 3D printing, and advanced materials, producing a lighter and stronger structural system. The jury felt that this collaboration exemplifies how new modes of design thinking can have a positive technological and ecological impact. Nature, through bio-mimicry, continues to reveal the most amazing secrets to help us to solve complex problems. Using this approach, these companies—in collaboration with universities—are working on air transportation of the future. Using cutting edge technologies—3D printing, generative design, and new materials—the project *Bionic Partition* is an impressive, innovative model that serves as a good example to be emulated.

Fairy Lights in Femtoseconds
Yoichi Ochiai with Digital Nature Group at University of Tsukuba and Utsunomiya University
Known as a magician of the digital era, Yoichi Ochiai has been exploring new potential by integrating art and the latest science & technologies. In this latest project, he creates a work that impresses scientists and artists alike by engineering an ephemeral fairy floating in the air—a 3-dimensional holograph made by high-intensity femtosecond lasers that focus on one spot to change the air into plasma that functions as a plasmatic display. This exciting project allows us to imagine the blurring of boundaries between objects and holography, and we experience and gain a better understanding of another kind of mixed reality—a true fusion of the virtual and material worlds.

RGB|CMYK Kinetic · ART+COM Studios
Renowned Berlin ART+COM Studios create a beautiful harmony of nature and technology from ordinary elements—lights, sound, and mirrors—immersing the audience in this extraordinary balance. Five circle mirrors are floating, slowly moving, and cascading red, green, and blue (RGB) light onto the entire space, and the finely tuned kinetic controlled motion of the five mirrors turns the environment into an amazing installation of lights and sound. This artwork exemplifies how public spaces can be transformed, providing a space for inspiration that goes beyond strictly aesthetic interventions.

SPARKED: A Live Interaction between Humans and Quadcopters
Verity Studios, ETH Zurich, and Cirque du Soleil
SPARKED is a perfect example of the fusion of a great storytelling idea and emerging technology. Traditional musical performance meets cutting-edge drone technology to create a magical experience with a beautiful illusion. While watching this mesmerizing interactive choreography between the actor and a set of floating lampshades generated by drones, the audience gets pulled deeply into the whimsical narrative without a chance to question the technology behind it. Everything is organically blended in the story as one. In terms of technology, the detail of the computer controls in drones is mind-blowing, and this will certainly open the door for drone technology to many more applications in the future.

unfold · Ryoichi Kurokawa
Artists and scientists have been exploring data visualization for many years and diverse innovations have been made. We might feel that we are now very familiar with the development of data visualization, however, *unfold* takes it to another level due to recent research and discoveries about the formation and evolution of stars and the universe. The data includes the conditions of star birth and the history of galaxy life. The artist then translates this data and information to an immersive sensory installation with beautiful images and sounds. This project truly shows how effectively art can display the scientific discovery through an immersive technology.

V2_ · Institute for the Unstable Media
Over the last 20 years the Rotterdam based transdisciplinary institute V2_Institute for the Unstable Media built up an international reputation through its innovative research at the intersection of art and technology. What makes it interesting for STARTS is how V2_ has been involved in developing technological tools for specific art projects. V2_ both produces art and also facilitates the production of art by offering technical support to interested artists and scientists. Their open platform helps to share, discuss, and disseminate their findings and knowledge. V2_ also explores the social impact of technology and advises universities, research institutes, art museums, and companies.

Water-based Digital Fabrication Platform
Mediated Matter Research Group, MIT Media Lab
A robotically controlled 3D printing system is designed to shape constructions with biodegradable composites. The work foresees the emergence of direct digital fabrication that allows multi-material and multi-scale structured objects. It also questions the status quo of industrial manufacturing processes, that are generally characterized as wasteful and highly energy intensive. The *Water-based Digital Fabrication Platform* sends a clear message: it is time to design sustainable, environmentally conscious but functional processes from products to architecture.

WCMC Discovery Wall
Squint/Opera and Hirsch & Mann
Discovery Wall is a whole new kind of digital installation utilizing thousands of mini screens and lenses to provide two different experiences to the viewers.

From a distance, we see a big projection screen of a beautiful visual and letters on the building wall. Then, up close, we realize that it consists of thousands of circular acrylic discs and we can look deeply into each of these. Inside, we get to learn about medical discoveries and scientific research by Weill Cornell Medical College. Not only is the idea and the concept brilliant, but the technology and experiments carried out by artists and engineers to make this possible are innovative and impressive for expert and lay audiences alike.

We Make Money Not Art · Régine Debatty

Since 2004, *We Make Money Not Art* has been at the forefront of transdisciplinary art practice, reporting projects and capturing the diverse art practice in technology, science and culture. Triumphant in defying categorization, Régine Debatty's invaluable perspective continues to frame the ever-changing landscape of art and technology. A valuable resource for students, practitioners, curators, and educators globally, *We Make Money Not Art* drives critical discussion and sets agenda for arts professionals and newcomers alike. In a world that overwhelms us with data and information daily, to search and to find is not that easy, especially when it comes to the exponential area of new technologies and their applications. Régine Debatty has the instinct to find a unique style to share her vision of contemporary artists and their works that helps us discover technology in a new way. *We Make Money Not Art* is a platform for hidden gems of creativity and exploration and a source of inspiration for many of us.

STARTS Prize'16
Nominations

#FindingSomethingBondingSound
#WhiteMatter

Beyond Humans: Perception & Understanding of Actions of Others
Ramiro Martin Joly-Mascheroni

Apostroph
Manfred Hild, Mitsuru Muramatsu, Shunji Yamanaka

BlindWiki, Unveiling the Unseen
Antoni Abad

Casa Jasmina
Team Casa Jasmina

Crowdcrafting
Scifabric, http://crowdcrafting.org

D-CENT—Decentralised Citizens ENgagement Technologies
http://dcentproject.eu

Environment Dress
uh513 (María Castellanos & Alberto Valverde)

Floating Points—Silhouettes
Hamill Industries, Junior Martínez

Floraform
Nervous System—Jessica Rosenkrantz, Jesse Louis-Rosenberg

HACKberry
http://exiii-hackberry.com

Hortum machina, B
Interactive Architecture Lab, William Victor Camilleri, Danilo Sampaio

Instruments of the Afterlife
Burton Nitta (Michael Burton & Michiko Nitta)

Project Nimbus
Dave Lynch, Mike Nix

Nosaj Thing—Cold Stares ft. Chance The Rapper + The O'My's
Daito Manabe, MIKIKO, TAKCOM, ELEVENPLAY, Rhizomatiks Research

Processing Foundation
https://processingfoundation.org

Sentient Chamber
Living Architecture Systems Group

Time Displacement—Chemobrionic Garden Interactive generative (chemical) sound installation
Robertina Šebjanič, Ida Hiršenfelder, Aleš Hieng – Zergon

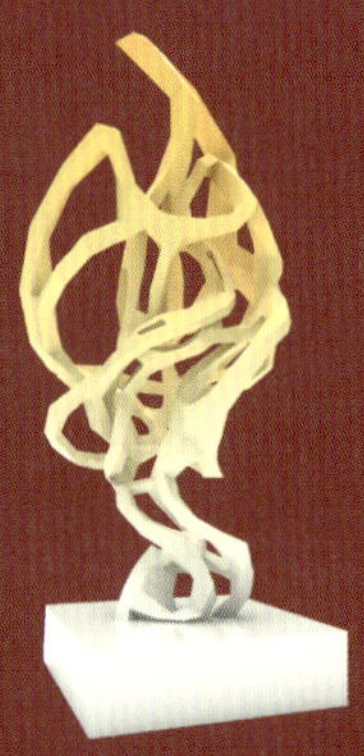

STARTS PRIZE´16

**Grand Prize
Artistic Exploration**

Awarded for artistic exploration and art works where appropriation by the arts
has a strong potential to influence or alter the use, deployment or perception of technology.

Magnetic Motion
Iris van Herpen

Iris van Herpen explores the interplay of magnetic forces. By thoroughly examining the representation of dynamic forces of attraction and repulsion, the designer fuses nature and technology. Earlier this year, van Herpen visited CERN's Large Hadron Collider, whose magnetic field-exceeding that of the Earth by 20,000 times, provided inspiration for *Magnetic Motion.* "I find beauty in the continual shaping of Chaos which clearly embodies the primordial power of nature's performance," says Van Herpen describing the essence of the collection. Van Herpen stayed true to her spirit of bridging fashion and other disciplines by collaborating with the Canadian architect Philip Beesley and the Dutch artist Jolan van der Wiel. Beesley is a pioneer in responsive "living" sculpture, whose poetic works combine advanced

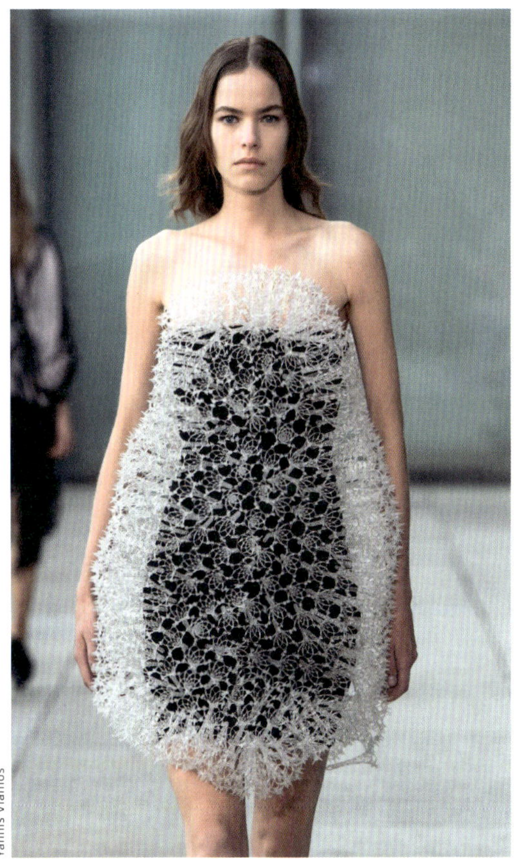

Yannis Vlamos

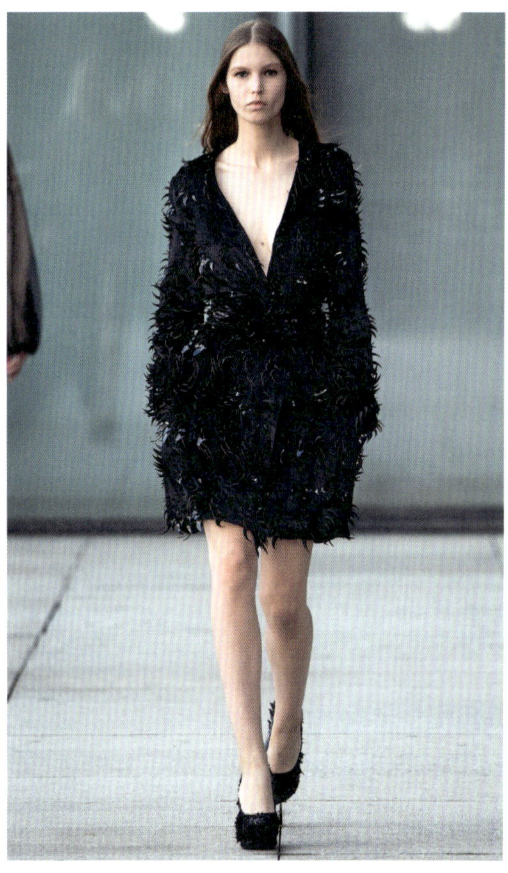

computation, synthetic biology, and mechatronics engineering. Van der Wiel is an artist and craftsman whose work with magnetic tension has resulted in dynamic sculptures and installations that bring to mind the power of volcanic eruptions. Both artists strive to erase the boundaries between nature and technology in their work, which coincides with the direction of van Herpen's creative aim.

The designer worked with techniques like injection molding and laser cutting on maze-like structures, 3D printing and intricate architectural handwork on dresses, jackets, trousers, skirts, and blouses, giving them dynamic shapes and surfaces that echo the body's movement. The three dimensional nature and the layering of the garments give them volume. Emphasizing light and shadow play, micro webs of lace both veil and reveal the luminescent glow of crystal forms, while triacetate feathers punctuate the soft drapes and volumes. The controlled structure of the clothes is offset by the chaotic structure of the accessories, where, due to the nature of magnetic growth, no two items are alike. The shoes, belts, necklaces, and clutches were "grown" using magnetic fields.

Magnetic Motion Collection in collaboration with the following artist's: Philip Beesley, Niccolo Casas, Jolan van der Wiel

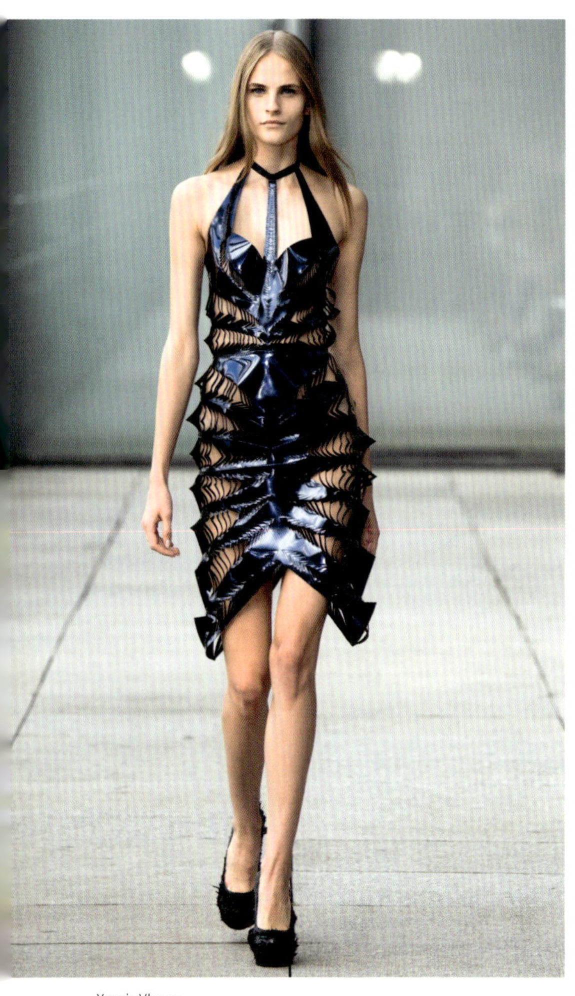

Yannis Vlamos

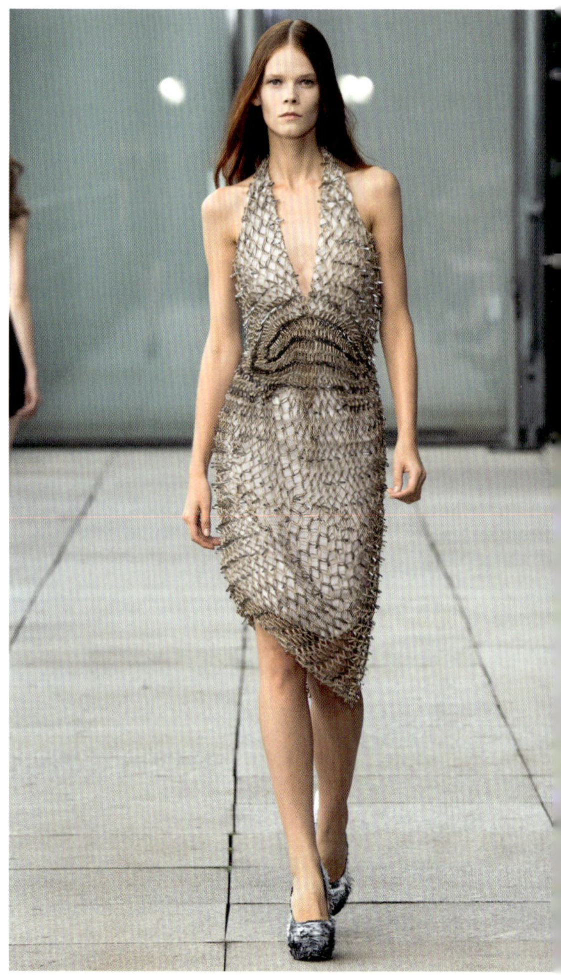

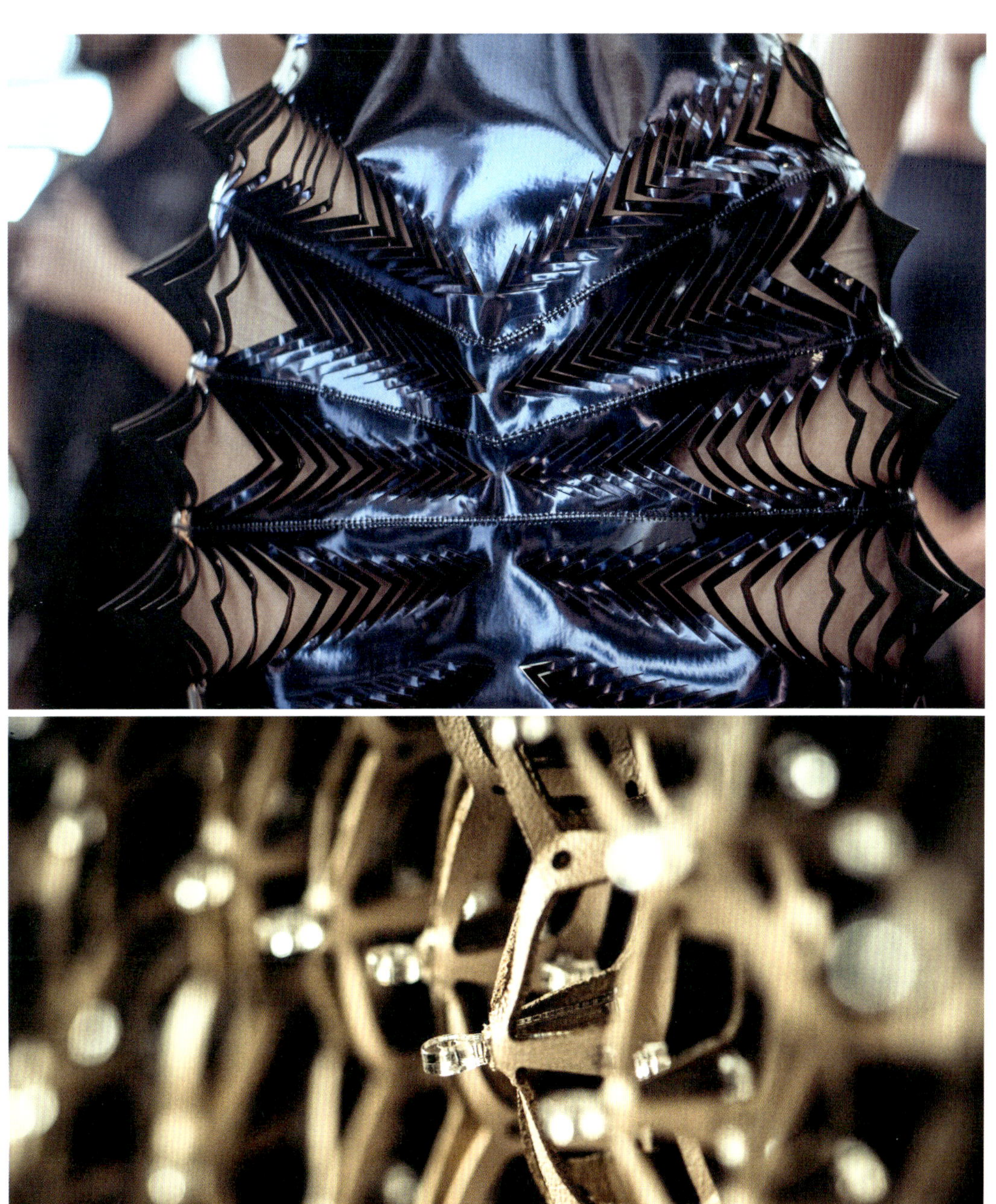

Morgan O'Donovan

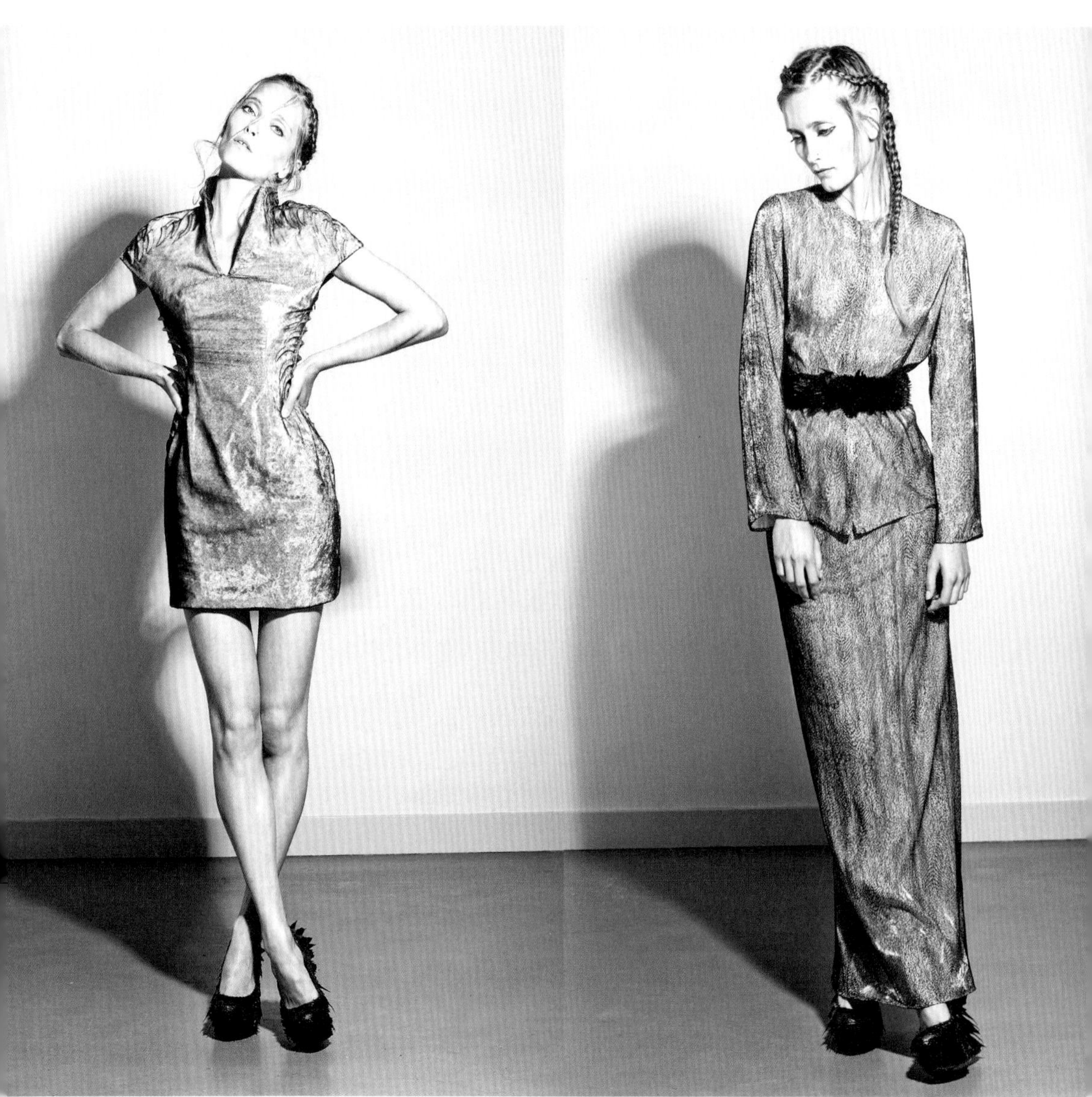

Courtesy of Iris van Herpen

STARTS Prize'16 · Grand Prize – Artistic Exploration

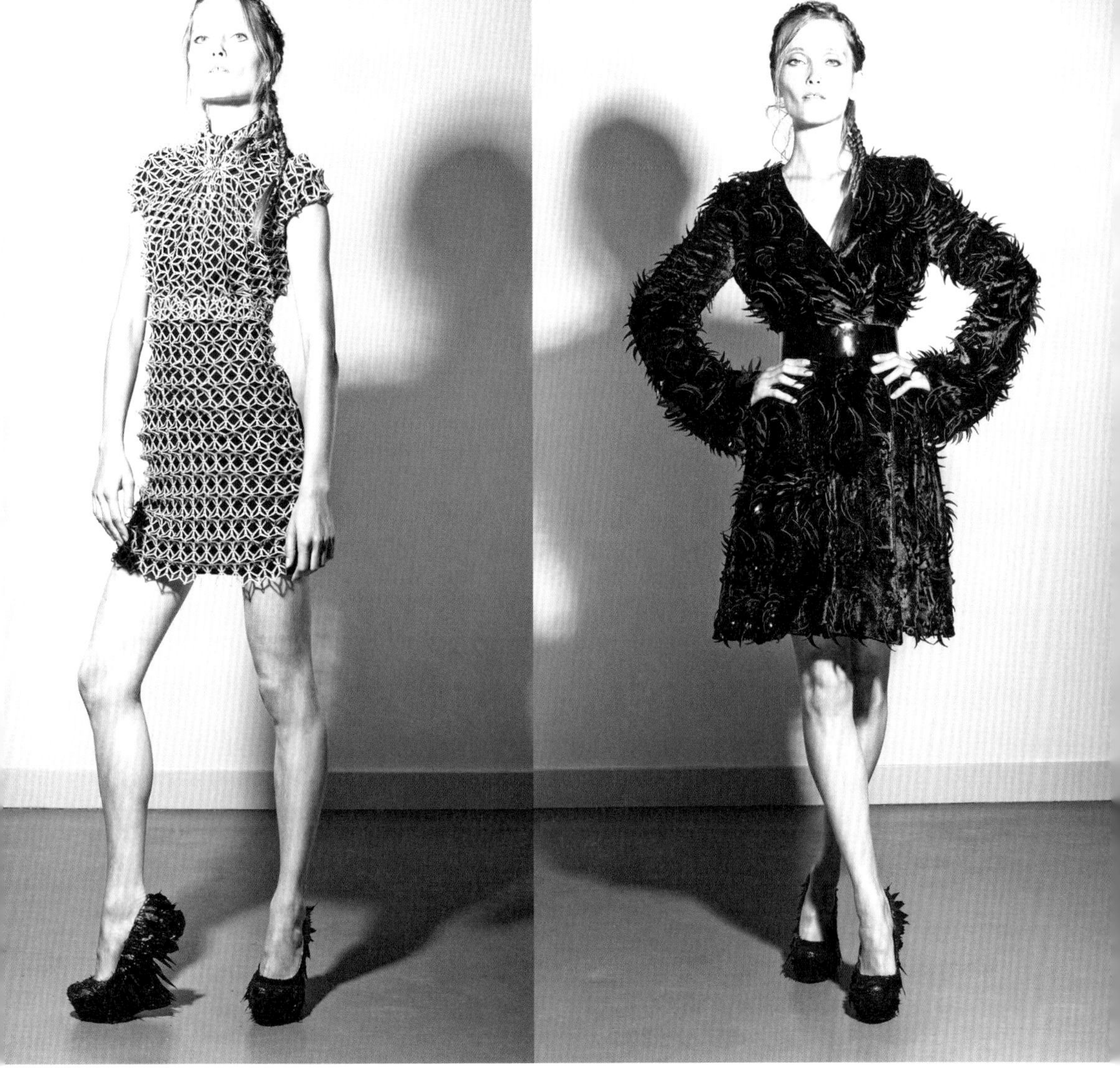

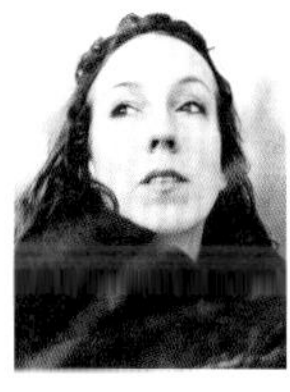

Iris van Herpen (BE), born in 1984, is a fashion designer. She studied Fashion Design at ArtEZ Institute of the Arts Arnhem and interned at Alexander McQueen in London and Claudy Jongstra in Amsterdam. Van Herpen immediately caught the eye with notable shows. In 2007, she started her own fashion label. Iris van Herpen creates women's wear collections. Her designs require every time a unique treatment of material or the creation of complete new materials. For this reason, Van Herpen prefers interdisciplinary research and collaborations with artists from various disciplines, often on a recurring basis. Since July 2011, she is a guest member of the prestigious Parisian Chambre Syndicale de la Haute Couture, which is part of the Fédération Française de la Couture. She participates in many international exhibitions and creates two collections a year. Her work has been recognized through awards, exhibitions, publications, and the mentioned guest membership.

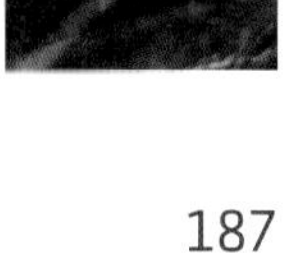

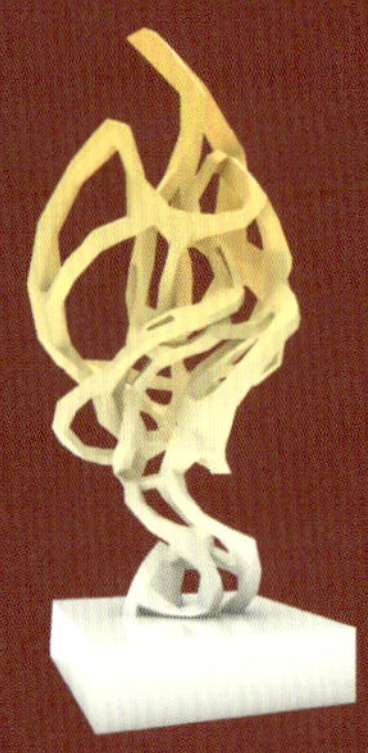

STARTS PRIZE´16

Grand Prize
Innovative Collaboration

Awarded for innovative collaboration between industry or technology and the arts that opens new pathways for innovation.

Artificial Skins and Bones
Artificial Skins and Bones Group

Nature's patterns, structures, and functions are an endless source of inspiration. We started off our project course *Artificial Skins and Bones* by looking into our body's design, and examining elements that may be applied to the design process of artificial bodies. The idea for this topic developed through our collaboration with Ottobock, the world market leader in prosthetics. Through workshops with their technicians and physiotherapists, interviews with amputees, and a visit to Ottobock's research and production hub in Duderstadt, we added additional topics to our agenda: the language of sensation, interaction with artificial body parts, and the aesthetics of artificial bodies and their relationship to the aesthetics of natural bodies.

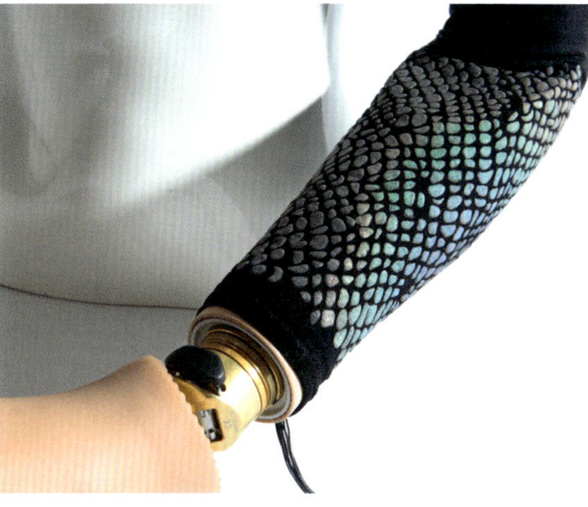

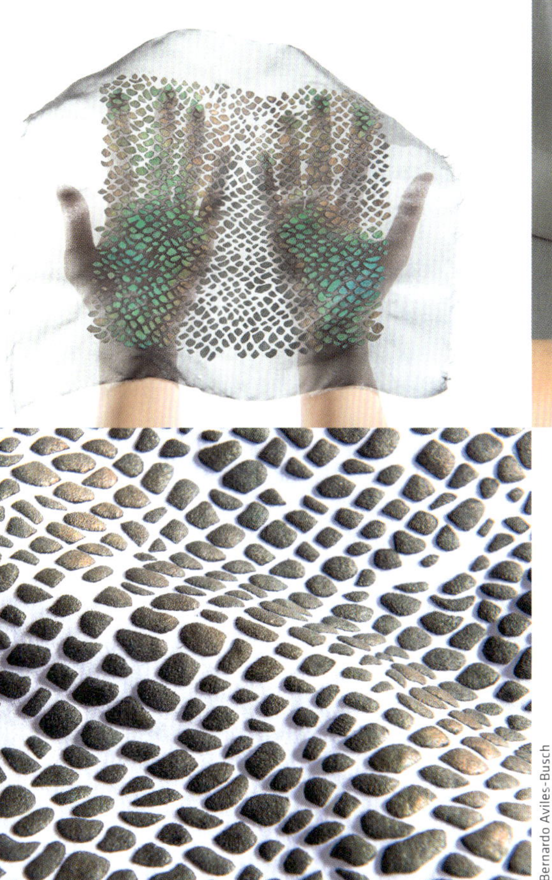

Visible Strength by Lisa Stohn and Jhu-Ting Yang proposes a flexible, creature-like textile surface that, like an octopus, changes its color and pattern in various ways through muscle stimuli.

Bernardo Aviles-Busch

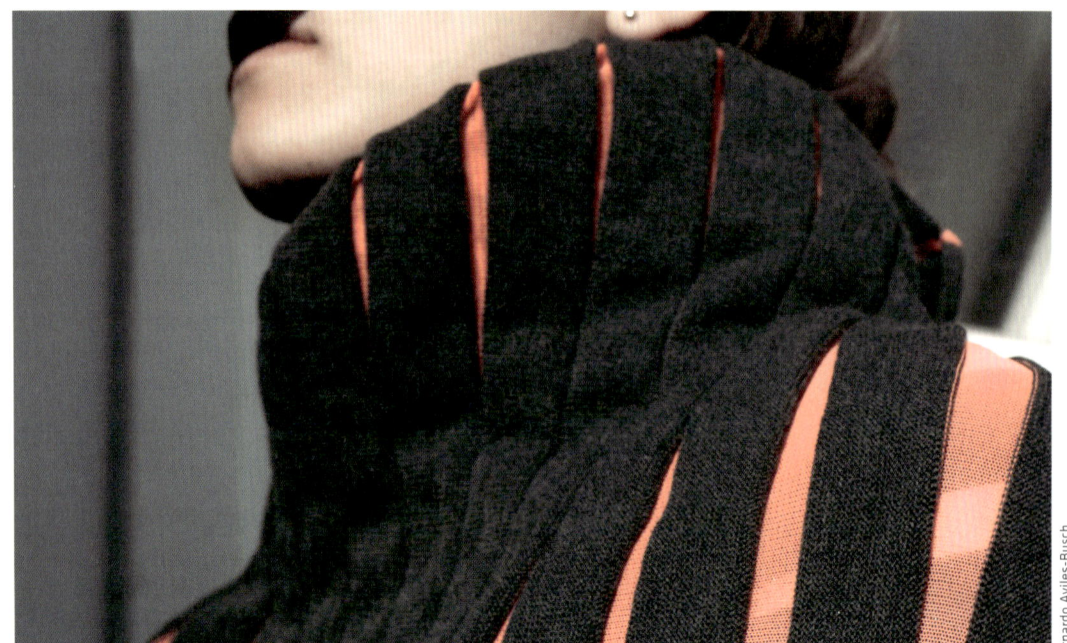

Bernardo Aviles-Busch

Trans.fur by Karina Wirth and Natalie Peter is the development of intelligent textiles, capable of altering moisture permeability by adjusting their surface structures. Inspiration for this project was the most versatile organ in the human body: skin.

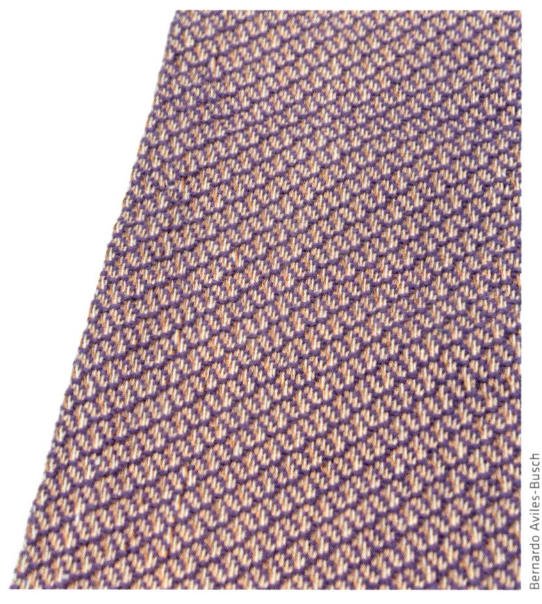

Bernardo Aviles-Busch

Technology, Temperature, and Textiles by Stephanie Natrass is an e-textiles material research project that embeds sensing and actuation into textile surface constructions.

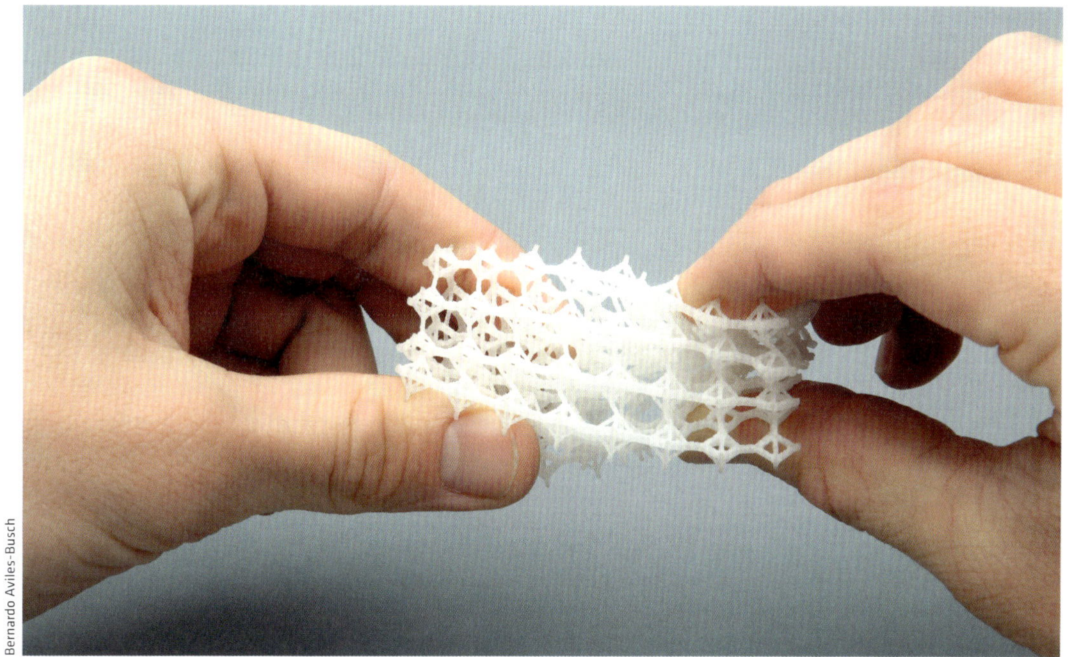

Bernardo Aviles-Busch

Naturanslation by Babette Wiezorek explores the nature and potential of organically inspired 3D grid structures by applying algorithmic design and 3D printing to microstructures.

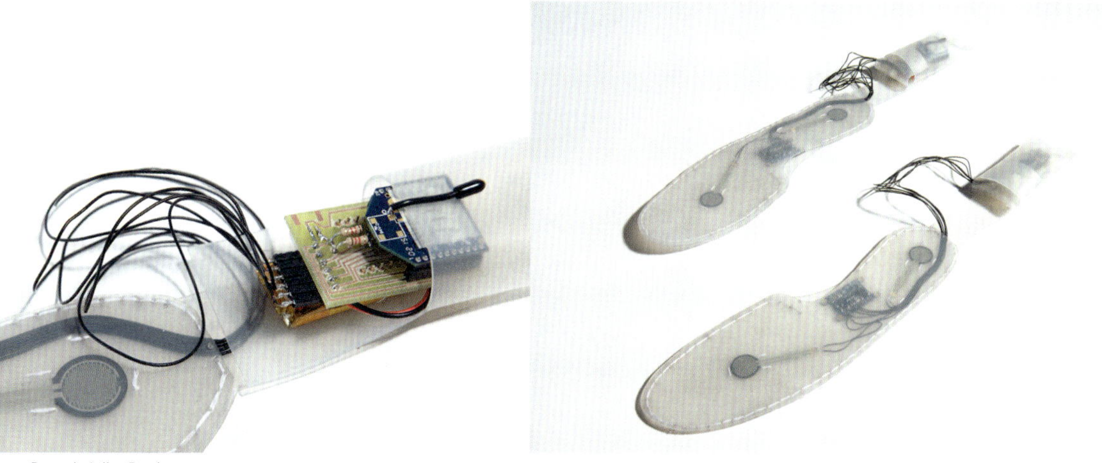

Bernardo Aviles-Busch

Audio Gait by Agnes Rosengren and Bernardo Aviles-Busch sonifies movements to aid the understanding of body balance while walking. The portable system is an easy learning aid for shin prosthetics training, which translates walking movements into auditory feedback.

Active by Hans Illiger looks into the rehabilitation process of lower limb amputees, and proposes a service design concept as well as a hardware solution for gathering movement data.

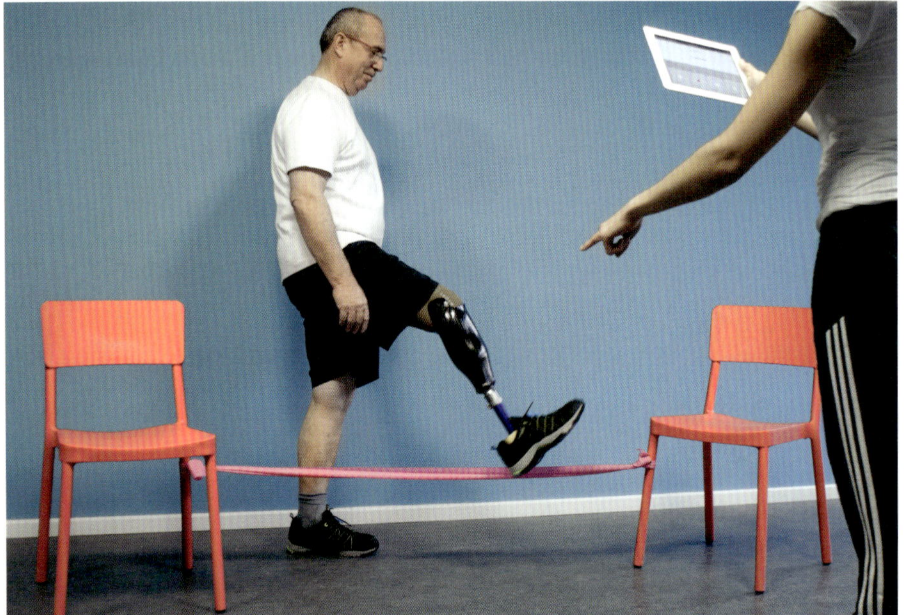

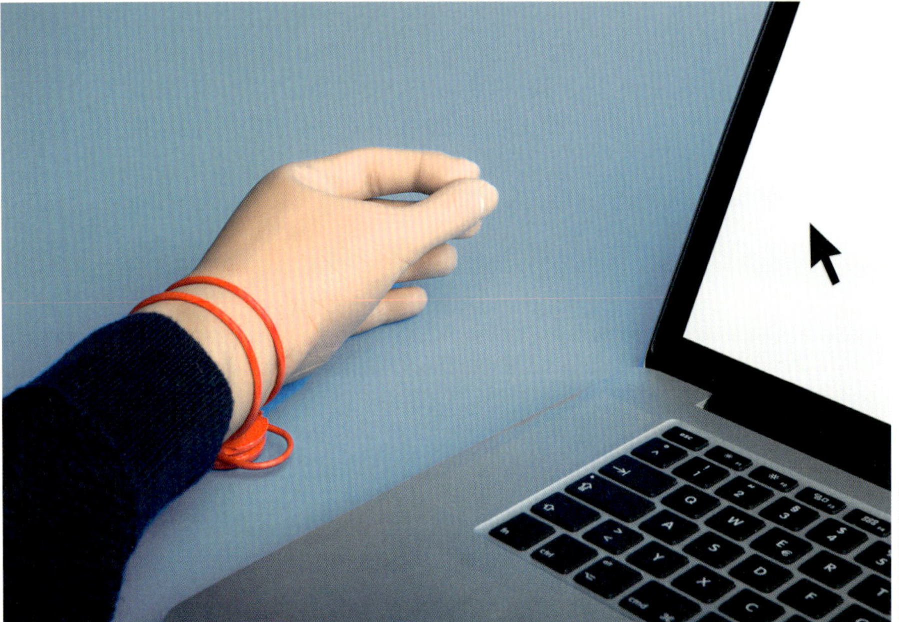

Shortcut by David Kaltenbach, Maximilian Mahal, and Lucas Rex is a customizable Human Interface Device (HID) for upper limb amputees. The bracelet detects sensory muscular impulses in the phantom hand, translating them into contactless and intuitive computer controlling.

STARTS Prize'16 · Grand Prize – Innovative Collaboration

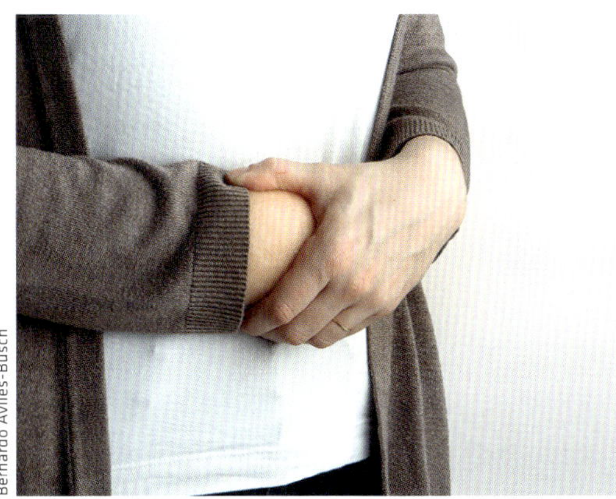

Bernardo Aviles-Busch

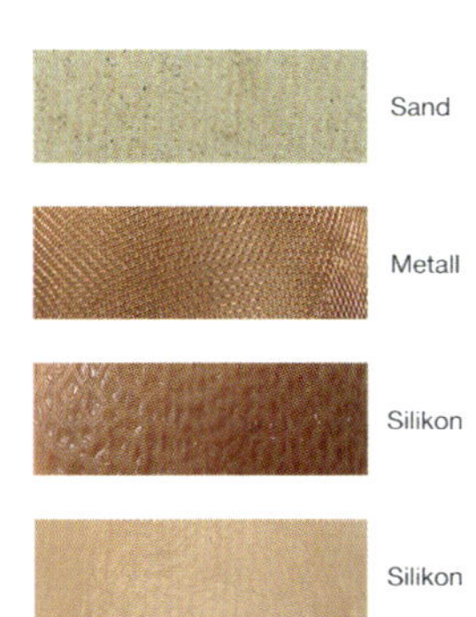

Sand

Metall

Silikon

Silikon

One of the most heated discussions during the ideation period was about the concept of Uncanny Valley. *The Aesthetics of the Uncanny* by Carmina Blank and Sandra Stark explores the delicate balance between familiar prosthesis design standards and uncanniness. The team researched how targeted material conception can help to understand and control this phenomenon, and can be taken into conscious consideration during the design process.

Tactile Sensation by Nina Rossow explores two possibilities of displaying information through tactile feedback: *Sens_mat* allows passive tactile recognition of materials when direct contact is not possible. *Sens_dia* simplifies descriptions in pain diagnostics and offers a non-verbal and body specific communication.

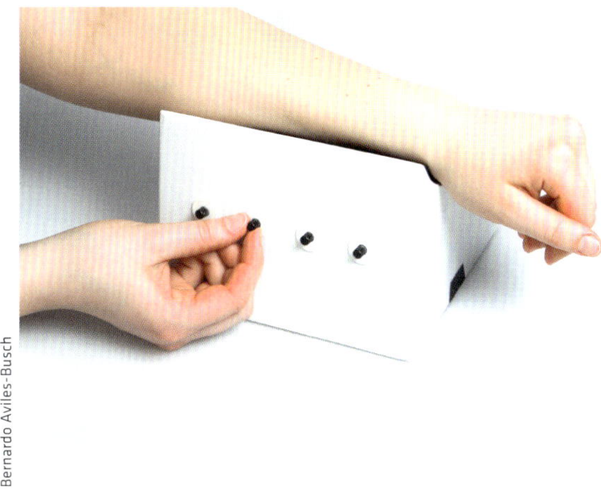

Bernardo Aviles-Busch

Artificial Skins and Bones Group
Course Instructors: Wolf Jeschonnek, Mika Satomi
Participating Students: Bernardo Aviles-Busch, Carmina Blank, Hans Illiger, David Kaltenbach, Maximilian Mahal, Stephanie Nattrass, Natalie Peter, Lucas Rex, Agnes, Rosengren, Nina Rossow, Sandra Stark, Lisa Stohn, Babette Wiezorek, Karina Wirth, Jhuting Yang

Main project partners
Weißensee Kunsthochschule Berlin
Fab Lab Berlin
Ottobock Healthcare GmbH
Makea Industries GmbH

The Artificial Skins and Bones Group (DE) is an interdisciplinary group of young designers from Weißensee Kunsthochschule Berlin. Their expertise ranges from textile, surface and product design to fashion and visual communications. In the *Artificial Skins and Bones* project the group freely explored the design of, and interaction with, artificial bodies and body parts. The projects presented illustrate a great variety of possible starting points, prototyping techniques, and application scenarios. We hope that the outcome is a valuable contribution to the future exploration of artificial bodies and prosthetic designs.

STARTS PRIZE´16 HONORARY

MENTIONS

Amsterdam Smart Citizens Lab
Waag Society

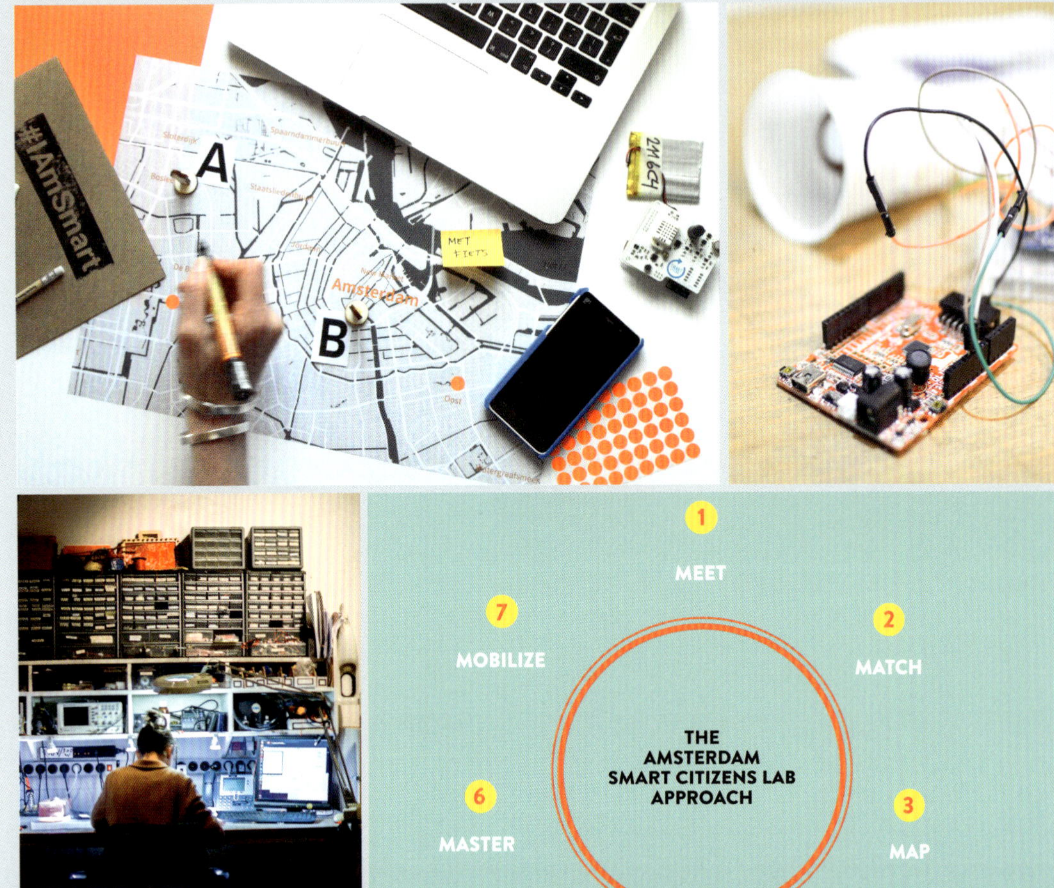

The *Amsterdam Smart Citizens Lab* empowers a vivid community of committed citizens to use inexpensive, open source technology to understand their environments (the air they breathe, the noise they hear, the water they drink & swim in, and the soil they grow on) better and to take action based on their findings. They are coached by experts and hackers who put their knowledge to use in answering the participants' questions, and help them to measure, analyze, and interpret data that would have been beyond their reach a few years ago. This is expected to lead to more engagement, more insight, better-informed dialogues between citizens and their governments, and in the end to more enjoyable, liveable, and creative cities.

While our environments have a large impact on our short and long term health, the data to understand them are sparse, obscure, and often inadequate. Pollution is measured in averages and then modeled to fill in the gaps, whereas their levels vary hugely from street to street and moment to moment. Some places can even be considered "toxic" during some moments of the day. Even so, the available data are taken to be "objective", whilst decisions made about

http://waag.org/en/project/amsterdam-smart-citizens-lab
http://www.meetup.com/Amsterdam-Smart-Citizens-Lab
http://waag.org/sites/waag/files/public/media/publicaties/amsterdam-smart-citizen-lab-publicatie.pdf

what to measure, their norms, and interpretations, are subjective and political. Citizens, meanwhile, suffer: from pollution, lack of knowledge and trust in measurement bodies, and from a lack of options to act.

The *Amsterdam Smart Citizens Lab* aims to provide a solution. It is open to inquisitive people who are interested in learning about their surroundings and want to team up to share their skills and time. Collectively they draft measuring strategies and campaigns, build or appropriate sensors, collect data, and interpret and act on the outcomes. The Lab builds on the existing infrastructures and communities from the Amsterdam Fablab & Open Wetlab, and consists of various meetings and group activities that last over long stretches of time. It was conceived and started by the Amsterdam-based media lab Waag Society, which has been researching and developing emergent technologies for social innovation for over 20 years. The Lab has attracted many partners (hackers, universities, city officials, official measuring bodies & the city of Amsterdam) to provide experts and expertise, and to learn from the outcomes.

From over almost a hundred enthusiasts at the start in 2014, the community has grown to over 600 that are currently registered at the meetup page. They are a mixed group of old & new Amsterdamers, including many people from abroad that are interested in contributing to the city they live in. The results, as well as the methodology, are described in Creative Commons Licensed publications and on the Web. Our aim is to extend and verify our methodology, thereby helping people all around the world to implement it, check it, expand it, and turn their own participatory sensing projects into a success.

We feel like we're part of the birth and growth of a movement of citizens that know where they can get the knowledge and support to use public networks of open source sensors and eventually use self-gathered data to make smarter choices. By embracing this bottom-up movement and enabling creativity, we want to facilitate citizens to maximize their capacity to act. With more data and more evenly distributed knowledge, we see impactful dialogues between citizens and governments arising. In short: we feel we are on to something and will continue in these efforts.

Waag Society runs the ASCL in conjunction with Gemeente Amsterdam, HvA, RIVM, SenseMakers, Alterra, AMS, Amsterdam Economic Board, KNMI, ECN, Fablab Amsterdam, and the Open Wetlab; and internationally with IAAC, Fablab Barcelona, Microgiants, FutureEverything, Dundee University, Peer Educators Network, Joint Research Center and others.

With special thanks to: Mara Balestrini, Ger Baron, Co de Boer, Pieter van Boheemen, Alessandro Bozzon, Jonathan Carter, Roberta Colavecchio, Guillermo José Rodríguez Fernández, Laurence Henriquez, Ester van der Geest, Christine van den Horn, Joske Houtkamp, Frank Kresin, Qijun Jiang, Folkert Lodewijks, Emma Pareschi, Edith van Putten, Cindy Regalado, Natasha de Sena, Pinar Temiz, Hester Volten, Maurice de Vries, Mathijs de Weerdt, Joost Wesseling and all the participants and supporters of the Lab.

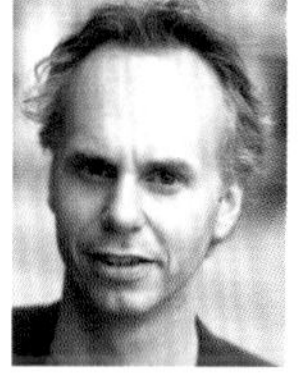

Waag Society—institute for art, science and technology—is a pioneer in the field of digital media. Over the past 22 years, the foundation has developed into an institution of international stature, a platform for artistic research and experimentation, and has become both a catalyst for events and a breeding ground for cultural and social innovation. Waag Society explores emerging technologies, and provides art and culture a central role in the designing of new applications for novel advances in science and technology. Artists and designers know better than anyone that they must question technology in order to get to the bottom of things, overthrow sacred cows, stimulate imagination and fantasy, create unexpected connections, and—above all—search for meaning. **Frank Kresin** is Research Director at Waag Society. His background is in Artificial Intelligence and Film making, and his interest in developing technology for societal goals. He was involved in many international programs, such as Apps for Europe, City SDK, CineGrid Amsterdam, Code 4 Europe and Making. Frank speaks, writes, and lectures on Open Data, Users as Designers, Living Labs, and Smart Citizens. He is a board member at ISOC.NL and The Mobile City

Bionic Partition: Generative Design for Aerospace

Airbus, APWorks, Autodesk, The Living

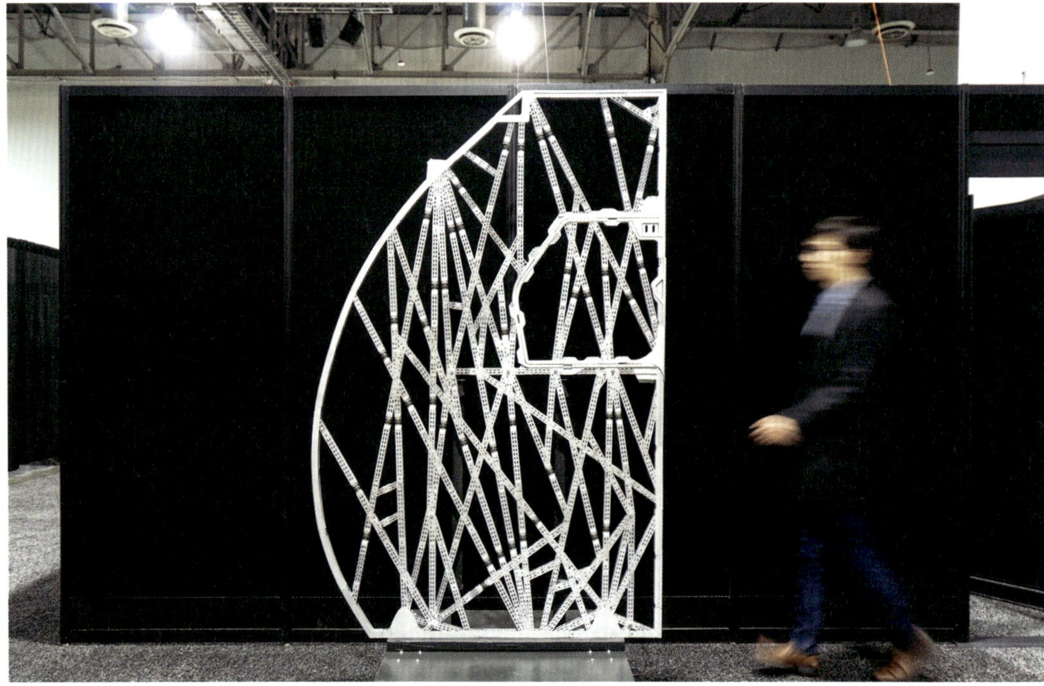

The *Bionic Partition* is the world's largest metal 3D printed airplane component. The partition is a dividing wall between the seating area and galley of a plane, and it is a challenging component to design because it must include a cutout for emergency stretcher access and it must hold a fold-down seat for cabin attendants. The new *Bionic Partition*— created through a pioneering combination of generative design, 3D printing, and advanced material— is almost 50% lighter than current designs, and it is also stronger. This weight savings translates to fuel savings and carbon reduction. The final design illustrates a novel use of "bio computation," and it demonstrates an ultra-high-performance result beyond typical engineering rules of thumb. The *Bionic Partition* is currently undergoing 16G crash testing as part of the process for certification and integration into the current fleet of A320 planes.

When slime mold grows, it creates a complex 2D network that is both efficient and redundant. It is efficient because it connects a given set of dots (food) with a minimal amount of lines. And it is redundant because each dot touches at least two lines—so if any line is removed, the dots remain connected in the network.

We developed an algorithm that uses the "biological algorithm" of slime mold to link critical connection points in an airplane partition. Then we ran a process of bio computation that generates, evaluates, and evolves tens of thousands of design options.

Combining our custom techniques of data science and bio computation, we can derive results that are both high performing and unexpected. The process is not about achieving cold-blooded efficiency. Rather it is about expanding our creativity.

The *Bionic Partition* is pushing the limits of several technologies, but it is on track for a real industry application this year. When applied to all A320 planes on backorder, this new design approach could save up to one million metric tons of carbon emissions per year.

The Living: David Benjamin, Danil Nagy, Damon Lau, Dale Zhao, John Locke, Ray Wang, Jim Stoddart, Lorenzo Villaggi
Airbus: Bastian Schaefer, Ingo Wuggetzer, Stefan List, Joerg Schuler, Peter Sander, Jens Telgkamp, Tobias Meyer, Martial Somda, Stefan Holst
Autodesk: Jeff Kowalski, Gonzalo Martinez, Ian Keough, Michael Kirschner, Huaijun Wu, Francesco Iorio, Ryan Schmidt, Sualp Ozel, Emmanuel Weyermann
APWorks: Joachim Zettler, Felix Rothe, Andreas Nick, Chris Seiffert, Angela Gruenewald

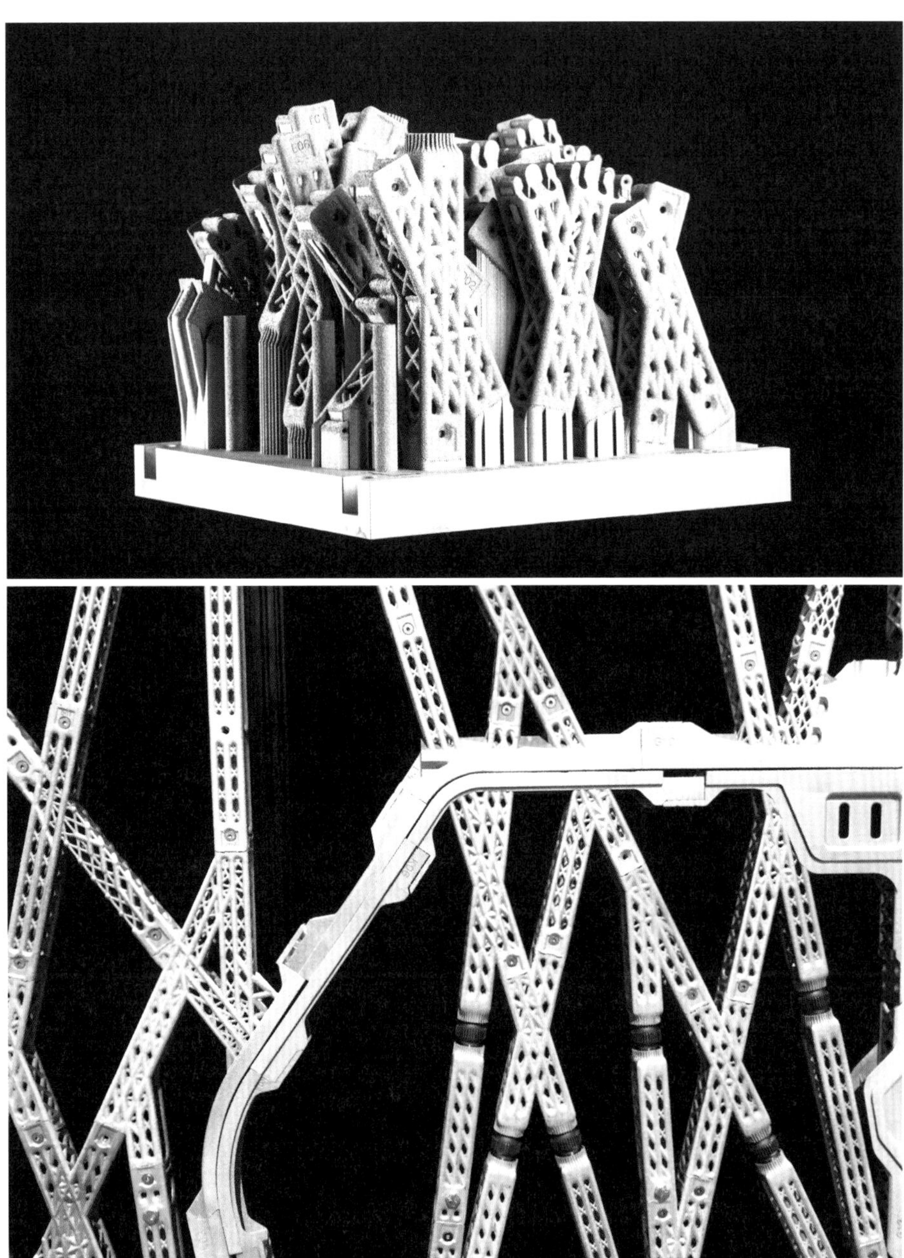

Airbus (DE), a division of Airbus Group, is the global leading commercial aircraft manufacturer with the most modern and efficient family of airliners. **APWorks** (DE) specializes in metallic 3D printing and covers the entire value chain, from optimized product design, to choice of materials, to qualified serial production. **Autodesk** (US) helps people imagine, design, and create a better world. **The Living** (US), an Autodesk Studio, applies generative design, biology, and new materials to real built projects in the context of technology, culture, and the environment.

Fairy Lights in Femtoseconds
Yoichi Ochiai with Digital Nature Group at University of Tsukuba and Utsunomiya University

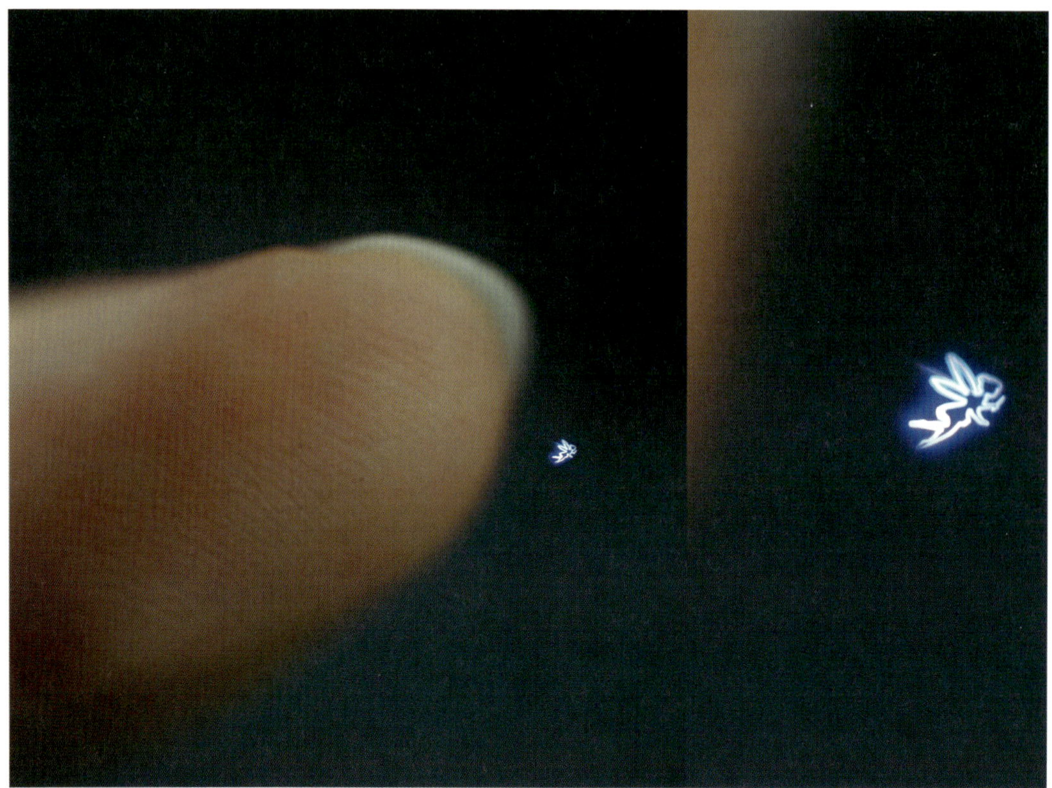

How can our imagination be materialized? From the dawn of humanity, imagination has been expressed in two ways: via images—by employing drawn images and motion pictures to form the protons for our eyes, and via sculptures—by fabricating statues and installations to materialize three-dimensional objects in the real world. In this project we explore the different methods to express our imagination via holographic synthesis on light fields. These light fields have been used as components of motion pictures for TV, movies, and Computer Graphics. We aimed to update these field quantities towards three-dimensional computational controlled matter.

In the art & science project *Fairy Lights in Femtoseconds*, compositions of light field technologies that use laser-induced plasma—30 femtoseconds ultra short pulse laser—are created. New artificial matter becomes tangible and visible new material. This project proposes a method of rendering aerial and volumetric graphics with computationally controlled femtosecond lasers. A high-intensity laser excites a physical matter to emit light at an arbitrary 3D position and it excites in an ultra short time period. Artistic applications can then be explored, especially since plasma induced by a femtosecond laser is safer than that generated by a nanosecond laser employed in conventional approaches.

We believe this project will melt the borders between matter and images. Moreover, tangibility, invisibility, and malleability are essential for digital societies and update our concept of matter.

Realized within the Digital Nature Group at University of Tsukuba and Utsunomiya University
Coauthors of the project research paper: Kota Kumagai, Takayuki Hoshi, Jun Rekimoto, Satoshi Hasegawa, and Yoshio Hayasaki.

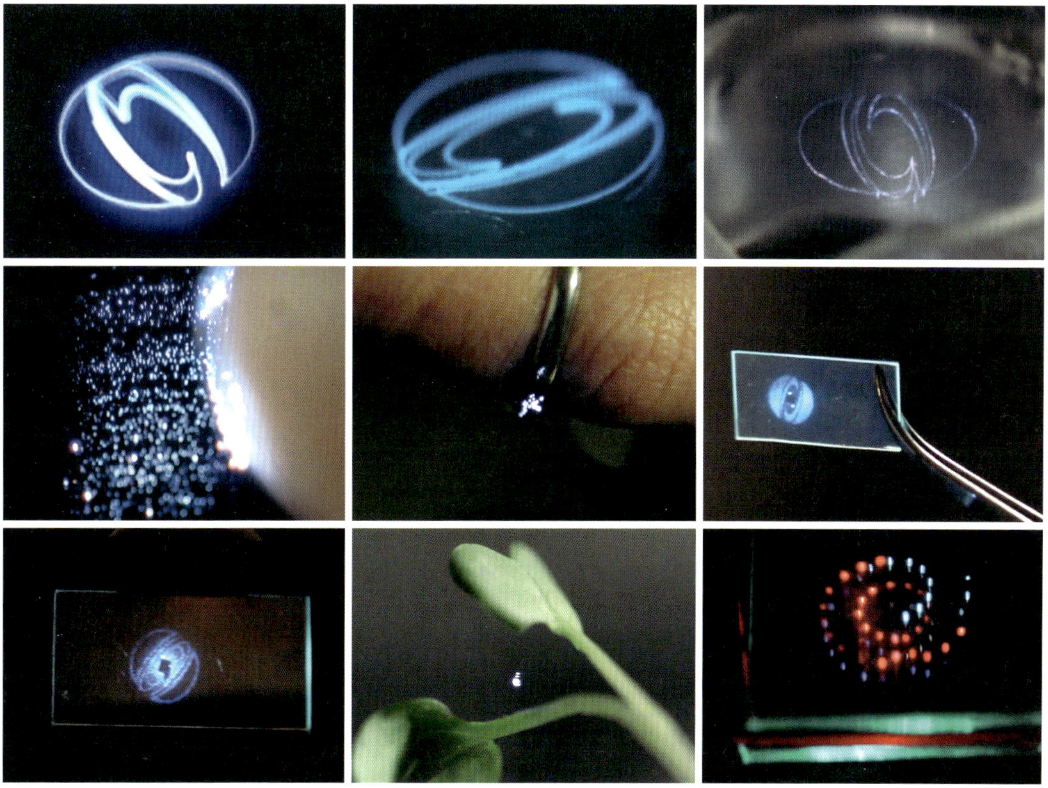

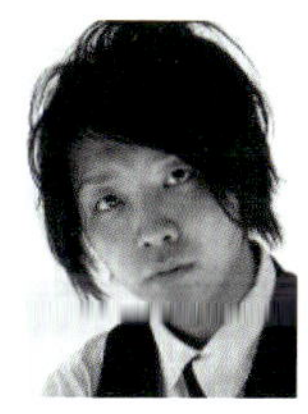

Yoichi Ochiai (JP), born in 1987, is a media artist and assistant professor of University of Tsukuba and Head of its Digital Nature Group. He holds a PhD in Applied Computer Science from the University of Tokyo. He works on new inventions and research through a mixture of applied physics, computer science, and art. He has a strong interest in post-pixel multimedia and conducting research towards his vision called Digital Nature—an alternative perspective of nature and humanity in the post ubiquitous computing era. He has received the Innovative Technologies Prize from METI Japan, the World Technology Award from WTN, and many more.

Fairy Lights in Femtoseconds · Yoichi Ochiai with Digital Nature Group at University of Tsukuba and Utsunomiya University

RGB|CMYK Kinetic
ART+COM Studios

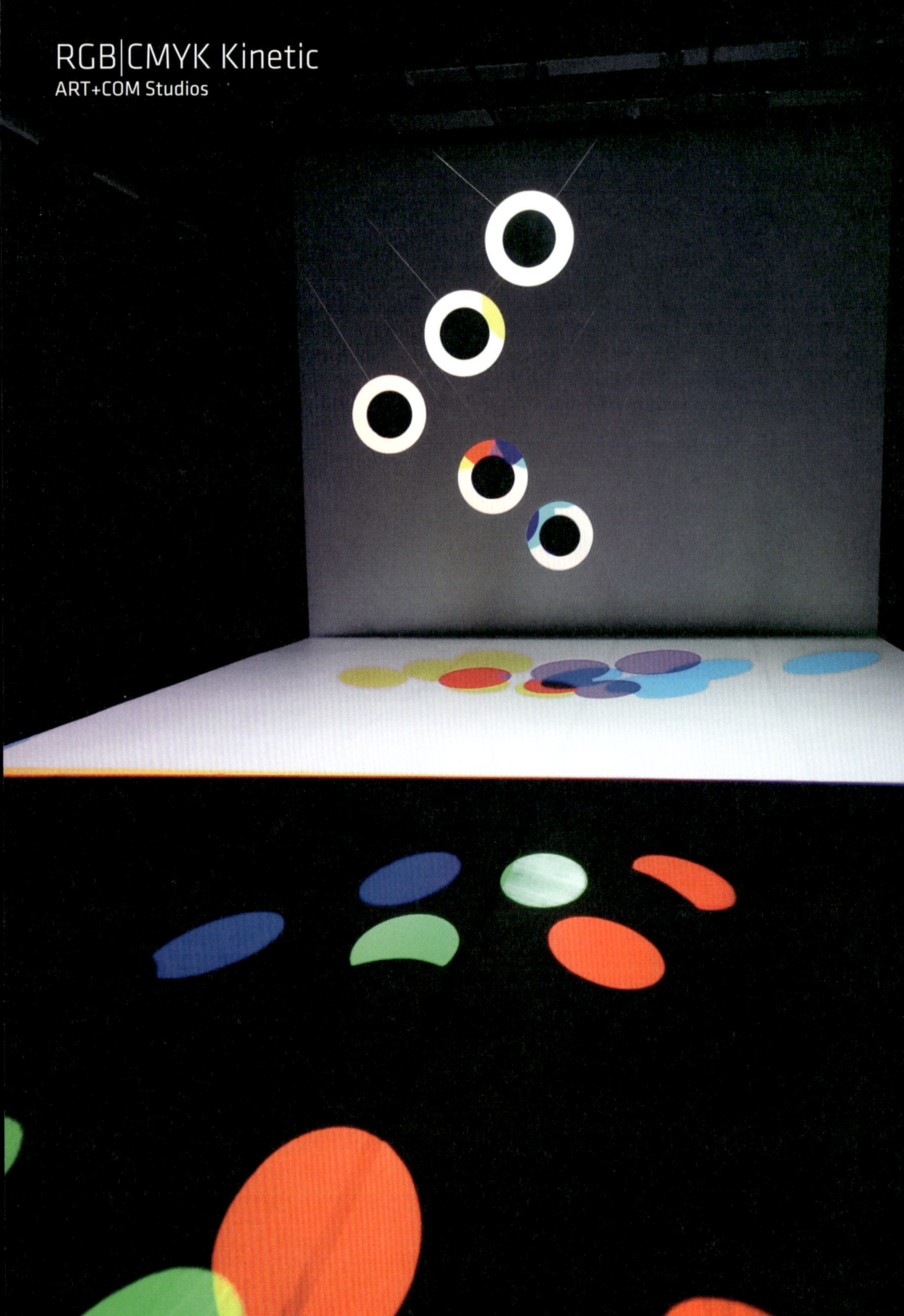

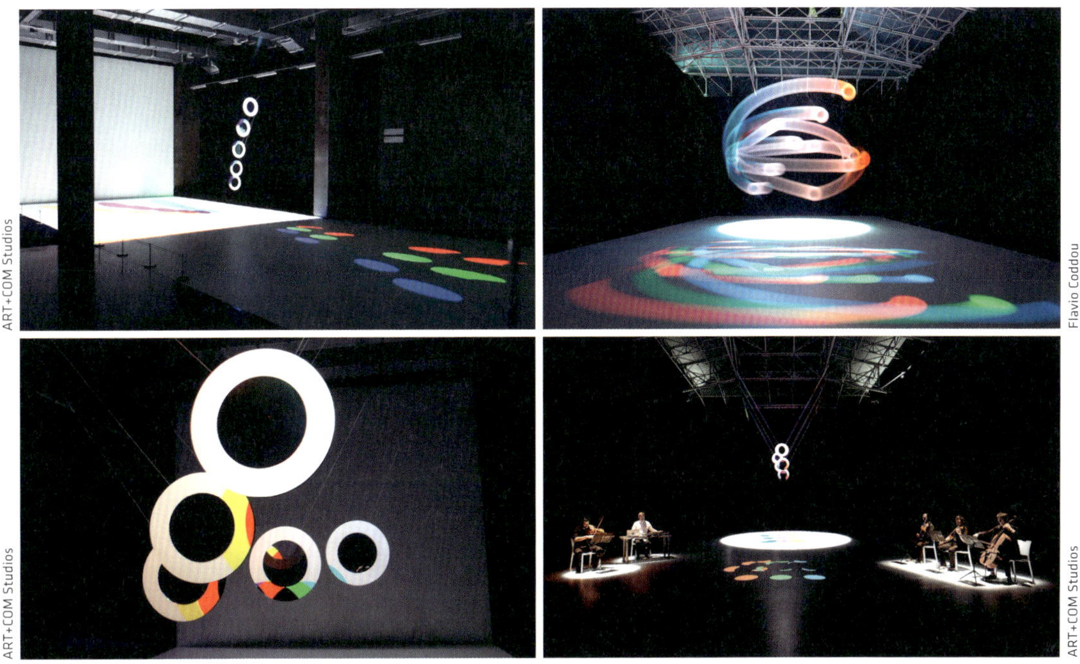

Flavio Coddou

ART+COM Studios

ART+COM Studios

ART+COM Studios

RGB|CMYK Kinetic is a poetic experience of color, movement, and sound. Simultaneously a suspended sculpture and a choreography of light and music, it has roots in two twentieth-century avant-garde traditions: kinetic art and light art. The inspiration for the work stems from the nature of light, particularly from the duality of additive and subtractive colors.

Five mirror-coated flat disks seem to float through space in unison. Three spot lights in the three primary colors, red, green, and blue (RGB), project a circle of white light on the floor. The discs reflect the light and cast colored shadows onto the floor. This set-up provides the basis for a poetic choreography and the immersive, spatial experience of colorful, synchronized lights and shadows moving in unison with the computative and weightless motion of the discs.

The colored ellipses on the ground are generated by reflecting and shadowing the spot lights. The mirror discs cast shadows behind them on the ground, and in these shadows the white light subtracts into cyan, magenta, and yellow (CMY). In front, the discs reflect the RGB light as individual colors onto the ground. With this the three additive primary colors (RGB) and the three subtractive primary colors (CMY) are created out of the white light.

The kinetic choreography is complemented by a musical score that unfolds in dialogue with the discs' movements. The three-part sound composition for *RGB|CMY Kinetic* was made by Icelandic musician, Ólafur Arnalds. The first part of the composition is based on the movements of the mirror discs: the varying heights of the discs in space modulate the five digital instruments. The following two sections of the composition interpret the computatively designed choreography more freely.

The installation *RGB|CMY Kinetic* was commissioned by Sónar and the Sorigué Foundation and premiered at SónarPLANTA Barcelona in 2015. Expanded by the dimension of black (the "K" in CMYK stands for key=mask=black), *RGB|CMYK Kinetic* is a work produced for the opening exhibition at the Asian Art Center in Gwangju, South Korea.
Sound: Ólafur Arnalds

ART+COM Studios (DE) designs and develops new media installations and spaces. We use new technology as an artistic medium of expression and as a medium for the interactive communication of complex information. In the process, we are improving the technologies constantly and exploring their potential for spatial communication and art. ART+COM e.V., founded in 1988, is today ART+COM Studios, working internationally in the field of art, communication, and research. *http://www.artcom.de*

SPARKED: A Live Interaction Between Humans and Quadcopters

Verity Studios, ETH Zurich, and Cirque du Soleil

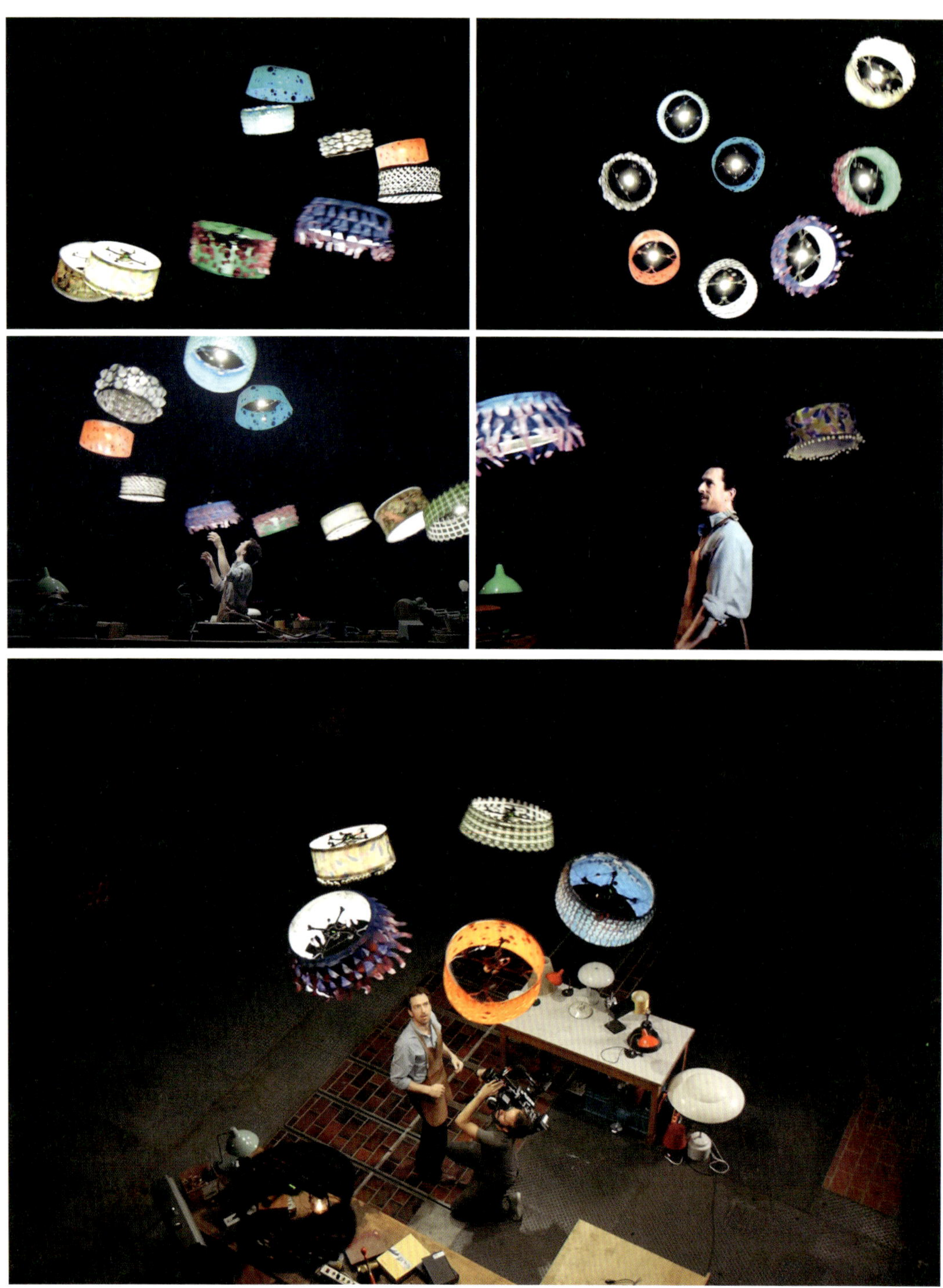

http://www.youtube.com/watch?v=6C8OJsHfmpI

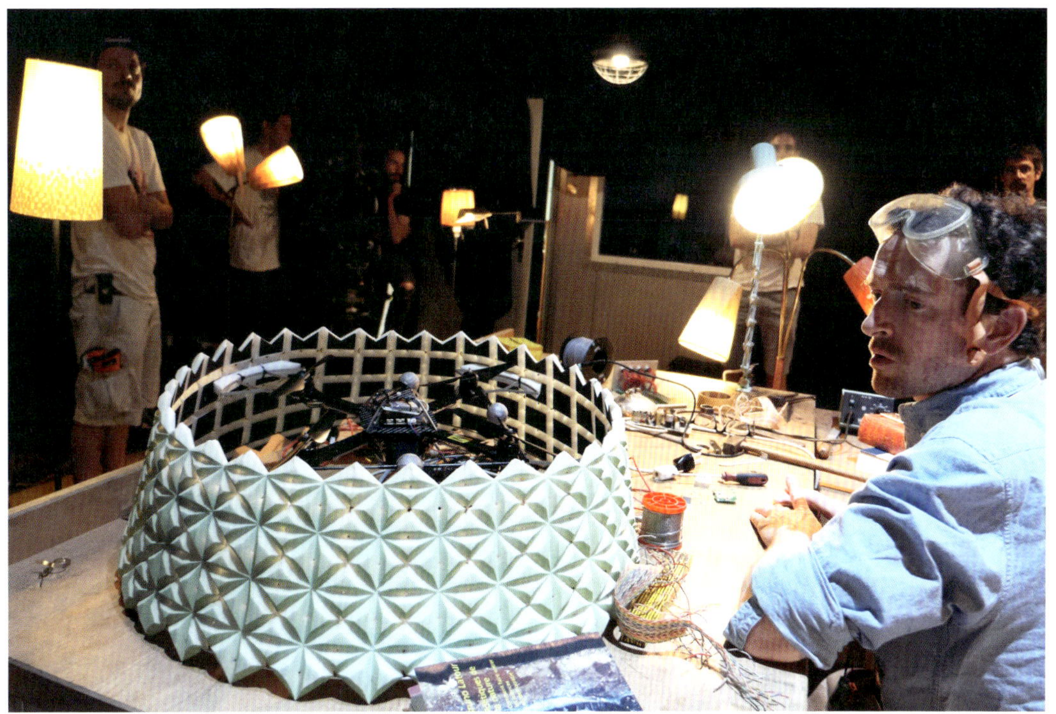

Verity Studios, ETH Zurich, and Cirque du Soleil have partnered to develop a short film featuring 10 quadcopters in a flying dance performance. The collaboration resulted in a unique, interactive choreography where humans and drones move in sync. Precise computer control allows for a large performance and movement vocabulary of the quadcopters and opens the door to many more applications in the future.

SPARKED: A Live Interaction Between Humans and Quadcopters was a highly democratic and highly collaborative process. Raffaello D'Andrea of ETH Zurich and Verity Studios, and Welby Altidor of Cirque du Soleil were the project leaders, but the true collaborative nature of this project is reflected in the fact that no participant roles are specified in the credits.

Ryoichi Kurokawa

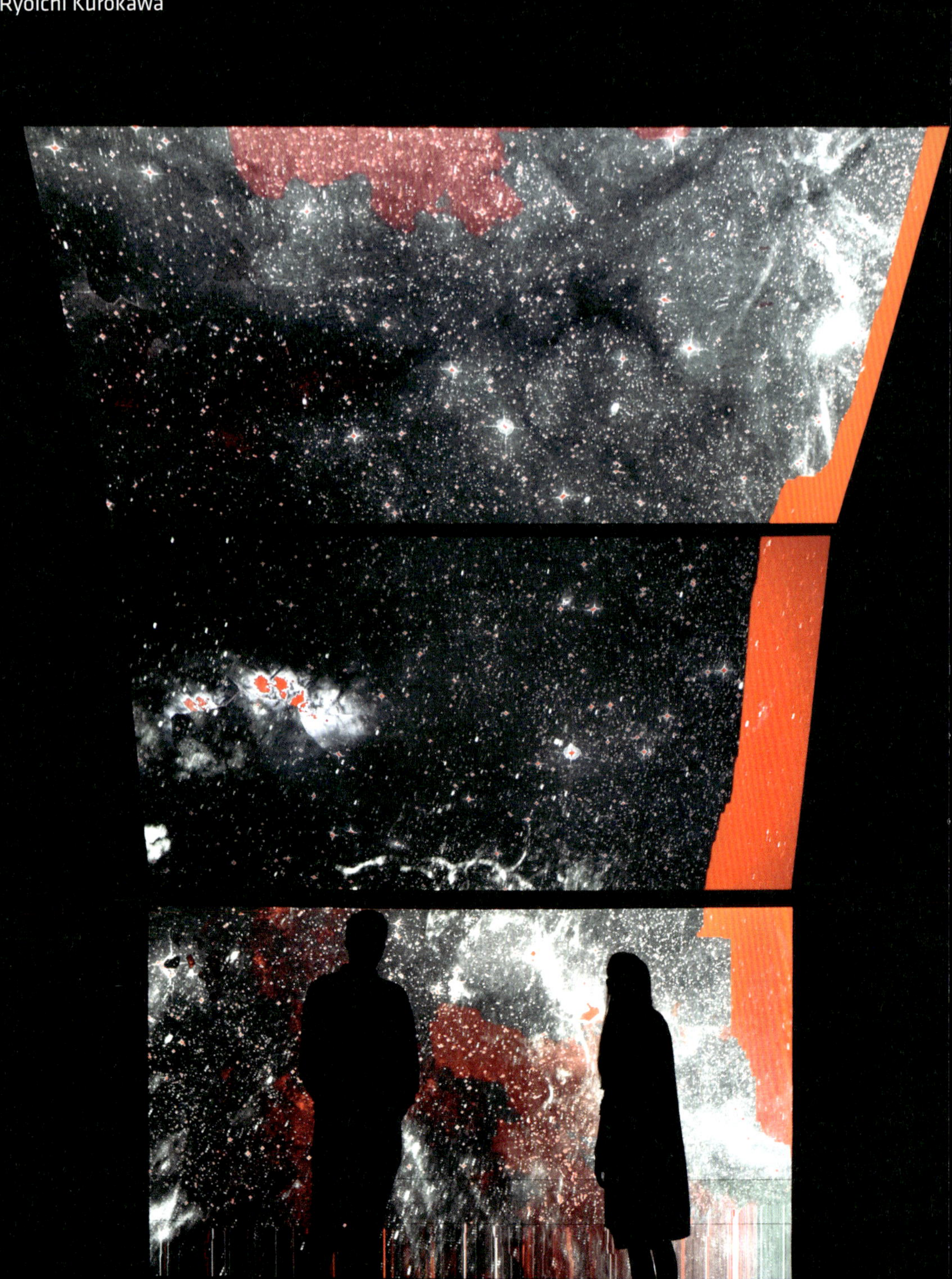

Inspired by the latest discoveries in the field of astrophysics, *unfold,* an immersive and sensory installation seeks to translate into sounds, images, and vibrations, the phenomena surrounding the formation and evolution of stars and galaxies.

With *unfold,* Ryoichi Kurokawa is concerned with the synesthetic, merging audible and visual materials, in the service of an art/science project inspired by recent discoveries. These findings have been made by astrophysicists at CEA-IRFU, based on data produced by the satellites of the European Space Agency and NASA, and more specifically by the Herschel space telescope. The telescope's observations of far infrared radiation have revealed some of the conditions of star birth and the history of the life of galaxies, over the course of 10 billion years. In addition to this data—that allows us to trace the cosmological history of star formation, especially the filamentary structure of molecular clouds where stars are born—the artist also based his logic on numerical simulations intended to model the universe and its structures, produced by astrophysicists at CEA-IRFU, with the help of supercomputers.

The project, created under the supervision of astrophysicist at CEA-IRFU, Vincent Minier, enables us to go beyond research and scientific discovery, in order to question the representation and publication of the data collected.

On this subject, Minier reminds us that although "the representation of these observations and their public sharing are generally done through beautiful colourised images," their coloration in no way refers to the actual color of the objects observed but is rather intended to represent "a light intensity, a density, a temperature or even a chemical composition." He comments that Kurokawa's work questions "the usual codes of nebulae at the atmospheric edge," to imagine new forms of visualization, "which enables the establishment of a pattern of results, a scientific interpretation, as well as an expression of the technology that is behind these results," more willingly playing "on the mathematical beauty" and the "immersion in the significance of this data."

Co-commissioned between FACT (Foundation for Art and Creative Technology), Stereolux et Salford University, with the support of CEA Irfu, Paris-Saclay (Alternative Energies and Atomic Energy Commission, Institute of Research into the Fundamental Laws of the Universe), Arcadi and DICRéAM (Dispositif pour la Création Artistique Multimédia et Numérique).

Concept, direction, composition, programming, design: Ryoichi Kurokawa
Producer: Nicolas Wierinck
Programming: Hiroshi Matoba
Scientific Advisor: Vincent Minier, astrophysicist at CEA Irfu, Paris-Saclay
Scientific Datasets: CEA (Herschel HOBYS, COAST, Frédéric Bournaud, Sacha Brun, Pascal Tremblin, Patrick Hennebelle, Rémi Hosseini-Kazeroni), ESA, NASA, BLAST Experiment, SuperCOSMOS H-alpha Survey
Produced by studio Ryoichi Kurokawa
Courtesy of White Circle

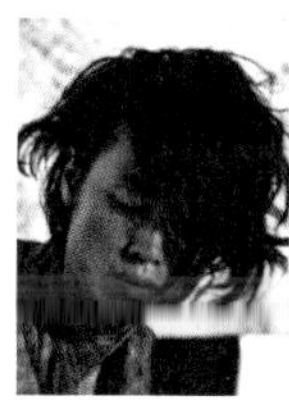

Ryoichi Kurokawa (JP), born in 1978, is a Japanese artist who lives and works in Berlin. Kurokawa's works take on multiple forms such as installation works, recordings, and concert pieces. He composes time sculpture with field recordings and digitally generated structures, and reconstructs architecturally audiovisual phenomenon. In recent years, his works have shown at international festivals and museums including Tate Modern, Venice Biennale, transmediale, and Sonar. In 2010, he was awarded the Golden Nica at Prix Ars Electronica in the Digital Musics & Sound Art category *http://www.ryoichikurokawa.com*

V2_
Institute for the Unstable Media

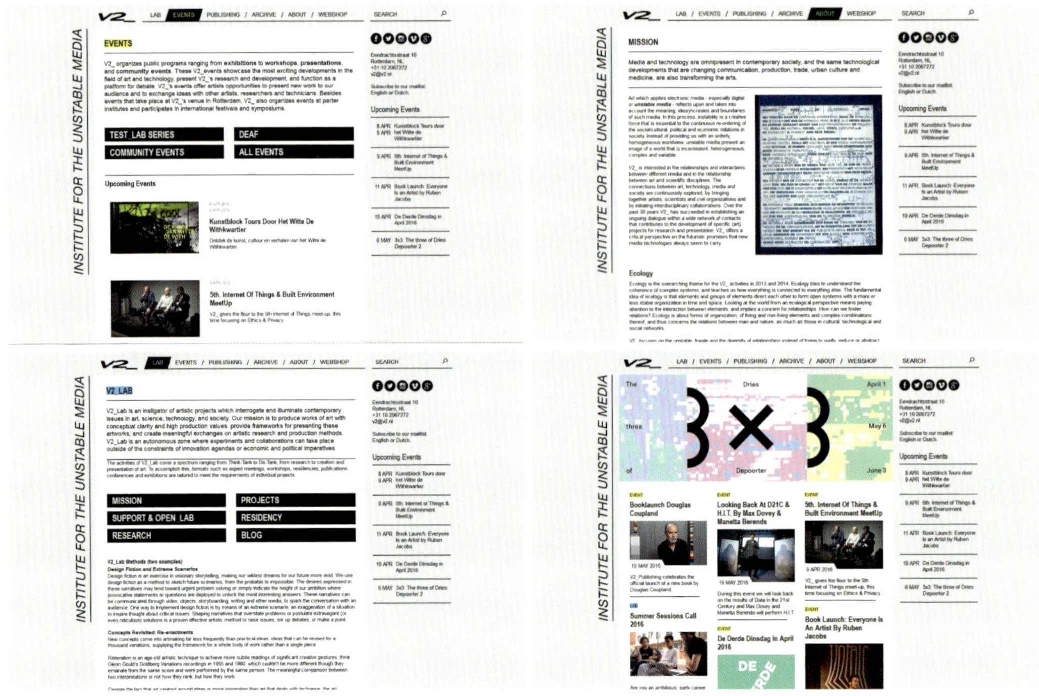

V2_, Institute for the Unstable Media is an interdisciplinary center for art and media technology in Rotterdam (the Netherlands). V2_ presents, produces, archives, and publishes research at the interface of art, technology, and society. V2_ offers a platform for artists, designers, scientists, researchers, theorists, and developers from various disciplines to discuss their work and share their findings. In V2_'s view, art and design play an essential role in the social embedding of technological developments. V2_ creates a context in which issues regarding the social impact of technology are explored through critical dialogue, artistic reflection, and practice-oriented research.

Unstable Media

Media and technology are omnipresent in contemporary society, and the same technological developments that are changing communication, politics, production, trade, urban culture, and medicine, are also transforming the arts. Art which applies electronic media—especially digital or *unstable*—reflects upon and takes into account the meaning, idiosyncrasies, and boundaries of such media. In this process, instability is a creative force that is essential to the continuous re-ordering of the social/cultural, political, and economic relations in society. Instead of providing us with an orderly, homogeneous worldview, unstable media present an image of a world that is inconsistent, heterogeneous, complex, and variable.

Interactions

V2_ is interested in the relationships and interactions between different media and in the relationship between art and scientific disciplines. The connec-

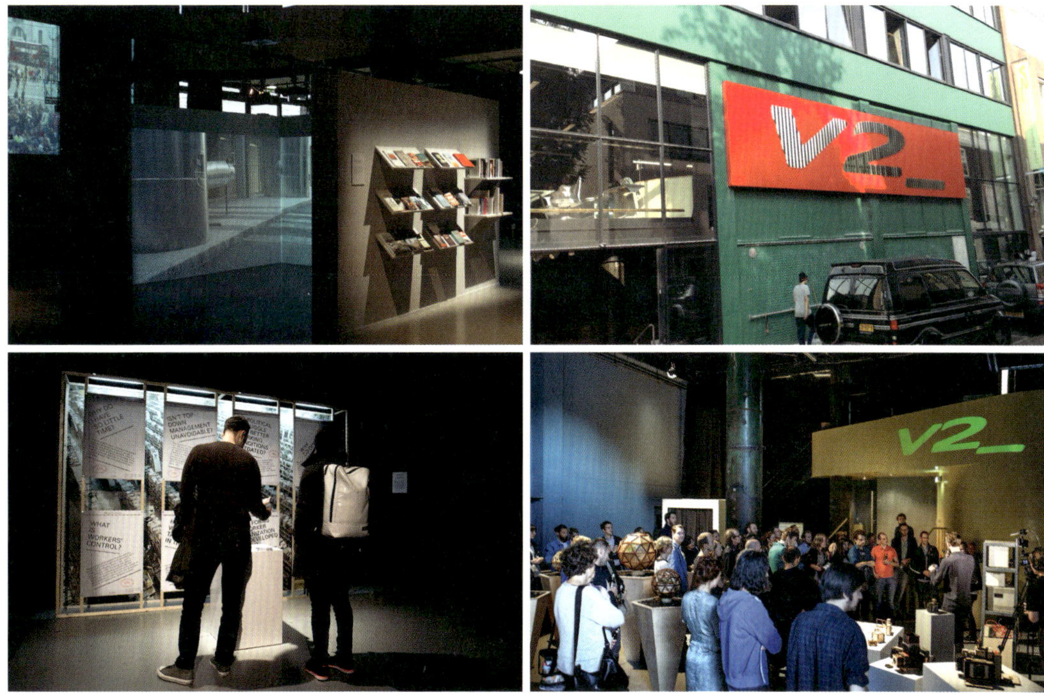

tions between art, technology, media, and society are continuously explored, by bringing together artists, scientists, and civil organizations and by initiating interdisciplinary collaborations. V2_ and its Lab are an instigator of artistic projects, which interrogate and illuminate contemporary issues in art, science, technology, and society. V2_Lab is an autonomous zone where experiments and collaborations can take place outside of the constraints of innovation agendas or economic and political imperatives. With its V2_Lab and the books published by V2_Publishing, V2_ offers a critical perspective on the futuristic promises that new technologies always seem to carry.

History

V2_ was founded in 1981 as an artist collective and multimedia center that transformed into a center for art and media technology. In 1994, it moved to Rotterdam and opened the V2_Lab in 1998 as an extension of its practices towards art production, research, and knowledge exchange.

V2_, Institute for the Unstable Media is an interdisciplinary center for art and media technology in Rotterdam (the Netherlands). V2_ presents, produces, archives, and publishes research at the interface of art, technology and society. Founded in 1981, V2_ offers a platform for artists, designers, scientists, researchers, theorists, and developers of software and hardware from various disciplines to discuss their work and share their findings. In V2_'s view, art and design play an essential role in the social embedding of technological developments. V2_ creates a context in which issues regarding the social impact of technology are explored through critical dialogue, artistic reflection, and practice-oriented research.

Water-based Digital Fabrication Platform
Mediated Matter Research Group, MIT Media Lab

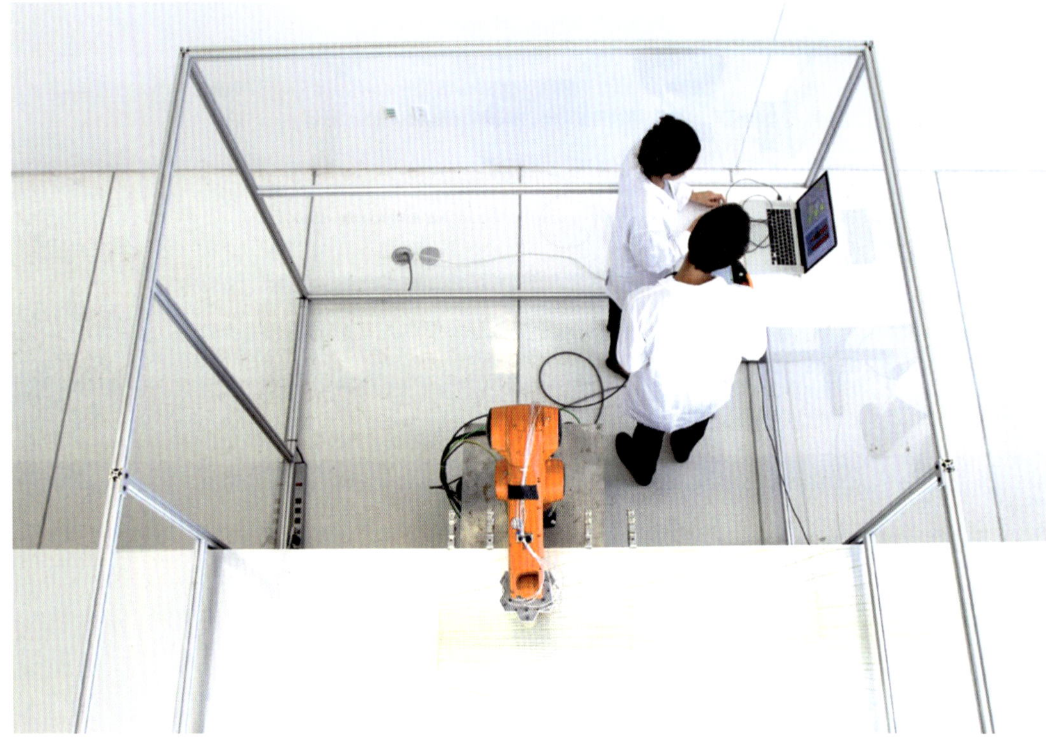

Nature is a water-mediated ecosystem. Through water Nature builds and demolishes as it enables life and guides material transformation over time. Omnipresent in inanimate and living matter, water is Nature's construction medium that gives shape, structure, and function to all organisms and natural formations; from the Great Barrier Reef single-cell micro-organisms generating energy through photosynthesis. And, to the ancients, water has been known to precede creation itself. Inspired by aqueous material formation, the *Water-based Digital Fabrication Platform* offers a new perspective on water-based manufacturing, combining an age-old crustacean-derived material with robotic fabrication and synthetic biology to form constructs that utilize graded material properties for hydration-guided self-assembly. A robotically controlled multi-chamber extrusion system is designed to deposit biodegradable composites with functional, mechanical, and optical gradients across length scales. A seamless computational workflow is implemented for the design and direct digital fabrication of multimaterial and multiscale structured objects. The workflow encodes for,

and integrates, domain-specific meta-data relating to local, regional, and global feature resolution of heterogeneous material organizations. Geometrically diverse constructs associating shape-informing variable flow rates and material properties to mesh-free geometric primitives are deposited. The structures are made of a *single* material system derived from chitin—the most abundant renewable polymer in the ocean, and the second most abundant polymer on the planet. Ground arthropod shells are transformed into chitosan, a chitin derivative, to form a variable property aqueous solution. Once printed, constructs are form-found through evaporation patterns given by the geometrical arrangement of structural members, and by the hierarchical distribution of material properties. Controlled wrinkling follows. Each component will find its shape upon contact with air, and biodegrade upon contact with water. Living matter in the form of Cyanobacteria is coated and impregnated onto chitosan samples to enable surface functionalization and impart additional properties such as water resistance and conductivity. Applications include the fabrication of fully recyclable products

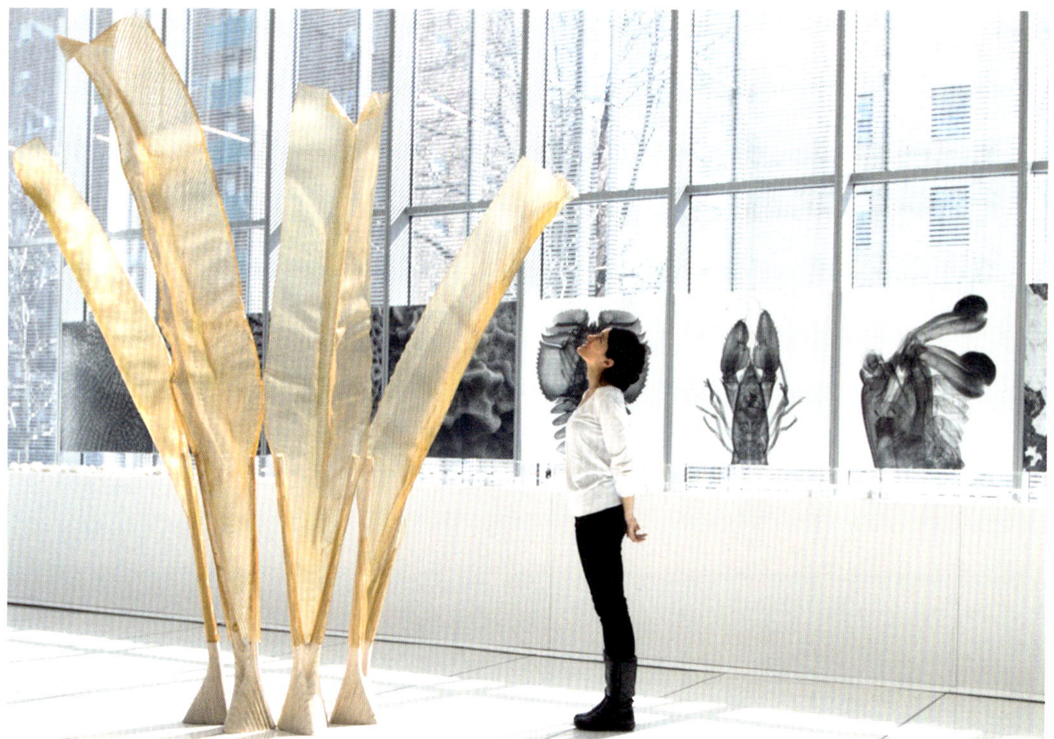

or temporary architectural components such as tent structures with graded properties. Proposed applications demonstrate environmental capabilities such as water storing structures, hydration induced shape forming and product disintegration over time. Derived from the ocean, shaped by water, and augmented by photosynthetic marine bacteria, these structures represent the transformation of a marine arthropod's shell into a treelike chitosan made skin that will ultimately convert sunlight into biofuel. The platform and its products demonstrate the *Material Ecology* approach to shape and property formation by design. It is a realization of the ancient biblical verse "from Earth to Earth," from water to water.

Research and design: The Mediated Matter Research Group at MIT Media Lab
Lead researchers: Jorge Duro, Laia Mogas, Daniel Lizardo and Neri Oxman (director)
Additional researchers: Markus Kayser, William Patrick, Sunanda Sharma, John Klein, Chikara Inamura, and Steven Keating
Collaborators: James Weaver, Javier G. Fernandez, Katia Bertoldi, Pamela Silver, Tim Lu, Allen Chen, Stephanie Hays, Eléonore Tham, Johannes Overvelde, and Dan Robertson.
Partially supported by TBA-21

The **Mediated Matter Research Group, MIT Media Lab** (US) focuses on Nature-inspired Design and Design-inspired Nature. We conduct research at the intersection of computational design, digital fabrication, materials science, and synthetic biology and apply that knowledge to design across scales from the micro scale to the building scale. We create biologically inspired, informed, and engineered design fabrication tools and technologies and structures, aiming to enhance the relation between natural and man-made environments. Our research field, entitled Material Ecology, integrates computational form-finding strategies with biologically inspired fabrication. Neri Oxman, Architect, Designer, and Associate Professor at the MIT Media Lab, heads the Mediated Matter Research Group.

WCMC Discovery Wall
Squint/Opera and Hirsch & Mann

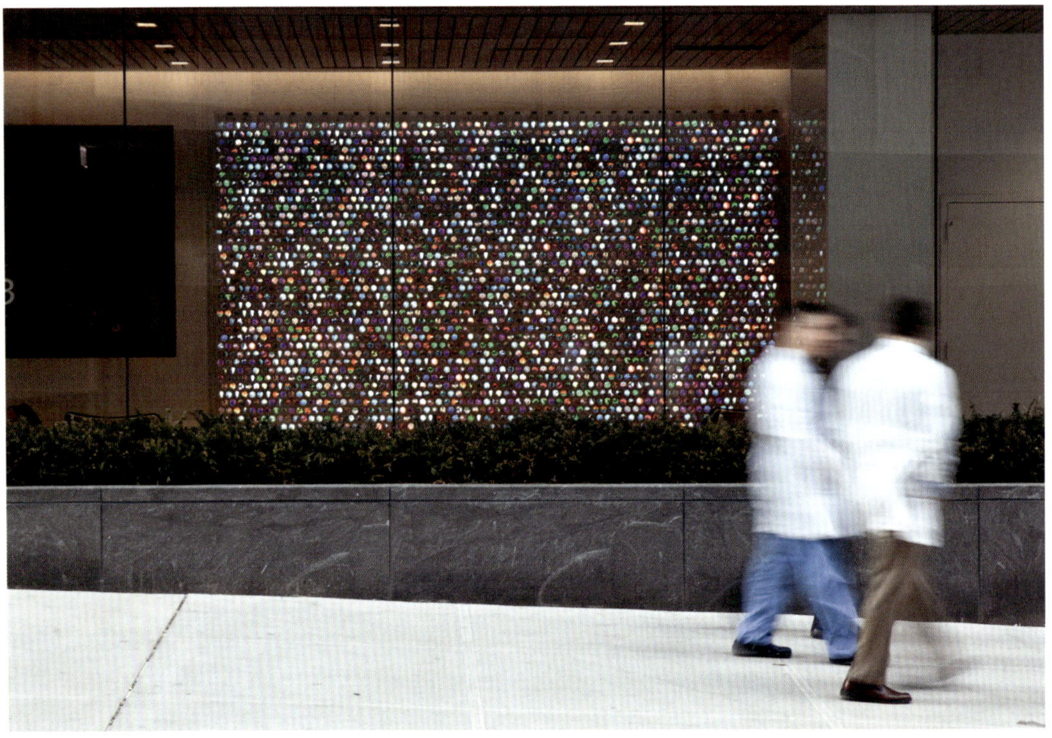

A wall-sized digital artwork created from thousands of tiny screens and lenses was designed by Squint/Opera in collaboration with Hirsch & Mann for the $650m Belfer Research Building in Manhattan, part of Weill Cornell Medical College (WCMC). The shimmering and animated foyer installation celebrates the college's research work.

The large-scale digital installation (4.6m x 2.7m) is comprised of 2,800 mini screens set in a grid pattern behind a panel of thousands of circular acrylic discs—a reference to the lenses used in medical research.

The purpose of the installation was to celebrate the support of the building's donors and promote the research and discoveries made in the building. The artwork was designed as an intriguing and beautiful object to be viewed close up in the lobby or seen from outside the building as a single image. Each screen has information about medical discoveries and other news fed from WCMC's website. The images and stories change constantly. Through the language of discovery passers-by are drawn in and encouraged to learn more.

The vision of New-York-based Ennead Architects was to commission an artwork that would promote collaboration throughout the building and give a light touch to the interior fabric. To achieve this, electronics were color-matched with stone cladding and circuit boards were mounted on transparent frames. The clear acrylic lenses magnify the stonework at oblique angles and focus the screens when facing square on.

During the commission Ennead Architects advised the client and briefed Squint/Opera to develop creative concepts. The concepts were delivered through a team of specialists brought together by Squint/Opera. Hirsch & Mann led the technology design, production, and delivery, The Cross Kings led the physical detail design and fabrication in Boston was completed by Design Communications Limited.

Squint/Opera worked closely with Hirsch & Mann to design and build all components from scratch. This involved creating many prototypes, which allowed the team to test ideas and communicate concepts to all stakeholders, taking them on the journey of developing a piece of art. The prototypes acted as a key discussion tool beyond drawings or presentations and allowed the team to refine the design and align with the architectural vision and the brief.

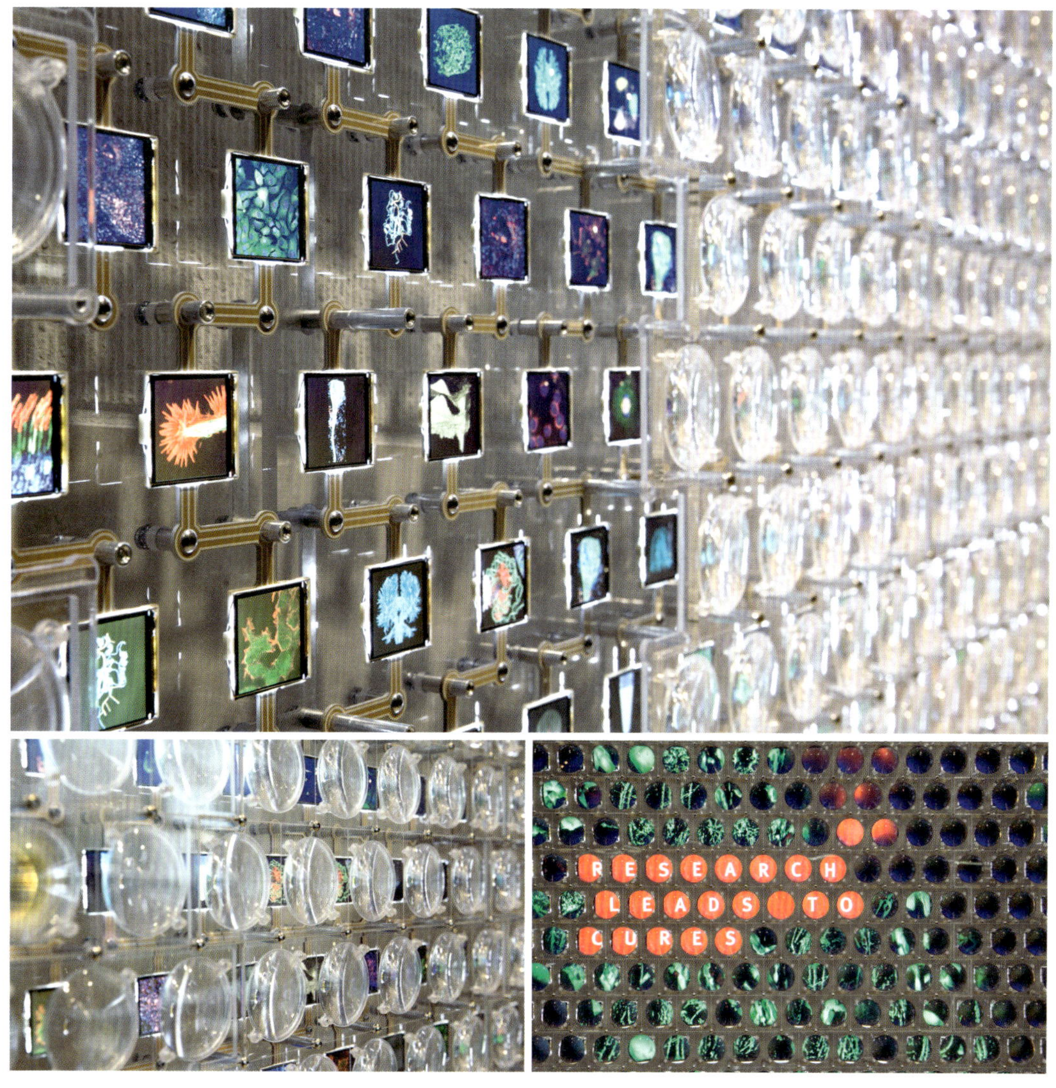

Squint/Opera (UK) is a creative agency and production house, working on exhibitions, films, animations, websites, print, and branding. Recent projects have included installations at the Milan Expo, the Victoria & Albert Museum, and the Imperial War Museum's First World War exhibition. Hirsch & Mann (UK) works at the intersection of people, technology, and businesses building compelling technology interactions between them. Their work includes the creation of electro mechanical wearables for Cadburys, building generative digital painting systems for The Whitney, and constructing a volumetric 3D LED display for Siemens

We Make Money Not Art
Régine Debatty

Brown Sound Kit. 'Toilet humour for gallery space'

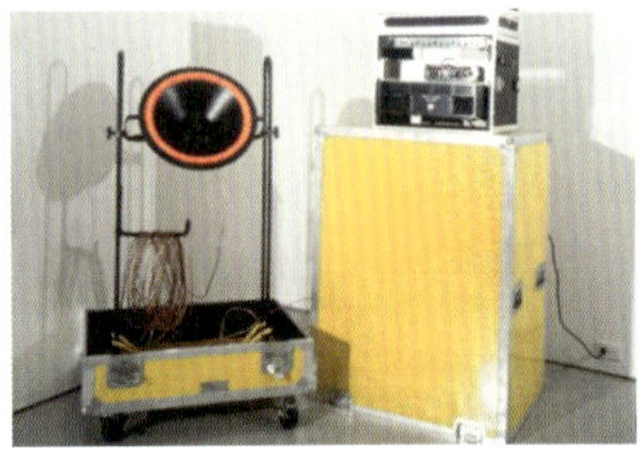

This piece of sound equipment emits low frequency infrasound waves, which causes those in its path to release the contents of their bowels—or more colloquially, to "shit themselves". This kind of sound cannon has its roots in sonic weapons first developed by the Nazis for the purposes of crowd control, and purportedly also by the French authorities during the Paris riots of 1968

Regine / June 24, 2016 / art in Antwerp, Art in Flanders, body, sound

Biometric Capitalism

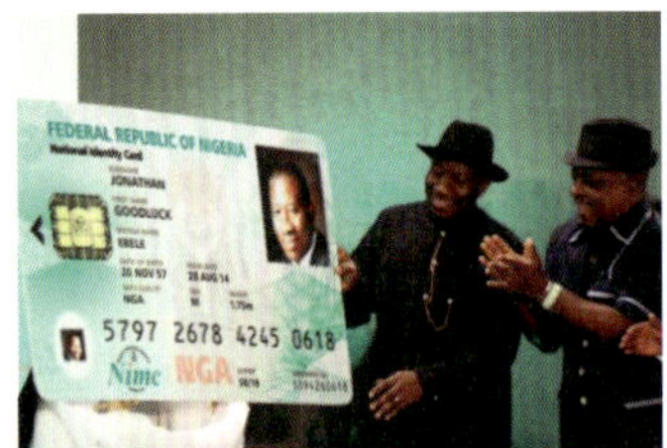

A new variety of capitalism is currently taking form on the African continent. States are being remade under the pressures of rapid demographic growth, conflicts over boundaries, security demands, and the offerings of multi-lateral donors and data-processing corporations. Much of this turns to enhanced forms of state surveillance that is common to societies across the globe, but the economic and institutional forms on the African continent are unusual

Regine / June 13, 2016 / art in Berlin, biometric, democracy, money, politics, video

Art, mathematics and a spider crab at the D'Arcy Thompson Zoology Museum

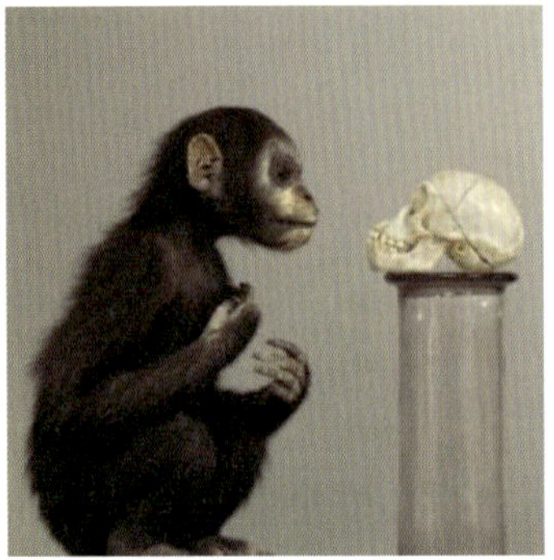

In spite of the loss of a large part of its collection, the museum remains a wonderful place to visit. For the historical specimens of course but also for a number of artefacts that are interesting from an artistic point of view

Regine / June 23, 2016 / bio, vintage

The Politics of Design. A *(Not So)* Global Manual for Visual Communication

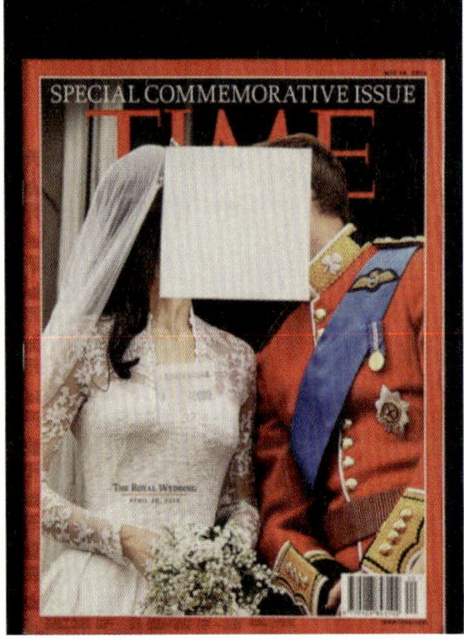

Grayson Perry. Flying penises, rude vases and teddy bears

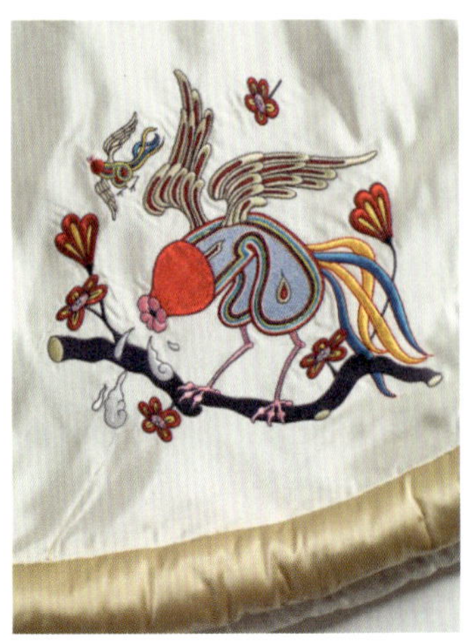

Perry can be a bit rude but he's never vulgar. He observes and satirizes British society, its classes, tastes and rituals but he does so with kindness. His vases look traditional but as you go nearer, you realize that they bear crude images and cheap tabloid headlines

Regine / June 20, 2016 / art

House Guests: where even plugs and bread crumbs have a mind of their own

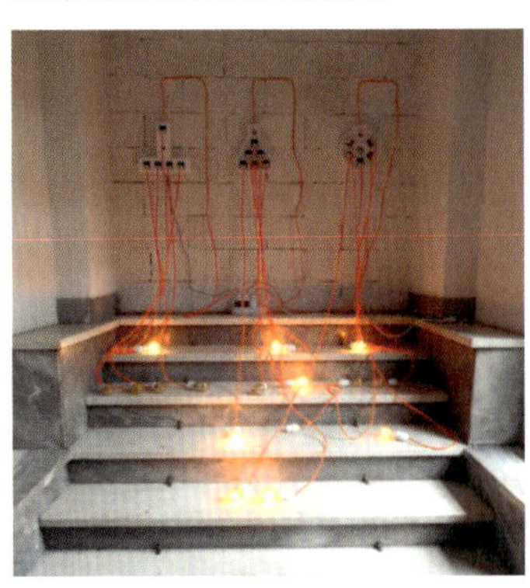

We Make Money Not Art is a blog that focuses on the intersection between art, science, and social issues. Created in March 2004, *we-make-money-not-art.com* investigates the work of artists, designers, and hackers who are using science and technology in a critical, socially engaged way. The blog is a personal one; it features interviews with artists and scientists, book reviews, reports from media art festivals as well as accidental explorations of contemporary culture at large.

Objectives of the blog:
· to present the many encounters of art and science in an approachable yet rigorous and critical way.
· to include media art in a broader cultural discussion.

Pictoplasma focus: Jim Avignon

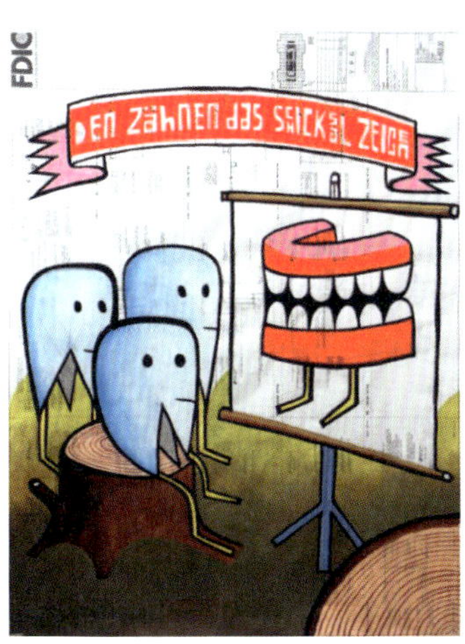

When he is not painting murals in Latin America, creating coloring books for children living in refugee camps or stealing Berlin's iconic and kitschy buddy bears, Avignon turns himself into "neoangin", a performer of electronic music that doesn't seem to take himself too seriously either.

Regine / May 5, 2016 / art in Berlin, Pictoplasma

Confessions of a Data Broker and other tales of a quantified society

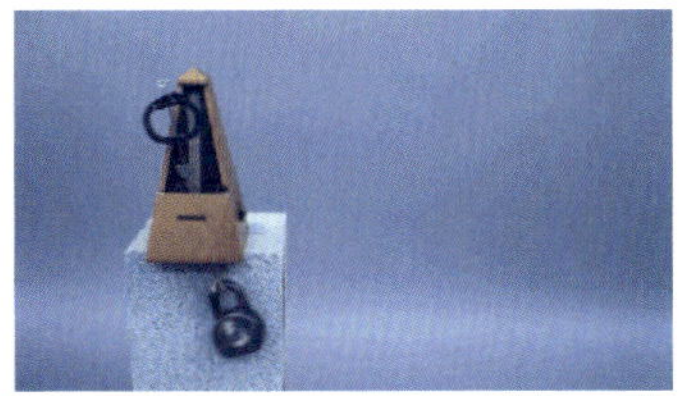

The objects, books, artifacts, gadgets and artworks offer a contemplation on autonomy as a disappearing modus operandi of political action, while workshops, discussions and demos focus on the devices we use every day: How do they work? What individual data traces do they capture? Where do these go, and what kind of control can one regain?

Regine / April 28, 2016 / activism, art in Berlin, biometric, life

Art in the Making. Artists and their Materials from the Studio to Crowdsourcing

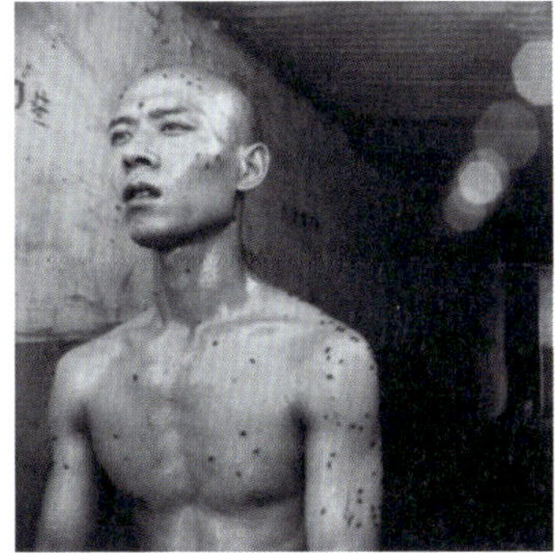

From painting to digital technologies to crowdsourcing, over the last few decades the means of making artworks have become more extraordinary and diverse. Yet we rarely consider the implications of how art is made

Regine / May 6, 2016 / art, book reviews

Order+Noise, a tug of war for motors, strings and rubber bands

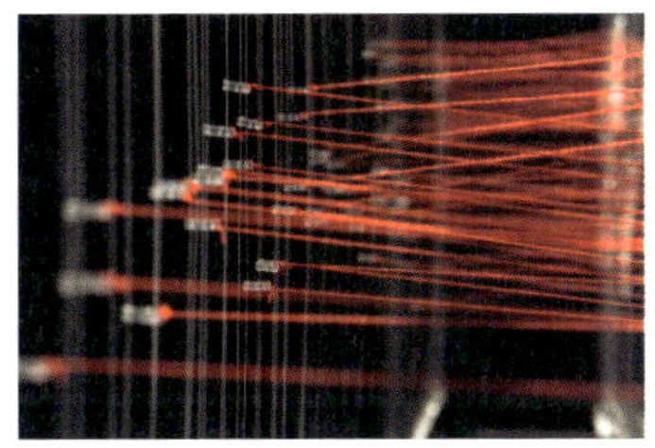

The installation's mechanical workings and network of strings allow us to explore the poetic potential of technology via its materiality, so that Interface I sits on the boundary between an imaginary field and an epistemological condition

Regine / April 29, 2016 / art in Berlin, installation

The Next Big Thing is Not a Thing

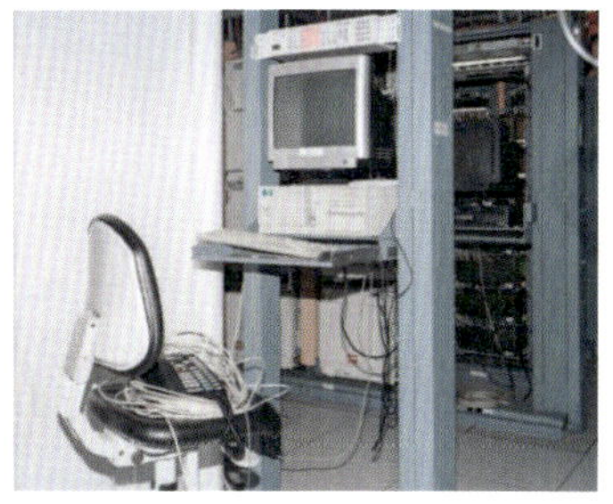

The exhibition questions the underlying myths within design, deconstructs its emerging signs, and examines how technology determines the future landscape of design

Regine / June 9, 2016 / activism, design, trends

CellF, the world's first neural synthesiser

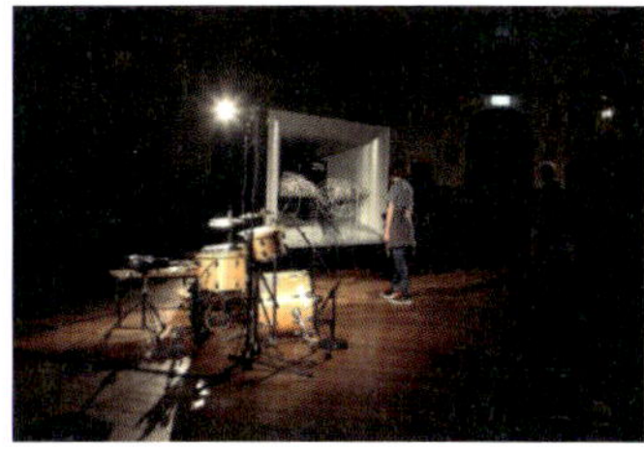

There is a surprising similarity in the way neural networks and analogue modular synthesizers function, in that for both, voltages are passed through components to produce data or sound. The neural interface we developed juxtaposes these two networks and in a sense creates a continuum that creates one unified network. With CellF, the musician and musical instrument become one entity to create a cybernetic musician, a rock star in a petri dish.

Regine / May 2, 2016 / bio, bioart, biotech art, body, performance, sound

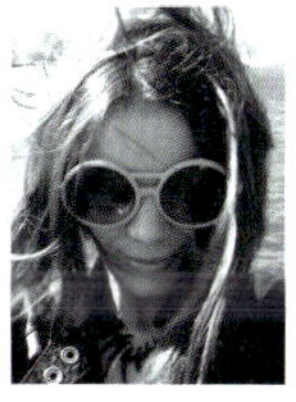

Régine Debatty (BE) is a writer, curator, critic, and founder of *we-make-money-not-art.com*. Régine is known for her writings on the intersection between art, science, technology, and social issues. She writes and lectures internationally about the way in which artists, hackers, and designers use technology as a medium for critical discussion. She also created A.I.L. (Artists in Laboratories), a weekly radio program about the connections and collaborations between art and science for the radio station Resonance which broadcasts on 104.4 FM in London (2012–2014), and is the co-author of the book sprint *New Art/Science Affinities*, published by Carnegie Mellon University.

STARTS
PRIZE´16

NOMINATIONS

#FindingSomethingBondingSound
#WhiteMatter

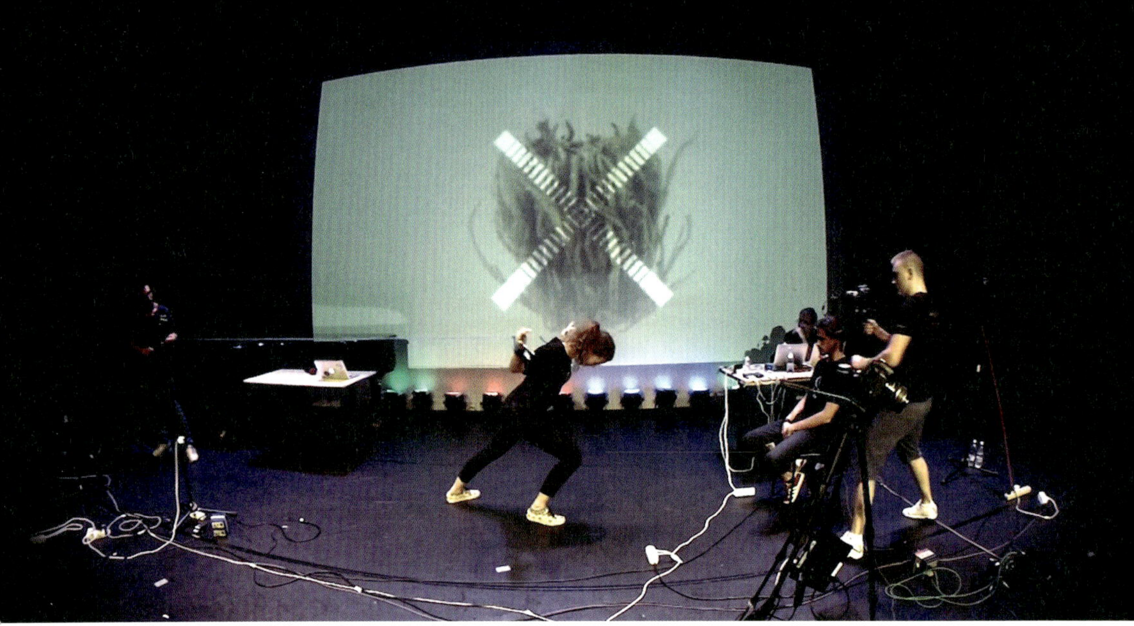

Is the mind separated from the body? *#FindingSomethingBondingSound* addresses this ancient philosophical question by using state-of-the-art technology to hack the brain & the body and translate their activity into sounds and images related to the deepest feelings, emotions, and motivations. In *#FindingSomethingBondingSound* the brain can act as an audiovisual sampling system and the body movements (gestures) act as an effects modulator. The mind controls audio and video samples organized in a playlist according to neurofeedback paradigms.

It uses states of mind, in 7 steps, from low arousal to high arousal, and the body gestures control some effects.

It uses several technologies including: Emotiv Epoc; R-IoT sensors (IRCAM); Audio Interfaces; Dj Mixers; Video Projectors, HoMy_EmoRAW (available at the Emotiv store); Max 7 (Cycling74); Live (Ableton), MnM/FTM filters (IRCAM). It also uses Video editors for non-linear editing and post-production.

www.muarts.tech/#!-findingsomethingbondingsound/oe56b

A Blue Vinyl / MusicBricks award incubation program project

#WhiteMatter is a collective formed by the MuArts (Francisco Marques Teixeira and Horácio Tomé-Marques) and RUMEX (Fanni Fazakas). **Francisco Marques-Teixeira** (PT). His passion is brain technology. He has been working with techie developers, geeky artists, and hackers who want to link the brain to the IoT and the digital world so we can enter in a transhumanism age and promote brain computer interactions. He wants to understand how this new media, mainly interactivity and immersion, can alter our brain. Currently he is the Neurofeedback director at Neurobios–Neuroscience Institute and partner at MuArts. **Horácio Tomé-Marques** (PT) Is a multidisciplinary artist and teacher (Multimedia and Performing Arts). His PhD research deals with the relationship between Music, Reason and Emotion where he uses Brain to computer interfaces and innovative arts approaches. It follows a dual framework: 1) science: that studies the brainwaves, synchronization, phase-lock, resonance; 2) art: artworks (e.g., live visuals, sound narratives) are anchored in the empirical findings. **Fanni Fazakas** (HU) is RUMEX, an audiovisual artist and music producer. RUMEX integrates music production, media design, and experimentation to form a unique visual and audio experience. RUMEX is also involved with new technologies of neuro and bio-feedback. RUMEX is project manager at the 4D sound and plans on using the brand new sound system for a live show. RUMEX graduated from Moholy-Nagy University of Art and Design where she studied Media Design.

Beyond Humans: Perception & Understanding of Actions of Others

Ramiro Martin Joly-Mascheroni

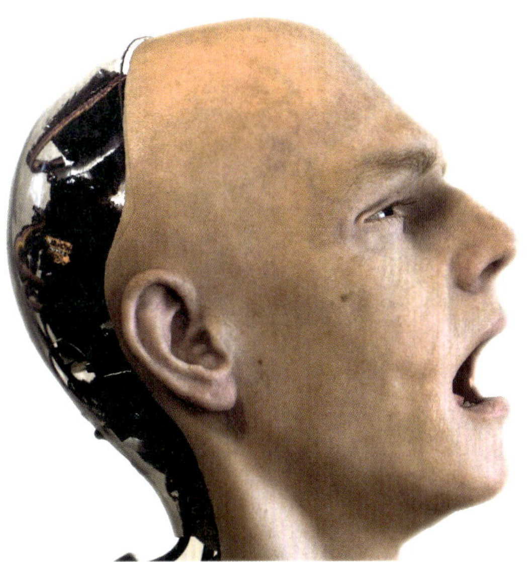

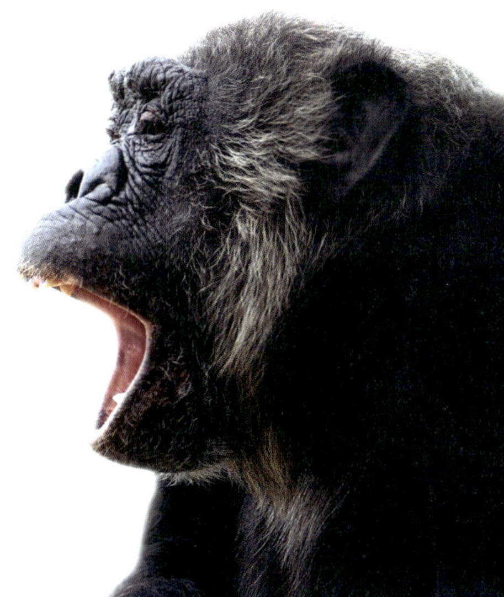

This is an open source project developed with blind individuals from The Royal National Institute for the Blind (UK), ONCE Foundation (ES), and Universidad de Buenos Aires (AR).It is a collaborative effort involving Art, Neuroaesthetics, Artificial Intelligence (AI) and Robotics. Using an android we explore the neural mechanisms and motor processes involved in the perception, interpretation, and portrayal of facial gestures and motor actions, crucial to social communication and interaction. The android yawning may invoke this motor action by triggering the urge to yawn. Robots and artificial agents have raised important moral and ethical concerns. Decision-making processes and moral judgements can be difficult challenges for us humans. How will AI deal with moral dilemmas? Can artificial agents such as androids solve moral dilemmas we can't solve ourselves? It is possible that we may be influenced by and follow the example of the "morally and ethically unaware" android we have created.

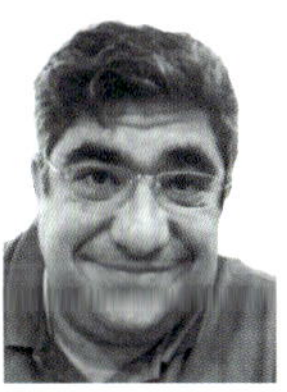

Ramiro Martin Joly-Mascheroni (IT) is a Psychology PhD student exploring how blind children and adults perceive actions. Within a comparative and evolutionary perspective he is investigating how human action perception differs from that of animals. He developed an android, as one of a series of tools used by blind individuals and stroke victims, to train, rehabilitate, and regain control of their own facial expressions, and to aid interpretation of others though biofeedback systems.

Apostroph

Manfred Hild, Mitsuru Muramatsu, Shunji Yamanaka

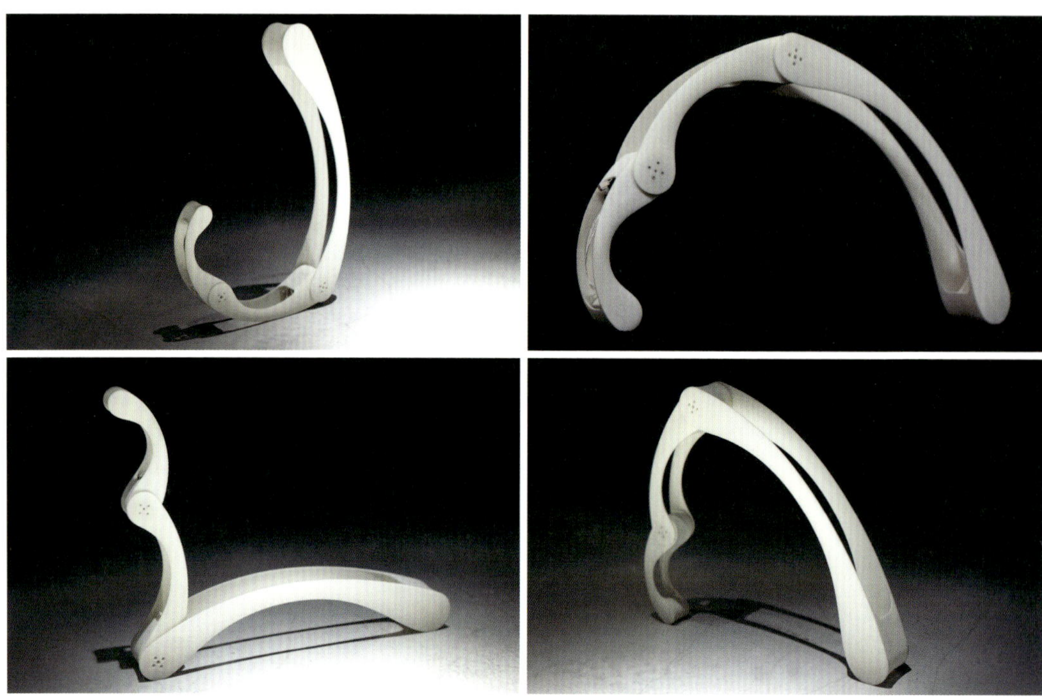

Apostroph is a prototype of a robot designed to study the intrinsic behaviors of living organisms. Standing up and counteracting gravity is characteristic of living organisms. We fight gravity and stand on our feet, adopting the posture that puts the least strain on our body joints. In *Apostroph*, the joint contains the motor which is programmed to resist external force. These motors rotate in the opposite direction to the rotation caused by gravity. *Apostroph* tries to lift its body, in the same way as a human being stands up. The unique movements of *Apostroph*—constantly transforming from a bridge-like arc, slipping just past its own skeletal framework, and rolling into a wheel—is a form of exploration to reach the point of stability, much like our own efforts to stand up on our own feet.

http://www.design-lab.iis.u-tokyo.ac.jp/projects/Apostroph/

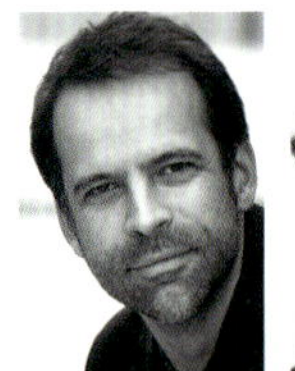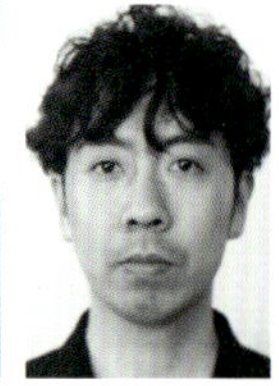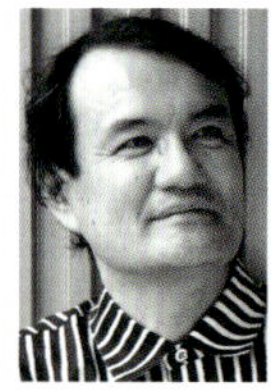

Manfred Hild (DE) studied mathematics and psychology at the University of Konstanz and got his doctoral degree at Humboldt-University of Berlin. Since 2014 he is professor for Digital Systems at the Beuth University of Applied Sciences Berlin. **Mitsuru Muramatsu** (JP) is a designer / researcher. He received the Master of Media and Governance and completed the PhD Program without a degree at Keio University. He won the Grand Prize in the interactive art category of the Asia Digital Art Award 2015. **Shunji Yamanaka** (JP) is a product designer / professor at the University of Tokyo. He has received many awards including the 2004 Mainichi Design Award, the iF Product Design Award, and the Good Design Gold Award.

BlindWiki, Unveiling the Unseen
Antoni Abad

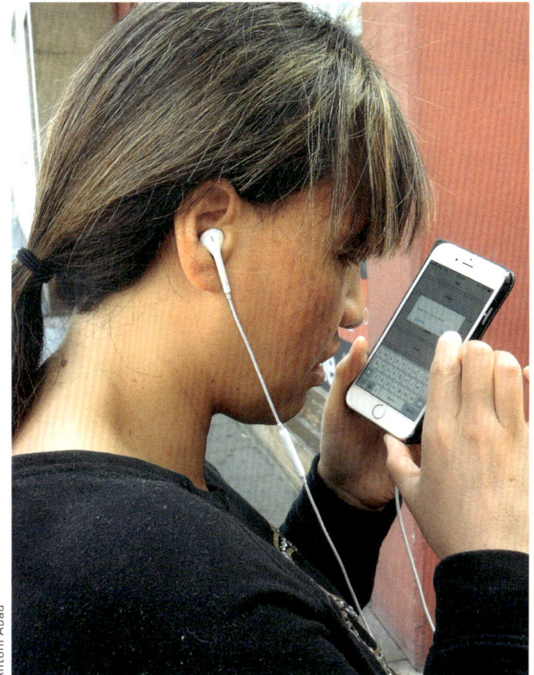

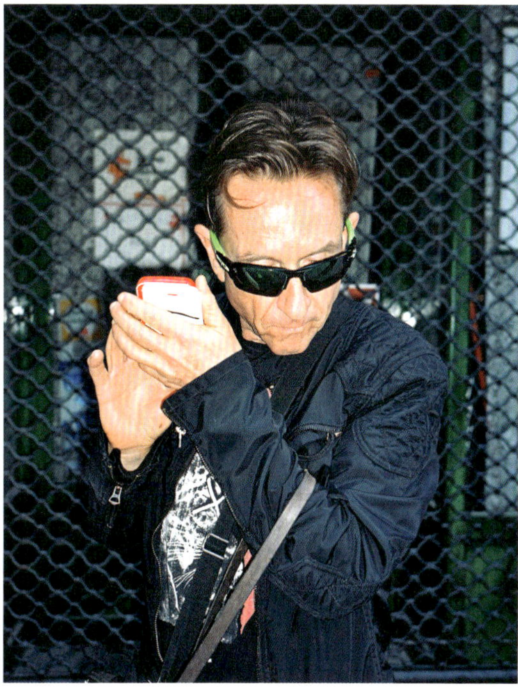

Antoni Abad

A community-based smartphone project that invites citizens who are blind or partially sighted to share their own experience on the difficulties and facilities they find in their day-to-day lives.

BlindWiki doesn't just provide information on barriers and accommodations, but is also a repository for storytelling posts. Designed to build a more nuanced location-specific overview of the cityscape—as experienced by people with vision loss who interact with it on a regular basis—*BlindWiki* collects experiences and opinions in order to produce a collaborative map of the unseen.

The app allows participants to record site-specific audio and to publish it to the *BlindWiki* platform.

Users have the opportunity to walk through their city with smartphones, receiving data that participants have previously tagged. The app triggers geo-located stories and tagged obstacles. The app not only allows participants to share their findings, but it also raises social awareness on the diverse perception of the visually impaired.

http://blind.wiki

Web programmer: Matteo Sisti Sette
App programmers: AKX Development
BlindWiki is supported by the 9th Berlin Biennale,
The Spanish Academy in Rome, Acción Cultural Española,
Institut Ramon Llull, Sydney Cervantes Institute, Cooperación
Española, La Sapienza Università di Roma, University of
Sydney.

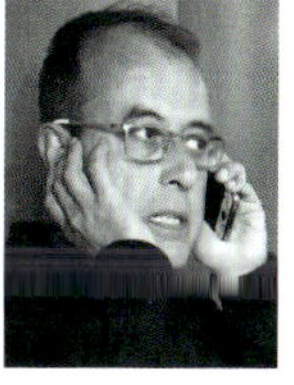

Antoni Abad (ES) is based in Barcelona. 2004–2013 he developed the *megafone.net* projects based on publications from smartphones of various marginalized groups in Spain, Switzerland, Brazil, Colombia, Costa Rica, Mexico, USA, Canada, and Algeria. His work has been presented at the following art biennials: Berlin 2016, Venice 1999, Lima 1999, Seville 2004–2008; Mercosul & Curitiba, Brazil 2009–2013. In 2006 he was awarded the Golden Nica of Prix Ars Electronica in the Digital Communities category.

Casa Jasmina
Team Casa Jasmina

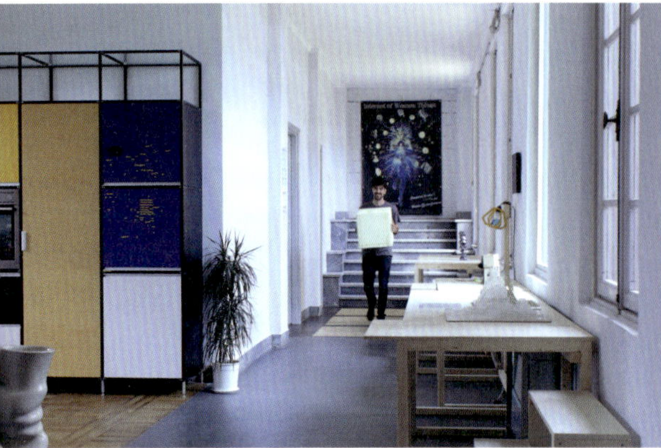
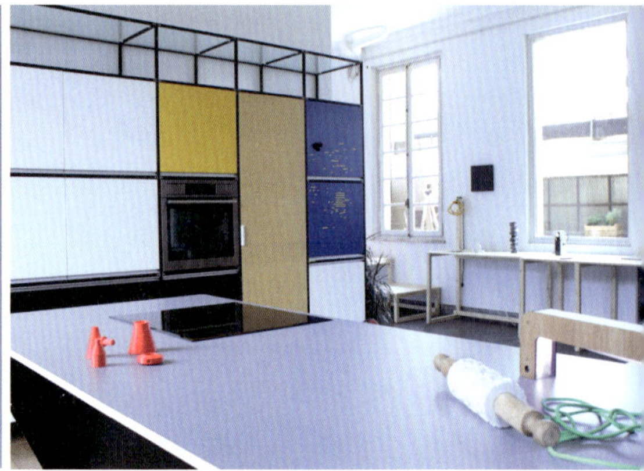

Casa Jasmina is a two-year pilot project in the field of domestic electronic networking, or the Internet of Things (IoT) in the home. The aim is to integrate traditional Italian skills in furniture and interior design with emergent skills in open-source electronics. The project is a showplace inside a large industrial building already shared by Toolbox Co-Working, Fablab Torino, and Officine Arduino.

Casa Jasmina has three main functions:
- A real-world test bed for hacks, experiments, innovative IoT, and digital fabrication projects.
- A curated space for public exposure of excellent artifacts and best practices.
- A guesthouse for occasional visitors to Toolbox, Officine Arduino, and Fablab Torino.

Casa Jasmina was founded in order to encourage:
- Makers, designers, digital artists, IoT experts, students, and universities to research, experiment, and use new technologies and new production methods related to open source and IoT.
- Factories, industries, corporate companies, and start-ups to be interested in IoT and to try to overcome the boundary between classical and open source production. Industries that will create tomorrow's living spaces.
- Ordinary people interested in testing the IoT in everyday life in the house of the future.

Although it resembles an apartment home, *Casa Jasmina* is actually a combination of lab, gallery space, and B&B, so it needs dynamic management. *Casa Jasmina* is not merely a kitchen, library, bedroom, and bathroom. It's a public interface for a larger IoT process of building things, acquiring and installing things, removing things, repairing and maintaining things, storing things, recording and linking to things, and, last but not least, getting rid of things. *Casa Jasmina* is an incubator, and its purpose is industry-boosting in the Torino and Piemonte IoT space. The successors of the *Casa Jasmina* project will be real homes with real, innovative products inside.

http://casajasmina.arduino.cc

Curators: Bruce Sterling, Massimo Banzi
Project manager: Lorenzo Romagnoli
Blogger: Jasmina Tešanović
Community manager: Alessandro Squatrito
Casa Jasmina is mainly supported by:
Arduino/ Genuino, Toolbox coworking, Fablab Torino
Casa Jasmina is also supported by:
Lavazza, Energy@home, Valcucine

Team Casa Jasmina consists of the curators and mentors Massimo Banzi and Bruce Sterling; project manager Lorenzo Romagnoli, who is also interaction designer and maker; product designer and community manager Alessandro Squatrito, and blogger and mentor Jasmina Tešanović. During the year students or freelancers collaborate with the team on the project. Apart from the core team, *Casa Jasmina* is open to people from Fablab Torino (the first Italian Fablab) and their projects, interaction and product designers who are interested in Internet of Things or open source projects. *Casa Jasmina* is active on the IoT council and organizes meetups and panels. The entire project is open source, anybody can visit *Casa Jasmina*, can be a guest, can try out all the projects inside.

Crowdcrafting
Scifabric, http://crowdcrafting.org

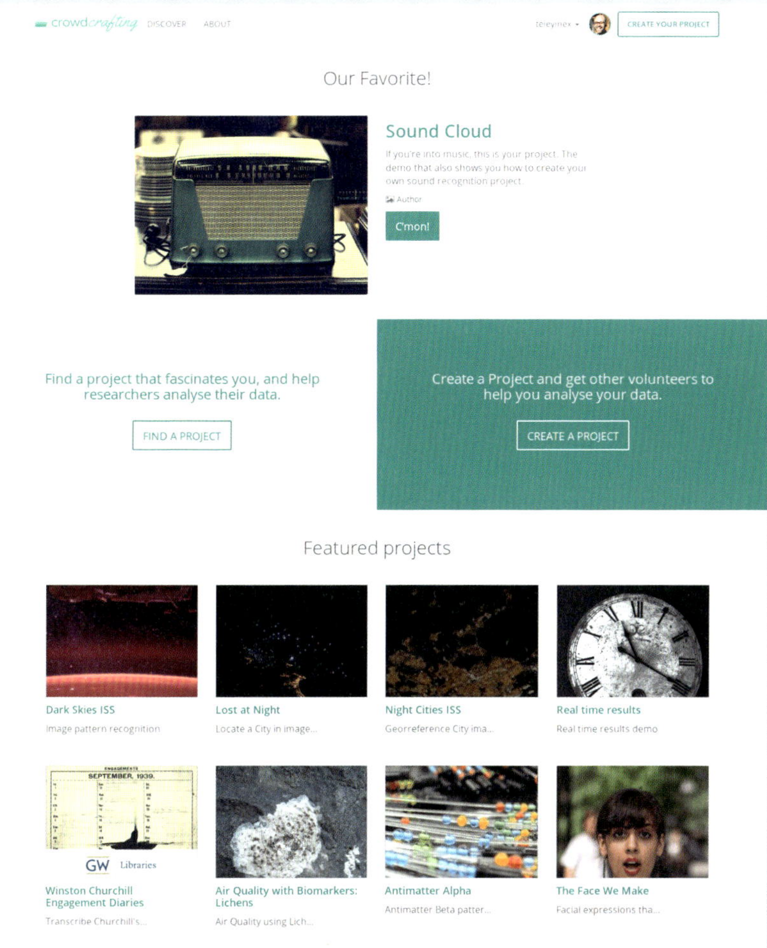

Crowdcrafting is a crowdsourcing, citizen science or microtasking platform developed by Scifabric and powered by PYBOSSA—our open source technology, where researchers or citizens can create a research project in a matter of minutes without having to develop a single line of code, since we provide the templates and tools that will help them kick start a project in minutes, replicating the scientific method. *Crowdcrafting* was born at a hackathon in Cape Town, South Africa, in 2011. In partnership with our key collaborators, such as CERN, United Nations (UNITAR), and the University of Geneva, we have reached out to and inspired many people to get involved in research.

Founder & CEO: Daniel Lombraña
Marketing & Content: Clara Sánchez-Puga
Senior Developer: Marvin Reimer
UX/UI Designers: Álvaro Suarez Pérez, Jorge Correa
Business Development: Mar Ramis
Communications: James Doherty

Scifabric is a Spanish-UK based company that develops technologies for the creation of platforms to collect, analyze, and enrich data. These international research projects explore the use of crowd-based methodologies. We have already developed humanitarian works, collaborated in the research against cancer, recovered a huge collection of archaeological findings, studied light pollution or how gravity interacts with antimatter, to name a few of the possibilities that our platform offers. All these projects are developed with our PYBOSSA technology, and all the data is open and available to anyone. *scifabric.com; pybossa.com*

D-CENT Decentralised Citizens ENgagement Technologies

http://dcentproject.eu

D-CENT is a Europe-wide project that has brought together citizen movements and grassroots organizations that have revolutionized democracy in Europe in the past years, and is developing the next generation of open source, distributed, and privacy-aware tools for direct democracy and economic empowerment.

D-CENT grows longer-term alternatives to today's highly centralized platforms and power structures, and promotes the development of knowledge, digital infrastructures, and data for the common good. It values privacy and security, and is built on open source code and open standards.

D-CENT tools form a federated and distributed architecture—they can be combined in many ways to support democratic processes. The tools enable citizens to be informed and get real-time notifications about issues that matter to them. They help to propose and draft solutions and policy collaboratively. They can be used to decide and vote on solutions and collective municipal budgeting.

D-CENT runs large-scale pilots in Spain, Finland, and Iceland to develop and test the tools. These pilots have involved thousands of citizens across Europe in municipal decision-making, policy and budgeting. The pilots are engaging democratic organizations and citizen-led coalitions like Podemos, Ahora Madrid, Barcelona en Comù, Open Ministry and Citizen Foundation.

The project has run following experiments: Participation and open consultation platforms in Barcelona and Madrid *(decide.madrid.es)*, Participatory budgeting platform *(beta.yrpri.org)*, Notification service *(decisions.dcentproject.eu)*, and a collaborative policy making platform *(objective8.dcentproject.eu)*.

D-CENT is also developing a blockchain toolkit to manage community trust, reputation, and provide a blockchain reward scheme that is auditable and transparent. *D-CENT* has contributed actively to the development of open social web standards, an open standardization effort led by the W3C.

D-CENT has done extensive research on new forms of democracy, citizen empowerment, and participation. An integrated techno-socio-economic analysis has been carried out on organizational models of emerging social movements, new economic models based on knowledge commons, distributed social networking, identity systems, new models for citizen control of personal and social data, privacy and security by design.

Coordinator: Francesca Bria

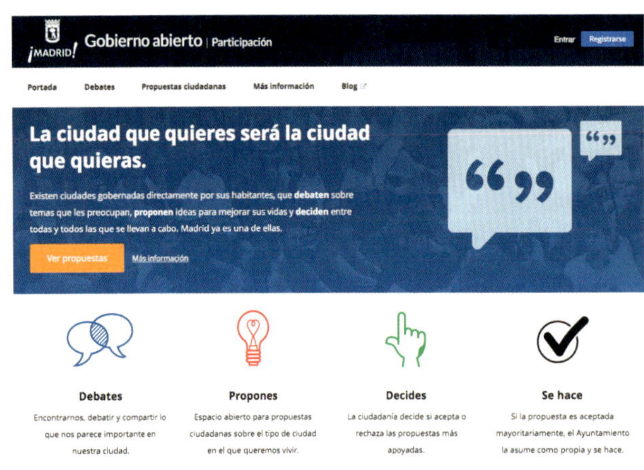

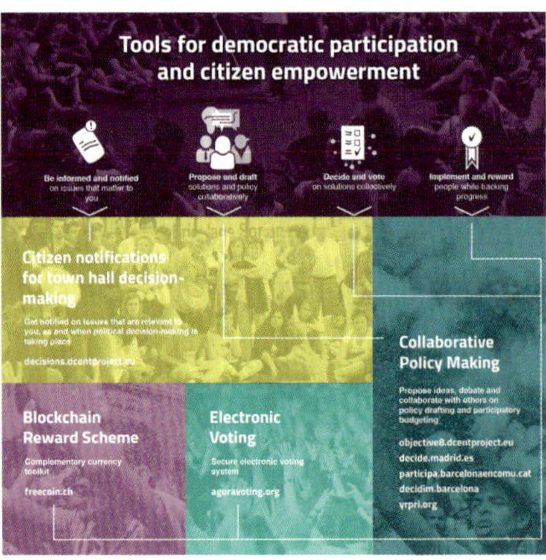

D-CENT has a strong international network as its consortium: Nesta (UK), Citizens Foundation (IS), CNRS - Centre d'Économie de la Sorbonne (FR), Dyne.org (NL), Forum Virium Helsinki (FI), International Modern Media Institute (IS), Open Knowledge Foundation (UK), Open University of Catalunya and Eurecat (ES), ThoughtWorks (UK), and World Wide Web Consortium (FR).

Environment Dress
uh513—María Castellanos & Alberto Valverde

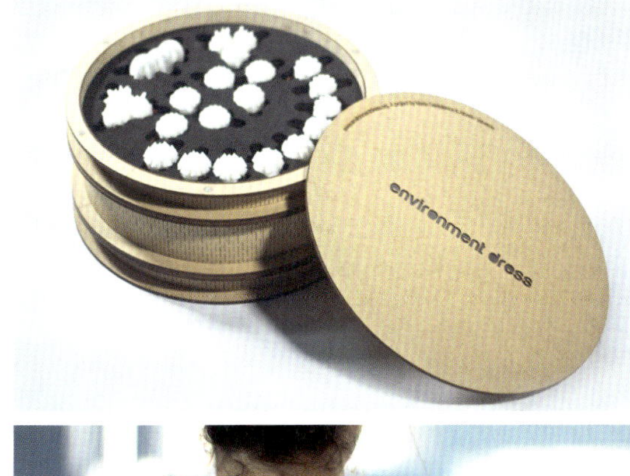

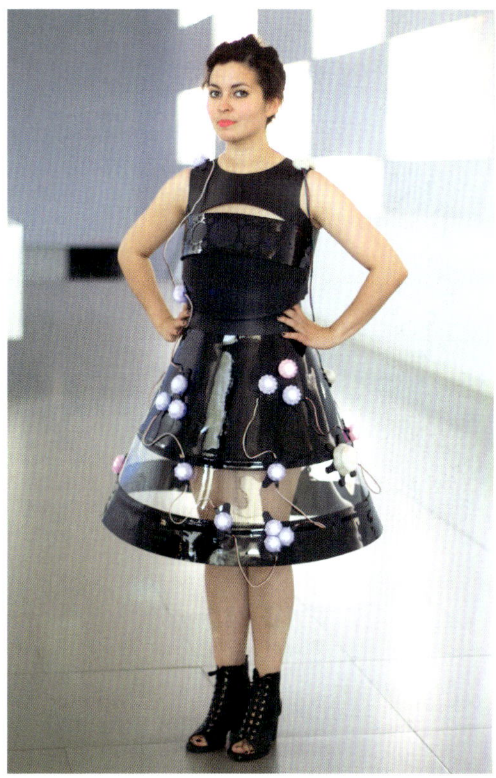

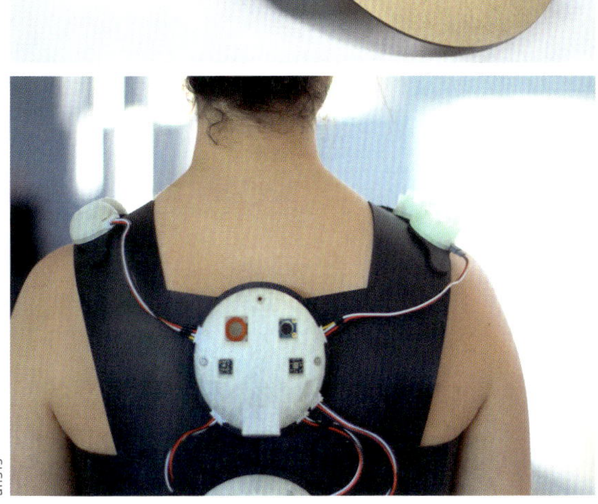

Environment Dress is a smart dress that measures the aggressiveness of the environment to analyze how it affects people's mood and behavior.

The natural sensors of our body are not able to alert us to external environmental factors. However, through the use of technology, we can know how these factors affect us and anticipate them. *Environment Dress* is a wearable equipped with sensors that analyze issues such as variations in noise, temperature, atmospheric pressure, ultraviolet radiation, or the amount of carbon monoxide present in our daily lives. All of this geo-located information is connected to the user's mood via an app. In this way, thanks to so-called machine learning, the garment is able to learn and anticipate the emotions of its user, linking specific environmental conditions with our previously recorded emotions. *Environment Dress* is a project created in open code.

http://www.environmentdress.org

Project created thanks to the Next Things 2015-Conducta prize. Joint call of LABoral Centro de Arte and Telefónica I+D

uh513 is composed of María Castellanos and Alberto Valverde. **María Castellanos** (ES) has a degree and a PhD in Fine Arts from the University of Vigo. She investigates the body, specifically the perception and sensory deficiencies of human beings. She focuses on the hybridizations between cyborgs and wearables as a paradigm for the expansion of human sensory capabilities. **Alberto Valverde** (ES) is an artist and technologist with a solid experience in system design, creating interactive environments, web design, and robotics. He has also taught courses on multimedia to Fine Arts students at the University of Vigo. In his work, he investigates chaos as a form of order.

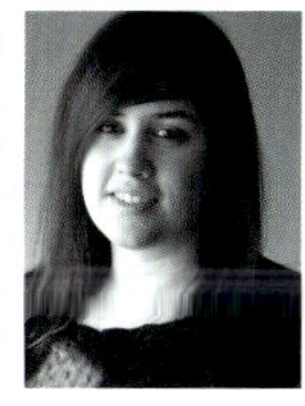

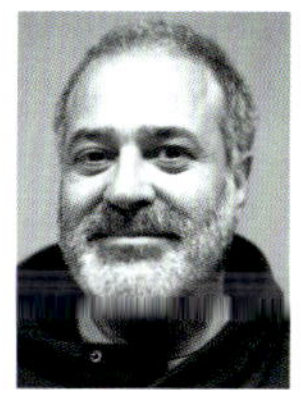

Floating Points—Silhouettes
Hamill Industries, Junior Martínez

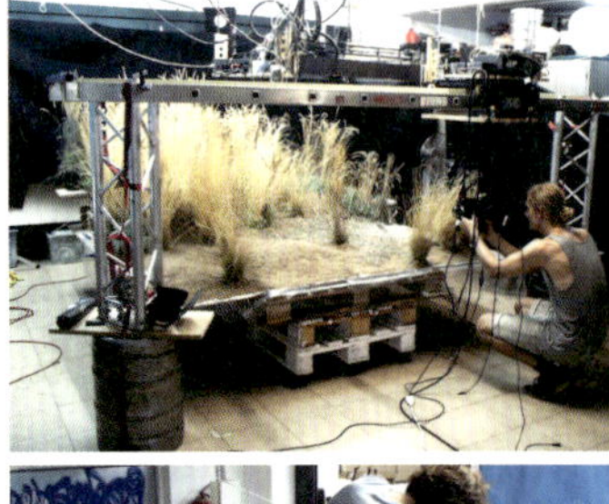
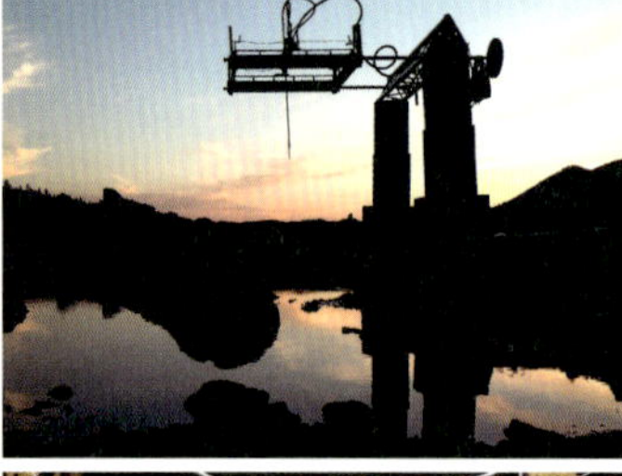
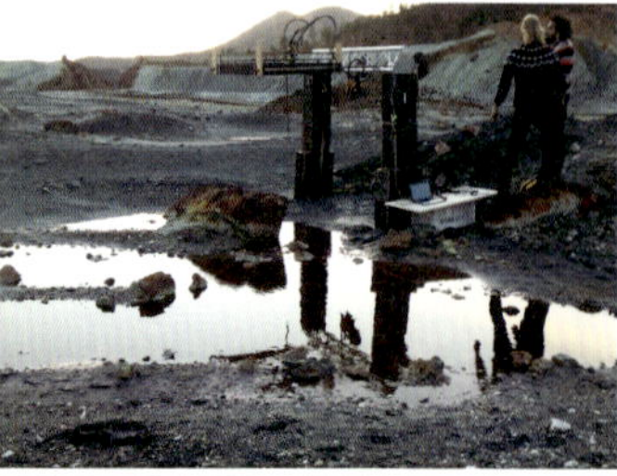
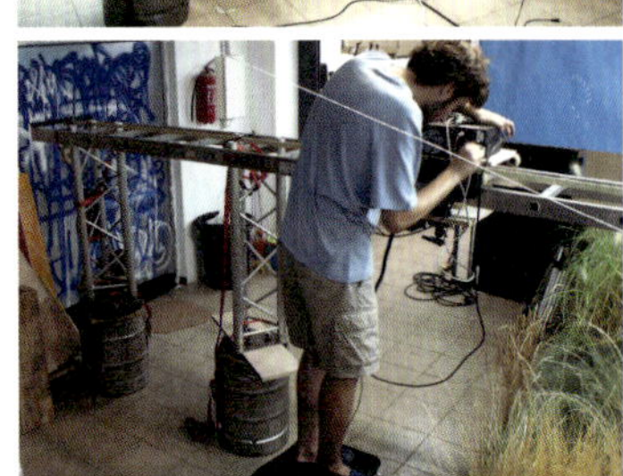
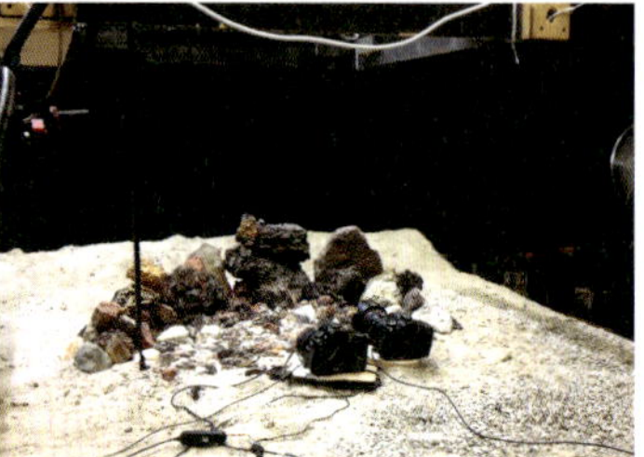
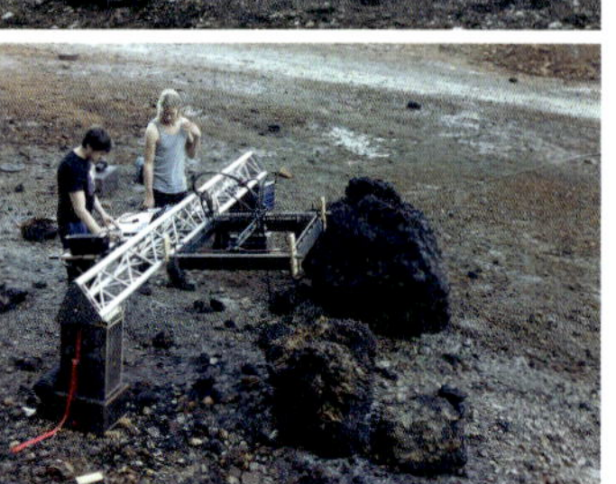

The experimental music video for Floating Points (the name under which English musician and neuroscientist Sam Shepherd performs), portrays an abstract oscillating light that evolves through the music in different life forms. All lights are in-camera produced effects that are made by a self-developed light paint machine. We've created a piece that, both in content and in its implementation, speaks of an analogue universe. Technique and form merge to bring out the geometry of Floating Points' sound, which, as a living being, mutates and creates a particular ecosystem. We invented a light-painting machine capable of reproducing light forms in motion, allowing us to film it with a camera, without the need of postproduction. The machine was also capable of controlling other aspects such as camera shutter release, lights, and fog machines, and a self-built motion control system. We wanted to make a video that involved a technical challenge and allowed us to conceptually explore the artistic complexity of Floating Points' sound, so we could reflect its music in a visual way.

It took us 6 months of work divided between development and shooting (outdoors and indoors).

http://vimeo.com/158610637
https://vimeo.com/141986621

Music by Floating Points
Direction: Junior Martínez and
Hamill Industries (Pablo Barquín & Anna Diaz)
Director of Photography: Nathan Grimes
Music by Floating Points

Hamill Industries is composed of Pablo Barquín and Anna Diaz, who are directors, art directors, passionate makers and mix-media artists. They love in-camera effects and combine old and new visual techniques. They focus on the conceptualization, design and development of audiovisual projects, installations, and spectacles. **Pablo Barquín** (ES) founded his first studio, Physalia, where he acquired recognition in the motion-graphics world and stood out for his crafted visual projects in which a wide range of different filming and interaction techniques combined in unique and spectacular ways. **Anna Diaz** (ES) graduated in audiovisual communication from the Universitat Pompeu Fabra, spent time studying at the Free University of Berlin, and started her professional career at XCENTRIC (CCCB). **Junior Martínez** (UK/VE) is a diverse director and illustrator, as comfortable behind the camera as he is behind the pen. He has a passion for graphics and studied graphic design at Prodiseño (Escuela de Comunicación Visual y Diseño) in Caracas before joining a print design studio. Jun founded the No-Domain design studio in 2003, active for over 10 years, before eventually embarking on a solo career in 2013, directing video clips, spots, and special audiovisual projects. Jun has been awarded at San Sebastian's El Sol festival and Grand Laus in Barcelona, and his work has been featured in Stash, Onedotozero, Motionographer, and Vimeo Staff Picks, amongst many others.

Floraform

Nervous System–Jessica Rosenkrantz, Jesse Louis-Rosenberg

Floraform is a generative design system inspired by the biomechanics of growing leaves and blooming flowers which explores the development of surfaces through differential growth. We created a simulation of a differentially growing elastic surface that functions as a digital garden. Within the system, we can explore how biological systems create form by varying growth rates through space and time.

Many of these experiments have been materialized as 3D-printed sculptures and wearable adornments.

We consider this work a kind of digital gardening, except instead of growing plants we're cultivating algorithms. We developed a set of mechanisms that allowed us to control, manipulate, and sculpt the growing process. These act as a set of material and environmental conditions that we can vary through space and time to produce finely differentiated structures.

http://n-e-r-v-o-u-s.com/projects/sets/floraform/

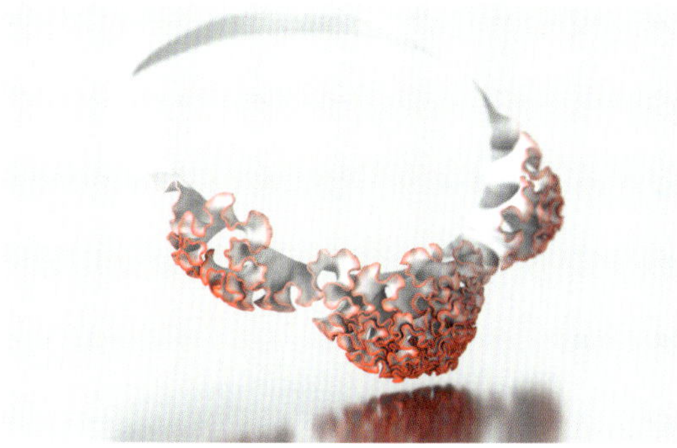

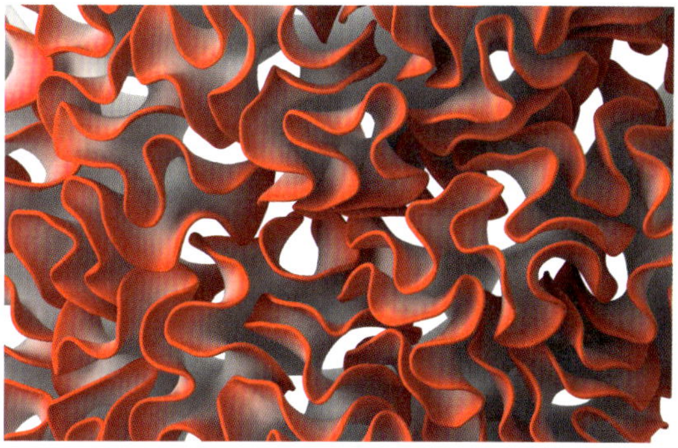

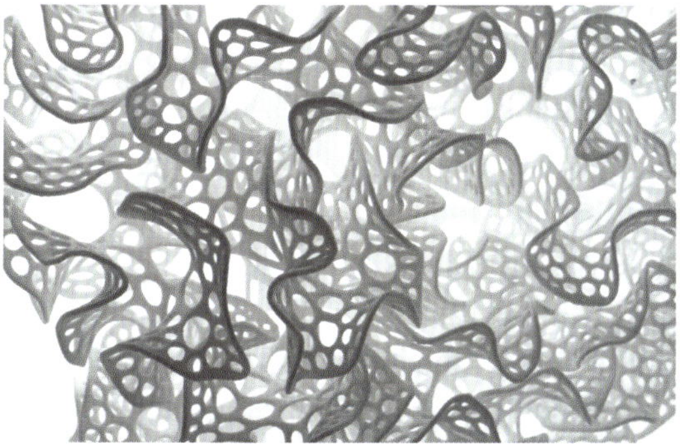

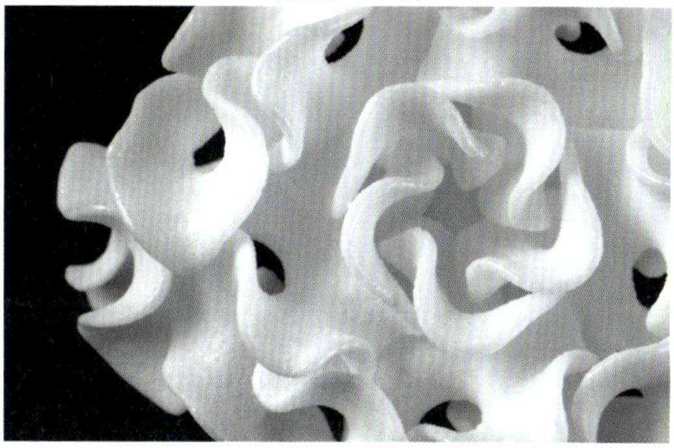

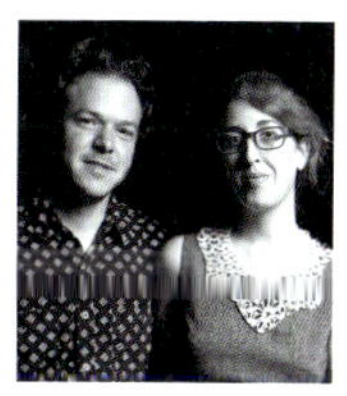

Nervous System (US) is a generative design studio that works at the intersection of science, art, and technology. Designers **Jesse Louis-Rosenberg** and **Jessica Rosenkrantz** create using a novel process that employs computer simulation to generate designs and digital fabrication to realize products. Drawing inspiration from natural phenomena, they write computer programs based on processes and patterns found in nature and use those programs to create unique and affordable art, jewelry, and housewares.

HACKberry
exiii, http://exiii-hackberry.com

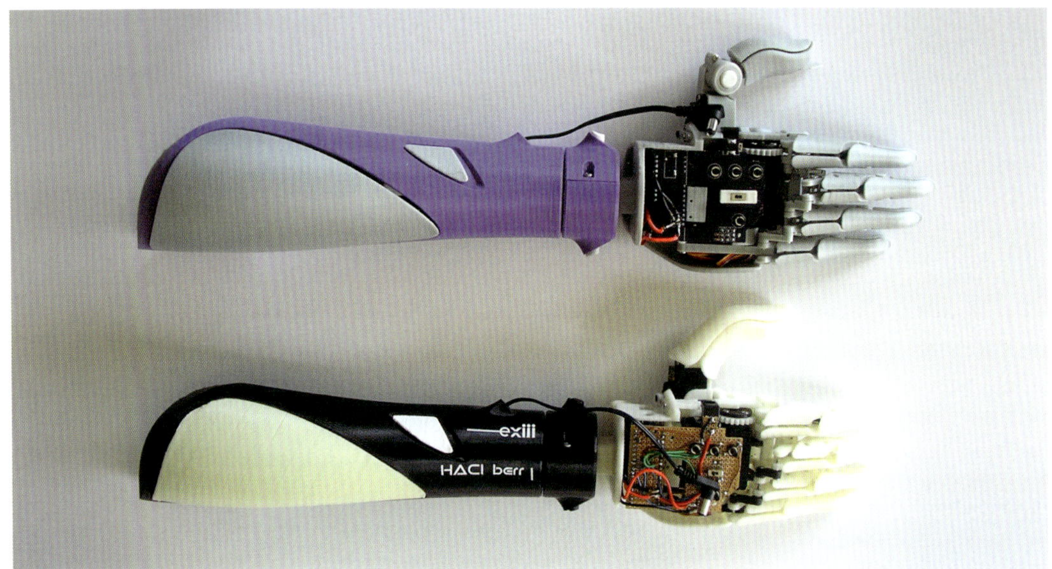

HACKberry is an open-source 3D-printable bionic arm (i.e. motorized hand that a person missing a hand can control intuitively via muscle signals in their residual arm). All the technical data including 3D CAD file, software code, circuit diagram, and bill of materials are disclosed as open-source under Creative Commons license. In this way, private developers around the world can replicate and customize it for whoever it can help in their local area. Since its launch in May 2015, many sub-projects have branched out globally, refining the quality of the hand and growing local communities. For example, a child-size version was created in Poland while a girl in the U.S. was provided with a *HACKberry* produced by a local makers community.

It is noteworthy that *HACKberry* and its precedent models *(handiii, handiii COYOTE)* have received several international design awards including the James Dyson Award in UK, the iF Gold Award in Germany, and the Good Design Award in Japan, which has attracted both developers and potential users to join the open-source community.

http://exiii-hackberry.com

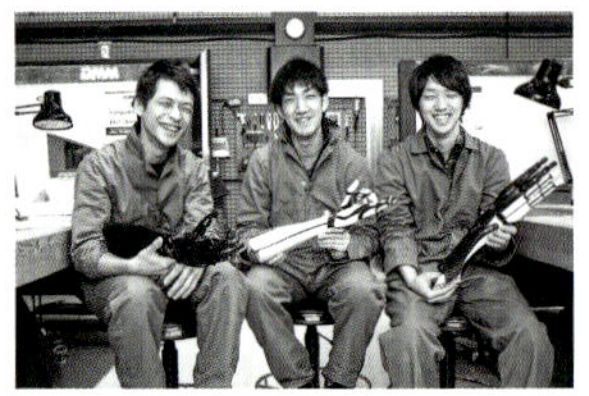

exiii (JP). In May 2013 Genta Kondo, Hiroshi Yamaura, and Tetsuya Konishi started to develop an affordable and fashionable bionic-hand—*handiii*—using a 3D-printer. In March 2014 they met Akira Morikawa, the first amputee to test *handiii*, and decided to start their own company, exiii, after receiving positive feedback. In March 2015, exiii demonstrated the 4th generation model *COYOTE* with Akira at SXSW, and their project received global media attention. In May 2015, exiii launched the 5th generation model *HACKberry*. All of its data is open source.

Hortum machina, B

Interactive Architecture Lab, William Victor Camilleri, Danilo Sampaio

Although plants lack nervous systems, they can, much like animals, become electro-chemically stimulated by their surrounding environment. Measuring this, we begin to understand the stimulus-response mechanisms that make up their primitive intelligence. Networked together we've harnessed their collective intelligence, exploring new forms of bio-cooperative interaction. The result is half garden, half autonomous vehicle—a cybernetic lifeform we've named *Hortum machina, B.* This three meter diameter geodesic sphere with a robotic core, encapsulating 12 garden modules, can shift its center of gravity, allowing it to gently roll around, controlled by the "thoughts" of the plants onboard. If the ones on the bottom feel like they need more sunlight, they "vote" to have the sphere roll over. If it becomes too hot for many of them, *Hortum machina, B* will find a cooler place in the shade. This is an autonomous, democratic, and networked living ecology of plants amplified by robotic agency.

http://www.interactivearchitecture.org/lab-projects/reearth
Collaborator: World Wilder Lab

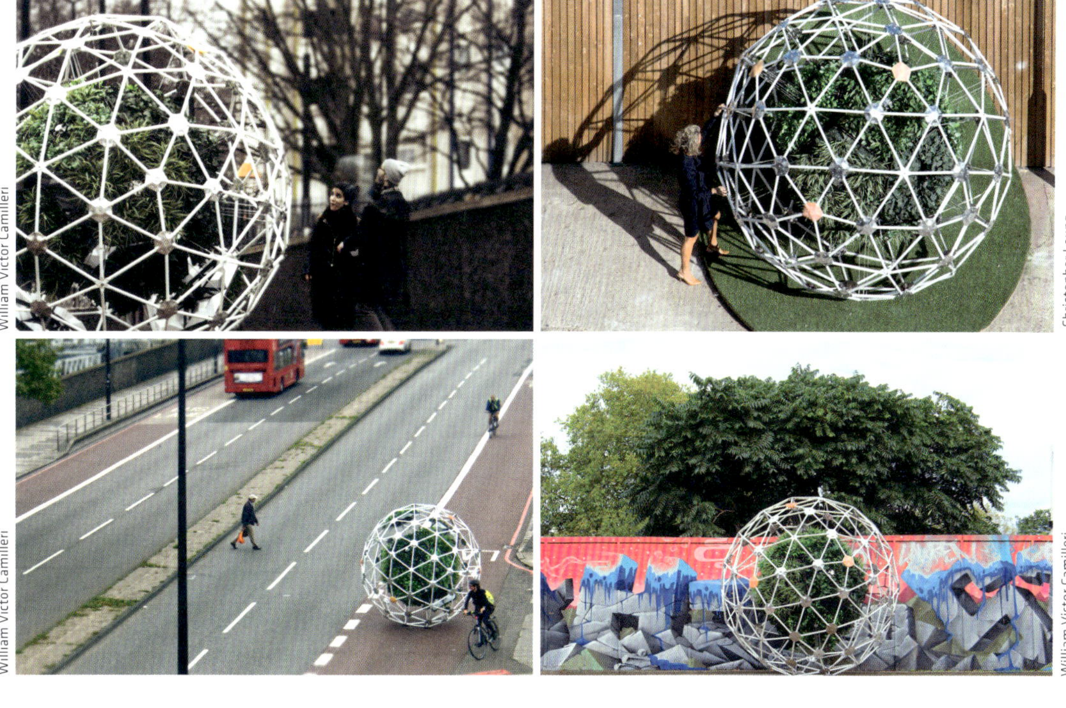

The Interactive Architecture Lab (UK) is a multi-disciplinary research group at the Bartlett School of Architecture (UCL). Research revolves around the behavior and interaction of things, environments and their inhabitants. The reEarth Project is led by William Victor Camilleri (MT) and Danilo Sampaio (BR), and supervised by Ruairi Glynn. Parametric Design and Fabrication was supported by William Bondin, Francois Mangion, and Thomas Powell.

Instruments of the Afterlife
Burton Nitta (Michael Burton & Michiko Nitta)

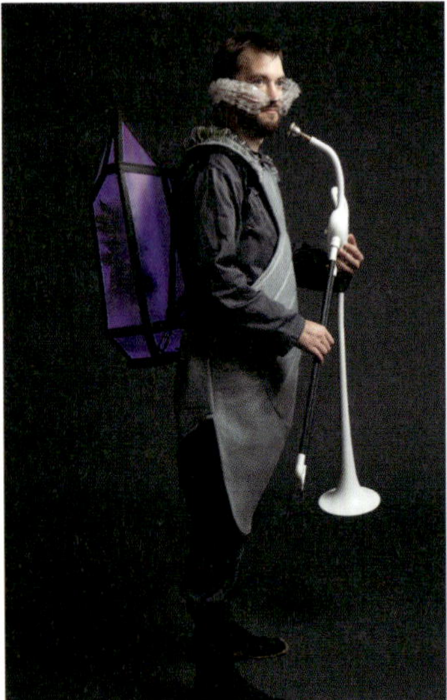 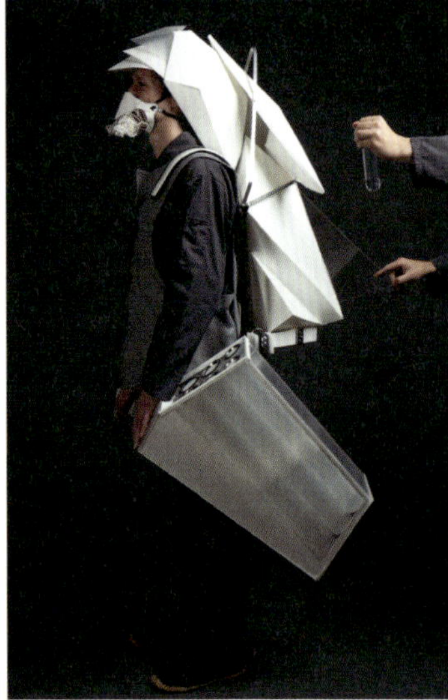 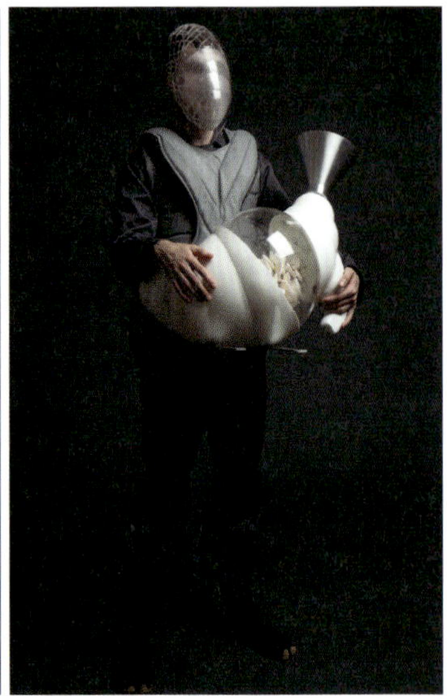

Burton Nitta

Instruments are created to transform contamination into valuable materials, by employing plants and engineered bacteria. Instead of mining material from geological sources and using fossil fuels that lead to environmental harm, could future generations use the contamination and pollution we leave behind to build their future world? Can they build balanced relationships with the natural world to be a no-waste civilization?

A series of new instruments use synthetic biology, plant science, and nanotechnology. Whilst cleaning the land, they remember the mistakes of the past and create materials to build a post-waste future.

The piece responds to the scientific research project, *Cleaning Land for Wealth* (CL4W), funded by the UK's Engineering and Physical Sciences Research Council and supported by Creative Outreach Resource Efficiency (CORE) at Loughborough University. The project involves science teams from universities at Birmingham, Cranfield, Edinburgh, Newcastle, and Warwick.

Burton Nitta in collaboration with:
Artistic team
Composer: Neil Luck
Musician: Lawrence Tatnall
Performer: Timothy Cape (Bastard Assignments)
Performer: Josh Spear (Bastard Assignments)
Actor: Emily Lloyd-Saini
Scientific team
Cleaning Land for Wealth (CL4W)
http://www.core-community.net/partner-projects/cl4w/
University of Warwick: Kerry Kirwan, Guy Barker, Maria Sotenko, Neale Grant
University of Edinburgh: Louise Horsfall, Matthew Edmundson, Michael Capeness, Virginia Echavarri-Bravo
Newcastle University: Adam Harvey, Valentine Eze
University of Birmingham: David Book, Dan Reed
Cranfield University: Philip Longhurst, Ying Jiang
Loughborough University: Creative Outreach For Resource Efficiency (CORE): Jacqui Glass
Supported by: Engineering and Physical Sciences Research Council

www.burtonnitta.co.uk/InstrumentsOfTheAfterlife.html

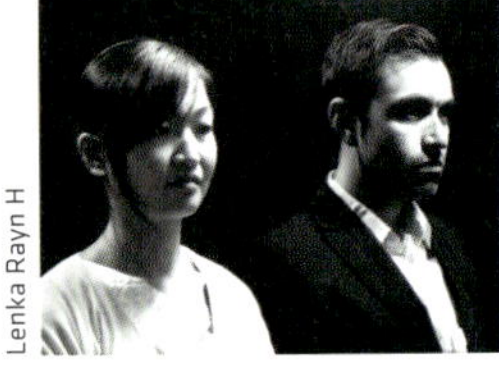

Lenka Rayn H

Based in London, **Burton Nitta** is an interdisciplinary art & design studio founded by **Michael Burton** (UK) and **Michiko Nitta** (JP) that collaborates with science and technology to investigate our future world and human evolution. Previous works such as *After Agri, Algaculture, The Algae Opera, The Republic of Salivation* and *The Instruments of the Afterlife* are published and exhibited internationally from MoMA, New York, to the V&A Museum, London.

Project Nimbus
Dave Lynch, Mike Nix

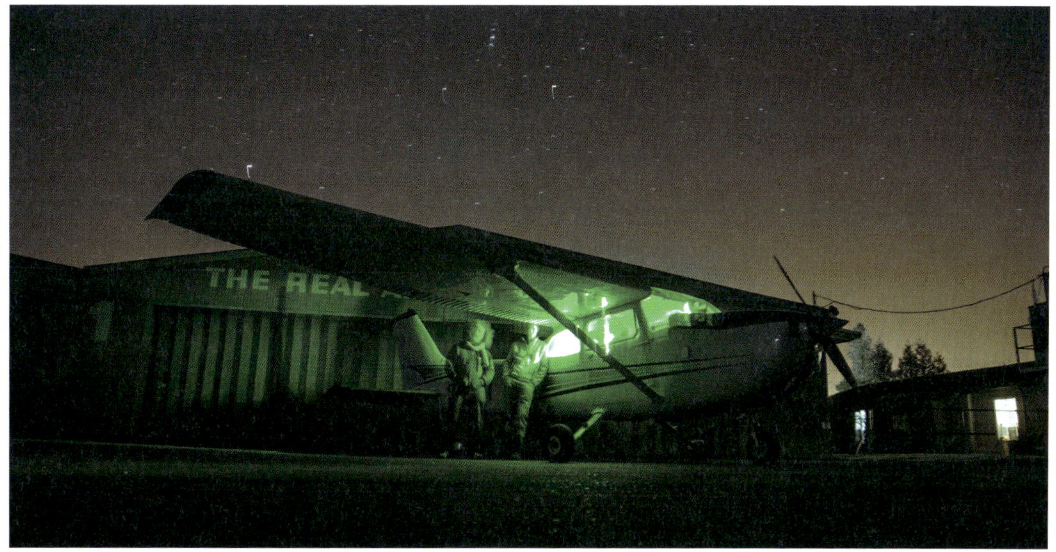

Project Nimbus achieved the inaugural projection of moving images onto clouds from aircraft. The image *Horse in Motion* by Eadweard Muybridge, 1878, is a shared cultural reference between art & science. Beyond the spectacle, genuine collaboration was underpinned by art as research, involving aviators, technologists, and cultural specialists, driven by the power of idea and joy of risk, giving freedom from commercialization.

Inspired by a proposed US military non-lethal weapon, the Laser Zoopraxiscope Mk6 is an open source cloud projector, combining historical and innovative projection technologies.

Through a pioneering journey of artistic and scientific enquiry, rapid prototyping and willingness to question, the blurring of art, science and maker cultures became the ultimate product. A moment of apparent physical impossibility revealed the fragility of inspiration—possibility, risk, commitment. *Nimbus* captures the innovation and optimism that pervade scientific and artistic research practice.

http:// projectnimbus.net

Collaborators: Aaron Nielsen, Vlad Strukov, Stephen Herbert, Ben Whitaker, Lawrence Molloy, Mark Pickles
Supported by: AND Festival, Octopus Collective, FACT Liverpool, Leeds Inspired, Arts Council England

Dave Lynch (UK) is an artist, director, and inventor working at the intersection of moving image, large scale interactive installation, performance, and projection. His practice combines elements of art, science, military, maker and media cultures as part of its tactics, technologies, and production. *Davelynch.net* **Mike Nix** (UK) is a physicist with a background in laser spectroscopy and molecular dynamics, previously working at the University of Leeds. He is involved in installation and performance based art with a scientific inspiration as influence, as part of an on-going interest in the coincidence and contrast of artistic and scientific methods in practice. Both Dave and Mike are part of Leeds (UK) based Art, Science, Maker Collective The Superposition. *http://www.thesuperposition.org*

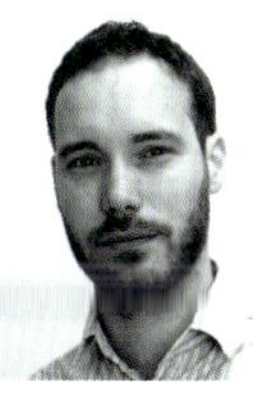
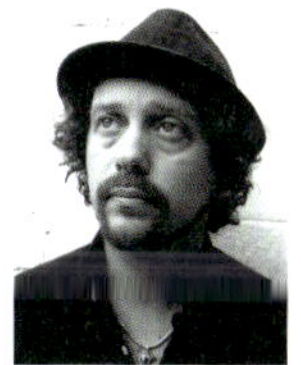

Nosaj Thing
Cold Stares ft. Chance The Rapper + The O'My's
Daito Manabe, MIKIKO, TAKCOM, ELEVENPLAY, Rhizomatiks Research

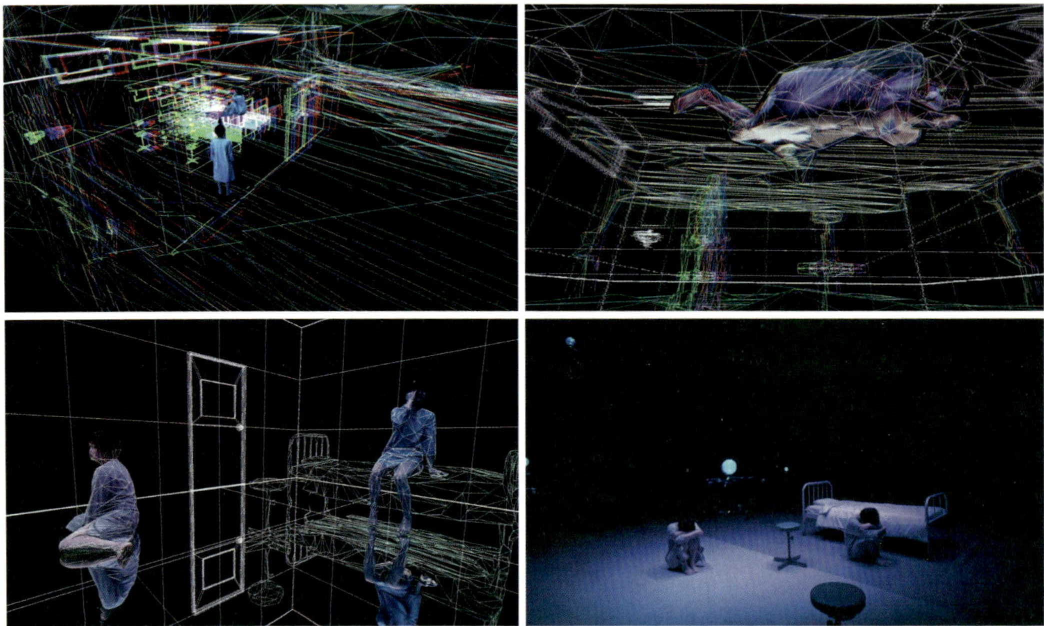

This is a music video of "Cold Stares," a collaboration between Los Angeles-based artist and beatmaker Nosaj Thing, who is actively working around the world, and rapper Chance The Rapper. A dance piece by two dancers was produced to express the message in the lyrics—their mental situation and conflict searching for reason of being and memories, wandering along the border between reality and illusion. This dance has been shown in two ways: the real world performed by people and the delusional world of CG. This film and editing system has potential for capturing various live performance and live sports broadcasts. In the future, we plan to use ultra wide band techniques to capture outdoor spaces, in place of motion capture cameras.

http://www.rzm-research.com/works/coldstares

Rhizomatiks Research: Daito Manabe, Motoi Ishibashi, Yuya Hanai, Katsuhiko Harada, Momoko Nishimoto, Youichi Sakamoto, Tomoaki Yanagisawa
ELEVENPLAY: MIKIKO, Kaori Yasukawa, Erisa Wakisaka
TAKCOM
P.I.C.S.: Takahiko Kajima, Syuhei Harada
McRAY: Akira Miwa, Kohki Okuyama, Akira Iio
Crescent, inc.
Yae-pon

Daito Manabe (JP) is a media artist, DJ and programmer. Daito founded Rhizomatiks in 2006, and since 2015 he has worked with Motoi Ishibashi on Rhizomatiks Research, which conducts projects for the purpose of R&D. **Rhizomatiks Research** (JP), researching into the relationship between human beings and technology, is an organization which introduces to the world, art and entertainment projects through collaborating with creators including artists, researchers, graphic designers, athletes, dancers, choreographers, directors, musicians, and engineers. **MIKIKO** (JP) is a stage director/choreographer, the artistic director and choreographer of world-famous Japanese artists, and choreographer/director of the dance company ELEVENPLAY. **ELEVENPLAY** (JP) was founded by MIKIKO in 2009 in hopes of creating dancers who possess highly artistic sense and creativity on top of exquisite techniques, body and spirit. **TAKCOM** (JP) is a director of the moving image and an artist based in Tokyo. He has garnered acclaim worldwide with gallery exhibitions and art festivals. From art gallery to advertising, he takes pleasure in pursuing artistic expression in all mediums and forms.

Processing Foundation

http://processingfoundation.org

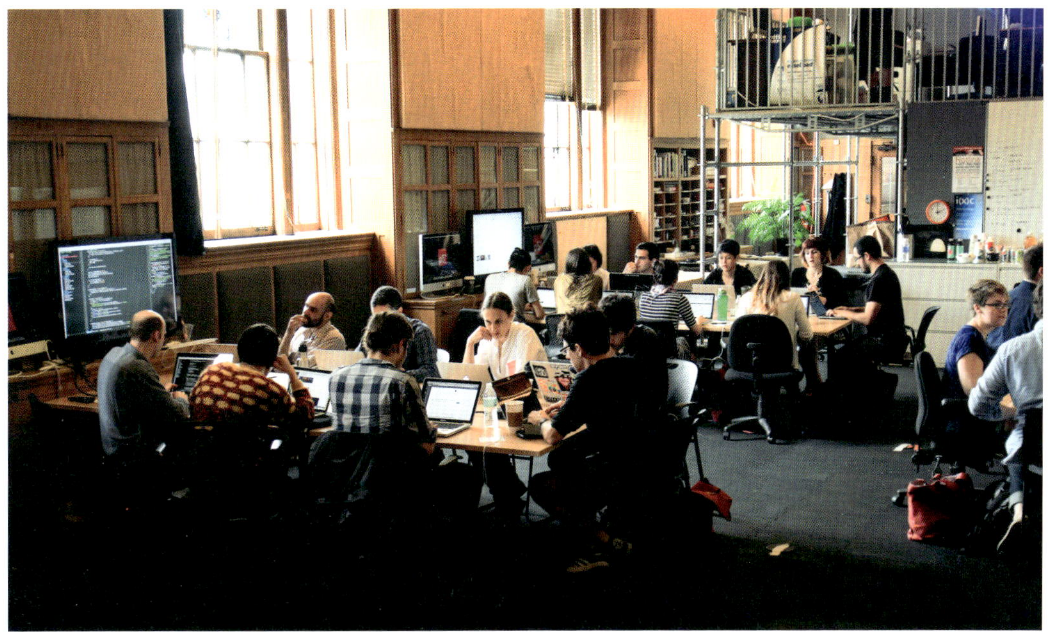

The *Processing Foundation's* mission is to promote software literacy within the visual arts, and visual literacy within technology-related fields. Our goal is to empower people of all interests and backgrounds to learn how to program and make creative work with code, especially those who might not otherwise have access to these tools and resources.

We do this by developing and distributing a group of related software projects, which includes Processing, p5.js, and Processing.py, and facilitating partnerships and collaborations with allied organizations and individuals, to build a more diverse community around software and the arts.

The *Processing Foundation* is specifically invested in expanding the communities of technology and the arts to include and support those who have not had equal access. At our core is the philosophy and politics of open-source software. We believe that learning to program is not about acquiring a certain skillset, but is instead a creative and exploratory process.

Board of directors: Ben Fry, Lauren McCarthy, Daniel Shiffman, Casey Reas
Director of initiatives: Johanna Hedva
Advisor: John Maeda

The *Processing Foundation* was founded in 2012 after more than a decade of work with the original Processing software. Over the years, Processing has reached and empowered not only artists and coders, but also designers, filmmakers, educators, musicians, performers, and students of all kinds.

Sentient Chamber
Living Architecture Systems Group

Located at the National Academy of Sciences in Washington D.C., *Sentient Chamber* is a free-standing pavilion integrating innovative near-living technologies developed by the Living Architecture Systems Group. *Sentient Chamber* is composed of a flexible meshwork canopy, housing a network of kinetic mechanisms that use dense arrays of microprocessors and sensors. These interactive systems offer interactions with viewers that include spatially imaged sound, light, and movement mechanisms. A curiosity-based learning algorithm in the software allows the sculpture to be aware of its audience, attempting to learn meaningful behaviors over time. The work explores an architecture capable of handling unstable conditions through artificial intelligence, attempting to offer practical methods for working with our increasingly complex built environment.

Living Architecture Systems Group: Philip Beesley, Matthew Chan, Rob Gorbet, Mike Hu, Mon Josef, Dana Kulic, Salvador Miranda, Clara Montgomery, Thomas Noussis, Jordan Prosser, Siubhan Taylor

http://philipbeesleyarchitect.com/sculptures/Sentient-Chamber/index.php

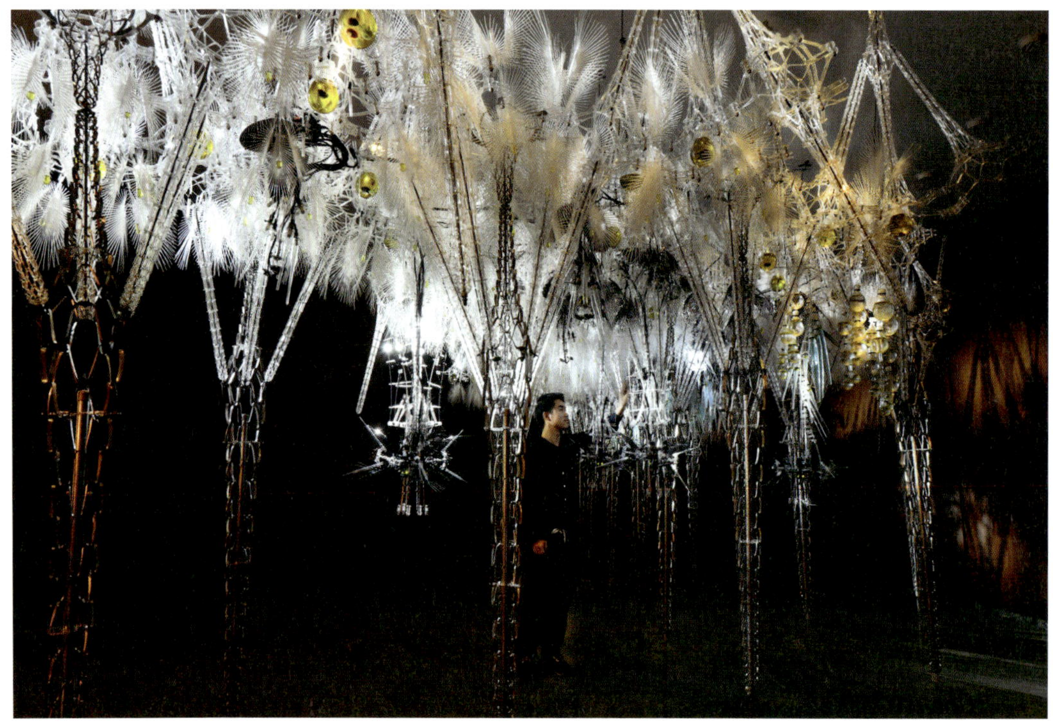

The **Living Architecture Systems Group** (CA) brings together pioneering international researchers and industry partners in a highly interdisciplinary research cluster dedicated to developing interdisciplinary working methods, innovative technologies, and new critical aesthetics within the emerging field of responsive architecture. Their work examines the integration of living and near-living qualities into our built environment through the interdisciplinary synthesis of technological systems.

Time Displacement—Chemobrionic Garden
Interactive generative (chemical) sound installation
Robertina Šebjanič, Ida Hiršenfelder, Aleš Hieng—Zergon

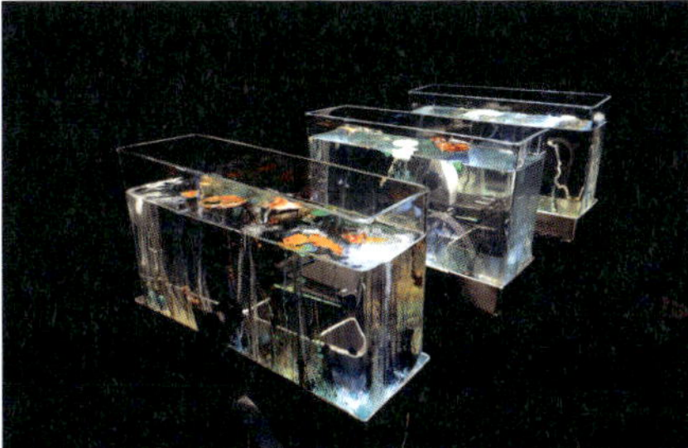

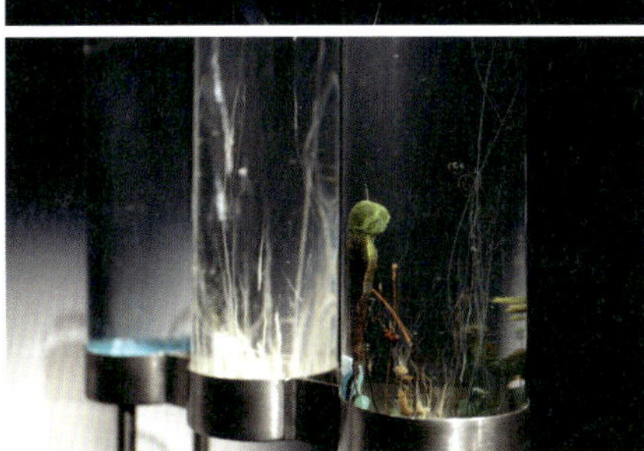

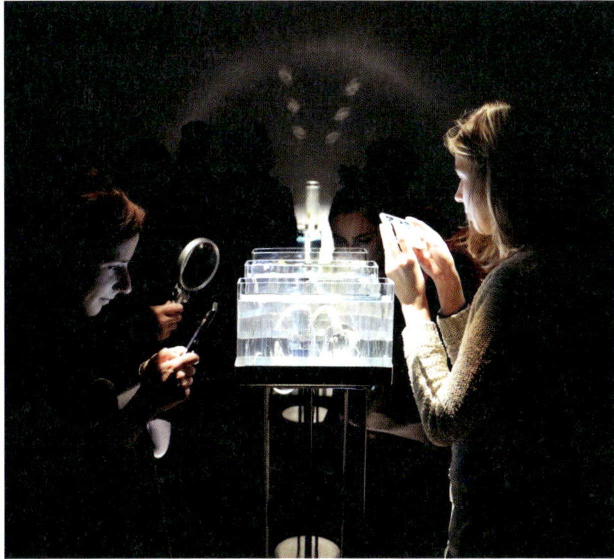

Katra Petriček

"In crystal we have a pure evidence of the existence of a formative life principle, and although in spite of everything we cannot understand the life of crystals —it is still a living being."

Nikola Tesla, 1900

Time Displacement—Chemobrionic Garden explores a relationship between hydrothermal chemistry, the passage of time, and the evolution of sound. The project consists of several small chemical garden formations in a water glass (sodium metasilicate) solution, to provide an insight into research on the origin of life and on chemical processes. The chemical reactions are monitored by cameras to detect changes in color and in shape by means of microcontrollers. The changes affect the code for live sound generation, and slowly alter the generative drone composition pervading the gallery space. The project's theoretical background is based on a paper entitled "From chemical gardens to chemobrionics", written and issued by a group of 21 scientists on 29 May 2015, a reiterating call for research into the principles of self-assembling structures, to produce—as they suggest—new insights into the origin of metabolism in Earth's early geological periods.

Artists (research and development): Robertina Šebjanič, Ida Hiršenfelder, Aleš Hieng—Zergon
Programming: Slavko Glamočanin
Production: Projekt Atol & LJUDMILA, 2015
Partner: Aksioma

http://robertina.net/time-displacement-chemobrionic-garden/

Robertina Šebjanič (SL) is an internationally exhibited artist, combining art—technology—science. Her ideas and concepts are often realized in collaboration with others, through interdisciplinary and informal integration in her work. She is a member of Hackteria Network, Ljudmila, UR Institute, and Theremidi Orchestra. *http://robertina.net/* **Aleš Hieng—Zergon** (SL) is a chemical engineer by profession as well as a DJ, a producer of electronic music, and a sound artist who also works in the field of audiovisual performances and DIY electronics. He is interested in sonic and audiovisual experimentations as well as club music. *http://zergon.org/* **Ida Hiršenfelder** (SL) is a Ljubljana based media art curator and sound artist. Her focus research areas are media archeology and archives of media art. She works at the Museum of Contemporary Art Metelkova +MUSM on projects related to digital archives. *http://beephlip.org/*

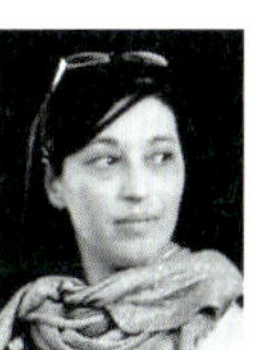
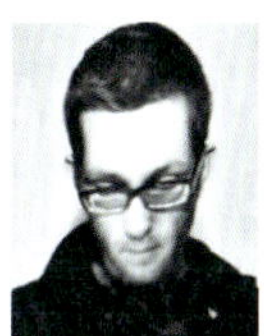
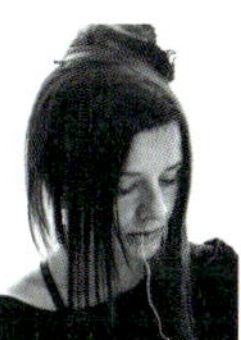

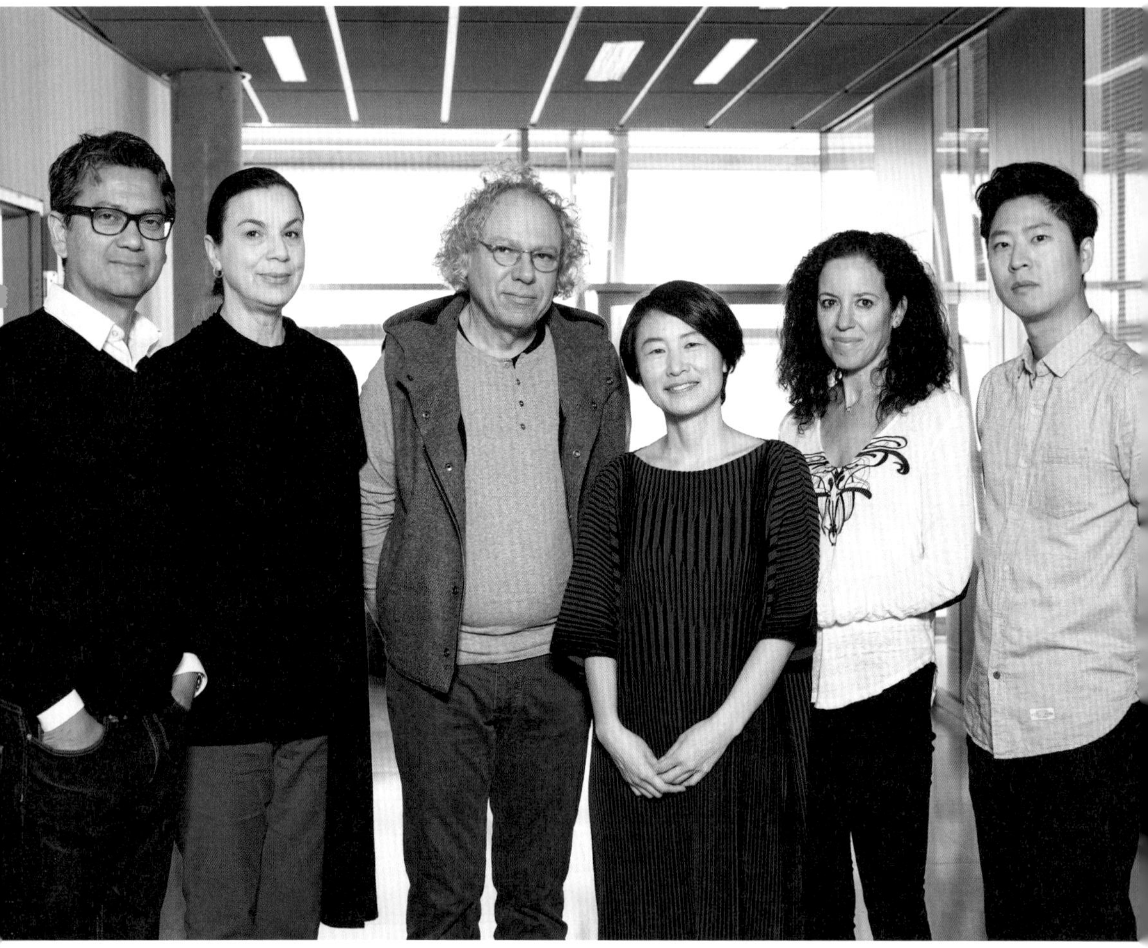

Ian Banerjee, Victoria Vesna, Alexander Mankowsky, Chiaki Hayashi, Yamina Aouina, Erick Oh

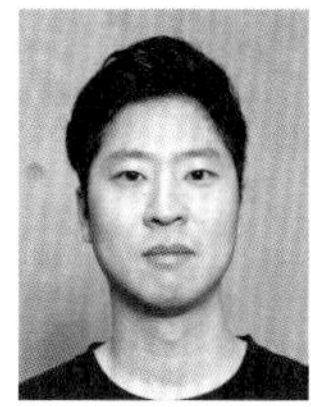

Erick Oh (KR) is a Korean filmmaker / painter based in California. His work has been introduced and nominated at Annecy Animation Festival, Hiroshima Animation Festival, Student Academy Awards, Zagreb Film Festival, SIGGRAPH, Anima Mundi, Ars Electronica, and numerous other international film festivals and galleries world wide. After receiving his BFA from the Fine Art Department at Seoul National University and his MFA from UCLA's film program, Erick joined Pixar Animation Studios as an animator in 2010. Erick's most recent independent animated film, *The Dam Keeper* was nominated for the Academy Awards in 2015. *www.erickoh.com*

Victoria Vesna (US), PhD, is an Artist and Professor at the UCLA Department of Design | Media Arts and Director of the Art|Sci center at the School of the Arts and California Nanosystems Institute (CNSI). With her installations she investigates how communication technologies affect collective 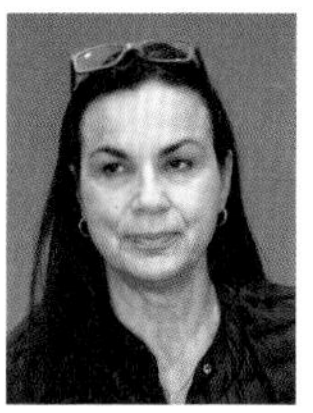 behavior and perceptions of identity shift in relation to scientific innovation (PhD, University of Wales, 2000). Her work involves long-term collaborations with composers, nano-scientists, neuroscientists, and evolutionary biologists, and she brings this experience to students. She is the North American editor of *AI & Society* and in 2007 published an edited volume–*Database Aesthetics: Art in the Age of Information Overflow* and another in 2011– *Context Providers: Conditions of Meaning in Media Arts.*

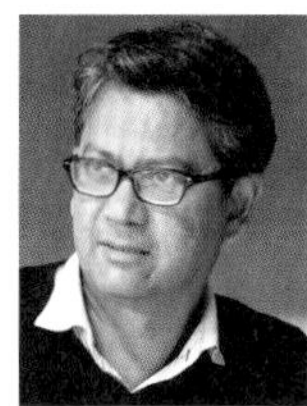

Ian Banerjee (IN/AT) is lecturer and research fellow at the Centre for Sociology (ISRA) at Vienna University of Technology. For 15 years he has been investigating global issues around urbanization with a special focus on urban innovation. For six years he has developed a keen interest in studying the interlinkages between urbanism and emerging educational practices. In 2015 he edited an e-book with Ingrid Fischer-Schreiber on *Digital Communities 2004-2014: Selected Projects from Prix ARS Electronica.*

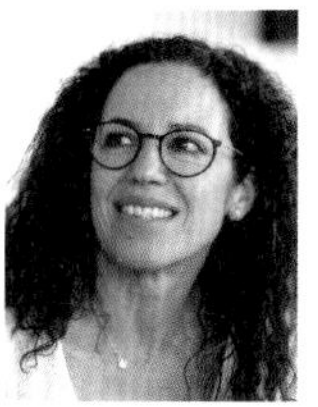

Yamina Aouina (DE/CH) has been involved with innovation and luxury for more than 10 years–first as an advisor for big Swiss watch making companies, then as Innovation Director at Cartier, and now as Head of Technology Intelligence at Richemont the Luxury Group. Through the different missions her experience had a common focus: aligning tradition, history, and outstanding craftsmanship with breakthrough technologies for the creation of fascinating products and experiences. As a member of Go-Beyond's business angle network she was closely involved in the start-ups of young entrepreneurs, helping them with their business development and financing, and she organized the first European Summit for sustainable investing.

Alexander Mankowsky (DE), born in Berlin 1957, studied Social Science, Philosophy and Psychology at the Freie Universität Berlin. In 1989 he started working in the Daimler research institute in Berlin. The multidisciplinary approach in the institute integrated a wide array of disci- 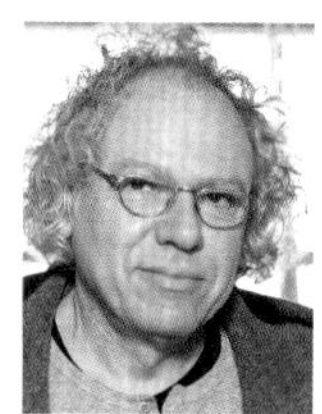 plines–from social sciences to artificial intelligence. He is currently working on Futures Studies, focusing on the ever-changing culture of mobility, the interdependency of social and technological innovation, and other aspects of envisioning paths into the future.

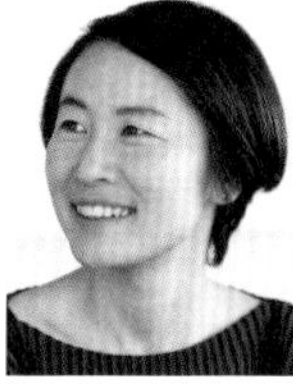

Chiaki Hayashi (JP) is the co-founder and currently the Representative Director of Loftwork Inc., which annually produces over 600 projects. She manages the operation of the company's creative platform Loftwork.com, which has 25,000 creators registered, FabCafe–a cafe with digital fabrication tools, and a material-centered co-working office MTRL. She is currently the Japan Liaison to the Director at the MIT Media Lab and has recently founded the company Hidakuma, which aims to promote and rebuild nature and local creativity.

STARTS Prize'16
Nomination Committee

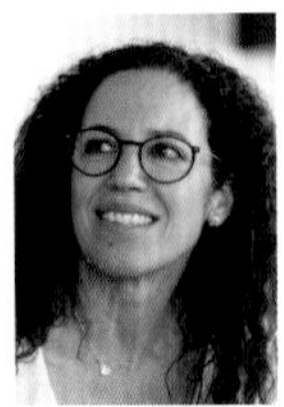

Yamina Aouina (DE/CH) has been involved with innovation and luxury for more than 10 years—first as an advisor for big Swiss watch making companies, then as Innovation Director at Cartier, and now as Head of Technology Intelligence at Richemont the Luxury Group. Through the different missions her experience had a common focus: aligning tradition, history, and outstanding craftsmanship with breakthrough technologies for the creation of fascinating products and experiences. As a member of Go-Beyond's business angle network she was closely involved in the start-ups of young entrepreneurs, helping them with their business development and financing, and she organized the first European Summit for sustainable investing.

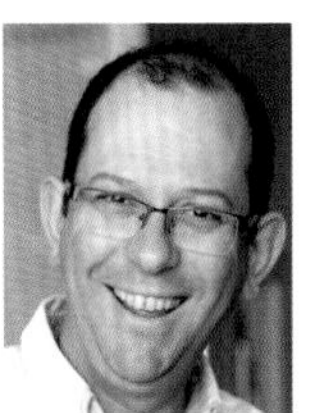

Luis Miguel Girão (PT), founder of Artshare, is a transdisciplinary artist and researcher. As a researcher he is generating support for EU and Transatlantic policy making in the field of the interface of art, science and technology. He is developing applications of technology as tools for artistic expression focusing on electromagnetism. Luis Miguel Girão is a member of the Planetary Collegium and of the Centre for Sociology and Music Studies at the Faculty of Social Sciences and Humanities of the New University of Lisbon. In 2007, he was awarded the Bolsa Ernesto de Sousa prize. He was coordinator of ICT ART CONNECT 2013 and of the European Commission's ICT ART CONNECT study program.

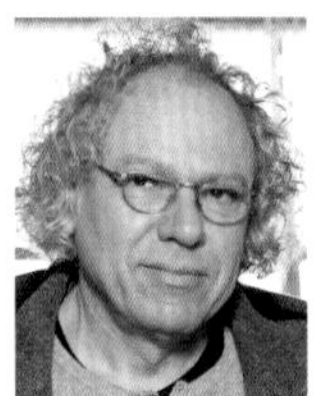

Alexander Mankowsky (DE), born in Berlin 1957, studied Social Science, Philosophy and Psychology at the Freie Universität Berlin. In 1989 he started working in the Daimler research institute in Berlin. The multidisciplinary approach in the institute integrated a wide array of disciplines—from social sciences to artificial intelligence. He is currently working on Futures Studies, focusing on the ever-changing culture of mobility, the interdependency of social and technological innovation, and other aspects of envisioning paths into the future.

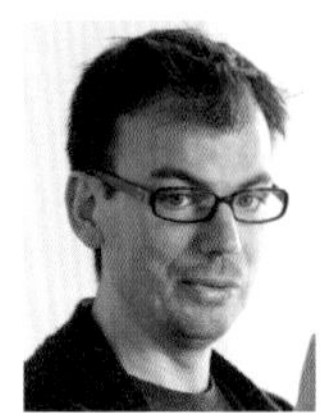

Filip Visnjic (UK) is a lecturer, curator, and a media technologist born in Belgrade now living in London. He is the founder and editor-in-chief of CreativeApplications.Net. The site tirelessly reports innovation across the field and catalogues projects, tools, and platforms relevant to the intersection of art, media, and technology. In 2012, Filip co-founded Resonate, a new educational platform and a festival located in Belgrade. He co-launched *HOLO*, a magazine about art, science and technology and is currently Director of Platform at FRAMED, working on a new canvas for digital art.

STARTS Prize'16
International Advisors

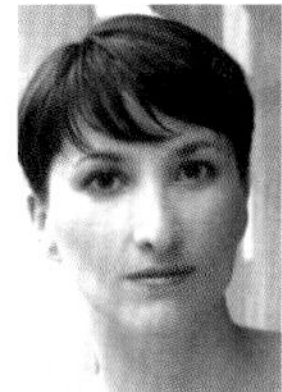

Jana Adamcová (CZ) is founder and chair of the Institute for Digital Economy. She has a master degree in Philosophy and German philology. She has 14-years' experience in the field of national level strategic management in both public and private sectors. Her expertise is R&D and industrial policy, public diplomacy and emerging industries such as cultural and creative industries and digital economy.

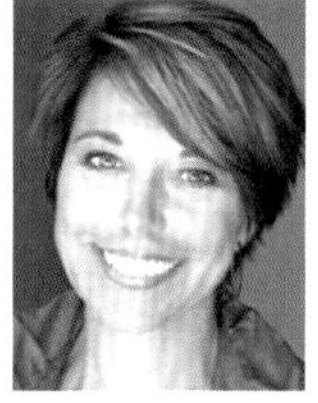

Anne Balsamo (US) has been an entrepreneur, author, educator, and new media designer at various times in her life and has recently taken the position as the inaugural Dean of the School of Arts, Technology and Emerging Communication at the University of Texas at Dallas. Previously she served as the Dean of the School of Media Studies at The New School in New York. She was a Full Professor at the University of Southern California where she held joint appointments in the Annenberg School of Communication and the Interactive Media Division of the School of Cinematic Arts. In 1998, she joined RED, the research-design group at Xerox PARC.

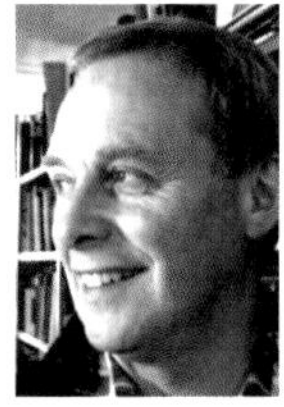

Peter Higgins (UK) trained as an architect and has worked for BBC TV. In 1992 he formed Land Design Studio who create exhibitions and visitor experiences including work for The British Museum, V&A, The Natural History Museum, Singapore Gardens By The Bay, and the UAE pavilion Milan Expo. He helped develop the MA Narrative Environments course at Central St Martins where he is visiting professor. In 2009 he was appointed a Royal Designer for Industry.

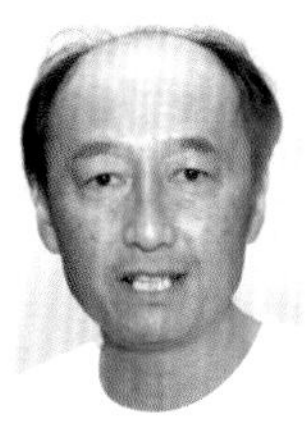

Hiroo Iwata (JP) has been conducting research projects on virtual reality. His research interests include haptic interface, locomotion interface, and spatially immersive display. He exhibited his work at the Emerging Technologies venue of the SIGGRAPH every year from 1994 to 2007 and received Honorary Mentions at Prix Ars Electronica 96 and 2001. In 2004 he launched the *Device Art* project and he has been in charge of the PhD Program in Empowerment Informatics at the University of Tsukuba since 2013.

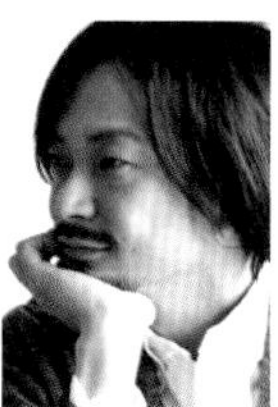

Daito Manabe (JP) is a Tokyo-Based media artist, DJ, and programmer. He founded Rhizomatiks in 2006, and since 2015 he has worked with Motoi Ishibashi on Rhizomatiks Research, which conducts mainly R&D projects. He also carries out collaborative projects with artists in various genres, focusing on programming and interactive design. Manabe was acclaimed internationally as one of the eleven key persons, including John Maeda and Hans Zimmer, selected for a special website to celebrate 30 years of Mac by Apple Inc.

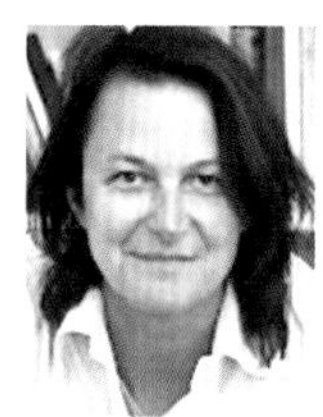

Elizabeth Markevitch (FR/DE) is an art professional and founder of ikonoTV, an international platform for visual arts broadcasting. She began her career restoring icons, after which she worked at *Vogue Hommes* Paris; since the '80s she has held numerous important positions in the international art world (Artemis Art Fund, Schröder Bank, Sotheby's). In 1998, she co-founded the first online art gallery eyestorm.com. This year, Markevitch Media is also launching ikonospace, a revolutionary new 3D software for gallery curators, art fairs, collectors, and museum exhibition designers.

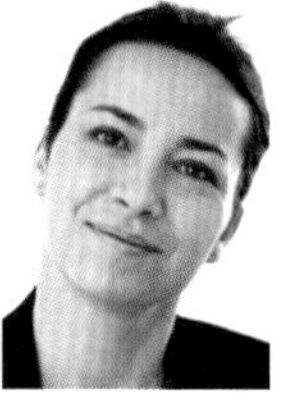

Simona Maschi (IT/DK) is a co-founder and director of the Copenhagen Institute of Interaction Design. Leading the overall organization at CIID, she heads a team that encompasses a world-renowned education, a cutting edge research group, an award-winning consultancy, and a very ambitious incubator platform. Simona is an expert in service design, scenario design, and design methods, and is passionate about using design to create real positive impact in people's lives.

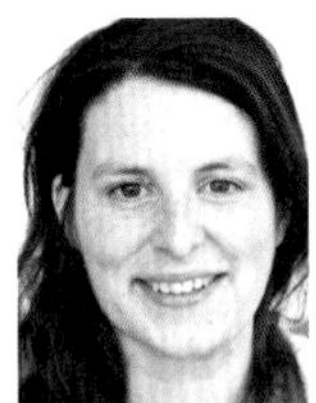

Lynn Scarff (IE) is the Interim Director of Science Gallery Dublin. She has over twelve years' experience in developing and leading public engagement projects in science, arts and education fields. Lynn comes from a background of work in the environmental and not for profit sectors and has developed a series of programs, exhibitions, events, books, TV and radio programs for these areas.

Thomas Schildhauer (DE) is computer scientist, marketing expert, and internet researcher. In 1999 he founded the Institute of Electronic Business—the first affiliated institute of the Berlin University of Arts. In his capacity as Professor at the Berlin University of the Arts, he holds the 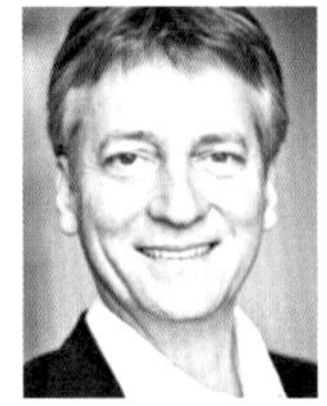 chair for Marketing with focus on Electronic Business, as well as conducting the Berlin-based Career College. As executive director of the Alexander von Humboldt Institute for Internet and Society, he is responsible for the research area Internet-enabled innovation. Since October 2012, he has held the position of Academic Director of iDeers Consulting, and he has been Chairman of the Council of Internet Sages, a scientific advisory board of the IEB, since 2013.

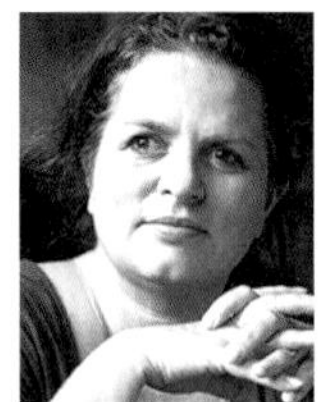

Marleen Stikker (NL) founded De Digitale Stad (The Digital City) in 1994, the first virtual community introducing free public access to the internet. She is founder of Waag, a social enterprise that consists of Waag Society, a research Institute for creative technologies and social innovation, and Waag Products, which launched companies like 7scenes, a mobile learning and gaming platform, and Fairphone, the first fair smartphone in the world. Stikker is also member of the supervisory board of WPG Publishers, an independent publishing group.

Maholo Uchida (JP) is a curator and exhibition development division manager of Miraikan (National Museum of Emerging Science and Technology) in Tokyo. She started her career as a curator of new media art and design, organizing several national and international exhibitions. She has devel- 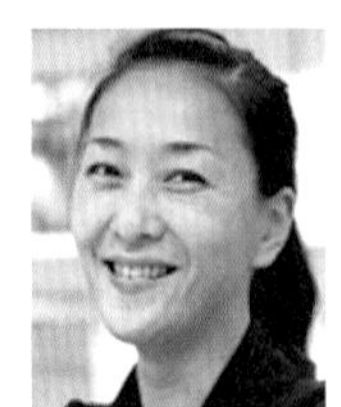 oped a new style of science museum, where activities and exhibitions are strongly oriented towards art, design, game, manga, and other forms of popular culture.

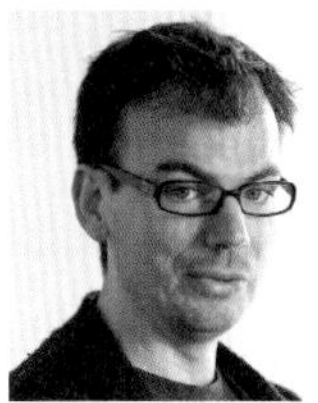

Filip Visnjic (UK) is a lecturer, curator, and a media technologist born in Belgrade now living in London. He is the founder and editor-in-chief of CreativeApplications.Net. The site tirelessly reports innovation across the field and catalogues projects, tools, and platforms relevant to the intersection of art, media, and technology. In 2012, Filip co-founded Resonate, a new educational platform and a festival located in Belgrade. He co-launched *HOLO,* a magazine about art, science and technology and is currently Director of Platform at FRAMED, working on a new canvas for digital art.

Ars Electronica 2016

Festival für Kunst, Technologie und Gesellschaft
Festival for Art, Technology and Society

Organization
Ars Electronica Linz GmbH

Managing Directors
Gerfried Stocker, Diethard Schwarzmair
Ars-Electronica-Straße 1, 4040 Linz, Austria
Tel: +4373272720
Fax: +4373272722
info@aec.at

Co-organizers

ORF Oberösterreich
Director: Kurt Rammerstorfer

LIVA—Veranstaltungsgesellschaft m.b.H.
Directors: Hans-Joachim Frey, Thomas Ziegler

OK Offenes Kulturhaus im OÖ Kulturquartier
Directors: Martin Sturm, Gabriele Daghofer

Partners
Anton Bruckner Privatuniversität
BOZAR Centre for Fine Arts Brussels
bug`n`play
c3
Campus Genius Award
Central Linz
Centre for the promotion of science
Crossing Europe
CUBUS
DIG gallery
Europe for Festivals, Festivals for Europe (EFFE)
Empowerment Informatics
Etopia
European Southern Observatory (ESO)
European Space Agency (ESA)
eutema
FAB Verein zur Förderung von Arbeit und Beschäftigung
Fachhochschule Oberösterreich – Campus Hagenberg
Filmakademie Baden-Württemberg
FMX 2016—Conference on Animation, Effects,
Games and Transmedia
GameStage
Gebärdenwelt.tv
GV Art London
Interface Cultures
International Students Creative Award
Japan Media Arts Festival
Kapelica Gallery / Kersnikova
Kepler Salon Verein zur Förderung von Wissensvermittlung
Klimabündnis Österreich Gmbh – Regionalstelle Ober-
österreich
Kunstuniversität Linz—Universität für künstlerische und
industrielle Gestaltung
LABoral Centro de Arte y Creación Industrial
LENTOS Kunstmuseum Linz
Mariendom Linz
mb21
OTELO Linz und Vorchdorf
QUT Queensland University of Technology
Saloon 2000
Science Gallery
Stadtwerkstatt
Südwind

Tourismusverband Linz
ULF–Unabhängiges LandesFreiwilligenzentrum
V2_ Institute for the Unstable Media
VHS
Wirtschaftskammer OÖ
Wissensturm
Zaragoza City of Knowledge Foundation
ZusammenHelfen in Oberösterreich

Directors Ars Electronica: Gerfried Stocker, Christine Schöpf
Head of Festival: Martin Honzik
Technical Head: Karl Julian Schmidinger
Head of Finance & Organization: Veronika Liebl

Production Team: Joan Bairam, Christl Baur, Katharina Bienert, Klaus Birklbauer, Lisa Brandstötter, Elise Brokensha, Florina Costamoling, Roman Dachsberger, Leopold Eckl, Hannes Franks, Marion Friedl, Bettina Gahleitner, Felix Ganzer, Sandra Gaßner, Rosi Grillmair, Nathan Guo, Julius Jell, Verena Christine Jurkovic, Juliane Leitner, Kristina Maurer, Hans Christian Merten, Antonia Mittendrein, Fabian Mühlberger, Manuela Naveau, Melvin Neumann, Michaela Obermayer, Emiko Ogawa, Hideaki Ogawa, Elvis Pavic, Pablo Peula, Christina Radner, Tina Reinthaler, Vera Reinthaler, Michael Sarsteiner, Louise Roux, Tamara Schürz, Shoko Takahashi, Tobias Thaler, Jochen Tuch, Olga Vad, Joschi Viteka, Nina Wenhart, Michaela Wimplinger, Susi Windischbauer, Carla Zamora

Co-curators
Ars Electronica Animation Festival: Christine Schöpf, Jürgen Hagler
Big Concert Night: Dennis Russell Davies, Heribert Schröder
Campus Exhibition: Wang Zhigang
Expanded Animation: Jürgen Hagler, Alexander Wilhelm
Interface Cultures Exhibition: Christa Sommerer, Laurent Mignonneau, Martin Kaltenbrunner, Michaela Ortner, Marlene Brandstätter, Fabrizio Lamoncha
Music Monday: Werner Jauk
Nightline: Salon 2000
Radical Atoms: Hiroshi Ishii
Music and Media Art / Music as Media Art: Volkmar Klien, Se-Lien Chuang, Andreas Weixler

Prix Ars Electronica 2016

Co-organizers

ORF Oberösterreich
Director: Kurt Rammerstorfer

LIVA—Veranstaltungsgesellschaft m.b.H.
Directors: Hans-Joachim Frey, Thomas Ziegler

OK Offenes Kulturhaus im OÖ Kulturquartier
Directors: Martin Sturm, Gabriele Daghofer

Idea: Hannes Leopoldseder
Conception: Christine Schöpf, Gerfried Stocker
Coordination: Martin Honzik, Emiko Ogawa
Technical Management: Karl Julian Schmidinger

Production Team: Katharina Bienert, Marion Friedl, Veronika Liebl, Kristina Maurer, Hans Christian Merten, Manuela Naveau, Elvis Pavic, Johannes Poell, Christina Radner, Remo Rauscher, Tina Reinthaler, Louise Roux, Jutta Schmiederer, Joschi Viteka

Press
Christopher Sonnleitner, Robert Bauernhansl, Martin Hieslmair, Vanessa Graf, Katja Nitsche

Marketing
Isabella Ematinger, Sara Fuchs, Eva Tsackmaktsian

Ars Electronica Linz GmbH

Managing Directors
Gerfried Stocker, Diethard Schwarzmair

Ars Electronica Center
Katharina Aichinger, Renata Aigner, Viktoria Aistleitner, Andreas Bauer, Reinhard Bengesser, Blanka Denkmaier, Johannes Egler, Erika Eiter, Julia Felberbauer, Melinda File, Johanna Firmberger, Andrea Fröhlich, Christoph Froschauer, Mitra Gazvini-Zateh, Christian Gerber, Elisabeth Gerhard-Mayrhofer, Dominic Gottinger, Nicole Grüneis, Anton Grünwald Beleda, Ulrike Gschwandtner, Harald Haas, Birgit Hartinger, Anna Haslehner, Florian Heiml, Barbara Heinzl, Thomas Hillinger, Susanne Hintringer, Florian Hofer, Sri Rahayu Hofstadler, Gerold Hofstadler, Eva Hofstädter, Philip Huemer, Thomas Jannke, Erika Jungreithmayr, Elisabeth Kattner, Herwig Kerschner, Viktoria Klepp, Martin Kneidinger, Karin Knoll, Michael Koller, Thomas Kollmann, Christoph Kremer, Andreas Leeb, Sabine Leidlmair, Magdalena Leitner, Juliane Leitner, Anna Katharina Link, Ulrike Mair, Reingard Medicus, Kathrin Meyer, Tanja Mikolasch, Clemens Mock, Horst Morocutti, Claudia Moser, Daniel Murina, Farzana Niazi, Heinrich Niederhuber, Michaela Obermayer, Benjamin Perndl, Svetlana Petrovic, Katharina Pilar, Armin Pils, Anna Polewiak, Ulrike Rieseneder, Michael Rottmann, Petra Saubolle-Hofmann, Alina Sauter, Birgitt Schäffer, Nina Schönberger, Thomas Schwarz, Fabian Schwarz, Stefan Schwarzmair, Elio Seidl, Manfred Seifriedsberger, Martin Spanka, Margarethe Stöttner-Breuer, Johannes Stürzlinger, Istvan Szabo, Bhoomesh Tak, Michaela Maria Tanzer, Michael Thaler, Thomas Viehböck, Florian Voggeneder, Raffaela Vornicu, Manuel Walch, Florian Wanninger, Stefanos Wasilakis, Stefan Weinknecht, Michael Wlaschitz

Ars Electronica Futurelab
Roland Aigner, Florian Berger, Patrick Berger, Chris Bruckmayr, Harald Dirisamer, Samuel Jakob Eckl, Barbara Erlinger, Maria Eschlböck, Peter Freudling, Matthew Gardiner, Rachel Hanlon, Roland Haring, Peter Holzkorn, Horst Hörtner, Andreas Jalsovec, Anna Kuthan, Christopher Lindinger, Martina Mara, Michael Mayr, Kristefan Minski, Stefan Mittlböck-Jungwirth-Fohringer, Martin Mörth, Otto Naderer, Nicolas Naveau, Kathrin Obernhumer, Hideaki Ogawa, Ben Olsen, Michael Platz, Erwin Reitböck, Jonathan Rutherford, Clemens Francis Scharfen, Simon Schmid, Claudia Schnugg, Markus Scholl, Shoko Takahashi, Marianne Ternek

Ars Electronica Festival / Prix / Exhibitions
Joan Bairam, Christl Baur, Lisa-Maria Brandstötter, Elise Brokensha, Florina Costamoling, Leopold Eckl, Hannes F. Franks, Marion Friedl, Sandra Gaßner, Rosi Grillmair, Franziska Gschwendtner, Martin Honzik, Verena Christine Jurkovic, Veronika Christina Liebl, Kristina Maurer, Hans Christian Merten, Antonia Mittendrein, Fabian Mühlberger, Peter Müller, Manuela Naveau, Melvin Neumann, Katja Nitsche, Emiko Ogawa, Elvis Pavic, Christina Radner, Tina Reinthaler, Vera Reinthaler, Louise Roux, Karl Schmidinger, Tamara Schürz, Carla Milena Zamora Campos

Ars Electronica Management Services
Robert Bauernhansl, Stephanie Danner, Bettina Danninger, Barbara Diesenreither, Isabella Ematinger, Michaela Frech, Sarah Fuchs, Bettina Gahleitner, Gerhard Grafinger, Martin Hieslmair, Julia Hofstätter, Andrea Huemer, Markus Jandl, Elisabeth Kapeller, Heinrich Klambauer, Stephan Kobler, Dominic Lengauer, Zulfija Magomedova, Peter J. Nitzschmann, Veronika Pauser, Christopher Sonnleitner , David Starzengruber, Daniela Thaller, Eva Tsackmaktsian, Michaela Wimplinger, Susi Windischbauer, Sebastian Zach

Ars Electronica Solutions
Michael Badics, Ina Badics, Cecile Bucher, Stefan Dorn, Gregor Fritsch, My Trinh Gardiner, Yvonne Hauser, Barbara Hinterleitner, Christoph Hofbauer, Martin Kaiser, Petros Kataras, Fadil Kujundzic, Thomas Lengauer, Pascal Maresch Johanna Mathauer, Kathrin Agnes Meyer, Harald Moser, Patrick Müller, Ali Nikrang, Dietmar Peter, Poorya Piroozan, Stephan Pointner, Andreas Pramböck, Gerald Priewasser-Höller, Gabriele Purdue, Andrea Rovescalli, Stefan Rozporka, Gerald Sixt, Markus Wipplinger, Claus Zweythurm

OK Offenes Kulturhaus im OÖ Kulturquartier

OK CyberArts Team
Directors: Martin Sturm, Gabriele Daghofer
Public Relations: Maria Falkinger
Technical Manager: Rainer Jessl
Curator: Genoveva Rückert
Exhibition Manager: Martina Rauschmayer
Production Manager: Aron Rynda
Technical Head: Andreas Kurz

Production Team: Jarno Bachheimer, Stefan Brandmayr, Attila Ferenczi, Alfred Fürholzer, Martin Haselsteiner, David Kraxberger, Bernhard Kitzmüller, Daniel Mandel, Andreas Steindl, André Tschinder, Hans-Jörg Weidinger, Gerhard Wörnhörer, Simon Wilhelm

Team: Verena Atteneder, Erika Baldinger, Katharina Baldinger-Hackl, Gerda Bauer, Renate Berger, Michael Dalpiaz, Walter Eckerstorfer, Max Fabian, Werner Friesenecker, Michaela Fröhlich, Andrea Gintner, Josef Gruber, Manuela Gruber, Stephan Hadwiger, Dominik Harrer, Sabine Haunschmid, Evi Heininger, Robert Herbst, Susi Heuschober, Maximilian Höglinger, Fritz Holzinger, Christoph Kaltenböck, Sabrina Kamenar, Simon Lachner, Barbara Mair, Judith Maule, Alexander Mauer, Franz Minichberger, Walter Mühlböck, Wolfgang Nagl, Maria Pachinger, Josef Pfarrhofer, Franz Pfifferling, Wilhelm Pichler, Angelika Pöschl, Franz Quirchtmayr, Gerda Sailer, Markus Schiller, Ulrike Schimpl, Helene Schoißengeyr, Marlies Stöger, Maria Venzl

LIVA–Veranstaltungsgesellschaft–Brucknerhaus

Directors: Hans-Joachim Frey, Thomas Ziegler
Team: Wolfgang Scheibner, Wolfgang Schützeneder, Ursula Kislinger

Kunstuniversität Linz–Universität für künstlerische und industrielle Gestaltung

Rector: Reinhard Kannonier
Vice-Rectors: Rainer Zendron, Christine Windsteiger

ORGANIZER

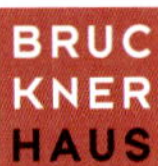 **ARS ELECTRONICA**

Ars Electronica Linz GmbH is a company of the city of Linz.

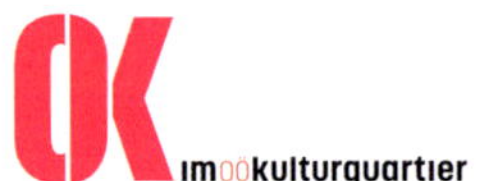 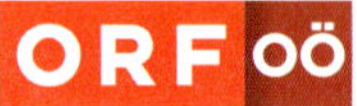 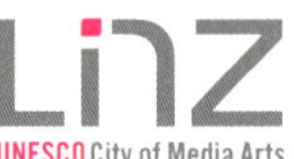

COOPERATION PARTNERS

1000 Worms
Anton Bruckner Privatuniversität
b00t Consultants
Berliner Technische Kunsthochschule (BTK)
BORG Bad Leonfelden
BOZAR Centre for Fine Arts Brussels
brotsüchtig
BTK—Hochschule für Gestaltung
bug'n'play
c3
Campus Genius Award
Center for Digital Music, Queen Mary University of London
Central Linz
Centre for the promotion of science
Crossing Europe
CUBUS
DIG gallery
DISK Berlin / CTM Festival
Donau-Universität Krems
Europe for Festivals, Festivals for Europe (EFFE)
Etopia
European Southern Observatory (ESO)
European Space Agency (ESA)
eutema
Experience Workshop Math-Art Movement
FAB Verein zur Förderung von Arbeit und Beschäftigung
Fachhochschule Oberösterreich – Campus Hagenberg
Filmakademie Baden-Württemberg
FMX 2016—Conference on Animation, Effects,
Games and Transmedia
GameStage
Gebärdenwelt.tv
GV Art London
hTh—CDN
Intel Corporation
Interface Cultures
International Students Creative Award
Japan Media Arts Festival
Johannes Kepler Universität Linz—Internationales GeoGebra Institut
Kapelica Gallery / Kersnikova

Kepler Salon—Verein zur Förderung von Wissensvermittlung
Klimabündnis Österreich Gmbh—Regionalstelle Oberösterreich
Kunstuniversität Linz—Universität für künstlerische
und industrielle Gestaltung
LABoral Centro de Arte y Creación Industrial
le lieu unique
Lehramt Bildnerische Erziehung—Kunstuniversität Linz
LENTOS Kunstmuseum Linz
Mariendom Linz
mb21
mehr demokratie!
Museo de la Universidad Nacional de Tres de Febrero
OÖ Familienbund
OTELO Linz und Vorchdorf
play:vienna
Quantum Reboot
QUT Queensland University of Technology
Resonate
Saloon 2000
Scholz & Volkmer
Science Gallery
Stadtbibliothek Linz
Stadtwerkstatt
Studiengang Raum & Design Strategien
der Kunstuniversität Linz
Südwind
Tourismusverband Linz
Trick-my-Film
ULF—Unabhängiges LandesFreiwilligenzentrum
Universidad Nacional de Tres de Febrero
Universität Salzburg
V2_ Institute for the Unstable Media
Volkshochschule Linz
Waag Society
Wanderkoch
Wirtschaftskammer OÖ
Wissensturm
youris.com
Zaragoza City of Knowledge Foundation
ZoopTEK
ZusammenHelfen in Oberösterreich

ARS ELECTRONICA RECEIVES SUPPORT FROM

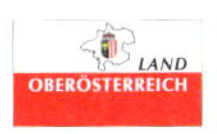

Land Oberösterreich

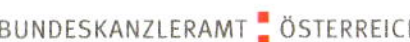

Bundeskanzleramt

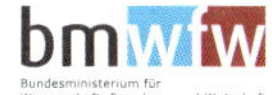

Bundesministerium für Wissenschaft,
Forschung und Wirtschaft

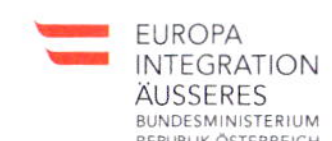

Creative Europe

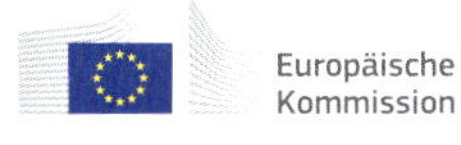

Europäische Kommission

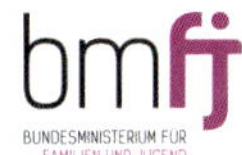

Bundesministerium für Europa
Integration und Äußeres

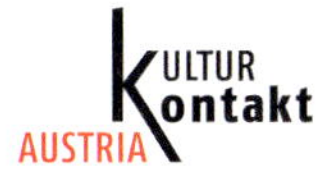

Bundesministerium für Familien und
Jugend – BuPP – Bundesstelle
Information zu digitalen Spielen

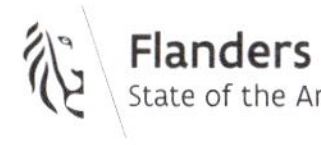

KulturKontakt Austria

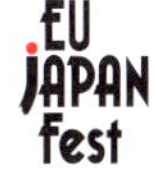

Botschaft Flandern

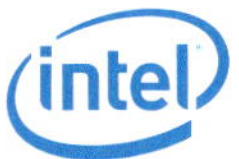

EU-Japan Fest
Japan Commitee

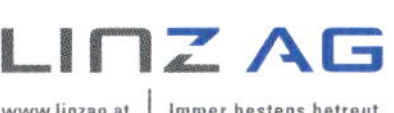

Creative Industries Fund NL
(CIFNL)

SPONSORS

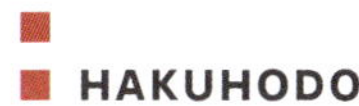

Intel and the Intel logo are trade-
marks of Intel Corporation in
the U.S. and/or other countries.

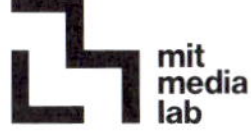

Linz AG

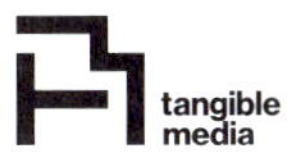

Hakuhodo

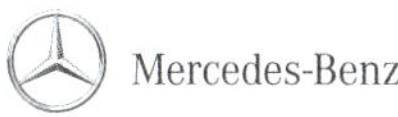

MIT Media Lab

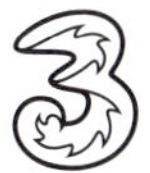

Tangible Media Group

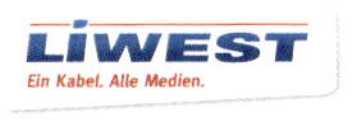

Mercedes-Benz

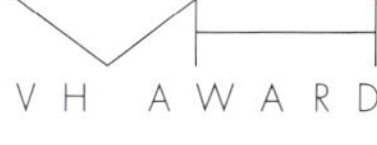

Hutchison Drei
Austria GmbH

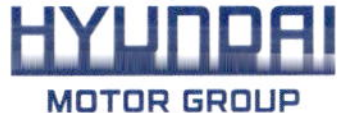

Liwest Kabelmedien GmbH

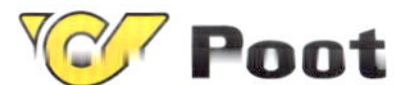

VH Award

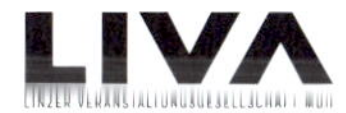

HYUNDAI MOTOR GROUP

Österreichische Post AG

LIVA – Linzer
Veranstaltungsgesellschaft mbH

SPONSORS

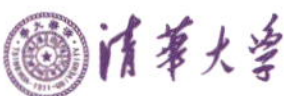

Tsinghua University

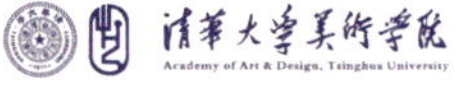

Academy of Art & Design,
Tsinghua University

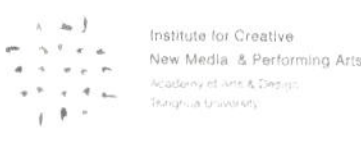

Faculty for Creative New
Media and Performing Art

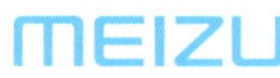

MEIZU

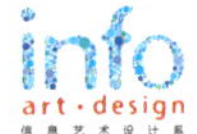

Department of Information Art &
Design (IAD) at Tsinghua University

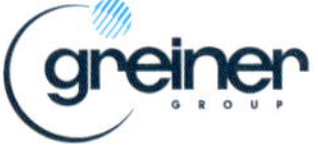

Greiner Holding AG

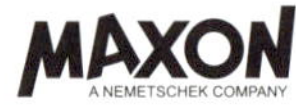

MAXON Computer GmbH

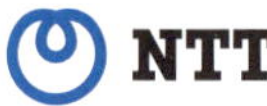

NTT

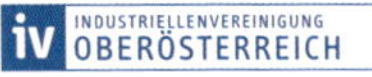

Industriellenvereinigung OÖ

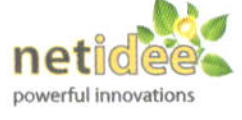

netidee

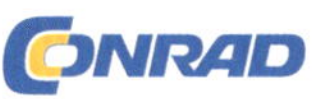

CONRAD
Electronic GmbH & Co KG

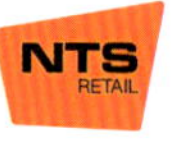

NTS Retail

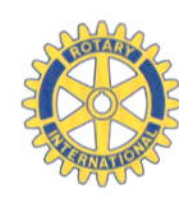

Rotary Club
Linz-Altstadt

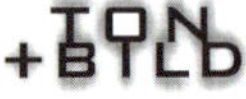

Ton + Bild

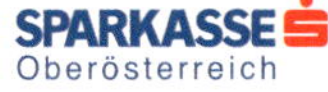

Sparkasse OÖ

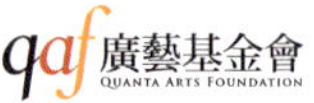

Quanta Arts Foundation

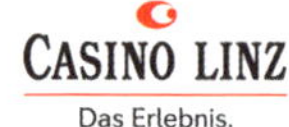

Casinos Austria AG

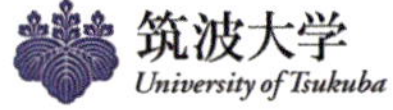

University of Tsukuba

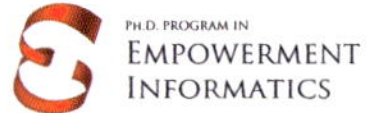

Empowerment
Informatics

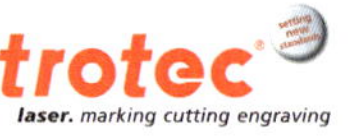

Trotec Laser GmbH

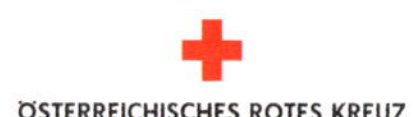

Österreichisches Rotes Kreuz

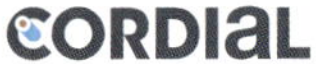

Cordial GmbH

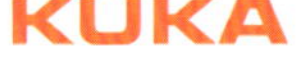

Kuka Roboter CEE GmbH

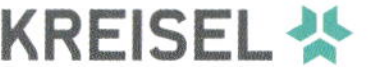

Kreisel Electric GmbH

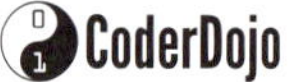

CoderDojo

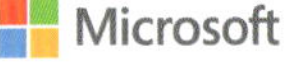

Microsoft Österreich

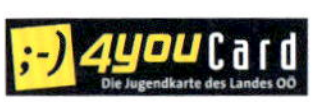

4YOUgend -
Verein OÖ Jugendarbeit

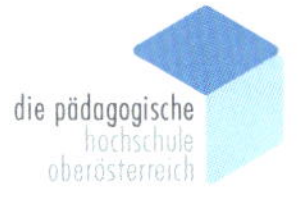

Pädagogische
Hochschule OÖ

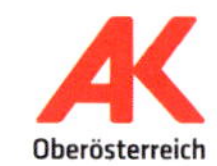

Arbeiterkammer OÖ

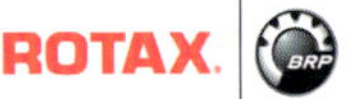

BRP ROTAX /
POWERTRAIN

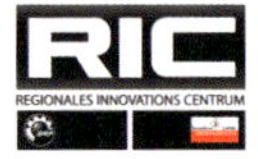

RIC GmbH

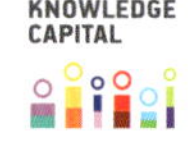

KNOWLEDGE CAPITAL

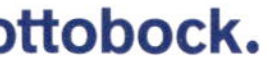

Otto Bock HealthCare
Deutschland GmbH

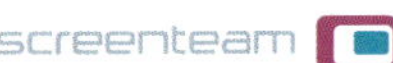

Screenteam GmbH

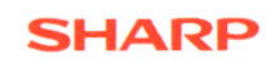

Sharp Electronics GmbH

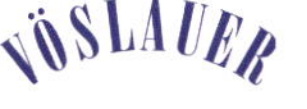

Vöslauer
Mineralwasser AG

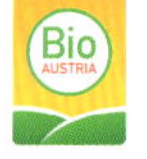

BIO AUSTRIA

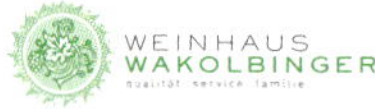

Weinhaus Wakolbinger

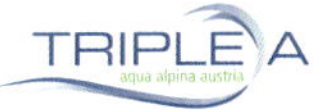
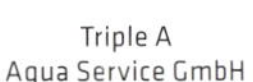

Triple A
Aqua Service GmbH

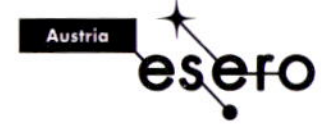

esero Austria

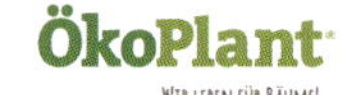

Baumschule Ökoplant GmbH

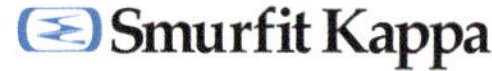

Smurfit Kappa Wellkart GmbH

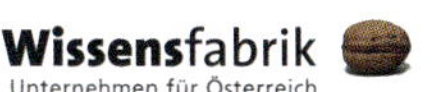

Wissensfabrik
Unternehmen für Österreich

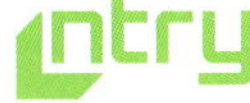

NTRY Ticketing OG

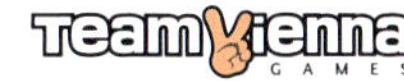

Team Vienna Games GmbH

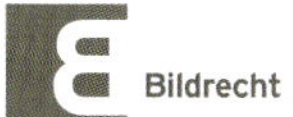

Bildrecht GmbH

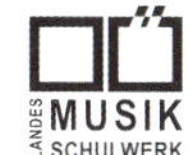

Oö. Landesmusikschulwerk

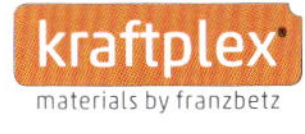

kraftplex
materials by franzbetz

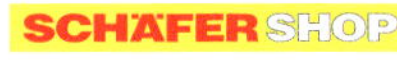

Schäfer Shop GmbH

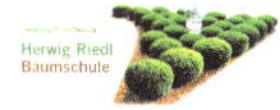

Baumschule Riedl

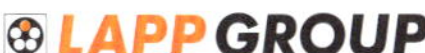

Lapp Austria GmbH

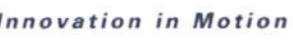

Miba AG

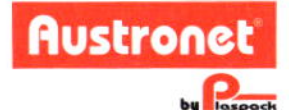

Plaspack Netze
GmbH

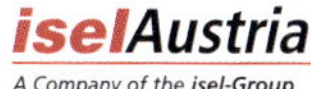

isel Austria
GmbH & Co. KG

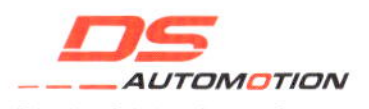

DS AUTOMOTION
GmbH

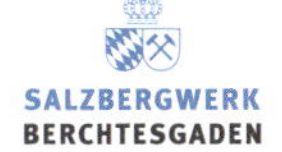

Südsalz GmbH

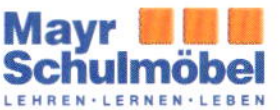

Mayr Schulmöbel
GmbH

CC4 Remarketing
GmbH

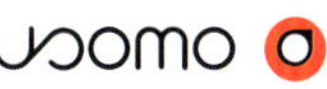

FRAMED immersive projects
GmbH & Co KG

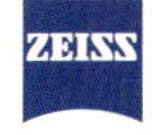

Carl Zeiss GmbH

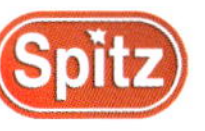

S. Spitz GmbH

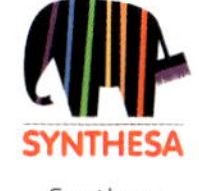

Synthesa
Chemie GmbH

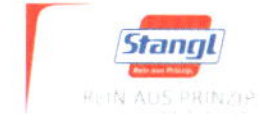

Stangl Reinigungstechnik
GmbH

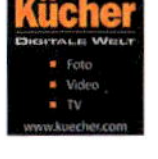

KÜCHER
Digitale Welt

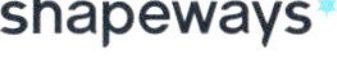

shapeways

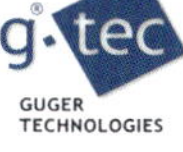

g.tec

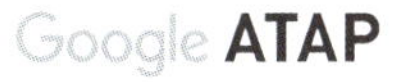

Google ATAP

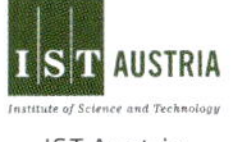

IST Austria

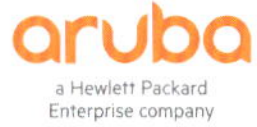

Aruba

PROJECT PARTNERS

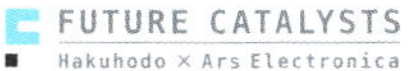

Future Catalysts

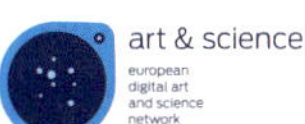

art&science

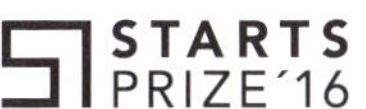

STARTS-Prize

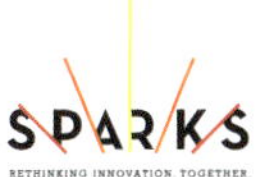

SPARKS-EU Horizon
2020 Project

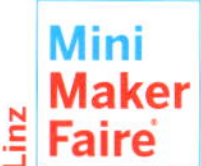

Mini Maker
Faire

MEDIA PARTNERS

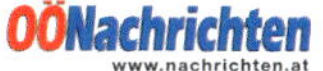

OÖ Nachrichten

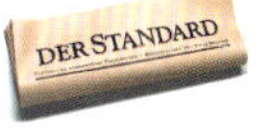

Der Standard

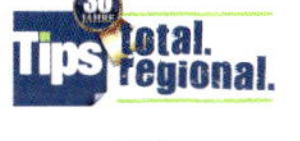

TIPS

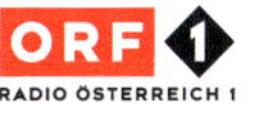

Ö1

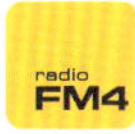

Radio FM4

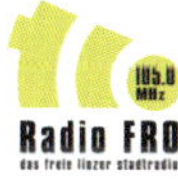

Radio Fro

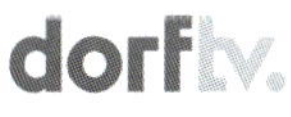

dorf TV

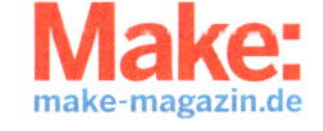

Maker Media

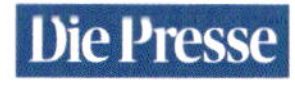

Die Presse

CyberArts 2016
International Compendium

Prix Ars Electronica
Computer Animation / Film / VFX – Interactive Art+ – Digital Communities –
Visionary Pioneers of Media Art – u19 - CREATE YOUR WORLD

STARTS Prize'16
Grand Prize of the European Commission honoring Innovation
in Technology, Industry and Society stimulated by the Arts

Editing: Jutta Schmiederer
Translations: (German–English): Mel Greenwald
Copyediting: Catherine Lewis

Graphic design and production: Gerhard Kirchschläger
Typeface: Klavika
Printed by: Friedrich Druck & Medien GmbH
Paper: Allegro Volume, 150 g/m², 300 g/m²
Photos: pp. 166–171; 238–240: Florian Voggeneder

© 2016 Ars Electronica
© 2016 for the reproduced works by the artists, or their legal successors

Published by
Hatje Cantz Verlag GmbH
Mommsenstrasse 27
10629 Berlin
Germany
Tel. +49 30 3464678-00
www.hatjecantz.de
A Ganske Publishing Group company

Hatje Cantz books are available internationally at selected bookstores.
For more information about our distribution partners please visit our homepage at www.hatjecantz.com.

ISBN 978-3-7757-4194-1

Printed in Austria

Cover illustration:
Front: *Uncanny Valley*, AlteredQualia + Fractal Fantasy (head scans courtesy of TEN24);
OpenSurgery – A do-it-yourself robot for domestic laparoscopy, Frank Kolkmann (Photo: Juuke Schoorl)
Back: *Artificial Skins and Bones Project: Visible Strength*, Lisa Stohn, Jhu-Ting Yang (Photo: Bernardo Aviles-Busch);
Magnetic Motion, Iris van Herpen (Photo: Yannis Vlamos)

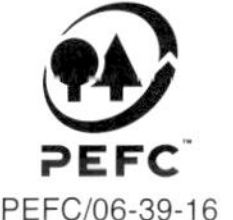

This product is from
sustainably managed
forests and controlled sources.
PEFC/06-39-16

printed climate-neutrally O ID: 11293-1607-1003